Social History of Africa

"Girl Cases"

Recent Titles in
Social History of Africa Series
Allen Isaacman and Jean Allman, Series Editors

Landed Obligation: The Practice of Power in Buganda
Holly Elisabeth Hanson

Creative Writing: Translation, Bookkeeping, and the Work of Imagination in Colonial Kenya
Derek R. Peterson

Slavery and Beyond: The Making of Men and Chikunda Ethnic Identities in the Unstable World of South-Central Africa, 1750–1920
Allen F. Isaacman and Barbara S. Isaacman

Paradoxes of Power: The Kano "Mamluks" and Male Royal Slavery in the Sokoto Caliphate, 1804–1903
Sean Stilwell

Re-creating Eden: Land Use, Environment, and Society in Southern Angola and Northern Namibia
Emmanuel Kreike

Mobilizing the Masses: Gender, Ethnicity, and Class in the Guinean Nationalist Movement, 1939–1958
Elizabeth Schmidt

Litigants and Households: African Disputes and Colonial Courts in the French Soudan, 1895–1912
Richard Roberts

Farmers, Traders, Warriors, and Kings: Female Power and Authority in Northern Igboland, 1900–1960
Nwando Achebe

The End of Chidyerano: A History of Food and Everyday Life in Malawi, 1860–2004
Elias C. Mandala

Invisible Hands: Child Labor and the State in Colonial Zimbabwe
Beverly Carolease Grier

Practicing History in Central Tanzania: Writing, Memory, and Performance
Gregory H. Maddox with Ernest M. Kongola

Fipa Families: Reproduction and Catholic Evangelization in Nkansi, Ufipa, 1880–1960
Kathleen R. Smythe

"GIRL CASES"
Marriage and Colonialism in Gusiiland, Kenya, 1890–1970

Brett L. Shadle

Social History of Africa
Allen Isaacman and Jean Allman, Series Editors

HEINEMANN
Portsmouth, NH

Heinemann
A division of Reed Elsevier Inc.
361 Hanover Street
Portsmouth, NH 03801–3912
www.heinemann.com

Offices and agents throughout the world

ISBN: 0–325–07092–X (cloth)
ISBN: 0–325–07094–6 (paper)
ISSN: 1099–8098

Library of Congress Cataloging-in-Publication Data

Shadle, Brett Lindsay.
"Girl cases" : marriage and colonialism in Gusiiland, Kenya, 1890–1970 / Brett L. Shadle.
p. cm.—(Social history of Africa, ISSN 1099–8098)
Includes bibliographical references and index.
ISBN 0–325–07092–X (alk. paper) ISBN 0–325–07094–6 (pbk: alk. paper)
1. Gusii (African people)—Marriage customs and rites. 2. Gusii (African people)—Social life and customs. 3. Women, Gusii—Social conditions. 4. Women, Gusii—Legal status, laws, etc. 5. Bride price—Kenya. 6. Marriage law—Kenya. 7. Kenya—Historiography. 8. Kenya—Colonization. 9. Kenya—Politics and government. 10. Great Britain—Colonies—Africa—Administration. I. Title. II. Series
DT433.545.G86S43 2006
306.81089′96395—dc22 2006015363

British Library Cataloguing in Publication Data is available.

Printed in the United States of America on acid-free paper.

09 08 07 06 EB 1 2 3 4 5 6 7 8 9

To Marie, Elliot and Alden, and to the memory of Mae Hardacre

Contents

Abbreviations and Foreign Terms

G-Gusii, S-Swahili

ACO	African Courts Officer
abd	abduction
ad	adultery
ADC	African District Council
Ag.	Acting
AG	Attorney General
AR	Annual Report
askari	policeman, soldier, retainer (S)
baraza	public meeting (S)
BCL	British Commonwealth League
bw	bridewealth
chache	lower areas of Gusiiland; Wanjare, Bassi, South Mugirango, Majoge (G)
CK	Central Kavirondo
CN	Central Nyanza
CNC	Chief Native Commissioner
CO	Colonial Office
COHS	Cardinal Otunga Historical Society
CS	Chief Secretary
cw	custody of woman
cwc	custody of woman and child(ren)
DA	Department of Agriculture
DAR	District Annual Report
DC	District Commissioner
DO	District Officer
DQR	District Quarterly Report

ebetinge	anklets worn by fully-married women (G)
egesirate	cattle herding villages (pl: ebesirate) (G)
engetare	anklets placed on runaway wives (G)
enyangi	final marriage ceremony (G)
etureti	informal dispute resolution body (G)
FL	Fawcett Library
Gov	Governor
ia	indecent assault
JA	Judicial Advisor
KNA	Kenya National Archive
LAC	Locational Advisory Council
LNC	Local Native Council
masaba	upper areas of Gusiiland; Getutu, North Mugirango, Nyaribari (G)
MFM	Iona and Philip Mayer Field Materials
MH	Mill Hill Archive
MIR	Monthly Intelligence Report
NCO	Native Courts Officer
NK	North Kavirondo
NN	North Nyanza
nsoni	sense/shame (G)
omogambi	clan leader (pl: abagambi) (G)
PACO	Provincial African Courts Officer
PC	Provincial Commissioner
PNCO	Provincial Native Courts Officer
PRB	Political Record Book
PRO	Public Records Office
RG	Ritongo Gesima
RH	Rhodes House Library
risaga	joint work party (G)
ritongo	court or tribunal (G)
RK	Ritongo Kuja
RM	Ritongo Manga
rug	Removing an unmarried girl from the custody of her parents without their consent (elopement)
SC	Senior Commissioner
SDA	Seventh-day Adventist
SJA	St. Joan's Social and Political Alliance
SK	South Kavirondo
SKAT	South Kavirondo Appeal Tribunal
SN	South Nyanza
SNAAC	South Nyanza African Appeal Court
SS	Secretary of State (for the Colonies)
WFL	Women's Freedom League
wimbi	millet (G)

List of Illustrations

Maps

Figures

Tables

Preface

I believe that this book had something new to say about Gusii history, even African history, but I will begin with something trite: This book has been completed only with the help of many, many people. I wish to thank all of you who have contributed, but if your name is missing, know that it is only because my obsession with cattle prices and court fees has crowded out most other information from my memory.

To begin with the money. My research and writing were supported at various points by a Hans Panofsky Summer Research Grant from the Program of African Studies at Northwestern University, a Boren Graduate Fellowship, a University Fellowship and a Dissertation Year Grant from Northwestern University, Bernadotte Schmidt and Littleton-Griswold grants, both from the American Historical Association, and Summer Research Grants from the College of Arts and Sciences, University of Mississippi.

I also wish to acknowledge the Office of the President, Government of Kenya, for granting me research clearance, and to the University of Nairobi for my affiliation. The Resident Magistrate in Kisii and the clerks and district magistrates in Nyamira and Keroka allowed me access to court transcripts and provided space for me to use them. The staff at the Kenya National Archive in Nairobi retrieved many files for me. Brother Anthony Koenig graciously allowed me to peruse the archives of the Cardinal Otunga Historical Society. At St. Joseph College Father Mol allowed me to look through the Kisii diaries of the Mill Hill missionaries, and also fed me excellent meals peppered with much laughter. Phillipa Bassett greatly assisted me in getting copies of the Owen papers from the CMS archive at Edinburgh University. I will always be grateful to Dr. Iona Mayer for allowing me to use the field notes from her and Philip Mayer's time in Gusiiland, and to Robert Mayer for his assistance.

My thanks to the departments of history at Northwestern University, Bowdoin College, the University of Mississippi, and Virginia Tech for their support in a variety of ways. The interlibrary loan staffs at each of these institution were of immeasurable assistance. David Easterbrook and the late Dan Britz at the Herskovitz Africana Library at Northwestern were always happy to help. I learned a great deal from fellow Africanist graduate students at Northwestern's Program of African Studies, under the guidance of Jane Guyer and Akbar Virmani. Ivor Wilks, Nancy Lawler and the rabble over which they ruled each Friday taught me much about Africa and collegiality. And, for the kinds of things only history department staff can give, my thanks to Carmelita Rocha, Paula Blaskovits, Charlotte Magnusen, Michelle Palmertree, and Betty Harness.

My dissertation committee—Jim Campbell, Karen Tranberg Hansen, and John Rowe—put up with far too much from me; hopefully they have long since forgotten my early, feeble attempts at being a historian. Jon Glassman deserves some type of award for taking on a graduate student who knew nothing about Africa and guiding him toward a Ph.D. I greatly appreciate his sharp insights and his unwillingness to accept anything less than my best (such as it was), and, aside from one slip at a dinner in Zanzibar (which I promised him I would never forget), for accepting me as a colleague. He and Jimmy have also taken in Marie and I as friends.

In Kenya the Onyancha family welcomed me into their home and their lives, despite my inability to eat my weight in *obokima*. Joel, always keep Bomachoge first. Esther, keep working hard. Evans Mageto also opened his home for many months to me and Marie, for which we are grateful. Ben Omwega assisted more than I could have expected and my research was greatly improved and much richer because of him. Arani Nyaberi is a true *omogaka*, and if there were still *etureti* all would defer to him. His knowledge of Gusii history, culture, and politics is unsurpassed and he shared it willingly with this wide-eyed outsider. For their continued and above-and-beyond the call help, thanks to Lynn Thomas, Derek Peterson, and Richard Roberts. From Jim Brennan I learned much, sometimes even about African history. He also insisted, almost obsessively, that I not view Gusii history as existing in a vacuum. Jeff Houghtby has been there since his days of wearing a clean blue suit to work every day. Lauri Allen, DeDe Hardacre, and Dutch and Ginger Featherston provided much moral support.

Thanks to all those who helped in ways large and small, and in ways that they may or may not realize: Jean Allman, David Anderson, Mike Bailey, Giulia Barera, Nancy Bercaw, Sara Berry, Tom Håkansson, Bob Haws, Win Jordan, Bethsheba Kemunto, Charles Kilonzo, Phillipa Levine, Gregory L. Mann, Robert Maxon, Kevin and Marty McCarthy, Suzanne Miers, Ken Moindi, the Mokogi family, the Neff family, Simon Newman, Pius Nyambara, Oluoch, the Onduso family, Steve Orvis, Emily Osborn, Susan Pedersen, Jeremy R. O. Prestholdt, Comrade Amy Randall, Jo Rose, Dave and Mags

Rose, Harvey Smith, Liz Thornberry, Mike Tuck, Calvin White, Jr., Luise White, and my graduate students at the University of Mississippi. At Heinemann, my thanks to Alexandra Goldmacher.

Despite all the advice I have been offered, mistakes will be found in the pages that follow. But who is to be blamed for these errors? In *How Europe Underdeveloped Africa*, Walter Rodney wrote that,

> contrary to the fashion in most prefaces, I will not add that "all mistakes and shortcomings are entirely my responsibility." That is sheer bourgeois subjectivism. Responsibility in matters of these sorts is always collective, especially with regard to remedying of shortcomings.

As attractive as it might be to parcel out blame to all those listed above, and as ill at ease as I am doing something Rodney so heartily scorned, I have internalized enough of the bourgeois world that I must take personal responsibility for my (our?) errors.

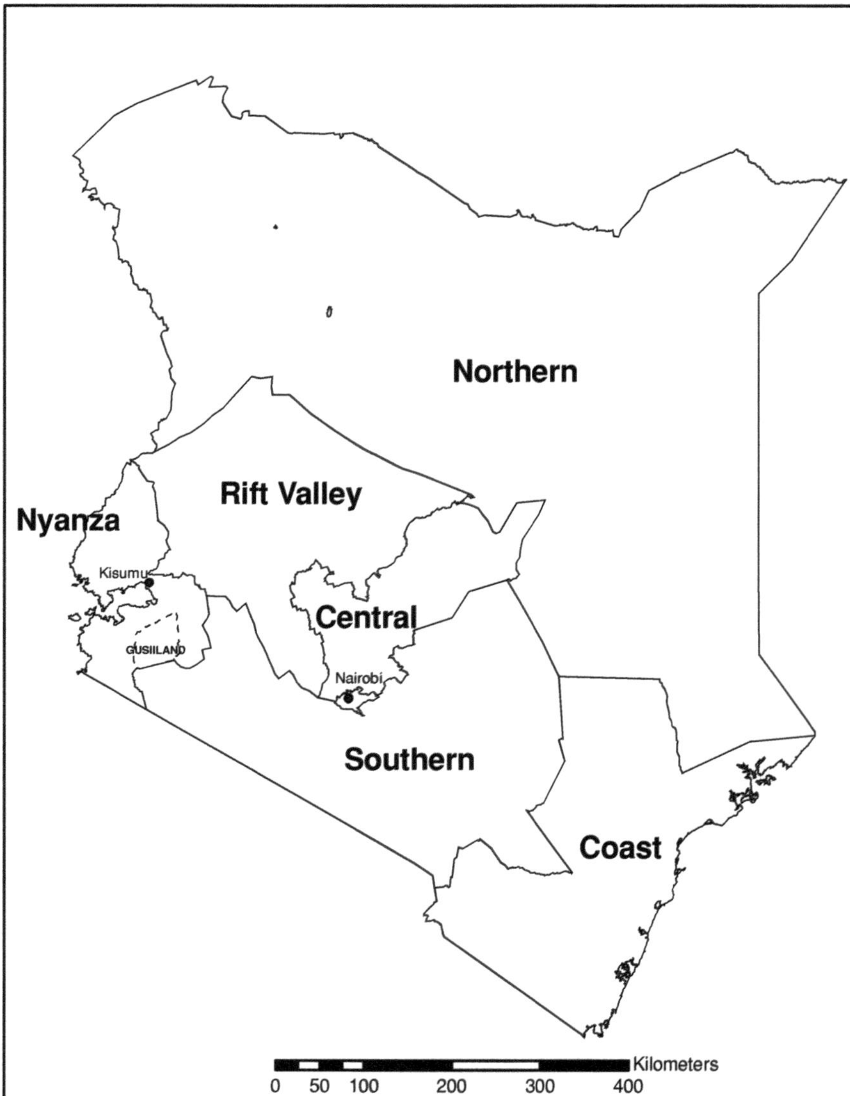
Northern
Rift Valley
Nyanza
Kisumu
Central
GUSIILAND
Nairobi
Southern
Coast
Kilometers
0 50 100 200 300 400

Map 1 Kenya

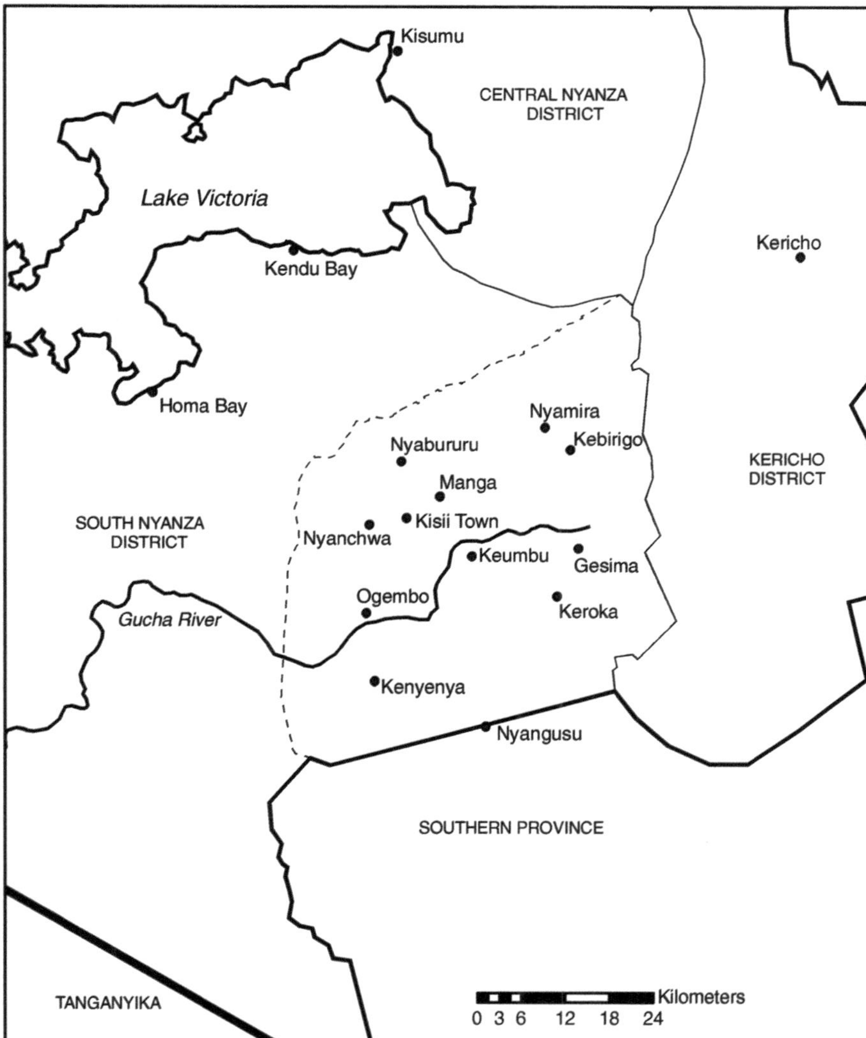

Map 2 South Nyanza

Introduction

"GIRL CASES"

In November 1937, K. L. Hunter, the top British official in the South Kavirondo district of Kenya colony, called a public meeting attended by several thousand Gusii men. Over the previous six months Gusii tribunal elders and members of the local African legislative body had grown agitated over the number of women abducted and raped, and the marked rise in women running off with lovers. Gusii elders had finally swayed Hunter, convincing him that gender and generational relations threatened to come unhinged, throwing Gusiiland into a spiral of lawlessness. "Girl cases," as Hunter called the disputes, could not be allowed to go unchecked. At the *baraza* (public meeting) Hunter gave the crowd a sound verbal thrashing, reserving special reproach for young men who abducted women, reducing themselves to the levels of "dogs and bitches."

Yet even as he berated Gusii youth, Hunter realized that he could not separate their transgressions from the already disturbed state of Gusii marriage. Young men abducted (with the intent to force a "marriage") or ran off with women because they could not afford to marry. Fathers had of late demanded so high a bridewealth from suitors that many youth simply did not have the cattle necessary to procure a wife. Unable to marry by legitimate means, bachelors got women illegitimately. Thus Gusii elders did not escape Hunter's wrath as he condemned them for driving up bridewealth and creating such a dangerous situation. After he finished his harangue several Gusii elders rose and seconded Hunter, urging their cohort to heed his words. Boldly, Hunter devised a new oath committing the assembled to do all in their power to restrict bridewealth and to prevent "girl cases."[1]

I find Hunter's *baraza* so compelling in part for the spectacle it must have been: a deeply tanned white man, undoubtedly clad in khaki shorts, chastising, in a South African accent, on behalf of the King, likely via an African interpreter, African boys half his age and gray-beards who could easily have been his grandfathers. More importantly, the *baraza* encapsulates the issues that were essential to the history of Gusii marriage for the three or more decades before and after 1937. Bridewealth—rising, falling, only to rise higher still, despite the best efforts of many Gusii and colonial officers. Marriage disputes—drawn forth in huge numbers by uncontrollable bridewealth. Colonial officials—inserting themselves into intra-African affairs. Gusii—young and old, men and women, sometimes acting cruelly and selfishly, usually trying to select from what were often a few poor options, and living out their dreams as best they could.

Hunter's *baraza* came at one of those historical moments that, in retrospect, mark the close of one era and the birth of another. Bridewealth was high in 1937 and the limit was needed and welcomed. Ten years later this would have appeared to have been a golden age of easily amassed bridewealth. "Girl cases" were on the rise, but their numbers would pale next to those of the following twenty to thirty years. Within a decade Hunter would concede that no pronouncement could ever limit bridewealth, perhaps embarrassed by his naivety in 1937. At the time of his *baraza* Hunter and his colleagues had only finished typing up reports filled with dire warnings of African women undermining social stability, corrupting public morality, and requiring tighter control by their fathers and husbands. A few years later one of Hunter's successors would blast Gusii patriarchs for buying and selling women like slaves under the guise of bridewealth. In this book, I describe from where the "girl cases" emerged and what became of them after Hunter's *baraza*, untangle the contentious struggles over marriage, and trace the trajectory of Gusii marriage from the turn of the century up through the 1960s.

"I WILL BE MARRIED BY MY WISHES"

In 1959 a woman named Nyabonyi came before the *ritongo* (Gusii court) to give evidence on behalf of her lover, charged with the crime of elopement. Her father accused him of taking Nyabonyi. She retorted that she had gone to the young man "of my own desire." "I had left home," she told the court, after "my father took me to [another man] by force, so that [my father] should be given cattle.... My father took me ... there to marry me by force without my consent." The clash between father's and daughter's ideas about marriage seemed unresolvable, but Nyabonyi believed their relationship could be mended. "I agree to return to my parents," she continued, "I will live there, so that I will be married by my wishes, but, if they marry me by force I will return to the accused."[2]

Nyabonyi's case was one of the thousands of "girl cases" that rent Gusiiland from the 1940s through the 1960s. Fathers and daughters, husbands and wives, young men and women all became enmeshed in passionate and often violent debates over what marriage meant, and what rights a woman could have in choosing her husband. Was a father's right to bridewealth and to arrange his daughter's marriage supreme? Could he force his daughter into marriage with a man she did not desire? Did wives have the right to desert such a husband, and daughters to elope? Could an abduction lead to a legitimate marriage?

What Nyabonyi and other Gusii women did not wish was to reject marriage entirely. Gusii women's goal was not to live an unmarried life. Quite to the contrary: they desperately wished to be married. Marriage meant adulthood. One could not truly be a man or woman without being married. An aging bachelor or maiden was a thing of pity, a perpetual child, unworthy of respect, and without status in their communities. They also recognized that there could be no marriage without bridewealth, for the two were inextricably intertwined. By running from fathers and husbands Gusii women did not reject bridewealth marriage, but only wished to make marriage on their own terms. Women and their lovers argued that women's choice in marriage partner was just as essential to a proper marriage as was the exchange of bridewealth.

Nyabonyi's case was sadly not unusual for her time, but this had not always been true. In the late nineteenth century and in the early decades of twentieth, Gusii women enjoyed certain rights in determining to whom they would be married. When suitors came to her home a young woman could choose whether or not marriage negotiations would be opened. After a honeymoon period of a month or two a woman could call off her union. The most elaborate custom practiced in the highlands, *enyangi*, which fully sealed a marriage, offered women the opportunity to end the marriage. Certainly, not all men respected their daughters' wishes, instead pushing them into undesirable marriages. Unhappy women exploited enmity between clans to escape unwanted husbands. Especially in the 1890s, when cattle plagues decimated bridewealth herds, some youth resorted to abducting women to be their "wives" and some fathers married off their daughters to any man with even one cow, or just a few goats. Once cattle numbers again began to build violent marriages declined, and remained at unremarkable levels for several decades.

The era of innumerable "girl cases"—roughly the 1940s through the early 1960s—was born of the union of two factors, one old, one new. First was the nature of Gusii bridewealth. Most men's primary source of bridewealth cattle was what they received from the marriage of a daughter or sister. A father thus had to ensure that what he received as bridewealth would, in turn, be sufficient to give as bridewealth. This generally worked well enough, for at any given time bridewealth tended to hover around a "going rate." For example, if the going rate was six cows a father could anticipate having to give six head for his son's wife, and so would ask six head for his own daughter. Rumors of an increase in the going rate complicated matters. If a man heard that other fathers were demanding high bridewealth he had better follow suit when marrying off his own daughter: should he abide by the present level, but the going rate increased, he would be left without enough cattle to make a new marriage.

More and more concerned fathers would up their bridewealth demands, and the going rate would indeed be forced higher.

The second factor behind the "girl case" epidemic was the colonial economy. New wealth circulating in Gusiiland, unevenly distributed, forced the bridewealth rate up to levels unseen for decades, if ever. The colonial economy was a cash economy. Taxes, clothing and other daily goods, education, litigation, and western medical treatment all required specie. For a time the sale of agricultural produce fulfilled these needs. From the later 1930s this would no longer be the case for all families. More men set out to sell their labor, but low wages precluded much in the way of building wealth. Not all Gusii were so unlucky, and by the time of Hunter's *baraza* a new class of men was emerging. Chiefs and other state employees, the educated and literate, the skilled or semiskilled—all could exploit the new economy. These men plowed their pay into highly profitable, newly introduced crops like coffee, or in business ventures such as grinding mills, retail shops, and transportation. During the war polygamists with plentiful land sold off bushels of maize and other crops in high demand by the army. Youth serving the empire returned with fat pay packets.

A gap emerged between the wealthy and the masses, one greater than had been common in earlier decades. Whether voluntarily or through hard bargaining these few well-off men gave bridewealth well above the going rate. Following the logic of Gusii bridewealth, other fathers felt compelled to increase their own demands. The going rate pushed upwards, a few men gave even more, and the rate pushed up again, reaching levels not seen since at least the 1880s, perhaps longer.

As bridewealth climbed and wages stagnated many young men found themselves without enough cattle to marry, and thus many young women found themselves without husbands. Indeed, by the early 1950s there were more single women of marriageable age than at any time in living memory. Chief Kirera introduced a bridewealth limit that held long enough for many young people to marry. Soon enough, however, a few fathers broke the limit, forcing others to follow suit, and again bridewealth rose. As futile as Kirera's limit eventually proved, his was the most successful of the many post-war attempts to keep down bridewealth.

Thence "girl cases." Many fathers in need of cattle—for a son's marriage or for a second wife—forced daughters into marriages with undesirable but cattle-rich men. Many such women ran away, refusing marriages created against their wills. Some returned to their homes, only to be forced back to their would-be husbands. Others went directly to new men. Many young lovers eloped, hoping to convince fathers to accept a more reasonable bridewealth at some later time. The most desperate young men abducted and raped women; should an abductee become pregnant she and her father would be likely to accept the "marriage."

Gusii tried all means of resolving their marriage disputes. Fathers tracked down and dragged home their daughters. Husbands did the same with their wives. Abducted women struggled to escape, and families exhausted themselves trying to find them. Fathers, husbands, and abducted women went to their chiefs for assistance, who might despatch an armed retainer *(askari)* to get the runaway or rescue the abducted. Others went to the *etureti*, unofficial local dispute resolution bodies, to try to hash out their disputes.

The many men and women who debated and fought over their marriages but failed to come to any resolution went to the African courts, in Gusiiland known as *ritongo*. *Ritongo* were staffed by Gusii men and empowered by the state to hear a wide range of cases, essentially everything other than dissolving Christian marriages, claims involving complex financial disputes, and the most serious crimes (such as murder). Under colonial law (but designated "customary law") it was a crime to live with a woman for whom one had not given bridewealth. The offended party prosecuted the case: fathers charged their daughters' lovers, husbands charged their wives' lovers, women charged their abductors. Other men made civil claims over "their" women, and women filed for divorce. It is in *ritongo* transcripts that we hear details of disputes and how men and women articulated their ideas about Gusii marriage.

Inside and outside the courts young men and women vigorously, if not always successfully, defended their interpretations of marriage: that both bridewealth and women's consent was essential to Gusii marriage. Fathers and husbands made their complaints ones of fact: of whether bridewealth had been paid or not. They refused to discuss anything else. Why a wife or daughter had run off was, for these men, irrelevant. Indeed, their language often denied women any role in illicit unions whatsoever. Women did not elope but were carried off, senior men insisted; they did not desert their husbands, but were caused to desert. Runaway wives, in turn, explained why their marriages were illegitimate. She had been forced into marriage, like Nyabonyi, or her husband had beaten her excessively. Couples explained why they had eloped, by and large because the young man lacked bridewealth and the woman's father had refused to compromise. Many couples tried to legitimize their unions by making bridewealth offers during court proceedings for it was, ultimately, bridewealth marriage that they sought. Few succeeded, for most of these men still lacked sufficient bridewealth—what had driven them into elopement in the first place.

Women's ability to consent to a union was not always denied. Certainly, senior men understood that women had the *capacity* to consent. They simply wished to deny women's consent held any significance. In abduction cases, however, the importance of women's consent came to the fore. Between initiation and marriage women enjoyed rights over their own bodies. They took lovers freely. So long as they did not question a father's right to make marriage—so long as they did not elope with their lovers—they would by and large be left alone. A woman's consent would be respected. Thus when an abductor took an unmarried woman (and abductees were all unmarried, for an abductor could not make marriage with a married woman) he violated *her* rights and she filed charges against him. Fathers and husbands (senior men argued) could use force to make and preserve marriage. Otherwise, women's wishes mattered.

Ritongo elders occupied a curious position. They were senior men. They were Gusii, they were married with children, some were polygamists. They were dedicated to the norms that gave senior men authority over women and juniors. Yet they were also worldly. They had stakes in businesses or cash crops, some were educated and Christian, and had regular interaction with British administrators. They could see beyond the individual cases that came before them and understood the larger context in which they made their decisions. Thus while *ritongo* elders tended to agree that he who had not given bridewealth had no claims over a woman, they did not always rule this way. In elopement cases elders often encouraged fathers to accept the union, drop the charge, and go examine the youth's cattle or to take out a civil suit for bridewealth. This was especially common if the couple had lived together for some time or if they had had children together. In a time of marriage crisis, *ritongo* elders thought it good to make marriages where they could.

In adultery cases too *ritongo* elders tried to balance out the rights of husbands with those of women. They found men not guilty, or handed down reduced sentences, for living with a woman who had had reason to leave her husband. If a man had not impregnated his wife or had not immediately sought after his runaway wife elders considered that he had not done what was expected of a husband. Nonetheless, a runaway wife had to return to the man who had given bridewealth.

The impact of colonialism was felt in many ways in Gusiiland. Across inter-war British Africa colonial officials dedicated themselves to preserving African society. Colonial rule functioned, they believed, only with the support and cooperation of "tribal" leaders who they assumed to be senior men. The temperament of colonial administrators, their social and educational backgrounds, also led them to appreciate strong patriarchal authority. African society under senior male rule had to be preserved. It was thus in the 1920s and 1930s that officials established African courts and extended them the power to fine (and in default of payment, imprison) young men in illicit relationships—young men who challenged senior men. But while colonial officials thought patriarchy to be a good thing and never really questioned its existence, particular manifestations of patriarchy would not go unchallenged. Colonial officials denied senior men the right to act in ways that upset the peace. Thus at his *baraza* Hunter chastised senior men just as much as juniors, pointing out that fathers' exorbitant bridewealth demands pushed young men into antisocial acts.

Despite living thousands of miles away from home, colonial officials could not perform their work in isolation from events in Great Britain. In the 1920s and 1930s, activists in Britain were becoming more vocal about the status of African women. In 1935–1937, trends in the colonies came into blazing conflict with those in the metropole. As state support for senior men was at its height, and as senior men were demanding and gaining new ways to regulate their womenfolk, missionaries in Africa and critics in Britain focused their energies on investigating and alleviating the status of African women. Kenya was at the center of the maelstrom. Archdeacon Walter Owen, head of the Church Missionary Society in a region just north of Gusiiland, shined light on examples of forced marriage and rallied public opinion in Britain. In the resulting uproar the Colonial Office was compelled to collect information from across its African empire on the status of women; colonial officials in the colonies were forced to justify and temper their policies toward women.

During and after the war administrative thinking toward women and marriage shifted and, as was true in previous decades, did so in relation to events taking place far outside Kenya. The nature of colonial rule in general underwent deep changes during the 1940s and 1950s. Strikes in British colonies in the Caribbean and in Africa, and the need to re-establish the British economy and to justify the British empire, all helped produce a dedication to "development." Rather than preserving the old it was now considered necessary to "modernize" and "develop" Africa.

Younger generations of Africans were making new demands for better schooling, more political representation, more economic opportunities. Similarly, a new generation of Britons began to enter the colonial ranks for whom perpetuating the "old" Africa seemed less an imperative. For many colonial officials development would include not just African economies but African social and cultural practices as well. Again, Hunter's *baraza* came at a turning point. Hunter did his best to stabilize bridewealth and bring some semblance of order to Gusii marriage. Less than a decade later, however, he encouraged fellow administrators to seriously explore the possibility of leading Africans to give up bridewealth. Marriage customs that administrators had defended as essential to tribal integrity and colonial stability now appeared outmoded, backward, roadblocks to new imperial goals.

Ideas about modernizing Africa also extended to the legal realm. Colonial officials formerly had either been satisfied with "traditional" African tribunals or had expended little energy overseeing them. As early as 1937, and with more ardor after the war, colonial officials undertook to revamp the African courts. New rules would be created and enforced, and new legal bureaucracies established to guide the courts toward a "modern" legal system. New and more highly educated elders would be appointed who could better follow new and more complex administrative regulations. This commitment to creating and enforcing court polices was where new administrative thoughts on women and marriage would have their deepest impact. Now, courts would no longer be able to physically force women back to their husbands or fathers, and fathers and husbands themselves had to track down their challengers, even fronting the money for the service of arrest warrants. At the same time, the number of women and men creating illicit unions forced administrators into this position—the state could not expend the time and finances to grant senior men extensive assistance. While the African courts remained indispensable to senior men's quest to uphold their vision of Gusii society, their success could not be guaranteed.

HISTORIOGRAPHY

"Runaway Women" and African Societies

Scholars have shown that the interwar years were particularly difficult ones for African women. While in the earliest years of colonial rule some women found European officials sympathetic to their plight,[3] in the 1920s and 1930s this would no longer be the case. Agricultural production by women in rural areas, it has been argued, was essential for the social and physiological reproduction of migrant wage-laboring men.[4] Confining women to their farms thus served the interests of capital as well as of rural patriarchs, always seeking new ways to retain their authority over wives and daughters. Indirect Rule, which was to preserve social stability and keep colonial rule on budget, required the cooperation of African rulers; these would be, Britons assumed, senior men. Thus colonial officials quickly saw the utility of an alliance with African elders, who similarly requested state assistance in controlling their womenfolk. Laws were tightened and the movement of women surveilled, scholars point out, by colonial administrators desirous of cementing the authority and loyalty of patriarchs. Colonial states established African courts for intra-African disputes. The courts were to apply "customary law," interpreted by court officials (senior men) in ways that were peculiarly beneficial to themselves. These courts lost little time in using their new authority to regulate the actions of women and junior men.[5] As Schmidt put it, in reference to the Shona in Southern Rhodesia, women were now "beholden to two patriarchies," to both African and European men.[6]

It is by now a given that at every power nexus the subordinated contest the relations that empower their superiors. Studies of peasants, workers, and slaves have proved that Africans resisted their exploitation, whether by Europeans or other Africans. But if the new state-senior alliance was as awesome as scholars believed it to be, how could women resist it? Archives readily provided examples. Colonial officials went through reams of paper deploring the actions of "runaway" women, those who left their rural homes for cities or the camps mushrooming around mines, women who rejected the new patriarchal order wholesale. These women brewed beer, sold sex and companionship, and some entered into a series of informal marriages with laborers. Other women converted to Christianity, seeking white missionaries willing to protect them from abuse by their "pagan" menfolk. The scholarship on "runaway women" burgeoned.[7]

We know rather less about the women who remained in their rural homes. In tracking the undoubtedly courageous and daring women who fended for themselves in urban areas scholars have given less attention to those women who did not "run away." By focusing on those who left to the cities or mining camps, and in trying to illustrate the pluck of such women, the historiographical question became why more women did not flee their homes. The unwarranted assumption that creeps into many analyses is that escape was the best or indeed the only option for women so oppressed. Scholars speak of women "who did *pry themselves* out of the rural areas,"[8] of "the *brave* and the *desperate* [who sought] an alternative to the oppressive social relations and deteriorating economic conditions of the rural areas,"[9] of women "discovering escape routes from rural drudgery and poverty."[10] The remaining rural women, it seems, were less brave or less desperate, or were simply unable to extricate themselves from the male forces holding them "hostage in the villages."[11]

Clearly, not all women who remained in their villages were "hostages." Women in Asante (in modern Ghana) rejected marriage, leading chiefs to "round up spinsters" and try to force them into their "proper" roles of wives and mothers.[12] Schmidt mentions women who used courts to sue for divorce and others who left their husbands and returned to their parents.[13] Lovett discusses the few Buha women who, faced with unwanted engagements or finding themselves in undesirable marriage, simply ran off with boyfriends or lovers.[14] Rather than going through accepted channels of complaint (fathers or court elders) women simply took matters into their own hands and made their own (informal) marriages. Nonetheless, as Allman and Tashjian explain, according to most of the historiography on eastern and southern Africa "opting out of marriage meant migration to colonial urban centers and, at times, the severing of ties with kin."[15]

In contrast to the prevailing historiography, I show that the vast majority of Gusii women neither left their homelands nor rejected the institution of marriage. Leaving Gusiiland for the city meant casting off the cultural norms in which they had been raised and which they accepted and embraced. Yet, unlike Asante women, remaining in their rural homes but choosing not to marry was not an attractive option for Gusii women. Their ultimate goal was marriage, but on their own terms. The historiography that has focused on women who rejected marriage and left their homes, or who remained near their homes but preferred not to marry, ignores the no less wrenching battles of women who stayed behind to fight over the nature of marriage.

The history of Gusii marriage can be seen as a series of debates—sometimes quietly resolved, sometimes played out over years, bitterly and violently—over the nature of Gusii marriage. Marriage disputes can best be understood as intracommunity struggles over defining an institution to which all parties remained dedicated. This approach owes much to pioneering work by John Lonsdale. Lonsdale demonstrates that Gikuyu (central Kenya) spent much of the colonial era trying to work out notions of "civic virtue." All agreed that to become an adult, young men needed land and family. As land pressure and relative poverty increased, as the wealthy became less willing to offer land to clients, many youth were left without the means to become "real men." Here, in part, was the origin of Mau Mau, an anti-colonial war for land and freedom, but also a Gikuyu civil war. It was not a civil war over the broad structures of Gikuyu society, Lonsdale shows, but over how (or if) youth could live their lives and succeed according to Gikuyu norms.[16] If Gusiiland never fell into bloody civil war, it was similarly wracked with conflict over defining Gusii marriage norms.

Generation

This book also contributes to the historiography of generation. Claude Meillassoux did much to focus attention on the central role of generation in African history. He argued that each generation in an agricultural community is indebted to previous generations, both for the food that nourished them before becoming workers and for the seed used in first plantings. In addition, senior men's dispensation of women means that they decide when junior men marry, forcing juniors to heed their elders' words. Scholars have widely accepted that the junior/senior divide constituted (and continues to be) one of the major fault lines in African societies. Generation has taken its place alongside the classic triumvirate of race, class, and gender as the main points of struggle in African social history. Nonetheless, as McKittrick notes, few scholars have pushed much beyond this basic framework.[17]

In particular, many scholars have wrongly drifted into a structural analysis of intergenerational relations. That is, scholars presume that fathers, as fathers, share one set of interests, and juniors, as juniors, have another, oppositional set of interests. (By and large, generation has dealt only with men.) Senior men might even work together as a class, as Henn argues: "It seems clear that patriarchs understand the need to take united class action to thwart the rebellious class struggles of their [female or junior male] dependents."[18] Yet the interests of all juniors and of all seniors do not always coincide and, to rephrase Linzi Manicome's insight on men and women, "to assume a fixed binary opposition between [juniors] and [seniors] suppresses the diversity within each of those binary categories."[19]

One of the commonest mistakes comes in relation to bridewealth. Many scholars argue that elder men purposely held up bridewealth to prohibitively high levels. In some cases, elders kept bridewealth "rates out of the reach of most young men," allowing themselves to marry multiple wives and extend their networks of clients.[20] Other elders supposedly saw high bridewealth as a way to stabilize marriage since a costly investment in marriage meant it would be less easily dissolved.[21] Or, as many scholars argue, elders manipulated bridewealth to reinforce their flagging authority over juniors. Young men returning home with their wage labor earnings put elders in a difficult position. Youth now had cash of their own to use as bridewealth, releasing themselves from reliance on their elders. Both to retain control over juniors and to tap into these new sources of wealth elders ratcheted up their bridewealth demands. Youth found their wage earnings less liberating than they had expected, and elders had access to cash otherwise outside their grasp.[22]

I argue, however, that we cannot necessarily attribute high bridewealth to a junior–senior conflict. Junior *and* senior men repeatedly and desperately sought ways to limit bridewealth. Gusii bridewealth rose *despite* the best efforts of many senior men, not because of their machinations. Gusii fathers understood that high bridewealth could create myriad social ills—including marriage disputes. Neither did senior men wish to keep their sons unmarried for too long. Certainly fathers and sons might debate the exact timing of marriage. But all fathers wished their sons to marry, to be real men. A man who died a bachelor brought a curse upon his family. Further, no matter how many wives and children a man had, without grandchildren his lineage (and thus his status as a revered ancestor) could not be assured. How much respect did a man deserve if he failed in his duties to his sons?

If fathers and sons were not always at each others' throats, neither did seniors always act as a cabal. Much social instability resulted from seniors refusing to work toward common goals. Gusii bridewealth rose in part because a few men exchanged higher than normal bridewealth. These men knew that their actions could lead to eclipsing of the going rate and all the ills that that entailed, but their individual desires overcame their concern for the state of Gusii society. Other men took up with women not their wives. Their particular circumstances—perhaps they were desperate for a wife, perhaps they simply wished to add another wife to an already successful homestead—proved more important than respecting the rights of another man over "his" woman.

Juniors too did not always act as we might expect them to have. They did not necessarily challenge their fathers over bridewealth. Gusii youth off at war or work willingly sent their money home to a father or brother to invest in cattle. Fathers were never to be excluded from marriage matters, and no youth would dispute the right of fathers to demand bridewealth for their daughters. At the same time, in striving toward their common goal—marriage—juniors could find themselves at odds with one another. When a young man eloped with or abduced a woman and did not give bridewealth, that woman's brother was left without the bridewealth he needed to form his own marriage. Junior men acting as brothers battled incessantly with junior men living in illicit unions.

Female Agency

Attributing too much explanatory power to intergenerational male conflict has also inadvertently put scholars in a position of denying women agency. Women sometimes appear only as things over which men fought. Young men are thus presented as the instigators of illicit relationships, who perhaps even used the unions as a way to strike out at senior men. Bonner, for example, argues that high bridewealth led *men* to seek alternative forms of marriage. I agree that high bridewealth helped produce a climate in which elopements flourished. But Bonner fails to consider why *women* may have wished to take part in these unions.[23] Similarly, Robertson argues that the upended social world of the 1930s "was used by those [Gikuyu men] who were landless to *secure* women."[24] But women were very clearly involved in elopements. As these scholars rightly point out, it was poor men who were most often involved in elopements, but it was women dedicated to their poor lovers who agreed to or proposed elopement. The silencing of women extends to discussions of abduction. As I show, women fought against, escaped from, and experienced a whole torrent of emotions because of abductions-cum-marriage. We should hesitate to say that "the commonest fate for a 'slave' girl was to marry her master" without also putting inverted commas around "marry."[25]

Clearly women were active agents in the making of illicit unions, but how did they choose to whom they would run? Scholars have shown that in many parts of Africa marriage can be consumed by struggles and negotiations over access to land, control of wages and cash crops, and responsibility for household expenses. This is in many cases close to the truth.[26] But analyses of African marriage have often also been intended as critiques of anthropology's structural-functionalist school that saw individuals following "involuntary, immutable bonds of kinship."[27] Scholars wished to denaturalize the assumption of the uncontested patriarchal head of the homestead, and put into question the notion "of the household as a unitary social actor."[28] Instead, it was pointed out that women have their own goals and strategies that often conflict with those of their husbands. African women do not blindly subsume their interests to those of the male-ruled homestead. However, scholars inadvertently invented a new model in which individual Africans are ruled by economic interests (broadly defined, including such things as land and people as strategic resources). That is, women acted not according to the demands of custom and kinship but according to some type of cost-benefit ratio.[29]

With such ongoing familial struggles over homestead resources one might be excused for wondering how husbands and wives manage to live together at all. Yet if marriage was simply a matter of resources many Gusii women acted rather irrationally. The men from whom they ran were wealthy—they had been able to give bridewealth—while the men to whom they ran generally were not. If not plentiful land and a household rich in cattle, what was a runaway woman after? The answer, in part, is a man with whom she shared an emotional attachment: love. The role of emotion in marriage has garnered little attention among Africanists, despite stray references in primary and secondary sources.[30] I show, however, that in the *ritongo* women and their lovers said that they loved *(kupenda)* each other. Many women in unwanted marriages explained their resistance in terms of lack of emotional attachment. A woman forced into a marriage by her father might explain that she did not love her husband, and women charging their abductors offered lack of love as evidence of their lack of consent. Court elders and many fathers accepted the latter argument. I have found it difficult to trace the history of emotion. That Gusii men and women before 1930s and 1940s shared emotional attachment cannot be denied; how Gusii understood emotions and how they expressed them is more difficult to reconstruct.

African Courts

Despite the recognized importance of African courts (they have been called the "cornerstone of indirect rule")[31] historians have done relatively little work on them. Anthropologists, especially in the 1950s and 1960s, published widely on African legal procedures.[32] Historical appreciation of African law emerged most significantly in the 1980s with Martin Chanock's and Terence Ranger's works on the codification of customary law.[33] They argued that colonial officials sought the "customary law" of each "tribe" they wished to rule. Indirect rule worked best if officials could implement laws recognized and accepted by the ruled. Yet most African societies had not employed an unalterable, uncomplicated set of laws. Colonial officials would not be deterred. They questioned elders for "customary law," overlooked inconsistencies, and codified the (new) law. As Kritisin Mann and Richard Roberts put it, the "invention and eventual codification of custom solidified fluid cultural and legal ideas and relationships into reproducible rules."[34] Not only reproducible, customary law was now "crystalized," unalterable (a point that has since been challenged by Sally Falk Moore, Sara Berry, and myself).[35] Scholars argued that since officials had consulted elder men—whom they expected to be the most learned in such matters—the new "customary law" put women and junior men at a distinct disadvantage before the courts. It was from here that much of the work on "runaway women" began; women were silenced in the powerful courts, and saw no avenue for resistance except escape.

Much of the subsequent work on African legal history, however, has focused on white courts. Chanock drew primarily on the proceedings in magistrates' courts or courts overseen by white administrators, as did many other scholars.[36] Yet transcripts from white courts pose special problems. The way Africans presented their cases in white courts certainly differed from how they spoke in African-staffed courts. What Europeans expected to hear and the evidence they found convincing would have shaped the complaints laid before them.

Moreover, the way whites heard cases (and thus transcribed them) often depended on the interests of their African translators.[37] Most significant, the vast majority of intra-African disputes were heard not by whites but by Africans. In Kenya in 1942, for example, 34,000 civil cases came before African courts of which fewer than 3 percent were appealed to British administrators. Only 0.2 percent of 60,000 criminal cases were so appealed.[38]

Several scholars have pushed beyond the limitations imposed by a reliance on white courts. Sally Falk Moore consulted some two thousand cases from chiefs' courts in Kilimanjaro (Tanzania), some from as early as the 1920s and on up through the 1970s.[39] Blessed with rich archives, historians of Asante have examined records of chiefs' courts in the colonial era. Jean Allman and Victoria Tashjian draw on court records to trace how men fought each other over the custody of women, and how men and women fought over the meaning of marriage and the distribution of conjugal property. Sara Berry similarly has mined Asante court records as a way to examine how people struggled over land rights.[40] Richard Roberts and Rebecca Shereikis have each used provincial Muslim courts in different parts of French West Africa to trace how women successfully sued for divorce in the early 1900s.[41]

The present study takes advances in the use of African court records and turns to local, in some ways more isolated courts. Asante courts were part of a hierarchy that led eventually to the court of the Asantehene (the king of Asante), a system that had strong roots in the nineteenth century. Such was not the case in Gusiiland. In earlier decades Gusii had taken disputes to *abanyamaiga*, neighborhood councils of elders. Gusii willingly turned to *abanyamaiga*, the wisdom of the elders respected by all. Yet if an individual refused to abide by a ruling of the *abanyamaiga* the elders could do little other than, in extreme cases, invoke a curse. *Ritongo* were entirely new. The British created the *ritongo* in 1937 and selected *ritongo* elders, sometimes in conjunction with Gusii commoners, more often not.[42] The *ritongo* enjoyed unheralded powers. Elders could impose fines of up to five hundred shillings, when a common laborer might earn shs. 15 or shs. 25 per month. A man unable to pay his fine could be tossed in a detention camp. In more serious cases, such as abduction or rape, the elders could send the offender to jail straightaway and tack on a fine for good measure (for which his sentence could be extended if he failed to pay it). Unlike the provincial courts studied by Roberts and Shereikis, *ritongo* served only Gusiiland, and Gusii went to no African courts other than the *ritongo*. Unlike Asante, few Gusii appealed, especially in criminal cases. Most of those who did appeal went only as far as the African appeals court in Kisii town, situated in the center of Gusiiland and staffed by elders selected from the *ritongo*.

Barbara Cooper has recently warned against the tendency in scholarship on gender and the law to overdraw "the importance of formal institutions of mediation such as colonial courts in recasting the nature of marriage and gender in Africa." It is in the local, unofficial tribunals, she argues, "that one gets a sense for how fluid and uncontainable the definition of local practice can in fact be, and the ways in which both women and men deploy a range of discourses about gender, family, and marriage."[43] True enough, but the *ritongo* offer an exceptional way of overcoming Cooper's concerns. Gusii courts straddled the two domains of local tribunals and colonial courts. In procedure and sentencing the *ritongo* were made to follow administrative dictates, which distinguishes them from Kilimanjaro courts, which "could scarcely have been closely supervised in operation."[44] *Ritongo* elders made their *judgments*, however, with relatively little oversight by and virtually no reference to their British rulers. Transcripts have at most an administrator's initial or checkmark, and often not even that. With thousands of court cases flowing through the *ritongo*, as well as Luo and Kuria courts in the same district, administrators could not hope to keep tabs on how elders judged their cases. Indeed, in 1955 an official assigned to courts work had to undertake a special study in order to discover how courts were deciding divorce cases.[45] The elders were Gusii and made judgments according to local logic. The *ritongo*s' transcripts provide the history of "local practice."

SOURCES AND METHODS

This book draws heavily on civil and criminal case records from the three *ritongo* that served Gusiiland. *Ritongo* Manga (at Manga), *Ritongo* Gesima (at Gesima), and *Ritongo* Kuja (at Ogembo) each heard hundreds and thousands of cases annually. In 1997, I examined transcripts then stored at, respectively, the magistrate's court at Nyamira, the magistrate's court at Keroka, and the old district offices at Ogembo. (They may have since been destroyed, which was being discussed at the time I was using them.) I examined all extant transcripts concerning marriage disputes. They were entirely unorganized by year or type of case. Many cases had to some extent been damaged by insects or the elements, and a small number rendered entirely unusable. From *Ritongo* Manga only civil cases could be recovered. Other civil claims over women and divorce cases were later made available at the Nakuru branch of the Kenya National Archive. The field material of Philip and Iona Mayer contain summaries of several dozen other cases. Transcription began in *Ritongo* Manga and *Ritongo* Kuja in the mid-1940s, and in *Ritongo* Gesima from its founding in 1953. Most criminal cases I recovered date from the 1950s and early 1960s, although others were recovered from the 1940s. More civil cases have survived from the 1940s. In all, I collected information on approximately two thousand cases.

I looked at three types of criminal cases: "Adultery" (later, "removing a married woman from the custody of her husband without his consent"); "removing an unmarried girl from the custody of her parents without their consent" (i.e., elopement); and "indecent assault" (which included both rape and abduction). The state defined these as "quasi-criminal," in that the offended person (the father, husband, or abducted woman) filed and prosecuted the case, but a convicted man could be fined or imprisoned by the state. I also drew on civil claims over women and/or children (filed by fathers and husbands) and divorce petitions (filed by women). Transcripts of the cases varied from one to four or five pages. Some were brief (having been dismissed ex parte), others included testimony of the litigants and witnesses, cross-examination by litigants and questions by the elders. The transcripts were handwritten in Swahili (or, from about 1964, in English) by recording clerks or elders. The prosecutor or plaintiff first gave his or her evidence, followed by the accused or defendant, and any witnesses the parties might have. At the end of the transcripts are the elders' summary of the evidence, interpretation of the case, judgment, and sentence or ruling.

The *ritongo* transcripts proved invaluable to this study. Through litigants' testimony I was able to reconstruct how marriage disputes played out before they reached the courts. Litigants testified as to the varieties of married life, how and why women ran off, how men tried to recover them, how abductions were carried out and foiled. Through hundreds of cases I saw patterns emerge, even as individual stories proved unforgettable. The evidence also reveals how Gusii understood marriage. While few ever made this explicit—"marriage is made of bridewealth;" "marriage requires female consent"—it was central to all the disputes.

Transcripts from the *ritongo* are not without their limitations. To begin, we must wonder if everything said in court was actually, and accurately, put to paper. In only a handful of cases are failures in transcription obvious. The elders' judgment in one abduction case favored the complainant since, they stated, she had produced a witness and the accused had not. No such witness appears on the transcript, however.[46] In another case over custody of children the *ritongo* elders found in favor of the plaintiff: they wrote that they were "following the evidence of Maisiba [maternal uncle of the children] . . . who has said clearly before the court that three head of cattle remain at his home because of the children." (That is, the former husband kept the children instead of taking back his entire bridewealth.) But Maisiba's evidence was exactly the reverse: "I say truthfully that three cows remain as a debt at my home, but they were not left because of the children, no . . ."[47] Why this discrepancy? Was it a failure of transcription, or a conscious manipulation of the facts by the elders or the clerk? It is impossible to know. But such cases were, thankfully, a tiny percentage of those recovered. Testimony is also littered with references to the legal standing of the parties: "the defendant" *(mshtakiwa)*; "the complainant" *(mshtaki)*. This is certainly the work of transcribers, but does not put into question the content of the evidence presented.

Accusations of bribery constantly plagued the courts. Administrators harbored their suspicions and cast about, apparently without success, for means of rooting out corruption. Gusii lodged complaints orally and in writing, and most elderly Gusii today concur that the *ritongo* were rotten with corruption.[48] Yet it appears that the vast majority of corruption involved land cases. In marriage disputes fathers and husbands could expect to win without having to bribe elders, while men accused of adultery and elopement did not have the resources to proffer bribes. Moreover, while facts might be altered in transcription, or elders could be convinced to favor the words of one party over the other, the "facts" on the transcripts had to be ones that could have reasonably led to the judgment given. Should an administrator happen to review a case or if it was appealed the verdict had to be consistent with the facts, or "facts," on the transcript. Thus even if the evidence in any particular case was false we can still understand how elders understood marriage, what "facts" had to be assembled to identify a couple as married or not.

Translation poses another problem. Litigants and elders spoke in Ekegusii, while the transcripts were written in Swahili. The clerks and elders were all local and Ekegusii was their mother tongue. Schooling was conducted in Swahili as were any dealings with the government, and so most if not all court members would have had proficiency in that language as well. Indeed, by the 1950s the administration required Swahili literacy exams be taken by aspiring clerks and elders. On occasion the Swahili in the transcripts is awkward but rarely unintelligible. The consistency of phrasing over many years by dozens of different elders and clerks suggests reliable translation. Poor translation would have resulted in language and phrasing peculiar to each transcriber, some exceptionally convoluted, some with exceptional stylistic flourishes. This was not the case.

Many Gusii spoke to me about their lives—their work, their courtships, their marriages. They told of others', and their own, struggles to marry, to avoid marriage, to escape marriage. They told of what became of disputes that never reached the *ritongo*. Some told very personal stories of elopement and abduction. Theirs' were stories that appeared in no written document. While many individuals graciously shared reflections on their lives, language proved an impediment. Most elderly Gusii speak little or no Swahili, and I failed to learn Ekegusii. I relied heavily on Ben Omwega who provided a running translation during interviews and later transcribed and translated them. We subsequently discussed them in more detail, and in several cases returned to informants to discuss certain points in more detail. After I left Kenya, he conducted more interviews, following a loose questionnaire. In 2002 and 2004 I conducted more interviews with Ben, as well with Isaac Onyancha, Dennis Onyancha, and Arani Nyaberi. Several former colonial officials also answered my letters with reminiscences of their experiences in Kenya and in Gusiiland.

The published and unpublished work of Philip and Iona Mayer are foundational to any study of Gusiiland. They lived there from 1946 to 1949, he as a government anthropologist, she as his assistant (so identified for state employment, although she did much more than that title suggests).[49]

Their work was only partially constrained by administrative concerns, which included bridewealth and the resuscitation of communal working groups. The Mayers' inquiries covered much additional ground. They published extensively on Gusii society and culture (see the Bibliography). Their work held impressive insights in ways often well in advance of other anthropologists of their era. For example, P. Mayer described in great detail the rules that guided bridewealth exchange, but he insisted that these rules were debated, were not always followed, and that they changed over time.[50] Iona Mayer granted me permission to examine their unpublished field notes at her residence in Oxford; I am the first outside researcher to use these files. These contain a wealth of information, some of which the Mayers had not written up for publication: a series of interviews tracing the marital histories of dozens of Gusii families, notes on chiefs, transcriptions or summaries of *ritongo* cases (the originals of which no longer exist), and more. I am deeply grateful to Dr. Mayer for graciously allowing me use of her archive, and to Robert Mayer for his assistance in using them.

I drew also on the more commonly used archival sources. The Kenya National Archive (in Nairobi and on microfilm at the Center for Research Libraries, Chicago) holds colonial-era documents on topics large (the total reorganization of the African courts; administrative ideas on how to transform African society) and small (if fees for filing a court case should be five or seven shillings; details of individual marriage disputes). Drawing on hundreds of memoranda and correspondence from Gusiiland and elsewhere across Kenya allows us to piece together histories of bridewealth, marriage, colonial rule, informal dispute resolution, the courts system, cash cropping, and a whole host of other matters. Using the KNA in conjunction with Colonial Office records (held in the Public Records Office, London) allows us to trace larger, empire-wide discussions of the law and of African society.

Priests kept diaries (held at St. Joseph's College, London) of their daily work as well as matters pertaining to marriage and bridewealth, while Seventh-day Adventist missionaries discussed their successes and failures in the columns of the U.S.-based *Advent Review and Sabbath Herald.* Students at Cardinal Otunga Secondary School in Mosocho, under the guidance of Brother Anthony Koenig, have for decades collected oral histories of their Gusii and Luo elders and published them in the *Bulletin of the Cardinal Otunga Historical Society.* The Fawcett Library at London Guildhall University holds collections of papers from a variety of feminist groups intimately involved in the meetings, publications, and letters that forced multiple government inquiries into the status of women in Africa. Papers of Archdeacon Owen (part of the Church Missionary Society collection at the University of Birmingham) provide examples of marriage disputes in Central Kavirondo, just north of Gusiiland, as well as how administrators responded to these particular cases and to the larger issues of women's rights that Owen brought before them.

GUSIILAND

Gusiiland is beautiful. Gusiiland covers some 750 square miles of southwest Kenya, just south of the equator, surrounded by Maasai, Kipsigis, and Luo. The sharp equatorial sun is tempered by the cool air of steep hills, some 4,500–7,000 feet above sea level. The lower areas can receive fifty inches of rain per year, the higher elevations can top one hundred inches. Blessed with plentiful rain and rich soils Gusii enjoy miles of bright green tea bushes, coffee bushes, pyrethrum plants and always-plentiful fruits, grains, and vegetables. Touching many parts of Gusiiland, the River Gucha flows peacefully or gushes dangerously as dictated by the rains. Roads are alternately choked by dust or impassable from mud. With one of the highest birth rates in Kenya, the Gusii population has exploded from under 600,000 in 1979, to 1.2 million in 1996, to an estimated 1.9 million in 2005.

CONCLUSION

From 1890 to the 1960s marriage in Gusiiland wound its way through a tumultuous and emotionally wrenching history. In 1900, Gusii young people enjoyed some voice in how and to whom they would be married; by 1950, they were locked in polarized debates, violent struggles, and acrimonious legal battles with their seniors over the nature of marriage; from 1970, they eloped with little fear of social or legal repercussions. This book traces these changes and explains how the intersection of empire-wide trends in social and legal thinking, the ideas and policies of administrators in Kisii, Kisumu, and Nairobi, the colonial political economy, and the ideals and actions of individual Gusii shaped this history. How these transformations came about, and what they meant to the average Gusii man and woman, is the story to be told here.

NOTES

1. South Kavirondo (SK) District Annual Report (DAR) 1937; "War—Aspects and Reactions, 1939," SK Political Record Book (PRB); SK Monthly Intelligence Report (MIR) Dec. 1937.

2. *Ritongo* Kuja elopement case 935/59. The following abbreviations are used when referring to court cases: RG—*Ritongo* Gesima; RK—*Ritongo* Kuja; RM—*Ritongo* Manga; KAC—Kisii African Court; SKAT—South Kavirondo Appeals Tribunal; SNAAC—South Nyanza African Appeals Court; abd—abduction; ad—adultery; bw—bridewealth; cw—custody of woman; cwc—custody of woman and child(ren); div—divorce; ia—indecent assault; rug—removing an unmarried girl from the custody of her parents without their consent (i.e., elopement).

3. Marcia Wright, "Justice, Women and the Social Order in Abercorn, Northeastern Rhodesia, 1898–1903," in *African Women and the Law: Historical Perspectives*, eds. Margaret Jean Hay and Marcia Wright (Boston University Papers on Africa VII, 1982). See also Marcia Wright, "Bwanika: Consciousness and Protest among Slave Women in Central Africa, 1886–1911," in *Women and Slavery in Africa*, eds. Claire C. Robertson and Martin

A. Klein (Portsmouth, NH: Heinemann, 1997 [1983]); Elizabeth Schmidt, "Negotiated Spaces and Contested Terrain: Men, Women, and the Law in Colonial Zimbabwe, 1890–1939," *Journal of Southern African Studies* 16 (1990), 622–648; Judith Byfield, "Women, Marriage, Divorce and the Emerging Colonial State in Abeokuta (Nigeria) 1892–1904," *Canadian Journal of African Studies* 30 (1996), 32–51. Diana Jeater shows that this early attention to improving women's status reflected only one opinion among many held by white administrators and missionaries in Southern Rhodesia. *Marriage, Perversion and Power: The Construction of Moral Discourse in Southern Rhodesia, 1894–1930* (Oxford: Oxford University Press, 1993), esp. 64–87.

4. Harold Wolpe was one of the first to argue the importance of the rural reproduction of laborers for capital, though he has been critiqued for the omnipotence he granted capital interests and his failure to suggest how internal dynamics of rural societies affected migration patterns. Capitalists also had various ideas on this, and some in fact favored the transplant of family units to mining camps. "Capitalism and Cheap Labour-power in South Africa: From Segregation to Apartheid," *Economy and Society* 1 (1972), 425–456. See also Belinda Bozzoli, "Marxism, Feminism and South African Studies," *Journal of Southern African Studies* 9 (1983), 139–171; Jane Parpart, "Sexuality and Power on the Zambian Copperbelt: 1926–1964," in *Patriarchy and Class: African Women in the Home and the Workforce*, eds. Sharon B. Strichter and Jane L. Parpart (Boulder, CO: Westview, 1988); Elizabeth Schmidt, "Patriarchy, Capitalism, and the Colonial State in Zimbabwe," *Signs* 16 (1991), 732–756.

Much of the work on production and gender relations in southern Africa, especially for the precolonial period, drew on the work of Claude Meillassoux and his fellow French Marxists. For a review, see J. B. Peires, "Paradigm Deleted: The Materialist Interpretation of the Mfecane," *Journal of Southern African Studies* 19 (1993), 295–313, esp. 300–305.

5. Terence Ranger, "The Invention of Tradition in Africa," in *The Invention of Tradition*, eds. Eric Hobsbawm and Terence Ranger (Cambridge, UK: Cambridge University Press, 1983); Martin Chanock, "Making Customary Law: Men, Women, and Courts in Colonial Northern Rhodesia," in *African Women and the Law*, ed. Hay and Wright; idem, *Law, Custom, and Social Order: The Colonial Experience in Malawi and Zambia* (Portsmouth, NH: Heinemann, 1998 [1985]); Schmidt, "Negotiated Spaces and Contested Terrain."

6. Elizabeth Schmidt, *Peasants, Traders and Wives: Shona Women in the History of Zimbabwe, 1870–1939* (Portsmouth, NH: Heinemann, 1992), chap. 1.

7. Janet Bujra, "Production, Property, Prostitution: 'Sexual Politics' in Atu," *Cahiers d'Etudes africaines*, 17 (1977), 13–39; Julia Wells, "Passes and Bypasses: Freedom of Movement for African Women under the Urban Areas Act of South Africa," in *African Women and the Law*, ed. Hay and Wright; Marjorie Mbilinyi, "Runaway Wives in Colonial Tanganyika: Forced Labour and Forced Marriage in Rungwe District 1919–1961," *International Journal of the Sociology of Law* 16 (1988), 1–29; Parpart, "Sexuality and Power on the African Copperbelt"; Phil Bonner, "'Desirable or undesirable Basotho women?' Liquor, Prostitution and the Migration of Basotho Women to the Rand, 1920–1945," and Cherryl Walker, "Gender and the Development of the Migrant Labour System c. 1850–1930," both in *Women and Gender in Southern Africa to 1945*, ed. Cherryl Walker (Cape Town: David Philip, 1990); Luise White, *The Comforts of Home: Prostitution in Colonial Nairobi* (Chicago: University of Chicago, 1990); Belinda Bozzoli with Mmantho Nkotsoe, *Women of Phokeng: Consciousness, Life Strategy, and Migrancy in South Africa, 1900–1983* (Portsmouth, NH: Heinemann, 1991); Theresa A. Barnes, "The Fight for Control of African Women's Mobility in Colonial Zimbabwe, 1900–1939," *Signs* 17 (1992), 586–608; Jane Parpart, "'Where is Your Mother?': Gender, Urban Marriage, and Colonial Discourse on the Zambian Copperbelt, 1924–1945," *International Journal of African*

Historical Studies 27 (1994), 241–271. Some Haya women in Tanganyika went to urban areas, but eventually returned home and set up their own, female-headed households. Lesley Stevens, "Bananas, Babies, and Women Who Buy Their Graves: Matrifocal Values in a Patrilineal Tanzanian Society," *Canadian Journal of African Studies* 29 (1995), 454–480.

8. Barnes, "Fight for Control," 592, emphasis added.

9. Walker, "Gender and the Migrant System," 188, emphasis added.

10. Jeater, *Marriage, Perversion and Power*, 251.

11. Gisela Geisler, "Moving with Tradition: The Politics of Marriage among the Toka of Zambia," *Canadian Journal of African History* 26 (1992), 437–461, quote from 439.

If, as I argue, this distorts the history of rural women, why have scholars generally followed this line of thinking? In large part, I believe, it has to do with Western feminists' concerns. Scholars who took up the study of African women in the 1970s asked questions that arose from feminists' battles in the West. Shirley Ardener, for example, investigated examples of female militancy in Africa "not only for their own interest, but also to see whether they can throw any light upon the completely independent modern women's liberation movements with which we are now familiar in the West." Shirley Ardener, "Sexual Insult and Female Militancy," in *Perceiving Women*, ed. Shirley Ardener (London: Malaby Press, 1975), 29. Regarding the disproportionate attention "runaway women" have received, Lovett wonders if similar factors have not been at work: is it possible, she writes, "that in our quest for illustrations of female indomitability, resistance, and agency in the face of oppressive structure and social relationships, in our search for heroines, we have transformed exceptional behavior into expected behavior?" Margot Lovett, "On Power and Powerlessness: Marriage and Political Metaphor in Colonial Western Tanzania," *International Journal of African Historical Studies* 27 (1994), 273–301, quote from 284. For a critique of early feminist Africanist scholarship, see Nancy Rose Hunt, "Placing African Women's History and Locating Gender," *Social History* 14 (1989), 359–379.

12. Jean Allman and Victoria Tashjian, *"I Will Not Eat Stone": A Women's History of Colonial Asante* (Portsmouth, NH: Heinemann, 2000).

13. Schmidt, *Peasants, Traders, and Wives*, 115–117. See also Lovett, "On Power and Powerlessness," 293–294, 300; Thomas McClendon, "Tradition and Domestic Struggle in the Courtroom: Customary Law and the Control of Women in Segregation-Era Natal," *International Journal of African Historical Studies* 28 (1995), 527–561; idem, *Genders and Generations Apart: Labor Tenants and Customary Law in Segregation-Era South Africa, 1920s to 1940s* (Portsmouth, NH: Heinemann, 2002), chap. 5.

14. Margot Lovett, "Elders, Migrants and Wives: Labor Migration and the Renegotiation of Intergenerational, Patronage and Gender Relations in Highland Buha, Western Tanzania, 1921–1962" (Ph.D. dissertation, Columbia University, 1996), chaps. 6–7; idem, "'She Thinks She's Like a Man': Marriage and (De)Constructing Gender Identity in Colonial Buha, Western Tanzania, 1943–1960," *Canadian Journal of African Studies* 30 (1996), 52–68.

15. Allman and Tashjian, *"I Will Not Eat Stone,"* 148.

16. John Lonsdale, "The Moral Economy of Mau Mau: Wealth, Poverty and Civic Virtue in Kikuyu Political Thought," in Bruce Berman and John Lonsdale, *Unhappy Valley: Conflict in Kenya and Africa* (London: James Currey, 1992). Glassman shows how in the 1880s popular protests in coastal towns of Tanzania eventually led to the collapse of the Shirazi elite. Yet the commoners and slaves who took to the streets did not call for the overturning of the dominant order; they did not reject the patron-client ordering of society. Instead, they demanded more of their patrons—that patrons live up to what clients expected of them. Jonathon Glassman, *Feasts and Riot: Revelry, Rebellion, and Popular Consciousness on the Swahili Coast, 1856–1888* (Portsmouth, NH: Heinemann, 1995).

Steven Stern takes a similar approach to patriarchal relations in late colonial Mexico. He shows that women "did not challenge a right of patriarchal authority as such, and the logic of their practice did not rest on a premise of fundamental equality or ability or likeness of rights across the gender." Women thus "did not challenge the principles of patriarchal dominance as such but reinterpreted their operational meaning so markedly that conflict ensued on the practical issues that defined the meaning and limits of patriarchal authority in everyday life." Steven J. Stern, *The Secret History of Gender: Women, Men, and Power in Late Colonial Mexico* (Chapel Hill: University of North Carolina Press, 1995), 21, 97. Like Mexican women, Gusii women would not reject the broad schema of Gusii marriage but did question particular aspects or interpretations of Gusii marriage. This in contrast to Hodgson's thesis that the term "patriarchy" cannot be applied to precolonial Maasai societies:

> Although men, especially elder men, served as the primary leaders and arbitrators for their communities, the responsibilities and interactions of men and women were complementary and interdependent.... There is in fact no evidence that women perceived themselves or were perceived as the "property" or "possessions" of men. Instead [her source] presents substantial evidence of ... the pride of women in their identities as pastoralists and their deep satisfaction with their lives and relationships.

But it is not necessarily true, or even common, that women in a patriarchal society feel particularly unsatisfied with their lives. An imbalance of power, rights and responsibilities need not and often will not produce vocal critiques by the powerless. Dorothy L. Hodgson, "Pastoralism, Patriarchy and History: Changing Gender Relations among the Maasai in Tanganyika, 1890–1940," *Journal of African History* 40 (1999), 41–65.

In fact, few Africanists have addressed theoretical questions surrounding the term patriarchy. Its meaning is not mentioned in Stichter and Parpart, eds., *Patriarchy and Class.* Schimdt in *Peasants, Traders, and Wives*, footnotes Heidi Hartmann who (like many other scholars of the 1970s and 1980s) reified patriarchy and presumed that, despite differences among themselves, *all* men conspired to control women. Heidi Hartmann, "The Unhappy Marriage of Marxism and Feminism," in *Women and Revolution: A Discussion of the Unhappy Marriage of Marxism and Feminism*, ed. Lydia Sargent (Boston: South End Press, 1981).

17. Meredith McKittrick, "The 'Burden' of Young Men: Property and Generational Conflict in Namibia, 1880–1945," *African Economic History* 24 (1996), 115–129.

18. Jeanne Koopman Henn, "The Material Basis of Sexism: A Mode of Production Analysis," in *Patriarchy and Class*, eds. Stichter and Parpart, 48.

19. Linzi Manicom, "Ruling Relations: Rethinking State and Gender in South African History," *Journal of African History* 33 (1992), 441–465, quote from 454.

20. Jane I. Guyer, "The Value of Beti Bridewealth," in *Money Matters: Instability, Values and Social Payments in the Modern History of West African Communities*, ed. Jane I. Guyer (Portsmouth, NH; Heinemann, 1995), 123–124, quote from 114. See also her *Family and Farm in Southern Cameroon* (African Research Studies No. 14, Boston University, 1984), 38.

21. Jane Parpart, "Class and Gender on the Copperbelt: Women in Northern Rhodesian Copper Mining Communities, 1926–64," in *Women and Class in Africa*, eds. Claire Robertson and Iris Berger (New York: Africana Publishing, 1986), 120; idem, "Sexuality and Power on the Zambian Copperbelt"; Schmidt, *Peasants, Traders, and Wives*, 114.

22. Colin Murray, "High Bridewealth, Migrant Labour and the Position of Women in Lesotho," *Journal of African Law* 21 (1977), 79–96; Patrick Harries, "Kinship, Ideology, and the Nature of Pre-Colonial Labour Migration: Labour Migration from Delagoa Bay

Hinterland to South Africa, up to 1895," in *Industrialisation and Social Change in South Africa: African Class Formation, Culture and Consciousness, 1870–1930*, eds. Shula Marks and Richard Rathbone (Essex: Longman, 1982); Schmidt, "Negotiated Spaces"; idem, *Peasants, Traders, and Wives*, 85–86, 113–114; Lovett, "On Power and Powerlessness"; idem, "Elders, Migrants, and Wives."

23. Bonner, "'Desirable or Undesirable Basotho Women?'" 236.

24. Claire C. Robertson, *Trouble Showed the Way: Women, Men, and Trade in the Nairobi Area, 1890–1990* (Bloomington: Indiana University Press, 1997), 99. Lovett discusses young men who "eloped with those girls they desired to marry," although she also refers to "young couple[s]" who eloped. "On Power and Powerlessness," 296–197. However, Lovett later describes elopement as "a tactic" of poorer youth, "a potent weapon available to young men in their struggles with their elders." Lovett, "Elders, Migrants, and Wives," 261.

25. Igor Kopytoff and Suzanne Miers, "African 'Slavery' as an Institution of Marginality," in *Slavery in Africa: Historical and Anthropological Perspectives*, eds. Suzanne Miers and Igor Kopytoff (Madison: University of Wisconsin, 1977), 32. See also, for example, Greet Kershaw, *Mau Mau from Below* (Oxford: James Currey, 1997), 20, 68–69.

26. For an excellent example, see Allman and Tashjian, "*I Will Not Eat Stone.*"

27. Meyer Fortes, *Kinship and the Social Order*, quoted on page 91 in Jane I. Guyer, "Household and Community in African Studies," *African Studies Review* 24 (1981), 87–137.

28. Jane I. Guyer and Pauline E. Peters, "Introduction," *Development and Change* 18 (1987), 197–214.

29. Even in terms of sexual orientation, Shepard argues: "What I hope to show is that homosexuality may be a rational decision, bringing fuller participation in and better benefits from the society of which the homosexual is a member." Gill Shepard, "Rank, Gender, and Homosexuality: Mombasa as a Key to Understanding Sexual Options," in *The Cultural Construction of Sexuality*, ed. Pat Caplan (London: Routledge, 1987).

30. Wilson reported that in parts of Tanzania and Malawi Africans tirelessly repeated the axiom, "with us love is small." This was in fact not always the case. "In theory," she writes, "property overshadowed personal affection; in practice there were many cases in which property was subordinated to personal choice." Monica Wilson, *For Men and Elders: Change in the Relations of Generations and of Men and Women among the Nyakyusa-Ngonde People 1875–1971* (New York: Africana, for the International African Institute, 1977), 166.

I believe scholars also hesitate to attribute too much to emotion given older stereotypes of Africans being ruled by emotion rather than rational thinking. Historians have also shown that romance and individualism in marriage in modern Europe is a product of only the last two centuries, which perhaps suggested to Africanists that romance was peculiar to the West and thus not a factor in African history. For the most important early work in the European historiography, see Lawrence Stone, *The Family, Sex and Marriage in England, 1500–1800* (abridged edition) (New York: Harper, 1977), and for a more recent study, David I. Kertzer and Marzio Barbagli, *Family Life in the Twentieth Century* (New Haven, CT: Yale University Press, 2003).

31. H. F. Morris, "Native Courts: A Corner-Stone of Indirect Rule," in *Indirect Rule and the Search for Justice: Essays in East African Legal History*, H. F. Morris and James S. Read (Oxford: Oxford University Press, 1972).

32. See, for example, Max Gluckman, *The Judicial Process among the Barotse of Northern Rhodesia (Zambia)* (Manchester: Manchester University Press, for the Institute for African Studies, University of Zambia, 1973 [1955]); Paul Bohannen, *Justice and Judgement Among the Tiv* (London: Oxford University Press, for the International African Institute, 1957); Lloyd A. Fallers, *Law without Precedent: Legal Ideas in Action in the Courts of Colonial Busoga* (Chicago: University of Chicago Press, 1969). Earlier works

included compilations of customary laws of various peoples. See, for an East Africa example, Hans Cory and M. M. Hartnoll, *Customary Law of the Haya Tribe, Tanganyika Territory* (London: International African Institute, 1945).

33. Ranger, "The Invention of Tradition in Africa"; Chanock, "Making Customary Law": idem, *Law, Custom, and Social Order.*

34. Richard Roberts and Kristin Mann, "Law in Colonial Africa," in Kristin Mann and Richard Roberts, eds., *Law in Colonial Africa* (Portsmouth, NH: Heinemann, 1991), 4.

35. Sally Falk Moore, *Social Facts and Fabrications: "Customary" Law on Kilimanjaro, 1880–1980* (Cambridge, UK: Cambridge University Press, 1986); Sara Berry, "Hegemony on a Shoestring: Indirect Rule and Access to Agricultural Land," *Africa* 62 (1992), 327–355; Brett L. Shadle, "'Changing Traditions to Meet Current Altering Conditions': Customary Law, African Courts, and the Rejection of Codification in Kenya, 1930–60," *Journal of African History* 40 (1999), 411–431.

36. For example, Schmidt, *Peasants, Traders, and Wives*; McClendon, *Genders and Generations Apart.* Gocking looks at African courts that were molded very closely along the lines of British courts. Roger Gocking, "British Justice and the Native Tribunals of the Southern Gold Coast Colony," *Journal of African History* 34 (1995), 93–113.

37. On the role of translators and other African subalterns in the shaping of colonial rule, see Benjamin Lawrance, Emily Osborn, and Richard Roberts, eds., *Intermediaries, Interpreters and Clerks: African Employees and the Making of Colonial Africa* (Madison: University of Wisconsin Press, 2006 [in press]); Emily Lynn Osborn, "'Circle of Iron': African Colonial Employees and the Interpretation of Colonial Rule in French West Africa," *Journal of African History* 44 (2003), 29–50.

38. These statistics are compiled from Arthur Phillips, *Report on Native Tribunals* (Nairobi: Colony and Protectorate of Kenya, 1944).

39. Moore, *Social Facts and Fabrications.*

40. Allman and Tashjian, *"I Will Not Eat Stone"*; Sara S. Berry, *Chiefs Know Their Boundaries: Essays on Property, Power, and the Past in Asante, 1896–1996* (Portsmouth, NH: Heinemann, 2001).

41. Richard Roberts, "Representation, Structure and Agency: Divorce in the French Soudan during the Early Twentieth Century," *Journal of African History* 40 (1999), 389–410; Rebecca Shereikis, "Customized Courts: French Colonial Legal Institutions in Kayes, French Soudan, c. 1880–c. 1913" (Ph.D. dissertation, Northwestern University, 2003). Lynn Thomas also draws on pregnancy compensation cases from early independence-era courts. Lynn M. Thomas, *Politics of the Womb: Women, Reproduction, and the State in Kenya* (Berkeley and Los Angeles: University of California Press, 2003), 122–32.

42. Brett L. Shadle, "African Court Elders in Nyanza Province, Kenya, c. 1930–1960: From 'Traditional' to 'Modern,'" in *Intermediaries, Interpreters and Clerks*, eds. Lawrance, Osborn, and Roberts.

43. Barbara M. Cooper, *Marriage in Maradi: Gender and Culture in a Hausa Society in Niger, 1900–1989* (Portsmouth, NH: Heinemann, 1997).

44. Moore, *Social Facts and Fabrications*, 150.

45. Oliver Knowles, "Some Modern Adaptations of Customary Law in the Settlement of Matrimonial Disputes in the Luo, Kisii and Kuria Tribes of South Nyanza," *Journal of African Administration* 8 (1956), 111–115.

46. RG ia 51/61.

47. RG custody of children 159/59.

48. Shadle, "African Court Elders in Nyanza Province." See also Maurice Nyamanga Amutabi, "Power and Influence of African Court Clerks and Translators in Colonial Kenya: The Case of Khwisero Native (African) Court, 1946–1956," in *Intermediaries, Interpreters and Clerks*, eds. Lawrance, Osborn, and Roberts.

49. For biographical information, see William Beinart, "Speaking for Themselves," in *Tradition and Transition in Southern Africa: Festschrift for Philip and Iona Mayer*, eds. Andrew D. Spiegel and Patrick A. McAllister (Johannesburg: Witwatersrand University Press), and interviews by Alan Macfarlane, posted at http://www.alanmacfarlane.com/index.html. Accessed May 6, 2006.

50. Philip Mayer, *Gusii Bridewealth Law and Custom* (Rhodes Livingstone Papers, 18, Oxford, 1950).

1

Gusii Society and Politics and the Coming of Colonialism

As the nineteenth century turned to the twentieth, the Gusii highlands, like much of east Africa, had only recently emerged from a decade of famine and disease that struck humans as well as their cattle. Gusii society had undergone massive strain, but had survived. Rather than struggling for existence Gusii could now return to striving for successful lives. The definition of success: wealth in people. Gusii wanted spouses, children, extended family, dependents. The basic building block was marriage, from which sprang legitimate children, agricultural surplus, a polygamous homestead, and perhaps clients. With luck, these all built upon one another into a spiral of more and more people, wealth, respect, and power. Throughout the entire system one found cattle. Marriage existed only with the exchange of bridewealth, which (excepting some years in the 1890s) was composed primarily of cows. Cattle, bridewealth, marriage, people—all interrelated, all measures of success.

Elsewhere in the region the turn of the century saw an entirely new factor introduced into Africans' lives. Some areas (but not Gusiiland) had for decades been exposed to and taken part in the long-distance trade that stretched from the Indian Ocean coast to Lake Victoria, and beyond. By now it was becoming clear that the white men who had previously only passed through intended to stay. They took on some Africans as allies, using them in "punitive expeditions" against others. It would not be until 1907, however, that a Briton came to proclaim himself the ruler of Gusiiland and the surrounding areas. It would be another two decades until his successors felt sure of the reach of their authority. The African chiefs they appointed were ignored as much as possible, sometimes flat-out disobeyed, and on occasion physically attacked by Gusii. By the later 1920s, chiefs, with significant financial power and as directors of state violence, had begun to build up a grudging respect by commoners. In the meantime, Gusii continued in their search for people, in ways not dramatically different than they had in 1900.

SETTLEMENT OF THE HIGHLANDS AND "THE GUSII"

At the turn of the nineteenth century the highlanders' ancestors had, after migrating from farther north, established settlements in the Trans Mara.[1] Patrilineal clans organized themselves under several totemic identities: Bassi, Mugirango, Wanjare, and Basweta (internally divided into Machoge and Getutu sections). They lived in this region for about a generation, exchanging cattle raids with nearby Maasai, only to fall victim to a final, overwhelming attack by Maasai *moran*.[2] Scattered by the superior Maasai fighters, the clans fled in confusion. The Mugirango split in two, with one group of clans heading into the northern-most reaches of the highlands. Most Getutu clans took refuge in the highlands near Manga ridge. The Machoge, Bassi, Wanjare, and the remaining Mugirango clans sought shelter with Luo-speakers west of the highlands. They soon chafed under (what is recalled as) the oppressive ways of their patrons. First the Wanjare decamped to settle in the forests of the highlands. By the 1850s the Bassi, Machoge, and Mugirango joined them, later making their way further east and south. By the second half of the nineteenth century those who would become the Gusii had staked claims to the highlands, living in dozens of clans loosely affiliated under seven groupings: Getutu, Nyaribari, North Mugirango, Wanjare, Bassi, Machoge, and South Mugirango.[3] Boundaries in the region could still be quite loose: people, customs, and identities were not easily contained. The Wanjare intermingled significantly with Luo, and Bassi likely had origins in indigenous "Dorobo" peoples.[4] Kipsigis women escaped difficult marriage by seeking shelter in the highlands, and people were traded or pawned across the region in times of famine.[5] Some individuals or whole clans settled with other clans, sometimes of different totems.

Aside from one or two passing Swahili traders, the region thankfully remained outside the orbit of the deadly nineteenth century East African ivory and slave trades, but proximity to Maasai and Kipsigis raiders determined the type and placement of Gusii settlements.[6] Where attacks were relatively rare, Gusii built homesteads (composed of a man, his wife or wives, unmarried daughters, and sons' families—a patrilocal and patrilineal society) along the hills, sometimes within hardened mud walls. There were few, if any, concentrated settlements, although extended families might construct their homesteads near to one another. Each homestead farmed several plots interspersed with others' in a large field, stretching down the slopes from the homes. Toward the upper reaches of North Mugirango and Nyaribari, however, cattle raids forced the construction of fortified settlements. One hundred or more people might build their homes within them. Ndubi, a leader in North Mugirango, encircled his people within impregnable stone walls, parts of which are

Figure 1.1. Looking down the Gucha Gorge
Touring Gusiiland in 1912, geologist Felix Oswald found the scenery much more welcoming than the residents, who repeatedly declined to be hired on as porters. *Source:* Felix Oswald, *Alone in Sleeping Sickness Country*. London: Kegan Paul, 1915.

still visible today. A single passage, easily sealed by thorn branches, allowed entrance. Outside the walls were deep, wide trenches.[7] While their fortresses kept residents some distance from their fields, they also provided security against the depredations of their neighbors.

By the late 1880s Kipsigis' raids (primarily for cattle) had intensified, undoubtedly due to the ravages of cattle diseases in their own herds.[8] After having tasted defeat many times, in one of the few examples of interclan cooperation people of North Mugirango and Getutu, along with some Luo, clashed with Kipsigis raiders at the battle of Saosao. In this terrible battle—the river where the clash occurred was said to have run red with Kipsigis blood—nearly all the cattle thieves were cut down, and the Kipsigis could not undertake any further raids for some years.[9] Nonetheless, into the 1910s fortified settlements remained common.

Fear of attack also left large swaths of land unoccupied. Getutu alone was densely populated and heavy cultivation had by 1910 resulted in some deforestation.[10] The River Gucha marked the effective southern limit of settlement for South Mugirango, Machoge, Bassi, and Nyaribari.[11] It would be

Figure 1.2. Fortified Gusii village
In the late nineteenth and early twentieth centuries those who lived in areas susceptible to cattle raids often enclosed their homes within hardened mud and stone walls with a single, easily defensible entrance. *Source:* C. H. Stigand, *The Land of Zinj: Being an Account of British East Africa, Its Ancient History and Present Inhabitants.* New York: Barnes and Noble, 1913.

several decades into the colonial era before significant numbers of people moved into the virgin territory.

"The Gusii"

Individuals' daily interactions were mainly with clansmen, less regularly with those who shared a totem. Any people identifying themselves as "the Gusii" would have been hard to find.[12] When traveling along the southwest margins of the highlands in the 1880s, Fischer referred to the residents as "Kossowa," although the Luo in the region knew them as "Kissi."[13] Traders from the coast in the 1870s distinguished between the Kosova and the "Watu wa Manga" (people of Manga ridge, that is, the Getutu clans) "who resemble the Kosova in appearance and dress, and speak the same language." Past the Watu wa Manga were the "Wa-Irángi" (Mugirango) who "appear to be of the same race."[14] These northern Mugirango knew themselves only as Mugirango. An early British official found in 1905 that elders there knew the name "Kosova," by which neighboring Kipsigis pastoralists referred to them, while few recognized the Luo's term "Kisii."[15]

This is not to say that residents of the highlands did not recognize that they shared many customs and that their histories were often tied together. Most important was language. They spoke Ekegusii, a member of the Bantu language group which shares little in the way of sounds, grammar, and words with the Nilotic languages of the Luo, Maasai, and Kipsigis. They lived as a linguistic island in their hills, surrounded by the mutually unintelligible tongues of the plains below. (Of course, people along the borders often were to some extent bilingual.) At least in the early twentieth century residents of the highlands understood commonalities shared, on the one hand, by the Getutu, Nyaribari, and North Mugirango, and on the other by the Bassi, South Mugirango, Machoge, and Wanjare. The former collection lived in the higher, wetter "up-east" area known as *masaba*, the latter "down-west" in *chache*. Bassi, Machoge, and South Mugirango respected the Wanjare as ritual elders for having hosted them after their escape from Luoland. Thus, planting and harvesting was to begin in Wanjare, and then spread across the other three lands. No cleansing ceremony was carried out after the killing of a highlander, something required when a Kipsigis, Maasai, or Luo was killed.[16]

What most connected Gusii clans and highlighted boundaries were three core values: circumcision, *nsoni* (shame), and marriage. Only circumcision made men of boys and women of girls. Each neighborhood planned and carried out its own male and female circumcision ceremonies, bringing together a half dozen boys or girls. For all highlanders it was incomprehensible not to circumcise. While the rituals surrounding circumcision taught one *how* to be an adult, including some details of *nsoni*, only the knife *made* one an adult. One might jokingly insult a friend by calling him *yaa*, an uncircumcised boy, but to the wrong person such taunts could spark a physical confrontation.

Circumcision was essential and universal. Circumcision helped mark boundaries. Maasai and Kipsigis circumcised, but the Luo—with whom the highlanders had more regular and peaceful interaction—did not. Girls who cried at circumcision would be taunted that they would be married into Luoland.

Nsoni marked the second core value shared by "the Gusii."[17] *Nsoni* was shame, especially in regard to sexual matters.[18] *Nsoni* rules regulated the most mundane interactions between men and women, juniors and seniors—*abansoni*, people who shared *nsoni* relationships. Certain topics could never be mentioned in the mixed company of parents and children, real and classificatory; a father should never enter the home of his married son; *abansoni* must not shake hands or otherwise come into physical contact. Again, highlanders' identity was shaped in relation to their friendliest neighbors, the Luo, who were considered to have no shame, no *nsoni*. Luo (in Gusii eyes) had no regard for the most tense and tightly regulated relationship, that between father and son, and their clothing exposed much of their bodies. Gusii in the 1940s remarked with disgust that the Luo "even take their fathers' widows."[19]

The relationship that most closely linked the highland clans was marriage.[20] Clans were exogamous and perforce had connection with outsiders. They also preferred to extend kinship connections in different directions, creating links with people with whom there had previously been none. Hence the saying "We marry those whom we fight."[21] This was not meant literally, of course. Marriage required an ongoing relationship between families, at the very least for the replacement of deceased bridewealth cattle, or for the return of bridewealth should a wife die. Hostilities ruled out intermarriage between highlanders and Kipsigis or Maasai: how could one recover cattle from those with whom one fought, who even stole one's cattle? The Luo too could not be considered for marriage. Luo did not circumcise, which was essential to adulthood, and one could not marry a child. According to one elder, lack of circumcision was all that prevented Gusii from marrying Luo.[22] But this was enough. Families would thus marry into a clan which they trusted, that is, one that would respect shared marriage customs. Failure to abide by these customs carried implicit sanctions, as I. Mayer explained: "Any community that consistently refused to play the bridewealth game by the rules would have put itself outside the moral order."[23]

People of the highlands could also call each other *mwanyagetinge*, people of the *ebetinge*, distinctive metal and leather anklets worn by married women. After the exchange of bridewealth a final ceremony, *enyangi*, completed the marriage, and *ebetinge* could be affixed to the wife. *Ebetinge* could not be found among Luo, Maasai, or Kipsigis women. Yet *enyangi* required a further outlay of cattle, which some husbands could not afford for some years, if ever, and *ebetinge* were generally more common in *masaba* areas than in *chache*. This was explained in the 1940s as the primary distinction between *masaba* and *chache*: "they marry differently."[24] Differently in form, but not in structure.

MARRIAGE, PEOPLE, AND POWER

Marriage provided the foundation for Gusii society. "Big men"—the wealthy and important—built their success on the productive and reproductive powers of their wives. On a more basic level, only marriage gave men and women the chance to achieve any status in society, even simply to be considered an adult. Virtually all women, regardless of character, looks, or infirmity, at some point married, though perhaps did not fully marry through *enyangi*, and perhaps to men they did not especially like. Poor men had to wait some years before accumulating enough cattle to marry. Nonetheless, even if they recognized that they might not become polygamists or big men, bachelors had every expectation that they would marry. Gusii society simply had no place for aging bachelors: they were very nearly socially dead.

Bridewealth and Marriage

Marriage did not exist separately from bridewealth. The exchange of cattle legitimized a union. It linked two families, secured a woman's land rights at her husband's home, and granted a man legal rights over all children borne by his wife. While details of these rights were debated[25] the broad schema was not. Without bridewealth, any relationship between a man and woman was illicit: no one recognized it as anything but temporary, liable to be broken at any time, with neither party holding any rights over the other.

While Gusii did not expect bridewealth levels to remain stable over any lengthy period of time, exchanges at any given time tended to keep within a particular range: a certain number of cows, a bull or two, and (from the 1890s) goats. In a few circumstances, a woman might fetch a bridewealth less than that given for her agemates and sisters. A woman who had borne a child out of wedlock might attract a reduced bridewealth. P. Mayer tells us that some fathers were willing to accept fewer cattle for an especially homely or disfigured daughter, or from a suitor whom the father especially favored. By and large, however, at a particular time bridewealth exchanges across the highlands were of roughly similar amounts.[26]

What really mattered in a bridewealth exchange was that the cattle coming in would be sufficient for a man in the household, typically the woman's brother, to give bridewealth for his own wife. *Nyaika*, bridewealth, literally meant "replacement": bridewealth from a daughter used to replace her with a daughter-in-law or a wife.[27] A young man wishing to marry relied heavily on his (full) sister's bridewealth to provide enough cattle for his own marriage. Thus it was essential that a father receive the going rate, lest his son (or he himself) be unable to marry.[28]

The Importance of Marriage

Every man wished to marry many wives, father many children, and own many cattle. As parents would say to a newly circumcised son, come to ask their blessing, "Yes, my child, blessing of cattle and children!"[29] It was commonly said that "cattle were children and children were cattle."[30] So important were children that should a wife die childless the widower could legitimately demand the return of his entire bridewealth, one of the very few instances in which this was so.[31] Sons were essential for a man's future. Sons preserved a man's memory and ensured his status as a venerated and lineage-founding ancestor. Men sacrificed to their ancestors (primarily fathers and grandfathers) to appease them, but also to ask "their blessings 'for increase of people and cattle' so that 'we may get sons to remember us as we remember you.'"[32]

Both sons and daughters were desired. One proverb tells that a house with only daughters will not be poor in food and cattle (because of their labor and bridewealth) but loneliness will come to it once the girls marry and move away.[33] Fathers appropriated the labor of their sons, at least until the youths married, thus a homestead of many sons could claim and exploit the best farmland and pastures. Young men took up arms to defend home and herd, and through raids built up the homestead's herd. Youth helped to enforce decisions of councils of elders, and in numbers could induce others to accede to their fathers' opinions.[34] Although daughters shifted lineage affiliation upon marriage (and so did not carry on their fathers' names and memories) they too were essential to the success of the homestead. Fulfilling a homestead's bridewealth needs relied heavily on a daughter's bridewealth, such that (at least in the 1940s) "the proportion of daughters to sons in the individual family is generally the factor that determines plenty or poverty in cattle."[35]

The importance of children could be seen in the most mundane aspects of daily life. On a day-to-day basis girls assisted their mothers in burdensome household chores. A song collected in the 1970s was a woman's lament: "I have cows but no son/He cannot bring a wife to braid my hair."[36] A person without a child might call to mind the proverb, "S/he has died without [meat] in the hand with which to eat *wimbi* [the staple grain]": a family without children would not often slaughter a goat, for there were not enough mouths to consume all the meat.[37]

Bridewealth, not paternity, determined fatherhood, thus a bachelor could never truly have children (nor become an ancestor) no matter the number of his biological offspring.[38] Men and their biological children might share emotional ties, but in the end sons returned to their jural fathers for bridewealth and land rights.[39] As P. Mayer explained in the 1940s, "A man may be on excellent terms with his own [biological] children by another man's widow or wife, but if any choice has to be made he is far more likely to side with his own legal children even if they are not physically his."[40]

Even more than dying without progeny, the thought of dying a bachelor horrified men. Impoverished men living through extended bachelorhoods existed at the edges of society, accepting but unable to achieve the basic hallmarks of adulthood. A bachelor aged chronologically but remained a junior while his age-mates became respected elders; his advice went unheeded and unwanted at public functions. The very idea of an "adult bachelor" made little sense: an adult man was one who had at least begun to craft a homestead filled with wives, cattle, and children. The death of a bachelor even brought down a curse on his family. To prevent tragedy compounding tragedy, a bachelor was buried with a piece of wood and the words, "This is your wife." This was *okogirokia*, "to appease someone by not withholding his rightful dues," to give him in death what should have been his in life.[41]

Simply paying bridewealth would not necessarily ensure a man's status and progeny. *Enyangi* marked the final transfer of rights over a woman from her father to her husband. Until *enyangi* a father could return the bridewealth and end the marriage, but *enyangi* added an extra "religious and mystical element" that cemented the union. The *ebetinge* would then be affixed to the woman to identify her as married. Having completed *enyangi* granted a man the status to fill a respected role like a marriage priest. But *enyangi* required an extra payment of cattle, over and above the bridewealth already given. Some men could not immediately afford this and so put off *enyangi* for some years, and other marriages never reached this final stage. Marriage was always better than being single, but poor men still yearned for the status and security conferred by a *full* marriage.[42]

All men desired to be polygamists. As one elder put it in the 1980s, "to see many wives meant much happiness."[43] Obviously, more wives could bear more children. But polygamists increased their social and economic stature in other ways. Multiple wives could prepare food and beer enough to accommodate larger and more frequent *risaga* (joint work parties) than could a monogamous homestead. With agricultural tasks completed in a timely manner a wealthy homestead produced yet more surplus. Haughty polygamists reinforced the lesser standing of monogamists. As one proverb tells, "the monogamist sits by the doorway" during beer drinking sessions. If his only wife were to fall sick he would jump up hastily to run to her side, upsetting the long drinking straws of his comrades. He should sit by the door, then, where he would disturb no one. As explained by local chronicler Erasto Abuga, "People used to say that a man would be much more upset over the death of his only wife, than if he had two or three."[44]

Wealth, Wisdom, and Authority

Aside from polygamy, men had other avenues to gain the esteem of their fellows, and to translate this into authority within their communities. The wise and sound of judgment garnered accolades. This, some said, was preferable to wealth: "Riches go to sleep," a proverb told, "The wealthy/powerful come and go." A good name lasted longer.[45] Men cultivated and expressed wisdom when they gathered at a *tureti* hut. Over beer and meat the *etureti* discussed the world and sang. Their songs passed along knowledge to younger men, and the soloists were the men most well-versed in custom.

If wisdom was valued above wealth, wealth brought wisdom. The *tureti* was supplied by the local big man who had the resources to provide a steady supply of beer and food. A man who rarely came to singing sessions could not soak up the wisdom of the ancestors, something of which his comrades were well aware. Should an occasional visitor strike up a solo the chorus responded with stony silence.[46] What man would fail to regularly attend the *etureti* gatherings? The man who had to spend long days in the fields. The poor man, especially the bachelor, did not have the leisure time of the wealthy polygamists. The poorest even hovered outside the *tureti*, hoping for a taste of the leftover beer. When the elders called for a fresh pot of beer a poor man might come to remove the finished pot, otherwise the work of women. As he took the pot away he scraped out the last bits of (highly nutritious) beer.[47] Nothing could make more apparent his low status or more embarrass the poor man than scavenging the discarded beer of his wealthy, and wise, seniors. If the monogamist sat by the doorway, the poor and the bachelors never passed through the door.

AGRICULTURE, CATTLE, AND BRIDEWEALTH

Women performed the bulk of agricultural labor in Gusiiland's extremely fertile and well-watered soil. The essential crop was *wimbi*, millet. *Wimbi* was mixed with boiling water to form a solid, sticky, and highly nutritious staple, *obokima*, taken either by itself or with meat and vegetables. *Obokima* (now generally made of maize) remains so central to their diet that Gusii often translate it simply as "food." Other crops included beans and a variety of greens and fruits. The daily and recurring tasks of planting, weeding, and harvesting fell primarily on women, along with domestic tasks of cooking and childrearing. Women of a neighborhood worked together in *egesangio*, joint rotating work parties. When brush had to be cleared men stepped forward, and many also assisted their wives in the fields. Men also had their own plots, *emonga*, on which to grow crops. These they could use to supplement a wife's empty granary, or to trade for cattle or other goods. Women commanded the surplus of their plots, also used for trade.

Homesteads accumulated wealth through trade. From the late 1800s Gusii engaged in irregular but substantial trade with less fertile and more drought-prone Luo areas. Gusii exchanged beans and *wimbi* for livestock, pots, baskets, and marijuana. So essential was this trade for Luo clans that they looked upon the highlands as "a reserve store for food and annually dispose[d] of thousands of sheep and goats in exchange for grain."[48] Occasional disparities in weather conditions contributed to an intra-highland trade on a smaller scale. Neither Luo nor Gusii established permanent markets. Instead, Gusii women went on regular trading expeditions into the lowlands.[49] Moving in small groups, women (believed to be less likely to spy on enemy clans) carried out the bulk of this trade generally in safety.[50]

As in most other parts of eastern and southern Africa, the major motivation for disposing of surplus crops was to collect cattle. Some trade was necessary for household goods, but Gusii bartered chiefly for animals. While important for milk and meat,[51] cattle's primary use value was bridewealth. Given the time men spent with their herds and the role cattle played in ensuring men's success in life, the relationship between man and beast could become close, even sentimental. Men often named their cows as they might dogs, as evidenced by these from the colonial era: *Esimba* (lion), Major, *Toto* (child), Rhino. Most telling (and most touching) was the case of Nyamerere Abuga, who in the 1940s had named his favorite cow Nyarinda—a girl's name—because, he said, "I am fond of it."[52]

Aside from trade, Gusii had a few other ways to collect cattle. People with special skills, such as marriage priests and priestesses, circumcisers, blacksmiths, and practitioners of trepanation (cranial surgery), could be compensated with cattle.[53] Natural reproduction could help slowly build a herd, as related by a song collected in the 1970s:

> Cows were stolen but a thin one was left behind
> They said it was useless
> But from it came many calves
> And the owner said they were fools
> They should have taken the thin one too.[54]

A man in dire straits could perform agricultural labor for a more wealthy man, or assist a blacksmith and be rewarded with a cow.[55]

Young men also acquired cattle through theft. Gusii raided Kipsigis and Luo, as well as other Gusii clans, while Kipsigis, Maasai and (to a lesser extent) Luo youth also raided Gusii herds. Between initiation and marriage, and sometimes before initiation, neighborhood boys grazed cattle from *ebesirate* (cattle posts; sing. *egesirate*) situated past their homesteads' boundaries. There they guarded the cattle against raids by other groups, their huts protected by one and often two strong branch fences, and frequently by pits along the outer wall.[56] In the later 1800s, raiding constituted a normal activity of youth who dared traverse the no-man's land between different clan settlements. As an educated man put it in the 1940s, *ebesirate* were only for guarding cattle, although his words belied another activity: "No, it was not for stealing cattle though one could rob cattle which were going with only a few men."[57] One pious Seventh-day Adventist (SDA) elder who had spent his preconversion years herding cattle assured his readers that "stealing livestock is not the same thing as real stealing."[58]

Cattle theft remained common well into the colonial era. As late as 1914 many men carried weapons due to regular attacks by Maasai and Kipsigis.[59]

Gusii youth were certainly not blameless, and in fact colonial officials over the course of thirty years regularly commented on their proclivity for cattle theft. The Gusii were "most expert cattle thieves"[60] whose "principle occupation consisted of cattle raiding."[61]

CONTROL AND COOPERATION

Women's Status

If men chased after cattle and wives, women's success came primarily through their menfolk. Like men, for women marriage was essential. There was no word for adult maiden: *bomokungu* meant both wife and grown woman.[62] Only after *enyangi* did a "girl" fully pass into the ranks of "woman," although a "girl" who lived many years and raised children with a man might in generosity be referred to as a true woman by neighbors.[63] As it did for men, bridewealth ensured that a woman would be remembered "as the ancestress of a house and a lineage branch."[64]

Bearing children defined the successful wife. While young, children shouldered some of the burdensome daily tasks that consumed so much of a woman's time. For several years after her son's marriage a mother also commanded her daughter-in-law's labor. Sons promised their mother security and helped to support her in her old age. In polygamist homesteads, where co-wives and their sons might try to appropriate a widow's land or cattle, sons fiercely defended their mothers' interests. A woman without sons was a pitiable figure. Who would protect her interests and care for her in old age?[65] It was for these reasons that nearly all the cattle a woman might collect through trade was put toward her sons' bridewealth.

Although daughters moved away upon marriage their relationships with their mothers remained strong—one of the closest bonds women had. It was expected that a woman would regularly return to her mother to help in the fields or simply to visit. Mothers brought milk to their daughters; one of the bridewealth cows remained with the bride's mother as the "cow of greeting the daughter." If men thought of making marriage in terms of bridewealth, women considered distance also.[66]

After *enyangi* women did have a few options for more individuated status. The wife of a marriage priest had her own special duties in the ceremonies. Other women conducted female circumcision ceremonies, and some took roles as diviners or dispensers of specialized or ritual medicines.[67] A song collected in 1975 told of such a woman:

> Kemunto Ngina Ongone was a medicine woman
> When people went to war, she gave medicine to defeat the enemies
> They said whoever drank beer should give a little to that good
>   woman who made them strong.[68]

One woman apparently had a role or status enough to mediate a land dispute between Nyaribari and Bassi clans sometime in the 1850s, but nothing else is known of her.[69] In 1908, a youth speared and nearly killed a British officer, by all accounts at the urging of an older woman named Moraa.

Women who had not borne sons could trade agricultural surplus for bridewealth cattle with which to "marry." This bride was not a wife of the woman but of a fictitious son. She labored as did any wife, and took lovers on the side for reproduction (much the same as happened in the homestead of a sterile man). The older woman, "grandmother" to the offspring, had full rights over them, including contracting marriages and giving and collecting bridewealth. If the young "wife's" lover attempted to take her or their children, the senior woman would send him off, telling him "You were only kept as an Omosomba," a bought person.[70] It is not clear how many women were able to take advantage of this practice, and while it seems to have become rare by the 1950s it is not unheard of today.[71]

Marriage Disputes

Although not to the extent witnessed from the later 1930s, in previous decades dissatisfied women fled their homes to avoid or end unwanted marriages. This was most effective if she ran to a clan with which her father's and, if already married, her husband's clan were on poor terms. She might also run into Kipsigisland if she lived close to the border. The woman (and children if she had any) was certain to find a man willing to take her in, and over time her past would be forgotten or, more likely, not discussed publically.[72] What made this strategy successful was the lack of any overarching authority in the highlands. Other than his own initiative, a man could turn only to his *omogambi* (plural: *abagambi*), his clan's ritual leader, who had at his command only persuasion. The value of a "free" wife likely outweighed the moral appeals of another clan's leaders. One elder explained this strategy:

> When a woman ran to another clan, the husband could not claim her back because of enmity between clans. Before the colonial period there were many Kitutu [Getutu] women among the Majoge. They ran away from Kitutu. If [women had] differences with the[ir] husband[s] they could run here where the Kitutu could not follow them because the Kitutu and the Majoge clans were enemies.[73]

One man recalled a specific instance of a woman escaping her home in North Mugirango and seeking shelter in Getutu. Under cover of night, her male guardian came to kill his Getutu enemy, but was himself killed. From that point, men of North Mugirango never again dared trace a runaway woman into Getutu.[74]

Men had other ways of controlling women's movements. After performance of *enyangi* a wife's adultery brought on *amasangia*, a mystical uncleanliness that could wreak havoc on the homestead and possibly kill her husband, and make childbirth long and painful until the adulteress confessed her sin. *Ebetinge*, the anklets placed on women at the completion of the *enyangi* ceremony, displayed a woman's status.[75] A man should consider her off-limits: he should not abuse her nor take her as a lover. *Ebetinge* could not be removed without courting mystical retribution. A husband who tired of a wife continually running away, or who presumed his young, unwilling bride would not long stay with him, might forcibly affix to her *engetare*, solid metal versions of *ebetinge*. The expectation was that no man would give shelter to a woman so obviously disobedient and disagreeable and that the runaway woman, shamed and alone, would eventually return to her husband. At least by the 1930s they were used relatively rarely (so much so as to not appear in written sources) but served as a threat to would-be runaways.[76]

Nonetheless, *ebetinge* and *engetare* did not always ensure compliance with male authority. In theory a man would hesitate to take in a married woman, for someday his own wife or daughter might too run off and he would wish no man to harbor her.[77] But this golden rule worked much better in theory than in practice. Men's circumstances, needs, and interests did not always coincide. Some men cut off *engetare* in exchange for a pot of beer. Aging bachelors, desperate for wives, willingly took in runaway women.[78] Men of other clans saw such women as free additions to their homesteads' productive and reproductive powers. Other women simply removed *ebetinge* when they ran off, making it easier to be accepted by a new man.[79]

For wives who had already borne children options were more limited. A woman's and her sons' land rights were secure only at the home of the man who had given bridewealth. Only a legal father could be made to give bridewealth cattle for his sons and, it was said, young men "run home to father when the time comes to marry."[80] Should a mother run off her husband might be content to let her go, knowing that eventually she would have to return. More commonly, a discontented wife many years into a marriage would shift her hut to a distant corner of the homestead's land, signifying that she continued to cultivate and to claim land rights there, but that other marital (including sexual) relations were no longer practiced.[81]

Women had their own ways to keep their menfolk in line. A serious insult was to sing songs of widows or perform rituals otherwise restricted to widows, intimating that a wife wished her husband were dead. I. Mayer related a case of an impotent man who had committed suicide after his wife stopped cooking for him: cooking implied intercourse, and thus a refusal to cook (or, in turn, a man's refusal to eat) meant a refusal of conjugal duties.[82] Much more deeply insulting, and an act that might be used to end a marriage, was for a wife to throw human excrement in her husband's face.[83]

Fathers and Sons

One of the more regular sites where seniors and juniors battled were the *ebesirate* (cattle villages). During the initial wedding ceremonies (*egechabero*) girlfriends of the bride collected at the groom's *egesirate* for an overnight celebration. While not "strictly obligatory" in the elders' view, the young man normally slaughtered at least a goat and a bull to complement the beer provided by the girls, and often slaughtered many more of the family herd (though not cows, to be sure). The consumption of these animals bitterly divided youth (who saw this as an opportunity to raise themselves in the esteem of young women) and fathers (who, claiming custom did not require the practice, decried the unnecessary wasting of the beasts). Speaking with elders in the 1940s, P. Mayer concluded that this "conflict assumed considerable proportion in Gusii eyes."[84] In 1908, a British official expressed concern over young men who "forcibly take their fathers' cattle with them or keep them as their own, only occasionally allowing the latter to take a little of the milk."[85] When in the 1920s the *ebesirate* finally disappeared (more of obsolescence than repeated government attempts to repress them)[86] elders expressed little displeasure, relieved from "the trouble we used to have with our sons slaughtering beasts there without our approval, to entertain their girls."[87]

Siblings

Control over homestead resources produced conflict not just between husbands and wives, and fathers and sons, but between households as well. A polygamist reserved the right to transfer cattle between his wives' households. A son of marriageable age might lack bridewealth, perhaps because of an imbalance of sons and daughters in his household, or his sisters were many years from being married. Another household might find itself in the exact opposite situation, with plentiful cattle but no immediate demands on them. The homestead head could then transfer cattle from the latter to the former. This was not permanent exchange, but a loan: a debt, it was said, "can never die."[88] The borrower household *had* to repay the cattle. Debts could carry into subsequent generations, and given the vagaries of human and bovine reproduction, household disputes over the number and quality of cows to be repaid, and when, could strain relations between co-wives and half-siblings.[89]

Even within the household competition over resources was not absent: "brothers fight at the mother's breast" a proverb observed.[90] Brother competed with brother over cattle, as evidenced in one 1947 court case in which the plaintiff accused his brother of misappropriating his army remits. Rather than saving them until his discharge, the veteran charged, the defendant had purchased six goats then slaughtered them to pay his own poll tax. His brother tried to redirect blame on their father (there were only four goats, he claimed, and the father had been the one who slaughtered them) but the court found him guilty.[91]

The futures of brothers and sisters were tightly linked, and this was especially true of a woman and the brother who had used her bridewealth for his own marriage. These relationships could produce warm feelings or ugliness. When a woman was to have *enyangi* done her linked brother prepared a goat skin for her and had a voice in the selection of the cattle.[92] An eldest son could claim a heifer (*emesuto*) from his maternal uncle.[93] The woman herself might claim a heifer and, as elders told P. Mayer, he would give "it to her because he loved her. In those days the sister was respected and feared by her brother."[94] Yet a man's reliance on his sister's bridewealth could place great pressure on her to accept and remain in a particular marriage, regardless of what she might otherwise desire.[95] Refusing a suitor delayed a brother's marriage. By running from a husband a woman could force her brother to break his own marriage and reclaim the bridewealth he had given, in order to return the cattle he had received for his sister.[96] Thus some women suffered moral pressure and physical coercion to accept their fate from brothers more anxious to preserve their own marriages than to sympathize with unhappy sisters.

Nsoni

Nsoni both shored up the authority of senior men and helped to prevent conflict, causing people to avoid situations shot through with unbearable tension. As it has been explained in another context, in *nsoni*-type relationships "any tensions that exist or may arise are prevented from breaking, by open conflict, what should be a friendly relation."[97] Fathers and sons did not attend the same beer drinks, lest a drunken youth abuse his senior. Intimations of sex and reproduction between mothers-in-law and sons-in-law, and fathers-in-law and daughters-in-law, were reduced by *nsoni*. (Thus menopause allowed for the relaxation of mother-in-law–son-in-law avoidance rules.[98]) Members of alternate generations—grandparents and grandchildren—were not *abansoni*. No topic was off limits for discussion, and they could even see each other naked.

The authority of fathers was expressed, and reinforced, by *nsoni*. "The *nsoni* etiquette," I. Mayer explains, "set parent against child, in ways providing that children would always be presented with a dignified father image, and would not see their father in his other, free and easy manifestations."[99] From the outward manifestation of fatherly status flowed respect and deference. With *nsoni* sons were less likely to defy or attack their fathers—although, by the same token, fathers were less likely to find themselves in situations that might provoke defiance. Clearly, *nsoni* could not eliminate father–son conflict. Perhaps equally important was a senior's control over cattle and the contracting of his sons' marriages (although fathers were expected to act within certain cultural norms). As a last resort, a father could punish a son through a curse that broke fundamental rules of *nsoni*. Before his son, a father would expose his penis and say "With this I begot you, with this I disinherit you."[100]

POLITICAL POWER

Patron–Client Relations

Influence was garnered by those most well off. As the proverbs say, "The property of the pauper is used by the rich"; "The property of the poor monogamist is owned by the powerful man."[101] An effective means of becoming rich and powerful was to attract clients and become a "big man." The cattle-rich loaned out cows to kinsmen who would tend them and drink their milk. The owner of the cows both gained clients and avoided the loss of his entire herd if disease struck his homestead. Poor men sought out wealthy men for help with bridewealth, and people fleeing famine or warfare took shelter with big men.[102] Kibagendi, a Mayer informant, recalled how clients (even some Luo) came to him during a great famine. They got along quite well (according to Kibagendi), they intermarried, and he allowed them use of his cattle.[103] Like other dependents, male clients added to the homestead's defenses, and women to its productive and reproductive potential. All clients helped with food production, creating new wealth which could attract and support yet more clients.[104] Thus potential clients were welcomed with open arms. "[Gusii] long ago never killed a [stranger]," recalled one elder. "If they found someone loitering they would welcome him and give him cattle to marry or if there was a widow he would take her over [i.e., live and raise children with her]. [Gusii] wanted people."[105]

By building up patron–client networks, Getutu created the only chieftaincy in the highlands. Around 1820, Oisera fled to Manga ridge after the bloody battle with Maasai. There he and his followers settled, protected by the steep cliffs atop which they built their homesteads. Yet Luo and Maasai still attempted raids, and people deferred to Oisera as a judicial and military leader. His son, Nyakundi, ushered in a period of prosperity and expansion in the 1830s and 1840s, though the fortunes of Getutu ebbed and flowed over the rest of the century. Sometime in the 1870s or 1880s a succession dispute broke out, dividing Getutu between two competing chiefly lineages. While each remained powerful, Getutu's expansion was checked up to British conquest.[106]

Getutu's success came from the clients it attracted. After their dispersal by the Maasai, confusion reigned among all the Gusii clans. Many non-Getutu clans sought refuge under Oisera's patronage and paid him periodic tribute

Figure 1.3. Manga escarpment
The Manga escarpment is the most prominent physical feature of Gusiiland; from the top, one can sometimes glimpse sunlight reflecting off Lake Victoria forty miles to the north. *Source:* Felix Oswald, *Alone in Sleeping Sickness Country*. London: Kegan Paul, 1915.

of cattle and grain. As clients built Getutu's strength it attracted yet more clients.[107] Getutu was known to have the stomach of an elephant, able to swallow many clients.

Getutu's patron–client system was unique in the highlands. In other areas dislodged people might take shelter with in-laws, *abako*. Generally this would be for a short time only, although some did assimilate with their hosts and become part of that clan. By shaving their heads at the death of local prominents (demonstrating their membership in that community) and eventually adopting exogamy rules of the clan, they would no longer be identified as *abako*. In contrast, clients in Getutu were not *abako* but *abasomba*, "bought people." As true strangers exogamous rules were inapplicable and marriages could be contracted straightaway. Daughters of clients could be married to sons of hosts at less than normal bridewealth or patrons might provide bridewealth to clients.[108] More than other groups, Getutu offered physical protection and watched carefully the interests of their clients, intent on rapidly integrating them into patronage and pseudo-kinship networks.

Political Power

Apart from Getutu, authority was rarely concentrated in the hands of one man. At the local neighborhood level (*maiga*) the authority to resolve disputes lay with elders, *abanyamaiga*. Two dispute resolution bodies lay above *abanyamaiga*, the *etureti* elders and the *egesaku* elders, although older Gusii insist that the use of *etureti* as councils of elders came only in the 1930s. At the most, the *egesaku* adjudicated intraclan disputes.[109]

Only *abagambi* approached anything like the chieftaincy of Getutu. An *omogambi*'s duties were restricted to his clan's foreign affairs and ceremonial duties. A man could borrow his *omogambi*'s staff when going to hash out a dispute in another clan; this symbol of the *omogambi*'s authority would (hopefully) induce the local elders to give the man a fair hearing. *Abagambi* performed the ceremonies to introduce first plantings and initiate the harvest season, and called on rainmakers when their services were needed. Other than this, *abagambi* had very little power.[110]

One of the few cases in which senior men across the highlands worked together was toward the limitation of bridewealth. When it had reached a reasonable amount and needed to be capped, or had risen too high and needed to be reduced, elites worked together to establish a new standard rate. The earliest known attempt to reduce bridewealth was in the early 1890s in Getutu. Bogonko, a leading figure, gathered other elders and argued that the bridewealth rate—as high as 18 or more cows—was untenable, and suggested a reduction to 10. The other elders refused, charging that Bogonko acted out of self-interest. He had already married off his daughters at the higher rate, and thus could marry many wives if the rate were lowered. He cursed the lot of them, to which many Gusii attributed that decade's cattle epidemics. Bogonko posthumously reduced the rate after all.[111]

In 1903, following the lead of Ogeto (a Getutu *omogambi* and member of the chiefly lineage) Getutu elders agreed that the going rate be reduced from five or six head to three cows and a bull. Only one man raised his voice against it, and he was quickly shouted down. To seal the rate every elder spit into a hole, swearing that they must die if they did not abide by the limit. At least some *abagambi* of non-Getutu clans also ratified the new limit.[112] There may have been other such instances, as the district commissioner noted in 1921 that the Gusii "periodically enforced [bridewealth limits] before they were administered" by the British.[113]

THE ESTABLISHMENT OF COLONIAL RULE

Conquest and Gasuku

As in many other parts of the *pax Britannia* it was the rattling of a Maxim gun which marked the advent of British rule in Gusiiland. In 1905, under the pretext of punishing Gusii cattle raiders but also forcefully to introduce the Union Jack,

Figure 1.4. Gusii youth with spear
Throughout the 1910s it was not uncommon for a white traveler or missionary to be met by armed youth. *Source:* Felix Oswald, *Alone in Sleeping Sickness Country*. London: Kegan Paul, 1915.

a King's African Rifles column and African irregulars entered the highlands. Cattle confiscation in Wanjare and Getutu sparked pitched battles between Gusii and colonial forces, leaving at least 160 Africans dead. For the next two years the British remained occupied elsewhere in Kenya (then known as the East African Protectorate) and no administrators were dispatched to the area. Only in 1908 did the state post G. A. S. Northcote there. He was soon speared and nearly murdered by a young Gusii man (intoxicated, according to the British, or urged on by an older woman questioning her menfolk's bravery, according to Gusii). This and the killing of several African police and porters in western Getutu brought another expedition, this time attacking Gusii almost at random. White troops and guns ensured that the fighting in 1905 and 1908 would be bloody, while African irregulars wreaked havoc more widely—stealing cattle, burning homes and crops, and raping and abducting women.[114]

Winston Churchill, then Undersecretary of State for the Colonies, was aghast at the 1908 "punitive expedition," not for the disregard for African lives but for the implications the massacre might have for his imperial dreams. "No doubt the clans should have been punished," he wrote, "but 160 have now been killed outright *without any further casualties* on our side . . . It looks like butchery. If the H[ouse] of C[ommons] get hold of it, all our plans in [the East African Protectorate] will be under a cloud. Surely it can not be necessary to go on killing these defenseless people on such an enormous scale."[115]

London did not have the will, nor the men or the money, to rule their African colonies through violence alone. Only once after 1908 would the British again use deadly force on a large scale in the new South Kavirondo district, which stretched from the Tanganyika border up to Winan Gulf in Lake Victoria, encompassing Gusii, Luo, Suba, and Kuria peoples. Here as across Africa Britons urgently needed African intermediaries to carry out the daily business of colonial rule. From Northcote's arrival on through independence European administrators in South Kavirondo were few and their tenures brief. Administrators' annual reports incessantly bemoaned the lack of staff in the district and the routine turnover of those who were assigned there.[116] Between 1907 and 1957 the state made thirty-six appointments for the post of district commissioner (DC), along with another eight temporary appointments. Seven men served more than once, meaning that over fifty years thirty-seven different men headed up the district.[117] In just one year, 1951, four different men filled the post of DC.[118] Their white subordinates were rotated in and out of Kisii town (established by the British as their district headquarters) with equal frequency.[119]

Administrators freely admitted the costs of officers' limited presence in the district. In 1925, the DC acknowledged that "it is quite incorrect to say that the District as a whole is being administered." Matters thought to be of importance to Africans—economics, agriculture, health—"are merely being toyed with, if indeed anything whatever is being accomplished under these heads."[120] Muksero (a tiny group that had hived off from Getutu in the nineteenth century) was not far from the orbit of Kisii town, but District Officer Desmond O'Hagan touring there in 1931 noted that "no officer has been here for over a year, and I am certain that all is not well in this location." O'Hagan himself managed to stay there all of three days.[121]

With Europeans unable to visit outlying areas of the district with any regularity, it was left to their African employees to carry out day-to-day rule.[122] Up to the 1930s, the most important "indirect ruler" was Gasuku, chief translator in South Kavirondo. Gasuku, a Suba from Mfangano island in Lake Victoria, joined up with Europeans early on. His linguistic skills quickly made him indispensable to the administration.[123] Swahili would for some time be little known among Africans there, and administrators rarely learned local languages. Virtually all communication between the state and the masses passed through Gasuku's lips. He was, the DC wrote in 1920, of great help and his "intimate knowledge of the district" was of inestimable value to the administration, given the regular replacement of European staff.[124]

Figure 1.5. Kisii town from the southwest, 1997
Today a bustling trading and administrative center, Kisii town was established only with the advent of colonial rule. Locals still sometimes refer to Kisii as "Getembe" (the name of the valley in which the town is situated) or "Bosongo" (place of the white people). Nyanchwa Adventist Church is in the foreground, and Manga escarpment is in the distance.

The administration's utter reliance on Gasuku, and his greed for power and wealth, meant that he soon became the *de facto* ruler of the district. Catholic missionaries referred to him as "head chief" of the Gusii.[125] Commoners approached the state, and felt state power, via Gasuku. When sitting as a magistrate the DC adjudicated cases as presented by Gasuku in Swahili, which differed greatly from the cases presented by litigants in Ekegusii and Dholuo. In Gasuku's translation, the litigants' words often mattered less than the size of their bribes.[126] When appointing chiefs, administrators sought Gasuku's recommendation, which an interested party could have for a "gift" of cattle.[127]

Gasuku's reign over the district was known to everyone but administrators. Kisii town was known for many years by Gusii as *Getembe gia Gasuku*, Gasuku's town (*Getembe* being the name of the valley in which Kisii town was built). Gasuku bragged that the DC was a hyena, and that should anyone interfere with Gasuku, he would turn loose the "hyena."[128] These were not idle threats, and Gasuku was widely feared.[129] Those few who tried to expose his misdeeds failed miserably. Administrators dismissed bribery charges made against him as *fitina*, baseless accusations borne of petty politics.[130] More commonly, Gasuku prevented complaints from ever reaching white ears. His network of clients fed him information on those who would dare to challenge him, and with his informal yet inescapable control of police powers he ensured that his enemies would be arrested, beaten, and jailed.[131] Gasuku's extreme wealth was displayed in his very body, which grew larger as he prospered. Gasuku collected cattle enough to marry twenty-two wives from across the district and fathered enough children to populate Jogoo, a suburb of Kisii town.[132]

The administration well understood Gasuku's importance as mediator between themselves and the masses. Gasuku's retirement as translator in 1932 "removed a link in the chain of Government and native authority," the DC wrote, and Africans "have been somewhat puzzled throughout the year in adjusting their relations with the District Headquarters and officers on safari."[133] Gasuku subsequently retained a not inconsiderable amount of power, serving on the district appeals tribunal and as chief of the Suba location of Gwassi. By now the churches had begun producing a small but important number of men with Swahili and/or English, and Gasuku's successors could not replicate his achievements. The era of the African dictator over all of South Kavirondo had passed.

Chiefs

Aside from Gasuku, the administration relied heavily on chiefs and headmen, but finding men to fill these roles was not simple. The highlands were carved into eight locations (following precolonial clan affiliations) each under a chief.[134] Outside Getutu, only *abagambi* had held any authority, and that largely ceremonial. The British knew this full well,[135] and so sought out collaborators wherever they could find them. Some were *abagambi* who had early on befriended the British. Ombati of Muksero had traveled to Kisumu in 1900 to seek British assistance in his feud with Getutu clans, and the officer who ventured into North Mugirango in 1904 received a warm welcome from Ndubi in his fortified settlement.[136] Both were appointed chiefs. Nyamosi, born either on an island in Lake Victoria or in German East Africa, exploited his reputation as a wizard to rule Majoge.[137] In Getutu, a member of one branch of the mid-1800s chieftaincy was installed as chief, much to the disgust of the other. Administrators desperately sought men with any kind of legitimacy. The Provincial Commissioner of Nyanza (of which South Kavirondo district was a part) reported that they selected men "on account of their supposed medicinal or magical powers, or as being the principal or one of the richest elders in the district or because of some personal characteristic appreciated by the local people or the administration."[138]

Chiefs differed from precolonial elites in both their duties and the areas under their authority. Whereas each *omogambi* had headed a clan, colonial-era chiefs ruled multiclan locations. The colonial state devolved on chiefs a range of duties for which there were far too few Britons to carry out effectively, such as ensuring the completion of road work and assisting in the collection of taxes. Compared to the limited impositions *abagambi* had made, chiefly rule appeared quite onerous.

It ought not be surprising that chiefs often found it hard to carry out their duties and for some time lacked any legitimacy in the eyes of their subjects. Northcote was under no illusions as to chiefs' powers. "It is useless to think [chiefs] really rule their subjects," he wrote in 1909. "The chief at present can only enforce power through the DC." That anything was done toward taxation or road work depended almost entirely on the administration: "Without the European at [the chief's] back, these functions could not be performed."[139] The populace tended to prefer men the administration considered ineffective. At a 1926 *baraza* (public meeting) elders in South Mugirango recommended Wigara s/o Ogako to be chief primarily, District Commissioner S. O. V. Hodge believed, "for his weakness of character so that he would not interfere at all in the Location." Hodge selected another man.[140]

Cognizant of their tenuous hold on power, some chiefs simply did nothing, and lost their jobs because of it.[141] Other chiefs gamely tried to build support from below. Onchango, chief of South Mugirango in 1931, was notable because he was "stingy with food and hence . . .finds it difficult to keep anyone round him."[142] That administrators noted his failure suggests other chiefs more successfully distributed foodstuffs to followers, a means by which patrons of old had attracted clients.

World War I did nothing to stabilize chiefly rule. The state fed its hunger for Carrier Corps porters with the forced labor of young men, 34,000 of them from South Kavirondo. Chiefs' *askari*s swooped in at night, tying up unfortunate young men and marching them off to Kisii town.[143] "Whenever you see the fez capped [African soldiers or chiefs' retainers]," people cried, "they take our young men away." Potential recruits took shelter in the forests and did without water in their marijuana pipes so that the noise would not betray them.[144] The DC noted that in rounding up men for the Corps "the chiefs and headmen have generally done all that could be desired of them." Given the horrific conditions in the Corps (thousands of men died from exhaustion, malnutrition, and disease) those sent out from the district undoubtedly noticed their chiefs' efforts as well.[145] Elsewhere in the district Luo youth appeared unusually committed to Christianity, likely in hopes of protection from conscription—a hope dashed by the priest who "refused admittance" to "able-bodied men" needed for the war.[146] The forced mobilization of labor continued after the war. The DC ordered five thousand men out of the district to work in 1920, instructions carried out by chiefs and headmen.[147] These unwilling laborers were later observed in Kisumu linked by ropes around their necks.[148]

Given the coercive aspects of their rule it is little wonder that chiefs faced mounting challenges. In 1917, the DC found it necessary to impose a collective fine on Kitutu location for "grievous hurt" of Chief Onsongo, while in 1926 a court case was made against a man who attempted to attack the chief with a *rungu* (club).[149] Popular dissatisfaction with chiefs reached a crescendo in the cult of Mumbo.[150] Mumbo, a massive python said to live in Lake Victoria, promised followers that the millennium was impending, at which time Europeans and chiefs would disappear. As one DC noted of a 1933 manifestation of the cult, "the chiefs are evidently afraid of [Mumbo] and realize that they are the special object of hatred and scorn." Among the teachings common that year was that "the great snake is coming to destroy all the chiefs and particularly Aoga," assistant chief of Kitutu and brother of Chief Onsongo.[151] Aside from millennial predictions, everyday Mumboite activities threatened to undermine what little legitimacy chiefs might have accumulated. Some Mumbo adepts held public meetings, normally a function of chiefs. More insidiously, adherents gave tribute to Mumbo's spokesmen, who in turn held rousing feasts: this was the stuff of patron–client relations.[152] Earthly representatives of Mumbo threatened to supplant chiefs as would-be patrons. Many were eventually rounded up, tried, and deported from the province, with chiefs acting as the instigators of the repression.

With the difficulties chiefs faced exercising their powers and convincing people of their authority, for over a decade colonial rule in South Kavirondo remained insecure. At times the state admitted its inability to provide security to Europeans traveling through the area. When trader Richard Gethin arrived in Kisii town in 1914, it caused some consternation among the administration, since "strange Europeans [*sic*] were not at the time encouraged in South Kavirondo owing to the Mumbo trouble."[153] In September that year, invading Germans engaged the British in a battle in Kisii town, after which both sides retreated. The town was left empty of Europeans, and Gusii from the surrounding hills streamed in, looting shops and destroying administrative and missionary buildings. Faced with such an overt challenge the state quickly reverted to violence. According to one missionary, a King's African Rifles column was despatched with orders to shoot all male Gusii (150 were murdered), while they burnt one thousand huts and seized three thousand head of cattle.[154] Despite this overwhelming show of force, things remained touch and go. Some Gusii (while firing off captured German guns) tried to stampede and recapture the cattle one evening. Over the next several months many people ignored administrative directives to provide free labor for missionaries. Even four months later the DC informed a Catholic father that the state would not (or could not) continue to procure labor for the missions, but that they would have to use their own influence instead. Shocked and perturbed, the missionary wrote that "This shows weakness, they seem still to be afraid of the [Gusii]."[155]

Christianity and the Threat to Chiefly Rule

Christians proved to be another threat to chiefly power. Missions got a relatively late start in Gusiiland, as the Bible followed the flag, not the reverse. Catholics (mostly Dutch) arrived first, in late 1911, and British (and later American) SDAs two years later. Both denominations found their work slow going, not least because of their mutual hostility. Typical of SDA beliefs in this era, Adventist missionaries believed in a papist conspiracy that reached right down to backwater stations like Kisii. Gusii Adventists feared that merely touching a rosary could bring death.[156] It was rumored that missionaries or their African converts preached that Catholics were devils and polytheists.[157] Catholic missionaries too had little faith in their co-religionists, trying to limit the spread of "SDA or any other form of heresy."[158] None of this led many Gusii toward the Christian god, and the number of conversions in the highlands remained pitifully low. During the war little work was carried out. From 1914 to 1918 Catholics operated only in Luo parts of the district, while the administration banned the SDAs from the district until 1918, suspecting that they somehow had connections to the Germans. Only after the war did any Gusii become Christian. Catholics baptized their first batch of converts in 1920, and the SDAs did not have any confirmed followers until 1922.[159]

Gusii did not simply reject Christianity but were actively hostile to the missionaries. During the sacking of Kisii town the Catholic mission at Nyabururu and the SDA church at Nyanchwa were also overrun, the buildings heavily damaged and the contents looted or destroyed. The missionaries had managed to escape with the retreating administrators, although a priest had three attempts made on his life.[160] When the Catholics finally returned they were given a cold welcome by their Gusii neighbors. Only with great difficulty could the missionaries purchase food and other supplies, and their pleas for labor largely went unanswered.[161] On more than one occasion SDA mission Eric Beavon was confronted by spear-toting Gusii while touring the hills.[162]

Gusii hostility toward missionaries sprang from the same source as their hostility toward chiefs and white administrators. According to Gethin (admittedly a raconteur) missionaries were not above bullying the common African, forcing them to carry loads on safari.[163] Missionary justice was often administrative justice. The priests at Nyabururu regularly sent recalcitrant laborers to the DC for punishment. Whites socialized together, even sharing room and board if they carried on too late into the night.[164] Missionaries also seemed in cahoots with the chiefs. When women came to smear the walls and floors of the new buildings at Nyabururu, the priest gave their pay to their chief, in his innocence supposing the chief would equitably redistribute it to the workers.[165] Missionaries also made courtesy calls on chiefs when on tour, exchanging gifts as they did so.[166] To Gusii eyes, one white would have seemed much the same as any other.

Those few Gusii who associated themselves with Christianity, however, very clearly perceived the different lines of power and authority. Chiefs were clients of the administration, Christians were clients of the missionaries.[167] Gusii living at the missions performed labor for the church in return for room and board, clothing, and education, surely traditional patron–client relationships but with very new goods being redistributed.[168] According to Beavon, his Adventist converts introduced him as "our bwana."[169] *Bwana* is generally used as a term of respect for men, and Africans regularly referred to administrators as *bwana mkumbwa*, literally "big/great *bwana*," to emphasize the officer's status. To call a missionary "my *bwana*" clearly demonstrated that SDAs thought of Beavon, rather than the chiefs, as their leader and patron.[170] Some Christians asked that government orders be sent via their teachers rather than their headmen (chiefs' subordinates), even if the latter were also believers.[171]

Perhaps more opportunistically, some male converts claimed that their new status absolved them of the government demands made of their non-Christian brethren. This was especially true of required communal labor and being called out for wage labor.[172] Chiefs as well as administrators feared the implications of Christians' newly claimed status. In 1921, the DC derided converts' tendency to "consider themselves independent of tribal authority." The next year his successor noted that they were still "apt to ignore tribal authority and discipline" and could be "ill behaved." In a vague accusation so typical of besieged European administrators, the DC charged that some SDAs had presented "a thinly veiled disrespect to Government."[173] Perhaps understating the situation, the 1932 annual report noted that the chief of Bassi found converts "difficult to administer."[174]

Competing lines of patronage often carried over into violent struggles between "mission boys" and chiefs and headmen. Headmen were alleged commonly to round up Christians for forced work since they could be easily collected in groups at their separate villages or outschools.[175] Catholics in South Mugirango charged Chief Kereu and his headmen of demanding bribes in exchange for tax exemption and of extortion. The DC dismissed their complaints (they were just as much to blame, he told them, for having given the bribes) and thought their dislike for the chief arose from the fact that he was an "old pagan."[176] But the next year relations had fallen lower still. A "particularly nasty crowd of mission boys" tried all means to depose the chief, including witchcraft and poison. They succeeded in killing a headman, for which one of the culprits was hanged.[177]

Deserting Clients

Christians were not the only ones striving to remove themselves from chiefs' authority. So too were those who migrated to previously uninhabited areas south the Gucha River. In 1927, Luke Gasuku, his siblings and widowed mother left their home for the hills abutting plains frequented by Maasai herders and the preserve of elephants and hyenas. The administration lent them traps to eradicate the latter, and the *pax Britannia* helped control the former. Other migrants left to escape plague, to avoid forced conscription during the war, or to return to clans from which they had, for one or another reason, left.[178]

Already in 1910 *abasomba* were deserting patrons, which was "not regarded very favorably by the Chiefs," the DC reported, "who consider these people will dispute their authority, as indeed in some cases they do."[179] This became even more common in the late 1920s when many clients and dwellers began to desert their erstwhile homes and return to their original clans. Those *abasomba* not fully assimilated to the host clan but who had been given bridewealth by their patrons might leave behind a few cows to settle the debt and break the relationship.[180] Not all properly redeemed themselves, however, since a significant number of claims were being made for "dowry originally paid to 'slaves'" against their descendants.[181] About two dozen migrants to Kuria (near the Tanganyika border) were in 1931 sent back "under escort" to their residences in North Mugirango, having decamped "without leave of their chief and without paying their debts."[182]

Acceptance of Chiefly Rule

While it took some time, chiefly rule did become more accepted by the masses. Patron–client relationships must have had a large part to do with this. Chiefs' distribution of foodstuffs and other state largesse would have attracted some.[183] Chiefs also set up their own system of indirect rule, coopting local, neighborhood leaders or using headmen to act as intermediaries between themselves and the masses.[184] Chiefs also relied on clan affiliation to direct benefits toward certain essential communities,[185] and others married many wives to cement links with important families.[186]

The introduction of Local Native Councils (LNCs) in 1925 offered chiefs an avenue through which to draw on and redistribute state resources. LNCs were composed of a mixture of appointed chiefs and men elected by the masses (how exactly elections were carried out is never clear). The British envisioned the councils as a way to draw in local elites and make it appear to the commoners that Africans were part of colonial rule (although LNCs were chaired by the DC). LNCs would levy taxes and fees, set up and regulate markets, and fund schemes for infrastructural development. A good deal of money passed through the councils, and a good number of men had to be hired on as laborers, drivers, market police, and so on. Chiefs delivered LNC employment to clients and later distributed grants and loans to themselves and their fellow elites.

Chiefs also hoped to capture support from below by adopting ornamentation of colonial and precolonial leaders. Gusiiland had no ceremonies on which the state and senior men could draw to mix the "traditional" with the new order, legitimizing the new way of life and methods of rule.[187] Chiefs did clamor for the return of the staffs used by *abagambi* of old, and succeeded in gaining lion badges and "red flash[es]" on their hats, marks of colonial authority.[188] Headmen wore fezzes decorated with two interlocking 'M's (for *Mkubwa Mlango*, "sublocation head").[189] But most Gusii were far too savvy to be convinced that outward pageantry reflected real authority. They could not be fooled into thinking chiefs were anything more than they really were, that is, low level government functionaries.[190]

If the abilities of Gusii chiefs were often (to administrators) low, the best ones could be forgiven some level of corruption or injustice. In the 1920s it was felt that Gusii chiefs were easier to deal with than Luo not because they were less corrupt, but more progressive.[191] Musa Nyandusi of Nyaribari (ruled 1930–1964) was a chief regularly praised by administrators—"undoubtedly the most progressive Chief in the District"—and was awarded the King's Medal in 1934.[192] Musa's rule was intense and often unjust. Local politician John Kebaso, no friend of Musa, likely spoke for many in detailing the chief's failings. Writing to anthropologists Philip and Iona Mayer in the 1940s, Kebaso explained that "Musa is very clever, [he] talks sweetly to you and D.C. and everyone, but for robbing and cheating he is the best in Kenya." The DC always demanded firm evidence of corruption but, Kebaso claimed, in the one case this was provided (on bribery in relation to tax collection) the administrators released Musa on a technicality to avoid his sure conviction.[193] There is no corroboration for Kebaso's accusations, but they are not all that far-fetched. In 1931 the DC wrote of accusations swirling about of Musa "pushing a man into a river, of accepting bribes, etc." The DC's response? "He has a difficult task and requires a good deal of support and supervision . . ."[194] Four years later, Musa and Getutu Assistant Chief Ooga were described as "zealous[,] painstaking and energetic"—the type of chiefs so valuable to the administration. The DC continued: "I am not entirely satisfied of their justice and lack of corruption, but never the less I have no facts upon which to base the opinions [*sic*]." Neither did the DC seek out any such facts.[195]

Whatever their characters, chiefs were representatives of the state and had sole claim locally to the use of violence. After the battle of Kisii soldiers were no longer stationed in the district, and police operated only under white command in the reserves. The daily exercise of legitimate violence—violence employed by representatives of the state—fell to the chiefs. This came to be one of the most important tools in chiefs' struggle to gain mastery over their subjects. Local authorities, Kebaso charged, made their livings by "frightening people."[196] Chiefs' *askari*s, armed with clubs, helped to ensure compliance with directives. But commoners also availed themselves of chiefs' powers. Chiefs held regular *baraza*s where subjects could bring forward their disputes. If a piece of property had to be recovered or a wayward woman returned home, a commoner could request the chief to despatch armed *askari*s.

Figure 1.6. Chief Musa Nyandusi
Chief Musa Nyandusi's portrait gazes down at lawmakers in the meeting hall of the Gusii County Council; among the legitimate and illegitimate sources of power Musa exploited was the Council's predecessor, the African District Council, on which he sat.

Chiefs' decisions had financial, even life and death, consequences. The items the state demanded of Africans—cash, crops, and bodies—were collected by chiefs and their underlings. In putting together tax rolls, chiefs oversaw hut-counting and in part the granting of exemptions for widows, the infirm, and the desperately poor. Similarly, chiefs identified the young men who were liable to conscription for the army or wage labor, as well as releasing those they deemed unfit. They exploited their authority well: for a price, chiefs could miscount huts, convince administrators that a man should be exempt from his tax, or underestimate a man's ability to contribute to the war effort.[197] Accusations of chiefs interfering with the workings of the African courts were common.[198] Selection for the Locational Advisory Councils (essentially lower-level LNCs) often owed less to ability than to bribery.[199] Through patron–client relations, their special access to the state, and authority to use violence (to legitimate or illegitimate ends), chiefly rule became more or less accepted by residents of South Kavirondo.

CONCLUSION

For twenty-five years Gusii found colonialism alternately intensely disagreeable and oppressive, or unobtrusive and irrelevant. They married and exchanged bridewealth, and debated the nature of marriage and bridewealth, in much the same terms as they had before. They sought children and cattle, they cooperated and struggled over the distribution of homestead resources. The white government brought peace south of the Gucha, and some Gusii received special protection from God's earthly representatives. White men and their chiefly lackeys demanded cash and young men, and they were best avoided when possible. Even in the 1920s, however, and increasingly in the 1930s, much deeper changes could be felt. Chiefs began to claim a measure of legitimacy and the state evinced a much more active interest in Gusii social life—relations between youth and elders, men and women. Through chiefs and new courts, administrators tried to implement increasingly conservative views of African society. A new era was at hand.

NOTES

1. The following draws on William R. Ochieng', *A Pre-Colonial History of the Gusii of Western Kenya, from c. A.D. 1500 to 1915* (Nairobi: East African Literature Bureau, 1974).
2. Ochieng', *Pre-Colonial History of the Gusii*, 109–111.
3. Ochieng', *Pre-Colonial History of the Gusii*, 111–134, and chap. 4.
4. Ochieng', *Pre-Colonial History of the Gusii*, 59, 67–69; John Lonsdale, "When did the Gusii (Or Any Other Group) Become a 'Tribe'?" *Kenya Historical Review* 5 (1977), 123–133, esp. 128.
5. See W. M. Logan, "History of the Wakisii or Abagusii," Kenya National Archives (KNA): South Kavirondo District Political Record Book (SK PRB); Robert A. Manners, "The Kipsigis of Kenya: Culture Change in a 'Model' East African Tribe," in *Three African Tribes in Transition. Vol. I of Contemporary Change in Traditional Societies*,

ed. Julian Steward (Urbana: University of Illinois Press, 1972), 219–220; Philip Mayer, *The Lineage Principle in Gusii Society* (International African Institute, Memorandum 24, Oxford, 1949), 15; David Mokamba, Nyayiemi Moturi, Gabriel Metet, and David Achira, "The Kisii-Kipsigis Wars of the Late Nineteenth Century," *Kenya Historical Review* 2 (1974), 221–234; Zebedeo Okioma, "Nyamosi, First Chief of Majoge," *Bulletin of the Cardinal Otunga Historical Society* 78 (Nov. 15, 1979), 19–20; H. B. Partington, "Some Notes on the Kisi People," *East Africa Quarterly* 2 (1905), 328–329. See also elders' descriptions of the exchange of people in Robert A. LeVine and Donald T. Campbell, *Gusii of Kenya* (New Haven, CT: Human Relations Area Files, 1972), passim, and William Sytek, *Luo of Kenya* (New Haven, CT: Human Relations Area Files, 1972), passim. On the larger region, see Margaret Jean Hay, "Local Trade and Ethnicity in Western Kenya," *African Economic History Review* 11 (1975), 1–12.

6. T. Wakefield, "Notes on the Geography of Eastern Africa," *Journal of the Royal Geographical Society* 40 (1870), 303–328; Ontiri, in LeVine and Campbell, *Gusii of Kenya*, 32; Kiriago, in ibid., 162–163. Some traders were welcomed, some were aggressive and were attacked. James Morombasi and Barnabas Gabuna, "Trade in Kisii Before 1907," *Bulletin of the Cardinal Otunga Historical Society* 64 (1978), 3–8; N.a., "Neumann's Journey in East Africa," *The Geographical Journal* 6 (1895), 274–276; Judith Marianne Butterman, "Luo Social Formations in Change: Karachuonyo and Kanyamkago, c. 1800–1945" (Ph.D. dissertation, Syracuse University, 1979), 109.

7. Felix Oswald, *Alone in Sleeping Sickness Country* (London: Kegan Paul, 1915); C. H. Stigand, *The Land of Zinj: Being an Account of British East Africa, its Ancient History and Present Inhabitants* (New York: Barnes and Noble, 1913), 293; "[Notes?] taken in Majoge Village," Mayer Field Material (MFM): 4; Arani Nyaberi, personal communication, June 2002. Fortifications could also be found in Wanjare. Stephen Orvis, *The Agrarian Question in Kenya* (Gainesville: University of Florida Press, 1997), 41. Toward Luo areas enclosures were not necessary, and only ditches were used in Majoge. Felix Oswald, "From the Victoria Nyanza to the Kisii Highlands," *The Geographical Journal* 41 (Jan.–June 1913), 122; "Majoge Village," MFM: 4.

8. On the increase of cattle raids during famine and cattle epidemics in the 1880s and 1890s, see Kennell A. Jackson, "The Family Entity and Famine among the Nineteenth-Century Akamba of Kenya: Social Responses to Environmental Stress," *Journal of Family History* 1 (1976), 192–216, esp. 210; Bill Bravman, *Making Ethnic Ways: Communities and Their Transformations in Taita, Kenya, 1800–1950* (Portsmouth, NH: Heinemann, 1998), 55–58, 73; Richard Waller, "Emutai: Crisis and Response in Maasailand 1883–1902," in *The Ecology of Survival: Case Studies from Northeast African History*, eds. Douglas H. Johnson and David M. Anderson (London: L. Crook, 1988), 76–77.

9. See Mokamba, Moturi, Metet, and Achira, "The Kisii-Kipsigis Wars of the Late Nineteenth Century," 128–132. For Kipsigis traditions on the battle, see S. C. Langat, "Some Aspects of Kipsigis History before 1914," in *Ngano: Studies in Traditional and Modern East African History*, ed. B. G. McIntosh (Nairobi: East African Publishing House, for the Department of History, University College, Nairobi, 1969). Some years later Kipsigis professed to be frightened and constantly under attack by Gusii, and begged a white captain passing through to help them recover some of their stolen cattle. In the wake of Saosao Gusii clans may well have pushed their advantage over the Kipsigis, but the latter likely also exaggerated their grievances in hopes of securing white military support. Captain Gorges himself did seem cowed. The officer "refrained from any such business" of recovering Kipsigis cattle, and when he realized that the Gusii were "determined not to permit [him] to travel through their country in peace," he skirted the highlands. Sounding somewhat defensive as to why he avoided these "undoubtedly brave and warlike" people, Gorges explained he did not wish "to act in any way contrary to [his] instruction" and so ("unwillingly") he made his way around the highlands. G. H. Gorges, "A Journey

from Lake Naivasha to the Victoria Nyanza," *The Geographical Journal* 16 (July 1900), 78–89.

10. Oswald, "Victoria Nyanza to Kisii Highlands," 123.

11. Richard Gethin, "An Old Settler Remembers," 65, 144, Rhodes House (RH): MSS Afr. s. 1277; South Kavirondo District Annual Reports (SK DARs) 1919/20, 1920/21.

12. A point made first by Lonsdale, "When did the Gusii become a 'Tribe'?"

13. G. A. Fischer, "Am Ostufer des Victoria-Njansa," *Petermanns Mitteilungen* (1895), 42–46. My thanks to Dr. M. D. Bailey for his translation.

14. N.a., "Native Routes through the Masai Country, from Information Obtained by the Rev. T. Wakefield," *Proceedings of the Royal Geographical Society and Monthly Record of Geography*, 4 (1882), 742–747, quote from 745.

15. Partington, "Some Notes on the Kisi People."

16. P. Mayer, *The Lineage Principle in Gusii Society*, 15; Iona Mayer, "Studies in Gusii Kinship" (Ph.D. dissertation, Rhodes University, 1965), 19.

17. *Nsoni* has a deep ancestry within Bantu linguistic groups with versions such as *ntloni*, *nthoni*, and *hloni* found in parts of southern Africa. A. R. Radcliffe-Brown, "Introduction," in *African Systems of Kinship and Marriage*, eds. A. R. Radcliffe-Brown and Daryll Forde (London: KPI, 1987 [1950]), 58–59.

18. Makio Matsuzono emphasizes the sexual aspects of *nsoni* in "Adjacent Generations and Respect Attitudes among the Gusii," in *Themes in Socio-Cultural Ideas and Behaviour among Six Ethnic Groups of Kenya*, ed. Nobuhiro Nagashima (Kunitachi: Hitotsubashi University, 1981).

19. Iona Mayer, *The Nature of Kinship Relations: The Significance of the Use of Kinship Terms among the Gusii* (Manchester: Manchester University Press, for the Rhodes-Livingstone Institute, 1965), 2, 14.

20. My thinking here owes much to I. Mayer, "Studies in Gusii Kinship."

21. Cf. Butterman, "Luo Social Formations," 36, and (for East Africa more generally) John Lonsdale, "The Moral Economy of Mau Mau," in Bruce Berman and John Lonsdale, *Unhappy Valley: Conflict in Kenya and Africa* (London: James Currey, 1992), 329.

22. Some Gusii and Luo intermarried, "but Gusii [were in the 1940s] not proud of admitting to" such marriages. I. Mayer, "Studies in Gusii Kinship," 13. The lack of circumcision among the Luo also prevented their intermarriage with Kuria. Ann-Britt Bernhardsdotter, "The Power of Being: A Study of Poverty, Fertility and Sexuality among the Kuria in Kenya and Tanzania" (Ph.D. dissertation, Uppsala University, 2001), 29, n. 24.

23. I. Mayer, "Studies in Gusii Kinship," 34.

24. Philip Mayer, *Gusii Bridewealth Law and Custom* (Rhodes-Livingstone Papers, 18, Oxford, 1950), 8–9.

25. P. Mayer, *Gusii Bridewealth Law and Custom.*

26. Philip Mayer, *Two Studies in Applied Anthropology in Kenya* (London: Colonial Office, 1951), 21.

27. Similarly, the word *rika* was used for a woman a family might send to a son-in-law to "replace" his deceased wife.

28. P. Mayer, *Two Studies in Applied Anthropology*, 21.

29. Philip Mayer, "Gusii Initiation Ceremonies," *Journal of the Royal Anthropological Institute* 83 (1953), 9–36, esp. 24. See also Father Doyle, "Circumcision," Archives of the Cardinal Otunga Historical Society (COHS): MAA/KIS/GEN/1/6.

30. N. K. Nyang'era, *The Making of Man and Woman under Abagusii Customary Law* (Kisii: self-published, 1999), 5.

31. P. Mayer, *Gusii Bridewealth Law and Custom*, 46–48. However, if a woman died childless but postmenopausal, her widower could theoretically claim no cattle, since he had benefitted from her lifetime of labor. Similarly, if a woman proved sterile the couple remained married and her parents refunded her husband only part of his bridewealth.

32. Iona Mayer, "The Gusii of Western Kenya," in *Cultural Source Materials for Population Planning in East Africa, Vol. III: Beliefs and Practices*, ed. Angela Molnos (Nairobi: East African Publishing House, 1973), 125.

33. I. Mayer, "Gusii of Western Kenya," 127. See also Nyang'era, *Making of Man and Woman*, 83.

34. See N. Thomas Håkansson, "Grain, Cattle, and Power: Social Processes of Intensive Cultivation and Exchange in Precolonial Western Kenya," *Journal of Anthropological Research* 50 (1994), 249–276. For similar ideas as witnessed in the 1940s, see P. Mayer, *Lineage Principle in Gusii Society*, 32; I. Mayer, "Gusii of Western Kenya," 122.

35. P. Mayer, *Gusii Bridewealth Law and Custom*, 25.

36. Dobrin song collection, 85–346-F, cass 2206/Tape 3 song 5, Indiana University Archives of Traditional Music (IUATM).

37. Zebedeo Onguti, "Some Kisii Riddles, Sayings and Proverbs," no. 61, *Bulletin of the Cardinal Otunga Historical Society* 32 (July 25, 1970), 8–17; exegesis by Arani Nyaberi, personal communication, June 1999.

38. P. Mayer, *Gusii Bridewealth Law and Custom*, 57–58; P. Mayer, *Lineage Principle in Gusii Society*, 5, 21. In 1928 an administrator and a large gathering of elders came to the same interpretation, but this *baraza* was meant to clarify and codify four points "that have been dealt with in different ways by different barazas," suggesting that Gusii elders may have had conflicting interpretations. "Codification of Some Kisii Customs," March 27, 1928, KNA: PC/NZA 3/17/12/2.

39. P. Mayer, *Lineage Principle in Gusii Society*, 21; Ochora Ogoro, July 15, 1997.

40. P. Mayer, *Gusii Bridewealth Law and Custom*, 60.

41. I. Mayer, "Gusii of Western Kenya," 126. Marriage also meant simply having all the trappings of an independent household, including someone to cook and so on. Doyle, "Marriage," COHS: MAA/KIS/GEN/1/6. As Robertson notes, having a wife to carry out these chores could mean the difference between leisure time and constant work for a man. Claire C. Robertson, *Trouble Showed the Way: Women, Men and Trade in the Nairobi Area, 1890–1990* (Bloomington: Indiana University Press, 1997), 6.

42. Philip Mayer, "Privileged Obstruction of Marriage Rites Among the Gusii," *Africa* 20 (1950), 113–125, esp. 114–115; Benson Nyamari Moengi, July 22, 1997; Ochora Ogoro, July 15, 1997; Helen Kerubo, Nov. 17, 1997; Sabina Gesare, Oct. 6–7, 1998. In addition to donning *ebetinge*, it appears that only after *enyangi* could a woman put on the longer goatskin skirt of a married woman. Eric Beavon, *Sindiga, the Savage: A Tale of the Wilds* (New York: Harper, 1930), 105. Luo of South Kavirondo practiced something quite similar. Gordon Wilson, *Luo Customary Law and Marriage Law Customs* (Nairobi: Colony and Protectorate of Kenya, 1961), 112. The Kuria practiced a series of marriage rites known as *inyangi* which contributed to the "near sacred nature" of marriage. Lloyd A. Binagi, "Marriage among Kuria," *Mila* (Institute of African Studies, University of Nairobi) 5 (1976), 13–23, quote from 16.

43. Quoted in Håkansson, "Grain, Cattle, and Power," 260–261. Polygamy remained an important status symbol up through the 1950s (and is hardly unknown today). One survey in the 1940s found that about one-third of men were polygamists, most having married a second wife after the first had passed menopause. I. Mayer, "Studies in Gusii Kinship," 14, 56.

44. See the undated manuscript in the possession of Erasto Abuga of Central Kitutu. A similar explanation of the proverb is provided in Philip Raikes, "Monogamists Sit by the Doorway: Notes on the Construction of Gender, Ethnicity and Rank in Kisii, Western Kenya" (CDR Working Paper 92.7, Center for Development Research, Copenhagen, Oct. 1992).

45. Onguti, "Some Kisii Riddles," no. 61; exegesis by Arani Nyaberi, personal communication, June 1999.

46. My thanks to Arani Nyaberi for this point.
47. Onguti, "Some Kisii Riddles," no. 15; exegesis by Arani Nyaberi, personal communication, June 1999.
48. SK DAR 1907/08; G. A. S. Northcote, "The Kisii," SK PRB.
49. Sarah C. A. Birundu, "Gusii Trade in the Nineteenth Century" (B.A. thesis, University of Nairobi, 1973); Morombasi and Gabuna, "Trade in Kisii before 1907"; Frank W. Holmquist, "Peasant Organization, Clientelism and Dependency: A Case Study of an Agricultural Producers Cooperative in Kenya" (Ph.D. dissertation, Indiana University, 1975), 82; Ochieng', *Pre-Colonial History of the Gusii*, 68.
50. The only recorded instance when women traders were molested came in the early 1900s and prompted a devastating reprisal by their clansmen. Robert Maxon, *Conflict and Accommodation in Western Kenya: The Gusii and the British, 1907–1963* (Cranbury, NJ: University Presses of America, 1989), 29. See also Abel Nyakundi's unpublished history of the Gusii, "Okaba Omochakano Bw'Abagusii na Mogikoyo Omwambo," trans. by John M. Omwenga as "Being the Beginnings of the Kisiis and their Brothers the Kikuyus," 46, 64, COHS: MAH/KIS/PRE/6/1b. On women traders see Håkansson, "Grain, Cattle, and Power," 262–263; Birundu, "Gusii Trade in the Nineteenth Century;" Morombasi and Gabuna, "Trade in Kisii before 1907."
51. The loss of large numbers of cattle in 1890 forced people in the highlands to go without milk and meat, causing a "mild famine." Nyakundi, "Beginnings of the Kisiis," 62, COHS: MAH/KIS/PRE/6/1b. Many adults turned to the milk of goats and sheep, normally the preserve of children. [Notes] from Oscar, [first page marked] "Blood of Cattle," ca. 1947, MFM: 4.
52. "Cattle (Wanjare): Nyamerere Abuga. Trib. Elder. 15.1.47," MFM: 4.
53. SK DARs 1916/17, 1917/18; Birundi, "Gusii Trade in the Nineteenth Century."
54. Dobrin song collection, 85–346-F, cass 2205/Tape 2 song 32, IUATM.
55. Birundu, "Gusii Trade in the Nineteenth Century," 30.
56. Northcote, "The Kisii," SK PRB.
57. "Ebisirate (cattle villages), Nyangau, N.M.," MFM: 4.
58. Nyakundi, "Beginnings of the Kisiis," 49, COHS: MAH/KIS/PRE/6/1b.
59. Gethin, "An Old Settler," 54, RH: MSS Afr. s. 1277; Harold Beavon, Dec. 20, 2002. The administration had tried to discourage the carrying of spears, and with the assistance of "The Elders" young men no longer came armed to large gatherings and marriage and funeral dances. SK District Quarterly Report (DQR), Sept. 30, 1912. Kibagendi recalls the administration burning young men's shields, although it is not clear when this would have been. "Kibagendi," MFM: 4.
60. SK DQR Oct. 31, 1908
61. SK DQR Jan. 31, 1909. See also SK DARs 1910/11, 1912/13, 1913/14, 1924, 1929, and 1935.
62. I. Mayer, "Gusii of Western Kenya," 129.
63. P. Mayer, "Privileged Obstruction of Marriage Rites," 115.
64. Thomas Håkansson, *Bridewealth, Women and Land: Social Change among the Gusii of Kenya* (Uppsala Studies in Cultural Anthropology, 10, Uppsala, 1988), 58.
65. I. Mayer, "Gusii of Western Kenya," 124.
66. I. Mayer, "Studies in Gusii Kinship," 108, 122–123. Gifts of food and beer also kept up good relations with the son-in-law.
67. P. Mayer, "Privileged Obstruction of Marriage Rites," 115, 118; I. Mayer, "Gusii of Western Kenya," 129; Beavon, *Sindiga, the Savage*, 79. In one early report, an administrator wrote that Kitutu was the ultimate ancestor of the Getutu, and in parentheses noted that Kitutu was a woman. Northcote, "The Kisii," SK PRB. The Mayers' assistant identified the woman who ordered the spearing of an officer in 1908 as "one of those great women called Eting'ana—queen." "'Omomundkkane,' Oscar, Jan. 47," MFM: 18.

68. Dobrin song collection, 85–346-F, cass 2205/Tape 2 song 32, UIATM.

69. Logan, "History of the Kisii," SK PRB.

70. "'Status of husband and children in woman[-woman] marriage,' Nyangau Maguti of North Mugirango," MFM: 8.

71. Kisii (or Gusii) Law Panel, Dec. 10–11, 1962, COHS: MAA/KIS/LAW/1. For a review of woman-to-woman marriage elsewhere in Africa, see Kirsten Alsaker Kjerland, "When African Women Take Wives: A Historiographical Overview" (The Nordic Africa Institute, Poverty and Prosperity Occasional Papers 6, 1997).

72. For an example, see P. Mayer, *Lineage Principle in Gusii Society*, 25.

73. Quoted in Håkansson, *Bridewealth, Women and Land*, 66. Even if a woman could be tracked down, her husband might fail to bring her home: ". . . nobody would search for [a runaway wife]. Otherwise she would say 'I don't know you,' even if you were the real husband." Moanda, in LeVine and Campbell, *Gusii of Kenya*, 327.

74. Kiriago, in Levine and Campbell, *Gusii of Kenya*, 310; cf. Moanda, in ibid., 332.

75. Much like wedding rings, a comparison made by Chief Musa Nyandusi. SK Local Native Council (LNC), April 4, 1934.

76. Nyangau Kiage, June 16, 1997; Josiah Mochama, Jeremiah Ogechi, Elemeleck Chaga, Thomas Choti, July 16, 1997. Solid metal bracelets were also placed on runaway wives in Luo areas to the north, although the attendant mystical sanctions appear to have been more important than social ones. See Olive Owen, "Meeting of women at Ng'iya, June 7, 1944," Church Missionary Society Archive (CMS): ACC 83 O 22/1.

77. Ambros Bwoma, July 19, 1997.

78. Bethsheba Kemunto, June 23, 1997; Jepheth Ondieki, Sept. 23, 1997; Kerubo Kiage, Nov. 19, 1997.

79. Nyakango Obiero, Nov. 3, 1997.

80. P. Mayer, *Lineage Principle in Gusii Society*, 21.

81. I. Mayer, "Gusii of Western Kenya," 138.

82. I. Mayer, "Studies in Gusii Kinship," 73.

83. P. Mayer, *Gusii Bridewealth Law and Custom*, 53–54.

84. P. Mayer, *Gusii Bridewealth Law and Custom*, 23.

85. SK DAR 1907/08.

86. "Kibagendi," MFM: 4.

87. P. Mayer, *Gusii Bridewealth Law and Custom*, 18, 23.

88. I. Mayer, "Studies in Gusii Kinship," 29.

89. P. Mayer, *Gusii Bridewealth Law and Custom*, 23.

90. One administrator in 1961 remarked that, "Even within families there seems little unity, and brother will cheerfully knock brother on the head with a rungu [club] over a minor disagreement." Kisii DAR 1961.

91. RK civil (claim of goats) 16/47.

92. "'Enyangi,' discussion with Justino and Oscar," MFM: 8. Cf. Adam Kuper, *Wives for Cattle: Bridewealth and Marriage in Southern Africa* (London: Routledge and Kegan Paul, 1982), chap. 3.

93. Nyang'era, *Making of Man and Woman*, 55.

94. P. Mayer, *Gusii Bridewealth Law and Custom*, 33.

95. Cf. Ivan Karp, "Laughter at Marriage: Subversion in Performance," in *Transformations of African Marriage*, David Parkin and David Nyamwaya, eds. (Manchester: Manchester University Press, for International African Institute, 1987), 145.

96. P. Mayer, *Gusii Bridewealth Law and Custom*, 42.

97. Radcliffe-Brown, "Introduction," 54–60, quote from 60.

98. Iona Mayer, "The Patriarchal Image: Routine Dissociation in Gusii Families," *African Studies* 34 (1975), 269; Matsuzono, "Adjacent Generations and Respect Attitudes."

99. I. Mayer, "Patriarchal Image," 265.

100. Quoted in I. Mayer, "Patriarchal Image," 270. See also Håkansson, *Bridewealth, Women and Land*, 39. Nyang'era writes that the father might state "You will die or you will have no child or you will be an idiot." *The Making of Man and Woman*, 95.

101. I. Mayer, "Gusii of Western Kenya," 122–123; Robert A. LeVine and Barbara B. LeVine, *Nyansongo: A Gusii Community* (New York: Wiley, 1966), 70, 10.

102. One administrator claimed that men with very many wives "farmed out" some to poor bachelors, tying the poor men in as clients while the children remained the patrons' social offspring. K. L. Hunter, "Memories of an Administrative Officer," RH: MSS. Afr.s. 1942, April 1975.

103. "Kibagendi," MFM: 4.

104. Håkansson, *Bridewealth, Women and Land*, 62–64; idem, "Grain, Cattle, and Power," 260–261.

105. Kimaiti, in LeVine and Campbell, *Gusii of Kenya*, 70; cf. Nyagarama in the same volume, 5.

106. William R. Ochieng', "In Search of a State among the Kitutu in the Nineteenth Century," in *State Formation in Eastern Africa*, ed. Ahmed Idha Salim (Nairobi: Heinemann, 1984).

107. Ochieng', "In Search of a State among the Kitutu," 212.

108. P. Mayer, *Lineage Principle in Gusii Society*, 28–29.

109. At a 1954 meeting of the South Nyanza Law Panel (SNLP), members stated that *etureti* were clan elders who heard mostly land cases, and the *egesaku* were "group" elders, the meaning of which is unclear. Meeting of the Kisii section, SNLP, June 1, 1954, KNA: RR 8/10. Other evidence suggests that *etureti* operated on a much more local level, however.

110. Meeting of the Kisii section, SNLP, June 1, 1954, KNA: RR 8/10.

111. P. Mayer, *Two Studies in Applied Anthropology*, 22.

112. P. Mayer was told that "special meetings were held for the purpose, and [in the 1940s were] still distinctly remembered by old men in some parts (e.g. North Mugirango)." Mayer, *Two Studies in Applied Anthropology*, 22–23.

113. SK DAR 1920/21.

114. Maxon, *Conflict and Accommodation in Western Kenya*, 30–45; Joseph M. Nyasani, *The British Massacre of the Gusii Freedom Defenders* (Nairobi: Nairobi Bookmen, 1984).

115. Quoted in Maxon, *Conflict and Accommodation in Western Kenya*, 44.

116. See, for example, SK DQR June 1911; SK DARs 1917/18, 1919/20, 1925, 1928, 1938, 1939, 1944; South Nyanza (SN) DARs 1951, 1952; Nyanza Provincial Annual Report (PAR) 1913; Nyanza Province Intelligence Report (IR) Jan. 1930. In both SK DAR 1945 and SN DAR 1953 the district commissioners noted that administrative turnover was less than in previous years, with 1945 "nearly, if not quite, a record."

117. Paul Mboya, *Utawala na Maendeleo ya Local Government South Nyanza, 1926–1957* (Nairobi: East African Literature Bureau, 1959), 30–32.

118. SN DAR 1951.

119. Goan employees may have stayed longer, but they served primarily in clerical positions.

120. SK DAR 1925.

121. Safari Diary, Nov.–Dec. 1931, KNA: Adm 12/4/1. Seven years later the DC broke the district down into two parts: that within a forty-mile radius of Kisii town, and the remainder. The latter was much more "backward" than the former, primarily because of differences in contact with the government staff, expenditure of funds, and communication. SK DAR 1938.

122. A point explored in Benjamin Lawrance, Emily Lynn Osborn, and Richard Roberts, eds., *Intermediaries, Interpreters and Clerks: African Employees and the Making of Colonial Africa* (Madison: University of Wisconsin Press, [in press]).

123. One wonders if "Gasuku" was a nickname or simply serendipity: in Swahili *kasuku* means parrot. Of course, Gasuku was far from a parrot. The bird repeats verbatim what is said, a skill that Gasuku did often choose to employ.

124. SK DAR 1919/20. See similar comments in SK DAR 1920/21.

125. Nyabururu Diary, entry of Dec. 16, 1911, Mill Hill Archives (MH): Kisii Diaries.

126. See Brett L. Shadle, "African Court Elders in Nyanza Province, Kenya, c. 1930–1960: From 'Traditional' to 'Modern,' " in *Intermediaries, Interpreters and Clerks*, eds. Lawrance, Osborn, and Roberts.

127. Luke Gasuku (no relation), June 15, 2002. For a similar example, involving the appointment of a clerk, see Butterman, "Luo Social Formations," 138.

128. Luke Gasuku, June 15, 2002.

129. Luke Gasuku, June 15, 2002; Beavon, *Sindiga, the Savage*, 264.

130. Safari Diary, Feb.–March 1932, KNA: Adm 12/4/1; correspondence between Ag. DC SK, SC Nyanza, and Father Doyle, Aug. 1926, in KNA: NZA 15/14.

131. Luke Gasuku, June 15, 2002.

132. Luke Gasuku, June 15, 2002. Subsequently Gasuku became chief of the Luo location of Gwassi. An administrator later touring Gwassi noted that Gasuku's "features ... appeared to be reproduced literally in everyone [the officer] met." Terence Gavaghan, *Of Lions and Dung Beetles* (Elms Court, UK: Arthur H. Stockwell, 1999), 72.

133. SK DAR 1932.

134. Reduced to seven when Muksero was reintegrated into Getutu in 1933.

135. G. A. S. Northcote despairingly noted that the "Kisii and Bantu chiefs are practically non-entities, except in certain ceremonial functions." "The History of the District," Dec. 20, 1909, COHS: MAA/KIS/GEN/1/1. See also his 1907 diary, entries of April 30, May 8, 12, and 25, and June 7, KNA: DC/KSI 4/1.

136. Maxon, *Conflict and Accommodation in Western Kenya*, 27–32, 45; Partington, "Some Notes on the Kisi People."

137. Okioma, "Nyamosi, First Chief of Majoge"; Logan, "History of the Wakisii," SK PRB.

138. Quoted in Maxon, *Conflict and Accommodation in Western Kenya*, 35. At one point the best chief in South Kavirondo was thought to be Orinda (a Luo) who had no hereditary claims to rule whatsoever. SK DQR June 1911. For an essential study of chiefs, custom and indirect rule, see Karen E. Fields, *Revival and Rebellion in Colonial Central Africa* (Portsmouth, NH: Heinemann, 1997 [1985]).

139. Northcote, "History of the District," SK PRB. This may have been more true among the Gusii than the Luo. Northcote noted that the Luo were "easier to deal with than the Kisii owing to the fact that they respect and obey their Chiefs and headmen." SK DAR 1908/09.

140. Ag. DC to SC Nyanza, Sept. 29, 1926, KNA: PC/NZA 3/32/2.

141. Maxon, *Conflict and Accommodation in Western Kenya*, 49.

142. "Character of Chiefs," May 1931, KNA: KSI/26.

143. N.a., "Interview with Johana Otero," *Bulletin of the Cardinal Otunga Historical Society* 81 (1980), 3–9. SK DAR 1917/18. On nighttime abductions, see SK DAR 1914/15.

144. Shem Omasire, "Milestones in the History of Gusii: An Oral Tradition Perspective," *Bulletin of the Cardinal Otunga Historical Society* 100 (1983), 43–46, quote from 44.

145. DC quoted in Maxon, *Conflict and Accommodation in Western Kenya*, 70; Donald C. Savage and J. Forbes Munro, "Carrier Corps Recruitment in the British East Africa Protectorate," *Journal of African History* 21 (1980), 313–342. According to the DC in 1918, the Gusii were "very much more under the control of tribal authority than they were a year ago. I attribute this result largely to the collection of Carrier Corps. [*sic*] Porters." SK DAR 1917/18.

146. P. Scheffer, "History of Asumbi Catholic Mission," c. 1930, in Anthony Koenig, *The Beginning of the Church in South Kavirondo* (Mosocho, Kenya: Cardinal Otunga High School, 1985), 54.

147. SK DAR 1919/20.

148. Record of a meeting at Government House [between Archdeacon Owen and state officials], Oct. 22, 1930, PRO: CO 533/404/13.

149. SK DAR 1916/17; Native Tribunal Cases, South Kavirondo, returns for quarter ending March 1926, KNA: PC/NZA 3/33/6. In Luo areas commoners would assault chiefs' retainers if found alone. Butterman, "Luo Social Formations," 122.

150. The following discussion is based on Brett L. Shadle, "Patronage, Millennialism and the Serpent-God Mumbo in Southwest Kenya, 1912–1934," *Africa* 72 (2002), 29–54.

151. SK MIR Nov. 1933, KNA: Adm 12/4/4.

152. As one man explained to P. Mayer, chiefs complained, "Why do these people eat all this food instead of feeding us?" "Arita (frightened Mumboist)," April 10, 1947, MFM: 1.

153. Gethin, "An Old Settler," 57, RH: MSS Afr. s. 1277. Geologist Felix Oswald in 1912 found the Gusii "an aggressive race," "inhospitable and of sullen demeanour," and found himself the object of interest to "half a dozen spearmen" who appeared "not particularly friendly." Oswald could collect porters only by despatching an *askari* with a rifle, who was nonetheless nearly speared and knifed. Oswald, *Alone in Sleeping Sickness Country*, 141–142.

154. Nyabururu Diary, entry of Sept. 17, 1914, MH: Kisii Diaries. Gethin noted that the KAR troops spent more of their time seizing women than burning huts. Gethin, "An Old Settler," 96, RH: MSS Afr. s. 1277.

155. Nyabururu Diary, entry of June 23, 1915, MH: Kisii Diaries. See also entries of Nov. 3 and 20, 1914, and Jan. 20, 1915.

156. Jackson Abuya, Samuel Ratemo, Saul Omweri, Japhet Ratemo Getugi, Zachary Sunda, Peter Ndemo, Zachary Omwenga, and Joseph Onserio, "The Seventh-Day Adventists in Kisii District," *Bulletin of the Bishop Otunga Secondary School Historical Society* 41 (1972), 12–19, esp. 18.

157. Nyabururu Diary, entries of April 28 and May 7, 1915, MH: Kisii Diaries. According to Gethin, the SDAs found few converts since as far as he could tell "they were not very religious appearing to be far more interested in trading in Buffa[l]o hides . . . than they were in converting the African to their way of thinking." Gethin, "An Old Settler," 61, RH: MSS Afr. s. 1277.

158. Nyabururu Diary, entries for July 1913, MH: Kisii Diaries.

159. Maxon, *Conflict and Accommodation in Western Kenya*, 82. As late as the 1940s few Christians could be found away from the main mission stations. P. Mayer, *Lineage Principle in Gusii Society*, 4. Notably absent were women, normally the first converts missionaries made in Africa.

160. Maxon, *Conflict and Accommodation in Western Kenya*, 70–71.

161. See Nyabururu Diary, entries for Sept. and Oct. 1914, MH: Kisii Diaries.

162. Harold Beavon (son of Eric Beavon), personal communication, Dec. 20, 2002.

163. Gethin, "An Old Settler," 62, RH: MSS Afr. s. 1277.

164. Nyabururu Diary, entry for June 25, 1922, MH: Kisii Diaries.

165. Nyabururu Diary, entry for Dec. 21, 1911, MH: Kisii Diaries.

166. Nyabururu Diary, entries for Aug. 1912, during priest's *safari*, MH: Kisii Diaries

167. As elsewhere in Africa it was Africans rather than white missionaries who converted the most people, which had much to do with Christian Africans creating new lines of power. See Shadle, "Patronage, Millennialism, and the Serpent-God Mumbo."

168. E. A. Beavon, "Among the Kisiis in the Heart of Africa," *Advent Review and Sabbath Herald* (April 19, 1923), 12–13; Nyabururu Diary, passim, MH: Kisii Diaries.

169. Beavon, *Sindiga, the Savage*, 286.

170. But some chiefs also tried to use Christianity as a path to attracting followers. Martinus, upon appointment as chief of North Mugirango in 1931, had a special mass said "for his intentions to Government, to his conscience and to his people." (This sounded, an officer remarked, "fairly comprehensive!") Safari Diary, Sept. 1931, KNA: Adm 12/4/1.

171. SK DAR 1928.

172. SK DARs 1914/15, 1932.

173. SK DARs 1920/21, 1922. See also SK DAR 1924. Mission outschools also fell into repeated struggles (even violent ones) with their neighbors over land rights. See, for example, SK MIR April 1930; SK DAR 1932. On Christian threats to chiefs in Central Kavirondo, see Margaret Jean Hay, "Changes in Clothing and Struggles over Identity in Colonial Western Kenya," in *Fashioning Africa: Power and the Politics of Dress*, ed. Jean Allman (Bloomington: Indiana University Press, 2004), 77.

174. SK DAR 1936.

175. SK DAR 1927. See also SK DAR 1930.

176. Safari Diary, March–April 1933, KNA: Adm 12/4/1.

177. SK DAR 1934. He was not the only victim. At least one other chief, Bochuki of Bunyabassi (Kuria), was murdered. SK DAR 1932.

178. Safari Diary, Nov.–Dec. 1931, KNA: Adm 12/4/1; NPIR Sept. 1930; Philip Mayer and Iona Mayer, "Land Law in the Making" in *African Law: Adaptation and Development*, eds. Hilda Kuper and Leo Kuper (Berkeley: University of California Press, 1965).

179. SK DAR 1910/11.

180. SK DAR 1920/21; H. E. Welby, "Nyeribari," July 3, 1921, SK PRB; P. Mayer and I. Mayer, "Land Law in the Making," 28.

181. "Codification of some Kisii customs," March 27, 1928, KNA: PC/NZA 3/17/12/2. See also SK Safari Diary, April 1928, KNA: PC/NZA 3/26/4/4; "Kibagendi," MFM: 4.

182. Safari Diary, Nov.–Dec. 1931, KNA: Adm 12/4/1. The same diary reports that many people of Muksero were heading for greener pastures in Nyaribari, causing Headman Murera to complain that most of his followers were deserting him. See also Nyanza Province Intelligence Report, Sept. 1930.

183. For a comparison, see Marshall Clough, *Fighting Two Sides: Kenyan Chiefs and Politicians, 1918–1940* (Boulder: University Press of Colorado, 1990), 83–86.

184. Holmquist, "Peasant Organization, Clientelism and Dependency," 105–107; General Secretary, Kisii Union, to Provincial Commissioner (PC) Nyanza, Feb. 18, 1946, and PC Nyanza to General Secretary, Kisii Union, Feb. 22, 1946, both in KNA: Adm 8/33.

185. Provincial Native Council, July 20, 1933, KNA: Adm 7/13/1/2.

186. Musa Nyandusi (chief of Nyaribari, 1930–1964) married fourteen or more wives. Chief Onsongo of Getutu (ruled 1913–1936) was said to have had between twenty and forty wives, more than observers could keep track of, and more than he apparently could satisfy. Onsongo was able to spend only one or two days with each wife in turn, leading many to desert him and seek solace in other men. Bethsheba Kemunto 2002; Tangurera Omwenga, Aug. 6, 1997; Beavon, *Sindiga, the Savage*, 265. Using marriage to build legitimacy was found also among the Kuria chiefs. Kirsten Alsaker Kjerland, "Cattle Breed; Shillings Don't: The Belated Incorporation of the abaKuria into Modern Kenya" (Ph.D. thesis, University of Bergen, 1995), 225–226.

187. For a contrast, see Charles H. Ambler, "The Renovation of Custom in Colonial Kenya: The 1932 Generation Succession Ceremonies in Embu," *Journal of African History* 30 (1989), 139–156.

188. SK LNC meetings of Aug. 13–16, 1946, and Nov. 20–22, 1946; DCs' Meeting, Jan. 15–17, 1942, KNA: Adm 3/2/2; DC SK to PC Nyanza, Oct. 9, 1947; Joint LNC Meeting, Oct. 28–31, 1947, both in KNA: Adm 15/7/13/1/2.

189. Luke Gasuku, June 15, 2002.

190. P. Mayer, *Two Studies in Applied Anthropology*, 26.
191. SK DAR 1929. See also SK DAR 1924.
192. SK DAR 1934; Gavaghan, *Of Lions and Dung Beetles*, 74.
193. [John] Kebaso, "Investigation [into] Tribunals," n.d., MFM: 13. On other administrative reactions to accusations of bribery among chiefs, see Safari Diary, March–April 1933, South Mugirango, KNA: Adm 12/4/1; and among African Court elders, Brett L. Shadle, "African Court Elders in Nyanza Province, Kenya, c. 1930–1960: From 'Traditional' to 'Modern,'" in *Intermediaries, Interpreters and Clerks*, eds. Lawrance, Osborn, and Roberts.
194. SK DAR 1931.
195. SK DAR 1935. Abel Nyakundi, for many years recognized as the moral leader of Gusii SDAs and, in their youths, a friend of Musa, in 1987 explained the chief's methods: "On Mondays he had an 'office' at Keumbu. Those with reports came to him and he extorted money from them before the case was tried in their favour." Cleophas Ondieki, "Chiefs as Agents of Social Change in Gusii During the Colonial Period, c. 1905–1963," *Bulletin of the Cardinal Otunga Historical Society* 117 (1987), 9–25, quote from 12. See also LeVine and Levine, *Nyansongo*, 74–75.
196. Kebaso, "Investigation," MFM: 13.
197. SK DAR 1933; John Kebaso, "British Rule in Africa" c. 1949, KNA: Pub 1/1/4; Kebaso, "Investigation," MFM: 13.
198. Nyabiya s/o Anyona to Registrar, Supreme Court, Oct. 1, 1952, KNA: ARC(MAA) 2/9/16 I; Shadle, "African Court Elders in Nyanza Province."
199. Kebaso, "Investigation," and comment by Oscar, MFM: 13.

2

Colonialism and African Society to ca. 1940

As Gusiiland fell under the colonial yoke, it entered an imperial world in flux, socially, culturally, and politically. Gusii men and women would have begun to sense that the colonial realm could impact the way marriage and family disputes might be hashed out. Administrative officials in the 1920s and 1930s graduated from schools that taught them the benefits of patriarchy and social hierarchy, while the doctrine of Indirect Rule—by which Africans would be ruled through their "traditional" senior male rulers—led them to support patriarchs over youth and women. For example, these young Britons established tribunals in which senior African men, backed by the state, enforced their claims over sons, daughters, and wives. Colonial policies such as these did not escape the critical eye of British liberals, some serving in Africa as missionaries, many others observing from back home. Their agitation would result in, most spectacularly, a major inquiry from 1935 to 1937 on "The Status of Women in Africa." African women and youth too were unwilling to accept unquestioningly this particularly burdensome aspect of colonialism. Thus when officials wished to set out policy for stabilizing African society, they found themselves trapped between the various and often diametrically opposed interests of many individuals and groups, and between African and British cultural traditions that were frequently at odds with each other, traditions that were frequently contested by those who subscribed to them.

It was an unlikely collection of people who created this explosive interwar world: unhappy African wives and their unbending fathers and husbands; Archdeacon W. E. Owen, a tireless, hardheaded, and deeply compassionate Irish missionary in Central Kavirondo; conservative twenty-something administrators fresh from Oxford and Cambridge; vocal British feminists packing meeting halls in London; and governments—Labour and Conservative—trying to keep policy debates tucked away safely behind locked Colonial Office doors. Gusiiland was, on the surface, not integral to this story. Yet it was the Gusii, along with the hundreds of thousands of other Africans living under the Union Jack, who brought to life what might have otherwise been charged but empty debates among Europeans. Without senior African men tugging at administrators' sleeves, directing their attention to wild women and disrespectful youth, insisting on the need for more powerful African courts, administrators would hardly have known how to, or even if they should, put into action their deepening patriarchal tendencies. Without courageous Luo women deserting unwanted men and pleading for help from Owen or (more commonly, in the first instance) from his African mission teachers and pastors, the missionary would hardly have known that forced marriages existed at all. In turn, without Owen dashing off missives to the *Manchester Guardian* and feminist groups in London, British concern for colonized women (such as it was) would have ignored Africa in favor of child brides and immolated widows in India, or girl slavery in Hong Kong. Without intense pressure from feminist parliamentarians, mass meetings addressed by public figures and scholars, and articles in British, French, and American papers, the Colonial Office would never have been forced to undertake the collection of information from His Majesty's African possessions. District officers and governors would not have had so bitterly to defend themselves and their policies from prying, "ignorant and uninstructed" busybodies,[1] and could have quietly gone about their business of defending the integrity of patriarchal African societies. It was from this cauldron that came much of the institutional and legal framework for Gusii marriage disputes of the war- and postwar years.

THE CREATION OF A CONSERVATIVE CADRE

Early Colonialism

The conservatism of the interwar years proved so important in part because it marked such a significant change from the preceding era's dedication to reforming African societies. Britons in the last decades of the nineteenth century sought radically to alter African life in their colonies. While imperialists had always thought of colonies as sources of raw materials, it became a top priority with Joseph Chamberlain, Secretary of State for the Colonies from 1895. Chamberlain feared the rising industrial and naval power of Germany, and with a sense of urgency pushed for the development of Britain's colonial possessions.[2] In West Africa officials hoped to restructure local economies along the lines of a rational marketplace. Africans would work for wages, and communal land tenure—which was thought to allow men a refuge from wage labor—would be dismantled in favor of individual tenure.[3] The uneconomic socialistic life would be replaced by progressive and profitable individual enterprise.

Administrators who entered Kenya (until 1920, the East African Protectorate) at the turn of the century similarly held a deep faith in progress fueled by competitive individualism. John Ainsworth, an early and experienced officer, predicted that "the old tenets, superstitions and traditions will have to disappear and in place thereof there must evolve a black with individualistic ideals."[4] Indeed, it meant relatively little to purge Africa of the old ways. "We are not destroying any old or interesting system," commented Charles Eliot, Commissioner of the EAP, 1900–1905, "but simply introducing order into blank, uninteresting, brutal barbarism."[5]

In important ways not all early colonial officials so ardently wished immediately to upturn the old order. Despite the abolitionist propaganda that attended imperial conquest, British officials in Africa often wavered in their commitment to attacking slavery head on.[6] Afraid of the anarchy that might follow the release of hordes of slaves (when first freed, one official believed, "they become lazy and good for nothing")[7] many administrators refused to issue orders for wholesale emancipation. In places like Zanzibar and the Sokoto Caliphate in Northern Nigeria, where master classes directed profitable slave-based economies, colonial officers thought little could be gained, and much lost, if slaves were freed from all obligations to their owners.[8] Nonetheless, even here officials remained dedicated to a new type of organization of production. There was little question that slaves should eventually become wage laborers; the problem was how to inculcate in them the morality, sobriety, and subservience essential to a proper wage-laboring class.[9]

Officers' hesitancy to manumit slaves was even more pronounced when it came to female slaves. Concubines reflected their masters' wealth; their offspring increased households; they could be distributed to allies and followers.[10] To deny masters these slaves, many administrators concluded, would alienate the very men they wished to win over. Moreover, as scholars have pointed out, administrators did "not really [consider women] to be slaves; they were merely women."[11] Disputes between concubines and their masters were dubbed marital cases: they were, according to influential administrator Lord Lugard, "really rather a question of divorce than of slavery."[12] Escaped female slaves, an administrator in Sokoto insisted in 1908, would cause "the present social state [to] be, entirely, disorganised with the result that immorality and disease will increase enormously."[13] The British abolished Zanzibari slavery in 1897, except in respect to concubines who remained enslaved until 1909. Even then, the freedwomen's options were limited. If concubines chose freedom, they renounced claims to material support by their masters as well as to custody of children born under slavery.[14]

In the same way, administrators on the Kenya coast saw little reason to interfere with families pawning or selling children in the lean years of the 1890s. In 1899, the Reverend Douglas Hooper of the Church Missionary Society complained to Sir Arthur Hardinge, Commissioner of the Protectorate, of "the custom amongst the Wagiriama of selling children." Hooper alleged that the practice "had spread, under the guise of infant marriages, owing to the stress of famine."[15] Hardinge, though never at the cutting edge of abolitionist thinking,[16] nonetheless appointed a committee of investigation. It suggested five amendments to the "Giriama Marriage Laws and Customs":

1. That "Hunda" (the sum payable for a wife) be not payable until the girl has reached the age of puberty.
2. That no girl shall be forced to marry a man against her will.
3. That no woman may be taken away from her husband on the ground that her "Hunda" or any part of it has not been paid.
4. On the death of a man none of his wives shall be compelled to marry any of her deceased husband's relations against her will.
5. That no child may be taken from its mother against her will, until it is at least seven years old, and that, in the case of a widow, no one shall have the right to deprive her of her child under any circumstances.

Recommendations such as these were liberal enough, and illustrate the committee's willingness to wean the Giriama from "backward" marriage customs. Elsewhere, however, these innovations appeared less attractive. In 1905, Hooper wrote to Murray, the officer at Malindi, incensed that the law "appear[ed] to be a dead letter!" Murray denied any knowledge of the regulations, and suggested that they might never have been enacted. As for the proximate cause of Hooper's letter, African tribunal cases involving widows and underage marriages, Murray dismissed him brusquely: "I regret that I cannot recognize your right to interfere."[17] As it turns out, after the committee's report the Foreign Office had consulted with the India Office, which had had much (distressing) experience in matters of child marriage. It was disruptive and ineffective to legislate against child marriage was their conclusion.[18] The EAP government thus "decided it was better to avoid legislation on the subject" and the committee's recommendations were "never brought into force."[19] Reforms that disrupted social order would not be enacted.[20]

With these caveats in mind, British dreams of black individualism, combined with African women's own initiatives, ushered in a period in which many women successfully assumed new freedoms. One of the principle tools for transforming Africa, colonialists believed, was British justice. Africans were encouraged to bring cases to white courts, and many did so, testing the ways this new power could be exploited to resolve new or long-standing disputes. Despite the time consumed in hearing this flood of litigation Britons happily reported the number of cases as a sure sign that Africans appreciated colonial rule.[21] Among those who made the most of the courts were women, both free and enslaved. In Asante, in the Gold Coast, many women successfully secured divorces upon application to district officers.[22] One magistrate working at the relatively isolated station at Abercorn, Northern Rhodesia, at the turn of the century consciously set himself to the task of deciding cases with a strict eye toward equity, regardless of African men's opinions. The combination of multiple and shifting ethnicities, the incursion of missionaries, and a recession that made women more a liability than an asset enabled numerous women to come to the court with marital disputes and realize at least a less restricted life. Similarly, slave women appeared before white courts to prevent their sale or to redeem themselves.[23] These women were the lucky ones, for as the years passed and as the tenor of colonial rule in British Africa changed, so too did colonial policies toward women and young men.

The Interwar Years and the Shift Toward Conservatism

The outlook of British rulers in Kenya and across Africa underwent considerable modification in the 1920s. After World War I, Berman explains, Kenya's colonial government shifted from an agent of radical change to "a conservative apparatus of control, focused on the maintenance of the colonial political economy by short-term 'static adjustment.'"[24] The shift in administrative thinking had many causes. Perhaps foremost was the growing recognition by administrators of their inability (at least in the short term) to impose far-reaching changes on African societies.[25] Part of what brought about this realization was simply numbers: there were not enough white men to rule directly and intensively the African masses. In Kenya there was a mere one administrator for every twenty thousand Africans, in Gold Coast, the ratio was one to forty thousand, and in Nigeria, one to fifty-three thousand.[26]

The emergent ideology of Indirect Rule suffused colonial thinking. Africa, Europeans believed, was populated by "tribes"—discrete collections of people attached to unique cultural, political, and societal norms and ruled by strong chiefs.[27] According to Indirect Rule, colonialism could not succeed unless Britons tapped into the legitimacy of indigenous rulers. Administrators would issue instructions to a chief, who would then ensure that all his faithful tribesmen did what the state wished; a pyramid with British officials at the top, chiefs below them, and the masses at the bottom.[28] Anticipating future lines of thought, in 1910 Percy Girouard, Governor of the East African Protectorate, perfectly articulated these sentiments:

> If we allow the tribal authority to be ignored or broken, it will mean that we, who numerically form a small minority in the country, shall be obliged to deal with a rabble, with thousands of persons in a savage or semi-savage state, all acting on their own impulses, and making themselves a danger to society generally.[29]

Obviously, tribes could not be allowed to disintegrate—chiefs without tribes were not chiefs, and with neither chiefs nor tribes Indirect Rule, and colonial rule altogether, would collapse. Now, tribes and tradition, rather than individualism and progress, preoccupied colonial officers, and they took it upon themselves to protect the "organic communities" that were African tribes.[30]

There was also a growing sense among administrators that not only were they unable, but they also did not wish to change "traditional" Africa. This emerged with a new generation of officers. The first government men in British East Africa were of a very mixed lot.[31] Some were holdovers from the British East Africa Company and were kept on since they knew the terrain, or simply because they were present at a time when white men on the ground were few. A significant number of these first administrators—as much as one-tenth—came from South Africa, some after having fought in the South African War of 1899–1902. *Wanderlust* brought others to East Africa: one man had been a tea planter in Ceylon and spent two years exploring Australia before signing up with the colonial state; another had been a rancher in North Dakota.[32] As necessary as these men were—rapid turnover required constant infusion of new men,[33] and as yet few were recruited from Britain—their usefulness and effectiveness never went unquestioned.[34] Governor Girouard looked forward to the day when they could be done with the "cowpunchers."[35] Sir Clement Hill of the Foreign Office when visiting the Protectorate in 1903 disparaged civil servants as having been "enlisted from the gutter."[36] As war turned into peace, many of this motley crew retired or were put out to pasture.

The men who would fill the administrative ranks in the 1920s and 1930s were, in contrast, of a very select group. From 1910 to 1948, Ralph Furse occupied the crucial position in the Colonial Office of recruiting members of the colonial service. Furse had no doubt as to the type of man best suited to serving deep in the African bush. He would be self-reliant, able to rule Africans almost by force of will, an "outdoorsman with not too many brains and a great deal of commonsense."[37] Lord Lugard, champion of Indirect Rule, also wished to keep out "prigs" and "bookworms."[38] The public schools (equivalent to American private schools) as well as the universities at Oxford and Cambridge (known colloquially as Oxbridge) produced just such men. Most public schools were situated in rural areas or small towns, and the students who lived there often had rather little contact with the modern world, even the world outside their small social circle.[39] Moreover, students and their teachers believed public schools to be "adult life in microcosm."[40] As students advanced through their schools they climbed the hierarchy that was student life: senior students commanded deference, and exercised corporal punishment on the lower grades. The "hierarchical nature," Gartrell explains, "was unquestioned."[41] More than just authoritarian, the schools were very much masculine. If more relaxed than the public schools, students at Oxbridge remained surrounded by men; paternalism and patriarchy reigned supreme.[42] Thus the men who would enter the colonial service were men of action, not reflection; they appreciated a clearly structured, male-dominated society, with classes clearly demarcated; they expected to be respected by their charges, whom they would tutor with a paternal firmness. Their personalities helped shape the tenor of the inter-war period.[43]

The post-war disillusionment with civilization would have hit the Oxbridge fraternity particularly hard. Furse reflected that the men appropriate for the officer corps came from the class of families "most severely hit by the war."[44] Eton, one of the public schools that funneled its graduates to Oxbridge, sent off 4,852 men to the war; 1,157 did not return. The death tolls for Oxford and Cambridge were similarly high: of 13,403 Oxford warriors, 2,569 gave their lives; 13,126 Cambridge men went off to war for King George, and 2,364 died for him. Three out of every ten men of the Oxford class of 1913 lost their lives.[45] With the ghosts of their elders haunting their campuses, surely subsequent graduates reflected deeply on the fruits of "civilization."

The functionalist school in British social anthropology played its part as well. Functionalist anthropology, especially as conceived by its guiding light and most influential interwar anthropologist, Bronislav Malinowski, held that pieces of a culture exist because they serve particular purposes. Each custom could be understood only within its cultural context, in relation to other customs. The alteration of any one custom, therefore, has a ripple effect throughout the society. Given the complexities of a culture, the consequences of any single change could be dramatic, unforeseeable, and perhaps fatal to a society's integrity.[46] Functionalism fitted well with administrators' views of African societies, and Malinowski himself remarked that Indirect Rule was "a Complete Surrender to the Functional Point of View."[47] Officers fully believed that cultures—tribes—were self-contained units, logical in their own way. The implication was that change introduced from without, if not done with extreme care, could cause the disintegration of a society.

Granted, administrators constantly criticized and harbored suspicions of anthropologists, whose research (they charged) was too theoretical and dealt with issues largely irrelevant to day-to-day administration, and who (a Northern Rhodesian administrator said) spoke a tongue "quite unintelligible to the ordinary human."[48] While some cadets took courses in anthropology before heading to the colonies we cannot be sure how deeply these lessons sank into their brains.[49] On the other hand, while on leave some officers sat in on Malinowski's seminars.[50] Interwar officers paid greater attention to the customary law of marriage and the family, reading "with avidity" anthropological work on marriage and bridewealth.[51] Many scholars championed "practical anthropology," using their skills to help resolve problems in the colonies.[52] Margery Perham promoted functionalism in administrative circles, teaching officers at summer courses and at Oxford, meeting and touring with them in the colonies, and taking active part in committees at the Colonial Office. Her influence on administrators, Cell writes, was "solid and enduring."[53] Functionalism illuminated administrative minds and, if nothing else, gave their own ideas academic legitimacy.

This is not to say that colonial officials were content with the contemporary state of Africa, nor that they did not wish and expect to see African cultures "evolve" toward the western ideal. Indigenous religious beliefs would disappear in favor of Christianity, and literacy and western education would be widespread. Yet these changes would be long in coming. Africa had reached about the same stage as had the Britons before Roman invasions, they reckoned, and could be expected (over a shorter, but still lengthy period) to reach civilization. While this process could be nudged along, the best thing the government could do was preserve "law and order" and not allow Africans too quickly to lose the moorings of tribal institutions, becoming adrift in modern ways which they could not comprehend and in which they could not survive.[54] In 1929, Sidney Fazan, a district commissioner (DC) in central Kenya, insisted that changes in African law had to be guided and limited to only incremental change:

> . . . we must watch the course of progress, guiding here and restraining there, learning as we go. While we recognize that the communal spirit of native law must in the end give way before advancing individualism, we shall not surrender the fortress to the first onslaught of detribalism, but, as the years go on and one point after another is threatened, we shall decide where to protect the tribal custom and where to let it down gently.[55]

Donald Cameron, Governor of Tanganyika Territory, explained that, as the more barbarous aspects of African societies were eliminated, Europeans would "graft our higher civilization upon the soundly rooted native stock . . ."[56] The metaphor is telling, as Gartrell explains: "as any good gardener knows, sound growth cannot be forced, but must proceed at its own slow, steady pace. And if the graft was going to 'take,' the joint must receive special care and protection through the delicate period of partial fusion."[57]

This reversal from the previous commitment to revolutionizing Africa was neither immediate nor universal. Regarding young Luo men, the South Kavirondo DC in 1927 wrote with seemingly little alarm that "they will assimilate new ideas and no longer be content to abide by the Elders saying that what was good enough for them is good enough for the rising generation."[58] But such opinions were by now in a minority.

THE STATE AND THE PRESERVATION OF PATRIARCHY

Preserving tribes was tricky business. Tribes were, by all accounts, patriarchal. Surveying the situation, officers despaired that disputes between fathers and their children, between husbands and wives, were omens of a looming social crisis. The power seniors wielded over juniors, and men over women, was the glue by which societies and tribes were held together. Without it, tribes would dissolve into individuals, and the state simply could not control hundreds of thousands of individuals. Conflicts between genders and generations haunted British officers across the continent, evoking a vision of a vast, chaotic Africa with no social center, no tribal leaders, and no way for Britons to rule. Administrators began to exert more energy toward preserving family stability under the strong rule of fathers and husbands. As one officer put it, "women and children [took on a] new importance."[59]

Britons across Africa also believed that a properly functioning wage labor system required constraining women's movements. Agricultural production of women at home had to supplement the low pay of men laboring elsewhere. Moreover, administrators often had to induce or force African men into taking up migrant labor, their hesitation borne of fear that their wives and daughters would take lovers or, worse, themselves seek out new lives in mining camps or urban areas. Keeping women in rural areas would also help stave off the emergence of a dangerous and undesirable urbanized working class. As noted one South African official (likely speaking for British officials elsewhere), "For so long as wives and families are kept in their [homesteads], husbands, brothers and sons will continue to return to them."[60]

The women who had previously sought succor with administrators now appeared less like embodiments of the success of the colonial civilizing mission than harbingers of a disorderly and perhaps unrulable new Africa.[61] Desperate letters passed between officials. One administrator in Southern Rhodesia warned that if wives were allowed to flout their husbands' authority they would soon shrug off all "recognized authority, thus undermining all law and order," even, a colleague argued, "the whole existence of a nation."[62] A flurry of new laws and policies (such as the criminalization of adultery) were enacted to shore up the apparently flagging power of senior men. Women faced increasingly tight restrictions on their movements and choices.[63]

The story was no different in Kenya. The need to preserve law and order and suppress youthful promiscuity ended in violence in Maasailand in 1922. Young Maasai men and women passed time in the cattle herding posts and, according to Oscar Watkins, then the Acting Chief Native Commissioner, in order to win the hearts of young women youths were expected to

> blood their spears in human blood. . . .[Y]ou can see that an ambitious warrior anxious to take a high place in war and love is not likely to cut much of a dash either with men or maidens till he has killed. In fact the ladies are reputed to be very sparing of their favors, and very free with taunts, to him who has not killed.

Government attempts to disarm marauding youth and end their custom of "cohabitat[ing] as they pleased" led to a military expedition and the killing of several Maasai.[64]

In Kamba areas administrators strove to suppress "free love" between "warriors" and the girls who circulated between their huts every few nights. The shelters were torn down, and the girls were returned to their fathers.[65] Another officer prepared a report on "Dancing, Drinking, and Other Excesses," in which he expressed concern over youth who held parties, invited and paired off with girls, "Dance all day and night, and then sleep together."[66] In 1929 Sidney Fazan (now DC in South Nyeri) called local elders to a *baraza* to discuss "certain aspects of native custom," namely, matters pertaining to cattle, bridewealth, and penalties for adultery.[67] Most telling, consider the 1919/20 Annual Report from Kisumu district. In Section 8 of the report, titled "Political subjects in general," the DC wrote that "Under this head may be noted the signs of a prevalence of immorality" including "Illicit cohabitation with young girls."[68] Disobedient youth and women troubled elders, but for administrators these family disputes exposed cracks in the tribal foundations of the entire state—these were not private but political problems.

GENDER AND GENERATION IN GUSIILAND

Longer than their colleagues elsewhere, administrators posted to Kisii continued to worry over chiefs' precarious position. In the midst of outbreaks of Mumboism, rampant stock theft, assaults on chiefs and flat out rejection of government directives, administrators would not prioritize the righting of upset gender and generational relations. Only as Gusii chiefs slowly built the authority to rule without the fear of being clubbed or poisoned did administrators really turn more attention to (what they claimed to be) irreverent young men and women. Certainly, in the 1920s and 1930s senior men did not have full control over their charges, but this had always been the case. Whatever the truth of the matter, officials in South Kavirondo (as elsewhere) perceived a rising tide in immorality.

In 1932, District Commissioner C. E. V. Buxton worried that the Gusii had experienced "considerable disintegration of... tribal life in the past 30 years."[69] Having been in the district only eighteen months, part of a district administration only twenty-five years old, Buxton's observations should obviously not be taken uncritically. Even with the transfer of knowledge between old hands and new recruits, DCs had come and gone in Kisii with marked rapidity; colonial understanding of long-term continuities and changes in Gusii social relations was probably not terribly deep. Gusii elders may well have been prodding Buxton toward these conclusions, decrying how far their authority had fallen from the idyllic (and mythical) precolonial past.[70] But Buxton's willingness to listen to such complaints had much to do with new colonial concerns over tribal and family stability.[71]

A Local Native Council (LNC) debate one year later similarly reveals the nature of administrative concerns. According to the Swahili minutes of the meeting (the meetings were conducted in Swahili), members complained of young men who engaged in wage labor out of the district and refused to remit money to their families and who, upon returning home, ignored the instructions of their families. In the English version of the minutes, drawn up by the DC, the issues had been subtly altered: it was the "detribalization" of young men who "on their return to the Reserve were not subject to parental or tribal control" which vexed the council.[72]

In late 1937 the failure of some Public Works Department employees to doff their hats upon passing Chief Musa Nyandusi was cause for a *baraza*, at which the DC condemned the lack of respect youths showed not only to chiefs and administrative officers but also, significantly, to their elders.[73] That same year, Luo elders complained to District Commissioner K. L. Hunter that youth were engaging in excessive drinking and, more disturbing, when seniors disciplined juniors with "minor chastisement" the young men filed assault charges in the courts. Hunter explained that if the situation was as the elders stated, and if the elders' "minor chastisement" caused minor hurt only, then the young men would be informed that they fully deserved their punishment.[74] Preserving the authority of chiefs remained a perpetual preoccupation, but generational and gender disputes had become the new bogey to colonial rule in South Kavirondo as elsewhere.

African Tribunals

Dispute resolution bodies in Gusiiland in the shape of the *abanyamaiga* long preceded colonial rule. But with the coming of the British new legal arenas were established, with new procedures, new powers, and new kinds of elders.[75] Authority to hear local, intra-African disputes was first granted to headmen in 1902, and transferred to councils of elders by 1913. In South Kavirondo the tribunals underwent an overhaul in 1937, with some thirty-nine courts consolidated into nine, two of which served Gusiiland. The Gusii tribunals were now known as *ritongo*, one at Manga and the other at Ogembo, a change significant enough that 1937 was dubbed "*Ritongo*" in local tradition. (A third court was added fifteen years later at Gesima.) The tribunals' jurisdiction did not cover more serious criminal cases—murder, for example—or civil cases involving business matters or Christian marriages. Otherwise, the tribunals enjoyed authority over a whole host of disputes, from cattle theft to assault to boundary disputes, as well as elopement and adultery and (at first *ultra vires* but with administrative connivance) abduction and indecent assault.

From their first sitting the courts began flexing their muscles, exercising their new powers over women and junior men, often with the encouragement of the administration. District Commissioner H. E. Welby in 1920 urged the tribunals to use their authority to punish breaches of "native customs, especially those relating to marriage" and to "check the promiscuity among the women." The elders quickly followed his suggestion, fining and imprisoning men who "enticed" away married women. Luo tribunals took a liberal interpretation of the DC's directive, using it to bar "girls married young to old men leaving them for younger men." Some took even more extreme measures: the North Mugirango tribunal sentenced a runaway woman to twelve lashes, a sentence well beyond their powers but one carried out nonetheless by a headman and his *askari*.[76] One administrator on *safari* at Buregi location in 1928 recommended to the elders that they impose six months imprisonment for "going off with another man's wife"; at Mfangano, he confirmed a sentence of six months imprisonment for a man guilty of seducing a married woman.[77] The courts were used to control not just women, but junior men as well. In 1929, a DC told the story of a young man who "failed to bring back a cow immediately he was told to do so" by his father for milk, and so the latter dragged his son into a tribunal for punishment.[78] Also facing punishment were fathers who failed to obey marriage customs, such as those who accepted bridewealth but then refused to allow their daughters to join their new husbands.[79]

AFRICAN TRIBUNALS AND ADULTERY

With tribunals essential to the regulation of African society, administrators worked hard to defend their jurisdiction over gender and generational disputes, including adultery. Administrators and judicial officials in many British African colonies struggled over the question of how to deal with adultery: was it a civil dispute or a criminal act?[80] Many officers could not countenance criminally punishing a man for a private consensual sexual escapade (a vice indulged in by many an administrator). Yet officials also feared what would happen if cuckolded husbands could sue for compensation from their wives' lovers. In many, if not most, African communities, compensation had been the primary means of settling adultery disputes. Yet, administrators wondered, what would prevent a husband from encouraging his wife to take a lover in order to drag the unfortunate man before the courts to claim compensation? Surely this was prostitution, the money being laundered by the courts.[81]

In many parts of British Africa, criminalization eventually became the preferred method of dealing with adultery, in part because of husbands who complained of the trouble they had controlling their wives. In some colonies—Northern and Southern Rhodesia, the Gold Coast, Tanganyika (under both German and British rule)—the legal status of adultery was rather quickly resolved in favor of criminalization.[82] In Kenya the process followed a more crooked path. The Indian Penal Code, crafted by the British for their colonial rule over the subcontinent, had criminalized adultery.[83] With the adoption of the IPC for the East African Protectorate in 1897 all residents—European, Asian, and African—could theoretically be tried for this offense,[84] although it is not clear how often this law was applied. In South Kavirondo it seems that few adultery cases came before district officers. Between 1907 and 1928, eight people were convicted and four acquitted of adultery, compared with, for example, 178 people tried for assault.[85] Adultery complaints may have been more common in local tribunals, even though they were null: infractions against the IPC could not be heard except by Resident Magistrates or judges. This did nothing to prevent tribunals from punishing adulterers, however, as administrators made it a point to overlook these legal niceties.

When in 1930 the state introduced a new ordinance to replace the Indian Penal Code, adultery was not included, likely due to the influence of the Attorney General and others committed to sticking close to British legal traditions.[86] Under the law, therefore, adultery was decriminalized across the board. Two years later, however, the Governor discovered at Kisumu women imprisoned for adultery, a situation the Attorney General said he had twice observed in Fort Hall district. The latter suggested that DCs be informed that adultery could no longer be tried criminally but rather as a civil matter only. An August 1932 Chief Native Commissioner circular to this effect provoked in Nyanza an administrative reaction as swift as it was alarmist.[87]

The main thrust of officials' complaints was that with the decriminalization of adultery African social relations, and law and order generally, were rapidly falling to pieces. Similar warnings had been voiced in 1928 when it was proposed that civil claims regarding adultery be triable only before white officers. The DC of North Kavirondo had expressed his fear of the potential effect on law and order. He had noted that although "'Fornication' is the principle past times [*sic*]" in his district, there still existed circumstances in which sexual intercourse was considered an offence by "Native Customs." During 1927, the tribunals there had handled 127 cases of "illicit intercourses [*sic*]." Requiring all these cases to be heard by a white officer, the DC had warned, would defeat the ends of justice. A cuckolded husband would not walk fifty miles to lay his claims before a white officer, and now it was only the ease of going to a nearby tribunal "which prevents him from taking the law into his own hands."[88] District officers in 1932 echoed this fear. If adultery was converted to a purely civil matter wronged husbands would fall back on "retributive methods which can only be regarded as destructive of law and order."[89]

Breaches of law and order were worrisome enough, but the threat of gender and generational relations being up-ended thoroughly frightened district officers. Three months after the CNC's circular, the DC at Kisii duly noted that no person had been imprisoned for adultery, as per instructions. The reactions of patriarchs (according to the officer) were as to be expected. Numerous husbands and fathers had complained "that their wives and daughters have run away from their homes and refuse to return."[90] In North Kavirondo young men sneered at their elders: once they realized that they would not be imprisoned for adultery, they began "laughing at the idea of a civil claim."[91]

But it was not simply young men, but *poor* young men, who threatened the peace. A poor man could now "seduce" a married woman and face only a civil charge. This meant little, since a poor man had no property to lose.

The husband could have the judgment debtor jailed, but only by bearing the expenses of imprisonment. Few were willing or able to do so.[92] The plaintiff had no real option and could be given no recompense for his "loss."[93] When a poor man was sued for adultery his poverty made colonial justice a sham.

Administrators thus understood adultery not simply as a conflict between seniors and juniors, but one especially concerning seniors and poor juniors. It was poor young men "who more commonly commit the offense." Decriminalization had put "a premium on the commission of such anti-social acts, and makes it possible for penniless libertines to seduce married women with impunity."[94] "Obviously," snorted the North Kavirondo DC, "a youth without property is in a strong position."[95] Without the power of the state to keep them in line, poor men would feel free to engage in "anti-social acts," crippling senior men.

Yet even as they raged against "local Don Juans without any attachable property," administrators admitted that the genesis of the problem implicated senior men as well. In a telling admission, while arguing the case for recriminalization the Nyanza Provincial Commissioner (PC) said that perhaps "the root of the evil lay in the amount which is generally asked for in bride price."[96] Young men created illicit unions and "seduced" women because they could not marry, and they could not marry because elders demanded too many cattle as bridewealth—a complaint that K. L. Hunter would make five years later. Nevertheless, while administrators blamed both fathers and poor suitors for the social disruption, at the height of this crisis no officer suggested punishment for elders.

Recriminalization of Adultery

As the complaints poured in from his DCs, the Nyanza Provincial Commissioner pressed the case for recriminalization. At the November 1932 PCs' meeting he argued for reinstating imprisonment for adultery. The PCs from Coast, Turkana, Ukamba, and Rift Valley agreed, while those from Kikuyu and Maasai dissented.[97] Finally, in March 1933, the Attorney General relented. Adultery could again be tried as a criminal offense with three restrictions. It would be an offense against customary—not statutory—law, only men could be charged, and a sentence of imprisonment could be given only in default of payment of a fine.[98] Customary law applied only to Africans, and so only adultery between Africans was criminalized. African courts handled customary law cases, which meant adultery would largely be kept out of white courts. Unlike officials in other colonies, administrators here knew full well that they were not implementing hoary African customary law.[99] Instead, arguments in favor of criminalization rested on matters of law and order and preservation of the family. The African family could not survive on its own, and if customary law could not protect it innovative measures by the state would be required.

That adultery was classed under customary rather than statutory law was a matter of convenience.[100]

Nonetheless, administrative opinions on criminalizing adultery lacked unanimity. At the November meeting, the PC Kikuyu stated that in the past "Provincial Commissioners had arrived at the conclusion that one cannot legislate against 'runaway wives' as in theory the woman is a free agent."[101] This PC may have been a throwback to an earlier era, when the control of women did not so consume administrators. But in central Kenya and Kiambu district in particular administrators remained hesitant too extensively to regulate women's movement. Women had to have enough freedom to bring agricultural goods to Nairobi, a trade on which the city relied. Thus when the Kiambu LNC in 1928 proposed prohibiting women from going to Nairobi (which led to "prostitution and disease"), the DC declined to support this, saying that it was a "domestic affair" and that legislation was "incapable of controlling women's morals."[102] While the concerns of senior men did matter, of more significance was ensuring that Gikuyu women traders continued to supply Nairobi with desperately needed produce.[103] The differences in opinion between Central and Nyanza provinces disclose just how mercurial state support for senior men could be. The needs of downcountry cities mattered less in Nyanza, and administrators there led the charge against decriminalization.

FORCED MARRIAGE AND THE STATUS OF AFRICAN WOMEN

Colonial officials' hostility to African women's mobility reached its peak in the 1930s, even as metropolitan critiques of colonial policies toward women did the same. The histories of these countervailing trends overlapped only slightly, but as they came together they spawned impassioned missives and mass meetings by the critics, condescending memoranda and frustrated reports by officials. Twice in the decade activists in Britain forced the Colonial Office to undertake investigations into the status of African women. The first, in 1930–1932, began as an inquiry into female circumcision and the health of the colonized population, but what emerged was an attempt to determine if African women lived as if enslaved to their menfolk. The second investigation, which stretched from 1935 to 1937, was intended to discover the existence and extent of forced marriage of African women. Only with the outbreak of war were attentions turned elsewhere.

Feminism and Imperialism

With the rise of women's movements in late nineteenth-century Britain, feminists believed women's oppression to be universal and thus (theoretically) united women across racial and geographical lines. But feminism and the second British empire grew up together, and the feminist case was hopelessly entangled with questions of imperialism.[104] Thus to justify their claims on the state, women depicted their goals as contributing to those of the nation-state that, in turn, was inseparable from Empire.

Feminists' interest in empire only grew in the interwar years, and internationalism (in membership, organization and activity) expanded.[105] As suffrage was achieved in many countries (1918 in Britain, though only for women over the age of thirty) many women's groups lost their primary focus of activity, if not their raison d'etre. Other issues quickly emerged, such as disarmament and peace, and the citizenship of women married to men of other nationalities. By their very nature, these topics led women's groups to look beyond their national borders. The League of Nations injected a new sense of internationalism into politics generally, Rupp writes, by "open[ing] up new opportunities for members [of women's groups] to converge on Geneva and importune delegates" on a whole host of issues.[106] Of particular interest was the Advisory Committee of Experts on Slavery, which first met in 1934, and which periodically examined issues such as the status of women.[107] The interwar years, Rupp continues, marked "a moment of intense and anxious engagement with empire."[108]

While the interwar feminist movement attracted many supporters, a few groups and individuals stood out. Eleanor Rathbone (1872–1946) was one of the most public figures. While long concerned with suffrage and active in a number of organizations, from her election to Parliament in 1929 Rathbone zealously and tirelessly worked to improve women's status in Britain, India and Africa, always with an eye toward the dangers of "sex antagonism."[109] While Rathbone articulated herself in a style befitting an MP, Nina Boyle's words were those of a fighter. Boyle (1865–1943) rose through the ranks of the suffragist movement, by 1907 heading up the Political and Militant Department of the Women's Freedom League. In the interwar years she took up a new career as a novelist but also became a vigorous, vocal activist for the rights of women in Africa.[110]

Other women found their voices in such feminist groups as the St. Joan's Social and Political Alliance (St. Joan's Alliance, or SJA) and the British Commonwealth League (BCL). The former had been the Catholic Women's Suffrage Society (established in 1911), but changed its name and goals in 1923. Through public meetings and its organ *The Catholic Citizen* (with its long-time editor and writer, Christine Spender) the SJA delved into questions of slavery and the status of women in the colonial world. A French branch, established in 1931, kept St. Joan's in touch with developments in Francophone Africa. In the 1930s, under the leadership of Mrs. Laughton Mathews, the SJA became a leader in the debates over marriage in Africa.[111]

St. Joan's and over forty other women's groups came together under the umbrella British Commonwealth League, founded in 1925. The origins of the BCL went back fourteen years to the Australian and New Zealand Women Voters' Committee, active primarily in Britain to defend their own voting rights and to advance the suffragist cause in the metropole. While its activities lapsed for a few years after the war the 1924 British Empire Exhibition re-energized the movement, prompting the name change and more regular meetings and political ventures.[112] The new BCL, however, was composed of "Women's Societies in any part of the Empire" (including ones from Canada, Bermuda, Ceylon, India and South Africa) concerned with "the securing of equality of liberty, status, and opportunities between men and women" within the Commonwealth.[113] The need for the BCL, its charter explained, was that other societies could devote only limited attention to imperial issues; these could be better addressed by a group dedicated solely to them.[114] With such a varied membership, a wide variety of issues attracted BCL attention: child marriage in India, sexual abuse of children, prostitution, the nationality of married women, and the status of African women.

The 1933 centenary of abolition in the British colonies occasioned celebration, but the specter of enslaved women in the colonies cast a pall over self-congratulations. The St. Joan's Alliance called on the government to end all forms of slavery, including the bartering of women and children into domestic and other forms of slavery. A participant at a Catholic meeting noting the centenary asserted that still in Africa "'wives' were sold, and lent, and even willed away as portion of a man's property."[115]

Polygamy also struck the sensibilities of women's groups and missionaries. Monogamy was "among the finest achievements" of Western civilization, they said, and was central to Christianity.[116] Moreover, polygamy seemed to approximate slavery. In monogamous marriages, men often claimed the fruits of their wives' labor and sole access to them sexually. But a polygamous union was something altogether different: one man claimed these rights over many women. This, women's groups charged, was slavery by its most basic definition. Father Hughes, of the Catholic missionary order White Fathers, told a meeting how "wives in Africa represent slave-labor . . . [and] are also considered breeders of slaves."[117] Disgusting tales of men sexually exploiting their wives-cum-slaves flowed into Great Britain. One chief, Hughes related, had desired a rifle, yet lacked sufficient cash. Where to get the money? The chief sent forth his fifty wives to seduce young men; the chief then demanded compensation from the men for adultery, and was then able to buy his rifle. Other men skipped the legal niceties and simply prostituted their wives or magnanimously lent them out as sexual favors to their friends or workers.[118]

The levirate (widow inheritance) also seemed patently to be slavery. Among some African communities a widow might choose to marry, or, at times, be forced into marrying, a brother of her late husband. This practice helped ensure that a widow continued to have the physical and social support of a man, and that the deceased's lineage retained control over her productive and reproductive powers. Abuses of the custom did, of course, occur, but critics greatly oversimplified it. "Levirate," they insisted, was interchangeable with "slavery."[119] Critics made "freedom" for widows one of their rallying points.[120]

More than anything else, bridewealth proved to British activists that African marriage was in fact the enslavement of women. This required no explanation, only description: women were transferred in exchange for money or property,[121] which was the essence of slavery—the commoditization of people. Bridewealth, Christine Spender argued, was "the root of all evil where the African woman is concerned." It aroused "avaricious and possessive instincts," and gave rise to all the other agonies suffered by African women.[122] Bridewealth "was a curse" Georgina Gollock told a British Commonwealth League meeting, and she was greeted with applause.[123] Over and over again activists pointed out that under the very definition put forward by the League of Nations' slavery committee bridewealth marriage was slavery (although the committee itself studiously avoided delving into marriage customs).[124]

Recurring accusations of abuses of African women were not idle chatter of outraged but ineffectual liberals. Their meetings, speeches, petitions, and letters, steeped with platitudes though they were, nonetheless forced the hand of colonial officials.

Female Circumcision and Slavery

It was no accident that, while critics culled information from across Africa, a controversy in Kenya would become a focus of metropolitan attention. From the arrival of the first batch of white settlers just after the turn of the century, Kenya was a lightning rod for public and parliamentary attack. Land alienation for white settlement drew heated reaction in London, as did the lack of health care, education, and other social services for Africans. The controversy liberals raised over the "Northey Circular"—in which the government told chiefs to "encourage" young men to seek out wage labor, sounding too much like a call for coerced labor—caused a reversal in Nairobi's policy.[125] Two former employees of the Kenya government, Norman Leys and William McGregor-Ross, returned to Great Britain in the 1920s disgusted by what they had witnessed. Their lectures and writings held liberal attention on Kenya. When gold was discovered in western Kenya in 1933, some thirty-two questions were made in Parliament in February and March alone, while the Colonial Office received almost three hundred petitions and letters from individuals and groups, the vast majority championing African land rights against white prospectors.[126]

The question of female slavery broke onto the political stage with Kenya's Gikuyu female circumcision crisis of 1929–1930. In 1929, after years of criticism, John Arthur of the Church of Scotland Mission demanded that his parishioners and employees pledge not to allow their daughters to be circumcised. With the question also tied up with broader politics and the control of churches the result was a wholesale desertion of the church by its Gikuyu members, men and women. The matter quickly assumed enormous proportions as the countryside fell into various (if not always clear-cut) groups: missionaries and Gikuyu loyal to them, the Gikuyu "masses," leaders of the Kikuyu Central Association, and colonial officials scrambling to keep the peace.[127] In Britain, with questions of African health and population attracting new interest, the crisis—minus its political aspects—drew the attention of many activists.[128] On December 11, 1929, the Duchess of Atholl and Rathbone raised the issue in Parliament.[129] Over the next several months the Committee for the Protection of Coloured Women in the Crown Colonies (an unofficial group of MPs that included Rathbone) focused itself almost solely to the crisis and pressed the Secretary of State for the Colonies for action.[130]

Quickly enough, the question of female slavery arose. As described by Pedersen, in her speech before Parliament Rathbone "reminded the House of its long opposition to slavery and urged it to extend its solicitude to African women whose relationship to their husbands, she argued, often precisely mirrored that condition."[131] Pressure mounted on the Colonial Office to address the controversy. On February 12, 1930, representatives of forty-seven organizations gathered at Caxton Hall to discuss the status of African women. A series of powerful speakers, including Rathbone, Boyle, the Duchess of Atholl and a representative of the Anti-Slavery and Aboriginies Protection Society, took the podium. Despite a few dissensions the consensus of the meeting was that African women were little more than slaves.[132] In February Secretary of State for the Colonies Passfield received a resolution adopted by the Women's Freedom League calling for the "improvement of [African women's] present enslaved status," and another in March from Rathbone's National Union of Societies for Equal Citizenship protesting the "wide-spread existence of cruel and degrading conditions of slavery among native women . . . being tolerated under the British flag."[133]

In April, Passfield bowed to requests and granted an audience to a deputation from the Council for the Representation of Women in the League of Nations. Nina Boyle again was present, as was Rathbone, who charged that in many parts of British Africa "women are in fact treated as the property of their fathers and husbands," and that bridewealth "leads to abuses of the most revolting character." Passfield prevaricated, making no promises.[134] But in fact he had already on March 8 issued a despatch to Britain's African dependencies requesting information on the prevalence, consequences and possibility of ending female circumcision.[135]

What most rankled the men in colonial government offices was the first line of Passfield's penultimate paragraph: "It has further been represented to me that the status of native women is in some places scarcely distinguishable from that of slavery, and I shall be glad to receive your observations on this question in particular and in general on the status and conditions of native women . . ." Responses from Uganda, Somalialand Protectorate, Northern Rhodesia, Nyasaland, Zanzibar, and Tanganyika, and a report on the West African colonies, all denied that any such conditions held: "The status of women of the [Zanzibar] Protectorate is far removed from anything akin to slavery."; "Slavery is not practised in Nyasaland. Women are well treated and free."; "Far from being slaves the whole social life of the tribes centres round them and they have far more influence than the men."; ". . . the suggestion that in some places [the status of women] is 'scarcely distinguishable from slavery' is without foundation . . ."; the examples go on.[136] Those in Great Britain who equated bridewealth with the sale of women, Mitchell of Tanganyika seethed, were "ignorant and uninstructed."[137]

The real danger, Passfield was informed, was that women had *too much* rather than too little freedom. The Director of Medical and Sanitation Services in Nyasaland reported that the real predicament "lies in too rapid emancipation rather than any tendency to slavery."[138] Elder men and chiefs in Uganda felt the same.[139] All was well so long as women remained (or could be kept) in the positions reserved for them in their traditional societies. As traditional social bonds dissolved, however, women repudiated their patriarchal authorities. Women's exercise of new-found freedoms, administrators warned, "easily degenerates into licence." The imperative was, as Mitchell put it, "for more, and not fewer, restraints" on women.[140]

The results of the inquiry apparently caused few ripples. The Duchess of Atholl, previously one of the most outspoken critics of CO policy, had been "taken into confidence by the Colonial Office" which, Pedersen explains, allowed them more easily to "muzzle and manipulate her."[141] Men in the CO were hesitant to make the governors' responses widely available, for fear of re-awakening public interest. One official proposed that the Stationary Office sell it at "a fairly high price and not to advertise it."[142] The report was finally made available in 1932, as Colonial Number 65, *The Health and Progress of Native Populations in Certain Parts of the Empire*, to apparently little fanfare. Time had passed, the CO had done its bureaucratic duty of undertaking an official investigation,[143] and the situation in Kenya had calmed.

Over the next several years women's groups in Britain continued, albeit less frequently, to ask after the status of women in the colonies. A brief inquiry arose in 1931 following a letter to Drummond Shields from the Duchess of Atholl. She had been told by Donald Cameron (former governor of Tanganyika Territory, and rarely in sympathy with feminist causes) that "several native councils" there had limited the amount of bridewealth "that may be charged." Her Committee on the Protection of Women in the Crown Colonies favored the extension of this policy. She requested information on other colonies about bridewealth levels past and present, and the possibility of limiting it.[144]

The CO limited the matter to Kenya and Tanganyika. The governor of Kenya began his response seemingly in agreement with Atholl. Bridewealth was the root of overstocking of the reserves and continuous legal disputes over payment and repayment, and as such it served as "one of the greatest obstacles in the way of the advancement of the native peoples." Moreover, it tended to "degenerate into sale and purchase . . ." At this point, however, the Governor turned against Atholl's position. To outlaw bridewealth by "arbitrary legislation" would not only be ineffective, it would produce "chaos." Limiting bridewealth had been attempted before in Kenya (his specific example was Gusiiland) only to fail miserably. Most interesting, he explained that bridewealth helped keep women moral. "Without it," he assured London, "there would be promiscuity."[145] Social stability was more important than ending a custom admittedly sliding into the "sale and purchase" of young women.

Agitation over Forced Marriage, 1935–1938

A letter that appeared in the *Manchester Guardian* in 1935 sparked the next round of debate. "Under certain circumstances," wrote W. E. Owen, a missionary in Kenya, "native marriage customs seem to involve a kind of slavery for reluctant women." The attention of readers in Britain would immediately have been piqued by this phrase. But Owen did more than reiterate the rhetoric being bandied about in London. He had, he told his readers, witnessed the "enslavement" of a young woman. She had been "captured (forcibly)" and "bound by the ten or fifteen head of cattle her family receive." She had run off only to be "dragged back" to her husband, then beaten until welts were raised. In the end, wrote an outraged Owen, her "marriage" had been confirmed by a Native Tribunal, established and empowered by the British colonial state.[146]

Archdeacon Owen, head of the Church Missionary Society in Central Kavirondo District, was no stranger to controversy. An Irishman, Owen had begun his career in Uganda in 1904 before being appointed Archdeacon of Kavirondo in 1918. Owen believed himself Africans' "friend who will stand up for them to his own countrymen" with a reputation "good enough to command respect, even from pagans."[147] He called for African representation in the Legislative Council and argued that eventually Africans should govern their own affairs via the staffing of a Native Affairs Department.[148] Owen also defended African interests against exploitation by white settlers and the state on such as issues as forced labor and unfair and burdensome taxes and fines.[149] His work with Africans was not, however, uncomplicated. His attitudes were "laced with paternalism," as Strayer puts it.[150] He bitterly resented the growing independence of Alfayo Mango, a leading CMS adherent who would go on to found the independent *Roho* spirit church in the 1930s. As the champion of Africans' interests against other whites, Owen found it incomprehensible that Africans would wish to emancipate themselves from his influence.[151] Whatever his failings, Owen's work on behalf of African rights were significant enough to anger his superiors in the church, and administrators dubbed him "Archdemon Owen." He was, according to one officer, "an out and out Bolshevist, [who has] done a lot of harm."[152]

One area of particular interest to Owen was the plight of African women. In many ways Owen was far ahead of other missionaries in the vigor with which he fought women's oppression. To be sure, he was a man of his times.

Observing a *Roho* meeting at which young men fell into trances, Owen could not help but point out (what he thought to be) the barely-concealed perversions of the practice:

> The sex dangers are obvious. Those two lads with their heads and shoulders pillowed on the willing laps of hefty, lusty wenches, when they came round would be able to twist those same wenches round their fingers. Sex passions must be aroused under circumstances of darkness . . . which present every opportunity to grave temptation.[153]

His concern for girls being taken advantage of sexually existed without apparent tension with his belief that these same girls were "hefty, lusty wenches." Nonetheless, Owen was a true crusader; his agitation for women's rights brought Kavirondo to the center of attention among women's groups in Britain and, eventually, Parliament and the Colonial Office.[154]

Of course, absent the actions of African men and women, Owen would have been left without ammunition. The Archdeacon gained a reputation locally as a man who would give physical protection to women escaping the violence of forced marriage[155] and through whom one could gain access to a district officer, a feat otherwise not readily accomplished. Excepting the rare case in which he might come across, quite by chance, an actual abduction or the beating of an unwilling wife,[156] Owen became aware of disputes only at the initiative of women (or abducted women's fathers). One woman came to Owen only after having avoided being abducted three times by her former husband.[157] Another woman was first married off on July 31, 1942. She escaped three days later, only to be recaptured that same day. Over the next five months the process was repeated at least four times. Owen finally was made aware of her travails in February.[158] African women did not appeal to the British public or petition the Colonial Office, but without their initiative neither would have Owen.

Soon after Owen's letter appeared in the *Guardian* feminist groups marshaled their forces. Christine Spender for St. Joan's and Dorothy Innes for the British Commonwealth League both called for inquires.[159] In late October the SJA drafted a (questionless) "Questionnaire" for the government:

> (a) That in all territories under British jurisdiction it shall be laid down that a woman, whatever her race, shall not be sold by her father or alleged proprietor to a polygamist or anyone else;
> (b) that no marriage contract be made for a girl under 14;
> (c) or over 14 without her consent;
> (d) that there shall be no inheritance of widows by their husband's heirs.[160]

The CO's noncommital response stated that the laws and customs found in the Empire were so diverse that imposing the uniformity they desired was "out of the question."[161]

The critics remained unsatisfied. In October at a Conference of Representatives of Women's Organisations on Women's Demands at the General Election, Spender moved that the government ensure "(1) that a woman, whatever her race, is not a chattel to be sold . . . (2) that every woman must be a free agent to choose her own partner in life . . ."[162] The British Commonwealth League in November held a conference on "Marriage and Slavery."[163] In stark contrast to other meetings, however, nearly every speaker rejected the women-as-slaves equation. It was an influential collection of speakers: Louis Leakey, Jomo Kenyatta (a Gikuyu politician and student of Malinowski), Julius Lewin (scholar of African law at Witwatersrand University), Norman Leys (the former colonial official from Kenya turned colonial critic) and Professor W. Macmillan (late of Witswatersrand University and author of several works on colonial policies). Their conclusions broke down along three lines. First, claims to women's slave-like status were misguided. In fact, women's rights were closely protected. Leakey (a self-styled "white Gikuyu") pointed out that by Gikuyu law a man could not force his wife to have sex. Leakey and others also claimed knowledge of many women who had successfully rejected undesirable men. Second, favorable comparisons were made between the status of African and British women.[164] Indeed, on the question of the legal status of rape within marriage, Leakey pointed out that Gikuyu women were much better off than their British sisters.

The most divisive question was whether to address primarily the oppression of Africans by Europeans or the oppression of women by men. For many long-time liberal observers the Kenya situation had always been clear-cut: the government and the white settlers oppressed Africans. When African women's status vis-à-vis African men required comment many critics attributed gender oppression to the failures of colonial rule; better to ignore intra-African conflicts than to complicate the primary issue. Perhaps the most effective argument was that underlying problems—Africans' economic disadvantages, and the lack of education for African women—required more immediate attention. This was a criticism women's groups had run up against before, in the female circumcision debates in particular.[165]

While the meeting seemed to cool the ardor of some critics, Owen would not be silenced. Within a fortnight he fired off another letter to the *Manchester Guardian* describing more cases of forcible marriage.[166] But it was the case of Kekwe of Tanganyika, written up by Owen for the *Guardian* in June 1936, that most touched the British public. Kekwe, eighteen, was married off by her parents to an unwanted man. She ran off to her preferred mate, and when her "husband" came to retrieve her she repulsed him with what turned out to be a fatal knife wound. A British judge sentenced Kekwe to eighteen months imprisonment for manslaughter.[167] This, Owen wrote, was manifestly unjust: "The fact that 18-year old Kekwe was resisting in spite of the sanction of her family and tribe does not seem to me to invalidate her right to defend her physical person and her spiritual personality." "We must," he pleaded, "for the sake of African girlhood, teach the tribes that without consent there is no true marriage."[168]

The relative quiet of the previous months was shattered. On July 10, St. Joan's called on the Colonial Office for more information on Kekwe and on official procedures meant to prevent forced marriage. Intimating that Kekwe was only one example of an empire-wide tragedy, the SJA requested the latest reports from the mandated territories as they related to women.[169] The BCL wished to know "whether it is possible for girls and women in countries under the British flag to be forced to marry against their will," and in August the Women's Freedom League demanded to know if the Tanganyika judiciary had reversed Kekwe's sentence.[170] The men of the CO were not at all happy at the prospect of going another round with their critics. One Alfred Milner wrote the Colonial Minister asking him to imagine if Kekwe were his own daughter. Scrawled in the file by someone in the CO was a decidedly unsympathetic comment. The answer he would give Milner, the gentleman wrote, was that "if I was the parent I should be in charge and would approve" of the marriage.[171]

Against the Colonial Office's best wishes the battle was engaged. At the urging of the SJA, Rathbone posed a question in Parliament to Ormsby Gore, Secretary of State for the Colonies.[172] Alluding to Kekwe, she inquired as to what the government intended to do to prevent forced marriages. Ormsby Gore (who as an MP in 1929 had joined the legions attacking the CO) replied that women enjoyed perfect freedom to bring their complaints to officials. At the same time he made public that he had, one week earlier, sent a despatch to the governors of Britain's African dependencies.[173]

The men of the Colonial Office hardly took seriously feminists' complaints; indeed, they refused to take seriously feminist complainants. Commonly, the CO dismissed these women as "busybodies"[174] infused with self-delusions of righting all the world's wrongs, and who hoped to make themselves indispensable to the Colonial Office.[175] In following their questionable goals the groups put to use equally questionable tactics. They made "wild statements" and spread "mischievous propaganda."[176] Exasperated officials railed at the St. Joan's Alliance as a "fantastic body of females," and dismissed members of the British Commonwealth League as "ridiculous women."[177]

Nonetheless, the charges made by these "ridiculous women," who, after all, included MPs, had to be answered. In his despatch to the colonies Ormsby Gore inquired as to the frequency of coerced marriages, if women were able to appeal to an officer and what action he would take, and if any changes need be made to prevent serious abuses. When responding to Rathbone's question in the House, Ormsby Gore assured her that in "most African tribes the old idea of coercion is completely eradicated." He could be confident that his officials would prove him correct. In the despatch he noted that "the extent and evil" of coercion in marriage customs "are capable of exaggeration."[178]

Administrators and Forced Marriages in Kenya

Each governor received his copy of Ormsby Gore's despatch, and in turn sent memoranda to his officers in the field. Perhaps more than their colleagues elsewhere, officers in Kenya could hardly contain their frustration, hypersensitive as they were to outside criticism. Certainly even more exasperating, the whole conflagration had been lit by a man in their own backyard, the uncooperative, unco-optable, "Archdemon" Owen. Administrators did not draw up their responses in hopes of pleasing Rathbone *et al.*

District Commissioners in Nyanza and Central provinces, not surprisingly, challenged the veracity of Owen's assertions. Out of fifteen responses from the two provinces, thirteen DCs said forced marriages were either nonexistent, rare, or in decline. The Fort Hall DC admitted that in non-Christian marriages coercion did take place, sometimes involving physical violence, although "all natives" with whom he spoke agreed that more and more parents were respecting their daughters' wishes.[179] In Meru, the DC allowed that "Coercion is frequent."[180] Even these two men, however, did not consider forced marriage a pressing problem.[181]

In asserting the nonexistence of forced marriage administrators worked from a strict interpretation of "force." Their definition of forced marriage meant the use of physical violence and excluded threats of violence, moral coercion and societal pressure.[182] Thus the Kiambu DC could report that he had heard of no cases of "real coercion," while another administrator considered that no "undue pressure" was brought to bear on women in selecting mates.[183] The implication here was that some other type of coercion or pressure could legitimately be employed.[184] Only by expanding the definition of coercion to include nonviolent means could one DC grant that forced marriages were "frequent." "Generally speaking," he wrote, "it may be stated that coercion in Meru is produced by pressure of established custom rather than by individual violence."[185]

Other officers argued that once a woman ceased to resist her forced marriage, it ceased to be a forced marriage. The Fort Hall DC quickly qualified his admission of the existence of forced marriage by noting that the use of coercion was generally brief since (as the elders told him), "the girl soon settles down happily with her husband."[186] His successor felt the same. A missionary's letter dated January 1, 1940, charged that some female Christians had been forced to into marriage in "the latter part of 1939." The skeptical DC wondered that if a woman in such circumstances "has remained with her 'husband' since being 'forced' into marriage, surely she has condoned the offence . . . ?"[187] Even coercion did not always a coerced marriage make.

District commissioners also reassured Nairobi that those few women actually forced into marriage easily reclaimed their freedom. In some areas custom allowed prospective brides a recognized opportunity to reject an unwanted suitor.[188] Even in Meru (the DC wrote) where forced marriages were "frequent," a woman had merely to run off to another man, at which point her father's "powers of compulsion" ended.[189] According to Lambert, the Kericho DC, Kipsigis elders fretted over the women who, when forced into marriage, ended up deserting often to become prostitutes elsewhere in the Colony.[190]

As had Phillip Mitchell in 1930, with his frustration over "ignorant and uninstructed" critics, officers in Kenya castigated their adversaries in Great Britain for their naivety.[191] Some of the forced marriages which critics claimed to have witnessed, officers proposed, could likely be chalked up to peculiar African customs. In certain areas (Gusii, Luo and Gikuyu among them) when a groom came to collect his new bride she was expected to resist—to hide, cry, scream, and struggle. "[I]t is considered indecent for a girl to proceed to her husband without a fuss," the South Kavirondo DC reported. "Should she do so, she would be considered a girl of low character, used to co-habitating with men."[192] Many observers likely mistook these performances for forced marriages, Acting Governor Wade told London. He quoted one officer to this effect:

> Recently I was shocked when a girl was literally carried kicking and screaming into my camp. I intervened, ordered her to be put down and sent home unmolested. She was. Next day, she returned on her own, and I found her in camp living with the very man to whom she had been carried screaming. It was only after I had taken the parties before the headman to get the marriage voluntarily registered, that I discovered that the apparent resistance was part of the customary marriage ceremony, and my intervention a matter for the amusement of all concerned except myself.[193]

At the November 1935 "African Women and Slavery" meeting Jomo Kenyatta suggested that perhaps Archdeacon Owen had made just this mistake, a scenario so amusing as to provoke laughter from the otherwise earnest British Commonwealth League assembly.

As administrators never tired of explaining, every African tradition, no matter how seemingly bizarre, served its own purpose. The DC at Fort Hall was a particularly staunch believer of the internal logic of African custom and its ultimate ability to satisfy all members of the community, something British critics (he argued) could not comprehend. Some Kamba men in fact did not consult their daughters when arranging their marriages. Yet neither did they hand their daughters over to the highest bidder, "but generally to a compatible and eligible suitor."[194]

The comparison between marriage customs in Africa and in Britain was again made. The Fort Hall DC went to great lengths to show that African women were not so badly off after all. "Considering how many incompatible marriages are contracted in civilized communities," he wrote, the cases of

Kamba women unhappily wed were comparatively infrequent. Even child betrothals (which "obviously [have] objectionable features") did not necessarily make "more unsuccessful marriages than any system of marriage based on consent that has been devised by more civilized communities." Further:

> I regret that I cannot overcome the temptation to observe that some of our own people who have become so impatient in this matter should remind themselves that forced marriage still persists as a barbarous custom in the civilized countries of Europe. Many a young girl, even in Society circles, there is still driven to the altar, with her whole soul in revolt, by the mingled pleadings and brow-beatings of callous, self-seeking parents.[195]

Runaway Women

Ultimately, administrators argued, the more pressing problem was women loosening patriarchal controls. District commissioners at Thika and Kisumu reported that while they received few if any complaints of forced marriages, they heard very many cases of runaway women.[196] Eliminating forced marriages was of course necessary, but not at the expense of further circumscribing patriarchal authority. The DC at Fort Hall was most vehement about this. More Gikuyu women were acting on a growing sense of freedom and so, without any official interference, forced marriages were on the decline. But matters had gotten out of hand. "It frequently happens," he warned, "that an unwilling bride simply snaps her fingers at parents and husband and goes off to lead her own life elsewhere." A similar course of events, the DC wrote, had earlier been observed in Basutoland (Lesotho):

> [It is] an interesting question whether the Basuto woman has not gained too much independence for the general well-being of the nation. It is certainly true that she has now become extremely lazy, and that she dominates the husband of her choice and grossly neglects many duties in ordinary domestic life. It may well be that the misuse of the large measure of freedom which she has gained is one of the chief causes of the sad degeneration which the Basuto are now beginning to suffer.[197]

In his despatch to the Colonial Office, Acting Governor Wade admitted that in relatively "backward" areas forced marriages did take place. But generally, he wrote, few cases of coercion had come to official notice, and in any event no drastic intervention was called for. Indeed, Wade warned London, it could be dangerous:

> Interference with deep rooted tribal customs, however deplorable, must be done with great caution, as any sudden removal of parental control would have disastrous results and might in fact shatter the tribal social system.

Certainly forced marriages should be checked, but never to the point of endangering already fragile tribal structures.

The solutions administrators advanced were those that required the least state action. The voluntary registration of marriage, some proposed, would give women an official opportunity to declare their feelings. From the mid 1930s some officers took seriously the idea of registration, even compulsory registration if need be.[198] But the appeal of voluntary registration was that it allowed officers to give the appearance of intervention while doing little actually to limit parental control. As the DC Meru in fact admitted, "if established custom is strong enough to coerce a girl into marrying a man against her will," she could also be coerced into remaining silent at the registration of the marriage.[199]

The only real answer to forced marriage, as well as other objectionable socio-cultural practices, officers argued, was social evolution. As time passed and Christianity, education and new economic relations altered Africans' ways of thinking, forced marriages would become repulsive even to them. In some areas, DCs reported, this had already begun and "public opinion" had swung against coercing girls into marriage. Within a generation evolution would naturally result in the elimination of whatever abuses might still exist.[200] The active intervention women's groups advocated could only disrupt this process, perhaps retarding African social evolution and African women's advancement.[201]

Responses from the other colonies were much the same as those from Kenya.[202] While parents employed moral coercion, real—that is, physical—coercion was "very rare indeed."[203] Authorities generally uncovered those few cases that did occur and liberated the women. As in Kenya, the true social ill was that women were becoming too free. In Northern Rhodesia, the governor reported, "some anxiety is felt because girls are becoming too independent and are tending to flout the influence which parents may rightly exercise over them."[204] Philip Mitchell, now Governor of Uganda, repeated his earlier warnings. He agreed with statements made at the British Commonwealth League's "Marriage and Slavery" meeting, in that the trouble lay in the "breakdown of traditional moral restraints." Some few abuses did take place, but solutions might be worse than the problem. "Anything which tends to weaken [marriage customs]," Mitchell warned, "may result in far worse evils, for it is not excessive restraint which is the most serious danger for the women of Africa but excessive licence."[205]

The Demise of Forced Marriage Debates in Britain

Critics apparently waited patiently while the investigation was being undertaken,[206] but they did not quietly receive the governors' responses, published in a July 1938 White Paper, *Correspondence relating to the Welfare of Women in Tropical Africa*. On the 29th the *Manchester Guardian* summarized the "enlightening" responses from the governors. Reports that forced marriages were declining in number were "well enough as far as it goes." But could officials "explain away the very disquieting cases of which Archdeacon Owen gave details?"[207] Owen himself wrote up a critique of the White Paper,[208] and in late September, a missionary in Uganda wrote St. Joan's also taking issue with it. Whereas the despatch from that colony confidently stated that "cases of real coercion are very infrequent," the missionary "would have written 'cases of real coercion are frequent in some parts of Uganda.'" In fact, "We have even got our 'little martyr' . . . who was speared because she refused her proposed husband."[209] Christine Spender in the pages of *Catholic Citizen* also rejected claims made in the White Paper.[210]

On December 12, 1938, St. Joan's called a large public meeting to discuss forced marriage and the White Paper. The attendees' first order of business was to thank Government for undertaking the research, but they insisted that the White Paper "can only be regarded as a preliminary to further investigation and action." The CO should in fact "re-open inquiries and to invite evidence in the Dependencies from Missionaries and social organisations and individuals with special knowledge of the subject," with "the evidence of women" (whether African or British was not specified) being "particularly useful." Owen then came to the stage to refute, one by one, the claims made in the White Paper. As for Kenya, he said, the Governor's assurances that forced marriage was rare contradicted his personal experiences. In his own district Owen estimated coerced unions amounted to more than five hundred per year. The meeting was rounded out by Olive Owen (the Archdeacon's wife), Rathbone, Boyle and Hawarden, all of whom urged the government to do more, much more, to improve the status of African women.[211]

Within a month the CO was forced into a meeting with representatives of the SJA (including Owen, Laughton-Mathews, Spender, and Hawarden).[212] They raised no particularly new issue, and little was accomplished.[213] The CO had agreed to an informal talk only, if for no other reason than to quiet the group and the ever-vocal Owen. Perhaps to signal to the SJA that the moment had passed, it was decided within the CO that the Secretary of State for the Colonies would not meet with them. In his stead went Under Secretary of State Lord Dufferin who, while expressing sympathy with the SJA's cause, disclaimed any special knowledge of the situation and stopped short of making any promises. A brief inquiry was made in 1939 but it appears that little came of it.[214]

With the outbreak of war British interest in African women soon dissipated. Rathbone was already investing most of her energy in fighting fascism and championing the cause of Jewish refugees from Europe.[215] Into the early 1940s Owen continued to press the issue on officials in Kenya and post letters to metropolitan newspapers.[216] But attentiveness to the plight of African women was on the wane.[217] As was the case in the first war, when many suffragists dropped their cause to focus on defending the realm, dedication to the war effort quickly superseded activism on forced marriage. The matter was discussed at the SJA's 1940 annual meeting although it was given much less time than had been common previously. Through the rest of the war, indeed through the 1940s, the SJA and other groups did very little and often nothing in regard to Africa. During these years the leading lights of the movement also passed: Boyle in 1943, Owen in 1945, Rathbone in 1946.

CONCLUSION

While the earliest colonial officials could be welcoming to runaway women, officials in the interwar years were much less so. Trends in Britain helped bring about this shift, reinforced by the demands of senior African men. Adultery was criminalized, elders were granted tribunals to enforce their claims over women and juniors. Yet colonial officials could not act as freely as they may have wished. Bitter disputes between officials and gadflies made sure of this, as did the continued willingness of African women to dispute the authority of their husbands and fathers.

In Gusiiland, the marriage disputes that so exercised Owen and the others only emerged in any number from the 1940s. Men with plentiful labor, education, and access to the state were able to take advantage of the new colonial economy, while others saw their fortunes increasingly limited. The few wealthy helped drive bridewealth to alarming levels, locking other men out of the marriage market, and setting Gusiiland adrift in a sea of upset marriage relations. To reinforce their authority Gusii fathers and husbands turned to the chiefs and tribunals that the state had empowered in the more conservative interwar years. At the same time, colonial officials were themselves now more hesitant to become involved too directly in African social life. Thus despite many pleas they refused to help Gusii regulate bridewealth, undermining Gusii attempts to eliminate the cause of marriage disputes. It would be a turbulent postwar world.

NOTES

1. P. E. Mitchell, "Female Circumcision and the Status of Women in Tanganyika Territory," April 26, 1930, 63, enclosure in Donald Cameron to Secretary of State for the Colonies, May 22, 1930, reprinted in Colonial Number 65, "Health and Progress of Native Populations in Certain Parts of the Empire" (London: HMSO, 1931).

2. Denis Judd, *Empire: The British Imperial Experience from 1765 to the Present* (London: Harper Collins, 1996), chap. 15; Anne Phillips, *The Enigma of Colonialism: British Policy in West Africa* (London: James Currey, 1989), 27.

3. Anne Phillips, *Enigma of Colonialism*, chaps. 3–4; John Lonsdale, "The European Scramble and Conquest in African History," in *The Cambridge History of Africa,* Vol. 6, eds. Roland Oliver and G. N. Sanderson (Cambridge, UK: Cambridge University Press, 1985), 752–753.

4. Quoted in Bruce Berman, *Control and Crisis in Colonial Kenya: The Dialectic of Domination* (London: James Currey, 1990), 110.

5. Quoted in Berman, *Control and Crisis in Colonial Kenya*, 112. Eliot similarly characterized the Maasai: "Their customs may be interesting to anthropologists, but morally and economically they seem to be all bad." Quoted in D. A. Low, "British East Africa: The Establishment of British Rule, 1895–1912," in *History of East Africa*, Vol. II, eds. Vincent Harlow and E. M. Chilver (Oxford: Clarendon, 1965), 35.

6. Paul E. Lovejoy and Jan S. Hogendorn, *Slow Death for Slavery: The Course of Abolition in Northern Nigeria, 1897–1936* (Cambridge, UK: Cambridge University Press, 1993); Frederick Cooper, *From Slaves to Squatters: Plantation Labor and Agriculture in Zanzibar and Coastal Kenya 1890–1925* (New Haven, CT: Yale University Press, 1980), 24–46; Suzanne Miers and Richard Roberts, eds., *The End of Slavery in Africa* (Madison: University of Wisconsin Press, 1988).

7. George Abadie, Dec. 19, 1901, quoted in Lovejoy and Hogendorn, *Slow Death for Slavery*, 40.

8. Cooper, *From Slaves to Squatters*, chap. 2; Lovejoy and Hogendorn, *Slow Death for Slavery*. See also Martin Klein, *Slavery and Colonial Rule in French West Africa* (Cambridge, UK: Cambridge University Press, 1998).

9. Anne Phillips, *Enigma of Colonialism*, 29–30.

10. Paul Lovejoy, "Concubinage and the Status of Women Slaves in Early Colonial Northern Nigeria," *Journal of African History* 29 (1988), 245–266; Heidi J. Nast, "The Impact of British Imperialism on the Landscape of Female Slavery in the Kano Palace, Northern Nigeria," *Africa* 64 (1994), 34–73; Frederick Cooper, *Plantation Slavery on the East Coast of Africa* (Portsmouth, NH: Heinemann, 1997 [1977]), 195–198.

11. Lovejoy and Hogendorn, *Slow Death for Slavery*, 117, and see also 238–239, and 329, n. 124.

12. Quoted in Lovejoy and Hogendorn, *Slow Death for Slavery*, 117. For similar administrative conflation of female slaves as wives, see Jean Allman and Victoria Tashjian, *"I Will Not Eat Stone": A Women's History of Colonial Asante* (Portsmouth, NH: Heinemann, 2000), 22–23.

13. Quoted in Lovejoy and Hogendorn, *Slow Death for Slavery*, 117.

14. Cooper, *From Slaves to Squatters*, 223, 75, n. 12.

15. Summary of the correspondence, in R. B. P. Cator, T. W. Tilton, and H. K. Binns, to C. H. Crawford, Commissioner and Counsel General, Sept. 22, 1899, KNA: Jud 1/88. See also Hardinge to Crawford, March 18, 1899, in the same file.

16. Cooper, *From Slaves to Squatters*, 24, 37.

17. Hooper to Murray, Collector, Malindi, Feb. 20, 1905, enclosed in Murray to Chief Justice, Mombasa, Feb. 21, 1905, KNA: Jud 1/88.

18. Dagmar Engels, "The Age of Consent Act of 1891: Colonial Ideology in Bengal," *South Asia Research* 3 (1983), 107–134; Geraldine H. Forbes, "Women and Modernity: The Issue of Child Marriage in India," *Women's Studies International Quarterly* 2 (1979), 407–419, esp. 408–411; Charles H. Heimsath, "The Origin and Enactment of the Indian Age of Consent Bill, 1891," *Journal of Asian Studies* 21 (1962), 491–504; Mrinalini Sinha, *Colonial Masculinity: The 'Manly Englishman' and the 'Effeminate Bengali' in the Late Nineteenth Century* (Manchester: Manchester University Press, 1995), chap. 4.

19. Judge R. W. Hamilton to Collector, Malindi, March 30, 1905, KNA: Jud 1//88.

20. H. B. Johnstone, stationed just to the south at Mombasa from 1898–1899, reported on a marriage tradition that (he said) "practically prohibits child marriages." Moreover, marriage "outside the tribe" was limited since few girls wished to leave their homelands, and elders required "an assurance of the girl's consent before allowing her departure." H. B. Johnstone, "Notes on the Customs of the Tribes Occupying Mombasa Sub-District, British East Africa," *The Journal of the Anthropological Institute of Great Britain and Ireland* 32 (Jan.–June 1902), 263–272, quote from 266–267.

21. Martin Chanock, *Law, Custom, and Social Order: The Colonial Experience in Malawi and Zambia* (Cambridge, UK: Cambridge University Press, 1985), 104–105; Sean Hawkins, "'The Woman in Question': Marriage and Identity in the Colonial Courts of Northern Ghana, 1907–1954," in *Women in African Colonial Histories*, eds. Jean Allman, Susan Geiger, and Nakanyike Musisi (Bloomington: Indiana University Press, 2002), 121. For examples of this in South Kavirondo District, see the SK DARs for the first several years from 1908, and Robert Maxon, *Conflict and Accommodation in Western Kenya: The Gusii and the British, 1907–1963* (Cranbury, NJ: University Presses of America, 1989), 52–53.

22. This was true up to 1924, when "native" courts began to hear such cases. Allman and Tashjian, *"I Will Not Eat Stone,"* 143–145. Hawkins suggests that for northern Ghana in this period, colonial officials were more likely to support senior men. Hawkins, "The Woman in Question."

23. Marcia Wright, "Justice, Women and the Social Order in Abercorn, Northeastern Rhodesia, 1898–1903," in *African Women and the Law: Historical Perspectives*, eds. Margaret Jean Hay and Marcia Wright (Boston University Papers on Africa, VII, 1982).

24. Berman, *Control and Crisis in Colonial Kenya*, 113.

25. Cooper, *From Slaves to Squatters*; Anne Phillips, *Enigma of Colonialism.*

26. These numbers do not include those employed by the technical services—health, agriculture, police—who were not involved in the daily business of ruling Africans. A. H. M. Kirk-Greene, "The Thin White Line: The Size of the British Colonial Service in Africa," *African Affairs* 79 (1980), 25–44; Karen E. Fields, *Revival and Rebellion in Colonial Central Africa* (Portsmouth, NH: Heinemann, 1997 [1985]), chap. 1.

27. The historiography on the invention of "tribes" is large and growing. For a succinct description of British views on "tribe," see Landeg White, *Magomero: Portrait of an African Village* (Cambridge, UK: Cambridge University Press, 1987), 45–46.

28. Fields, *Revival and Rebellion in Colonial Central Africa*; Steven Feierman, *Pleasant Intellectuals: Anthropology and History in Tanzania* (Madison: University of Wisconsin Press, 1990). Of course, this worked better in areas where, unlike much of Kenya, chiefs predated colonial rule.

29. Quoted in Frederick Lugard, *The Dual Mandate in British Tropical Africa* (London: Frank Cass, 1965 [1922]), 139.

30. Berman, *Control and Crisis in Colonial Kenya*, 106.

31. For the general context, see Robert Heussler, *Yesterday's Rulers: The Making of the British Colonial Service* (Syracuse, NY: Syracuse University Press, 1963), chap. 1.

32. T. H. R. Cashmore, "Studies in District Administration in the East Africa Protectorate, 1895–1918" (Ph.D. dissertation, University of Cambridge, 1965), 15–18.

33. Between 1897 and 1907, for example, one-third of the officers died while on duty, mostly from disease. Cashmore, "Studies in District Administration," 36.

34. Cashmore, "Studies in District Administration," 18–19.

35. Quoted in Cashmore, "Studies in District Administration," 24.

36. Quoted in Colonel R. Meinertzhagen, *Kenya Diary, 1902–1906* (Edinburgh: Oliver and Boyd, 1957), 132.

37. Beverley Gartrell, "The Ruling Ideas of a Ruling Elite: British Colonial Officials in Uganda, 1944–1952" (Ph.D. dissertation, City University of New York, 1979), 200.

38. Lugard, *Dual Mandate*, 139.

39. Ross McKibben, *Classes and Cultures: England 1918–1951* (Oxford: Oxford University Press,1998), 244–246, 248–249; Beverley Gartrell, "Ruling Ideas of a Ruling Elite," 106, 114–115.

40. Heussler, *Yesterday's Rulers*, 90.

41. Gartrell, "Ruling Ideas of a Ruling Elite," 106, 109. Cf. Jeffrey Meyers, *Orwell: Wintry Conscience of a Generation* (New York: Norton, 2000), 20.

42. Heussler, *Yesterday's Rulers*, 111.

43. John W. Cell, "Colonial Rule," in *The Oxford History of the British Empire*, Vol. 4, eds. Judith M. Brown and Wm. Roger Louis (Oxford: Oxford University Press, 1999), 233; Meyers, *Orwell*, 21.

44. Heussler, *Yesterday's Rulers*, 34.

45. John Stevenson, *British Society, 1914–45* (London: Penguin, 1984), 95–96.

46. Adam Kuper, *Anthropologists and Anthropology: The British School, 1922–1972* (New York: Pica, 1973), 38–39; Bruce Berman, "Ethnography as Politics, Politics as Ethnography: Kenyatta, Malinowski, and the Making of *Facing Mount Kenya*," *Canadian Journal of African Studies* 30 (1996), 313–344.

47. Quoted in George W. Stocking, Jr., *After Tylor: British Social Anthropology, 1888–1951* (Madison: University of Wisconsin Press, 1995), 399.

48. The administrator is quoted in Stocking, *After Tylor*, 418. For a later example, the Provincial African Court Officer (PACO), Central, in 1952 weighed in on the question of whom to appoint as Kenya's government sociologist, an administrator or an anthropologist. He favored the former since the latter, he charged, were less interested in administrative problems than in making names for themselves in academic circles. "I am not sure," he wrote, "that I feel very happy about our present system of depending on the Young Marrieds of Illinois, fresh from the campuses and the Great American Way of Life, or strange Europeans who end up in Lunatic Asylums in Cracow." PACO to ACO, Oct. 11, 1952, KNA: RR 8/1. (The quote struck close to home for this recently married, recently arrived from Northwestern University, Illinois native sitting in the archives in Nairobi.)

49. Gartrell, "Ruling Ideas of a Ruling Elite," 146, 57.

50. Kuper, *Anthropologists and Anthropology*, 46.

51. H. F. Morris, "Indirect Rule and the Law of Marriage," in H. F. Morris and James S. Read, *Indirect Rule and the Search for Justice: Essays in East African Legal History* (Oxford: Oxford University Press, 1972), 221. See also Sally Falk Moore, *Anthropology and Africa: Changing Perspectives on a Changing Scene* (Charlottesville: University of Virginia Press, 1994), 20.

52. Stocking, *After Tyler*, 406–21.

53. Cell, "Colonial Rule," 247.

54. Berman, *Control and Crisis in Colonial Kenya*, 104–115.

55. "Memorandum Regarding the Development of Native Tribunals," RH: MSS Afr. s. 1792, box 37 (Matson Papers), File 5/1. S. H. Fazan. In the interim, Africans who appeared "civilized" would live under administrative suspicion. Administrators looked warily at the man "in trousers," who (officers thought) had gained only a smattering of education and a veneer of western style, and lorded it over his backward but steadier and more trustworthy brothers "in blankets." Berman, *Control and Crisis in Colonial Kenya*, 239.

56. Quoted in Gartrell, "Ruling Ideas of a Ruling Elite," 149.

57. Gartrell, "Ruling Ideas of a Ruling Elite," 149.

58. SK DAR 1927.

59. Quoted in Lynn M. Thomas, "Regulating Reproduction: State Interventions into Fertility and Sexuality in Rural Kenya, c. 1920–70" (Ph.D. dissertation, University of Michigan, 1997), 86.

60. Quoted in Thomas V. McClendon, "Tradition and Domestic Struggle in the Courtroom: Customary Law and the Control of Women in Segregation-Era Natal," *International Journal of African Historical Studies* 28 (1995), 527–561, quote from 540. There was here, as in many areas of colonial rule, a fundamental contradiction. Women needed to be kept at home, yet the sale of their companionship, food, and sex in urban areas helped passify laborers. Luise White, *The Comforts of Home: Prostitution in Colonial Nairobi* (Chicago, IL: University of Chicago Press, 1990); Claire C. Robertson, *Trouble Showed the Way:*

Women, Men, and Trade in the Nairobi Area, 1890–1990 (Bloomington: Indiana University Press, 1997). For Barnes, this "paradoxical" set of policy needs by the late 1930s critically undermined state attempts to control women's movements, and pushed the state to re-evaluate its regulation of women. Theresa A. Barnes, "The Fight for Control of African Women's Mobility in Colonial Zimbabwe, 1900–1939," *Signs* 17 (1992), 586–608. I argue below that in Kenya these goals appear less paradoxical if looked at the provincial, rather than the state level, and in Chapter six I suggest alternate reasons for the changes Barnes sees in these years.

61. So reflected Theodore Morison, a former Tanganyika district officer. In 1916 he was confronted with a father demanding punishment for his daughter who had repeatedly left her husband for another man. "My heart," Morison recalled in 1933, "was with the two children of nature." He convinced the father to accept the small bridewealth his daughter's lover could provide. "A very bad judgement, I am inclined to think," wrote Morison, "now that the boy and girl are out of my sight and sympathy." He easily imagined the elders in Tanganyika cursing his decision and resultant loosening of marital fidelity. "The Wachaga of Kilimanjaro: Reminiscences of a War-Time Officer," *Journal of the Royal African Society* 32 (1933), 140–147.

62. Quoted in Elizabeth Schmidt, *Peasants, Traders, and Wives: Shona Women in the History of Zimbabwe, 1870–1939* (Portsmouth, NH: Heinemann, 1992), 104.

63. James M. Ault, "Making 'Modern' Marriage 'Traditional': State Power and the Regulation of Marriage in Colonial Zambia," *Theory and Society* 12 (1983), 181–210; Chanock, *Law, Custom, and Social Order*; Margot Lovett, "Gender Relations, Class Formation, and the Colonial State in Africa," in *Women and the State in Africa*, eds. Jane Parpart and Kathleen Staudt (Boulder, CO: Lynne Rienner, 1989); Jane Parpart, "Sexuality and Power on the Zambian Copperbelt: 1926–1964," in *Patriarchy and Class: African Women in the Home and the Workforce*, eds. Sharon B. Strichter and Jane L. Parpart (Boulder, CO: Westview, 1988); Penelope A. Roberts, "The State and the Regulation of Marriage: Sefwi Wiawso (Ghana) 1900–40," in *Women, State, Ideology: Studies from Africa and Asia*, ed. Haleh Afshar (Albany, NY: SUNY, 1987); Elizabeth Schmidt, "Negotiated Spaces and Contested Terrain: Men, Women and the Law in Colonial Zimbabwe, 1890–1939," *Journal of Southern African Studies* 16 (1990), 622–648. Marjorie Mbilinyi argues that the state downplayed the oppression of women in the 1930s, and began more repressive measures to control women in the 1940s and 1950s It will be apparent in this chapter and Chapter six that I disagree with this periodization. Mbilinyi, "Runaway Wives in Colonial Tanganyika: Forced Labour and Forced Marriage in Rungwe District 1919–1961," *International Journal of the Sociology of Law* 16 (1988), 1–29.

The interaction between chiefs, senior men, and the state was not always so straightforward. Geisler argues that despite their desire to support senior men, white courts inadvertently destabilized them. This changed when courts were turned over to chiefs. Gisela Geisler, "Moving with Tradition: The Politics of Marriage among the Toka of Zambia," *Canadian Journal of African History* 26 (1992), 437–461. In Asante new restrictions were placed on women mainly by chiefs, although the state shared chiefly concerns if not their methods. Jean Allman, "Adultery and State in Asante: Reflections on Gender, Class and Power from 1800–1950," in *The Cloth of Many Colored Silks*, eds. John Hunwick and Nancy Lawler (Evanston, IL: Northwestern University Press, 1996).

64. Letter from Watkins to his wife, 1922, in Elizabeth Watkins, *Oscar from Africa: The Biography of Oscar Ferris Watkins, 1877–1943* (New York: Radcliffe Press, 1995), 138–139.

65. Ukamba PAR 1927; Teita DAR 1927.

66. Quoted in Margaret Jean Hay, "Changes in Clothing and Struggles over Identity in Colonial Western Kenya," in *Fashioning Africa: Power and the Politics of Dress*, ed. Jean Allman (Bloomington: University of Indiana Press, 2004), 74.

67. Arthur Phillips, *Report on Native Tribunals* (Nairobi: Government of Kenya, 1944), 279.

68. Kisumu DAR 1919/20.

69. SK DAR 1932.

70. This is a point discussed in Chanock, *Law, Custom, and Social Order.*

71. Buxton's concern for preserving family stability apparently did not extend to white families. Five year later he was called to court as a co-respondent in a divorce case, accused of having committed adultery with the petitioner's wife in Nairobi Game Park. His defense: "In the *Game Park*...? Preposterous! Too many ticks." Buxton's career ended soon thereafter. Charles Chenevix Trench, *Men Who Ruled Kenya: The Kenya Administration, 1892–1963* (London: Radcliffe, 1993), 104. Later still, Buxton purchased a farm in Kenya and became a proponent of settler self-rule, although not in as radical terms as some of his cohort. A settler proposal to forestall African dominance demanded that, inter alia, Africans have no elected representatives until they had achieved "Complete emancipation of women..." and "Eradication of the Bride Price custom." Buxton rejected this wholesale: such proposals "are based on lack of experience and understanding of the realities....[and] are dangerous because... they are attractive to those who have no knowledge of the situation or responsibility for the results." Clarence Buxton, *The Kenya Question* (Nairobi: East African Standard, 1948), 18–20. See also Gavaghan *Of Lions and Dungbeetles*, 150–151.

72. Gidion Magak and Martinus Maina were the two members to raise the issue: "[W]alishitaki ya kuwa vijana waliofanya kazi mbali na nchi zao, zaidi katika mashamba ya Wazungu, hawakutaka kulete shilingi, kwa jamaa zao. Na waliporudi kwao hawakutaka kusikia maneno ya Jamaa zao." SK LNC, April 1933. Swahili versions of LNC minutes were found for only a few meetings.

73. SK MIR, Nov. 1937.

74. SK Safari Diary, Nov. 1937.

75. For an overview of these changes, see Brett L. Shadle, "African Court Elders in Nyanza Province, Kenya, c. 1930–1960: From 'Traditional' to 'Modern,'" in *Intermediaries, Interpreters and Clerks: African Employees and the Making of Colonial Africa*, eds. Benjamin Lawrance, Emily Lynn Osborn, and Richard Roberts (Madison, WI: University of Wisconsin Press, [in press]); idem, "Law and the Nature of Colonial Rule: The Struggle to Control African Courts in Kenya," Department of History Faculty Research Seminar, Virginia Tech, April 21, 2006.

76. SK DAR 1921; H. E. Welby, "History of the District," 1920–21, SK PRB; Ag. Chief Native Commissioner (CNC) to Ag. SC Nyanza, May 14, 1929, and DC SK to PC Nyanza, May 30, 1929, both in KNA: PC/NZA 19/4.

77. SK Safari Diaries, Feb. and March 1928, KNA: PC/NZA 3/26/4/4.

78. SK DARs 1907/08, 1929.

79. DC SK to PC Nyanza, Feb. 26, 1927 KNA: PC/NZA 3/32/2.

80. Allman and Tashjian, "*I Will Not Eat Stone*," 174; Marc Epprecht, *"This Matter of Women is Getting Very Bad": Gender, Development and Politics in Colonial Lesotho* (Pietermaritzburg: University of Natal Press, 2000), 127; Martin Chanock, "Making Customary Law: Men, Women, and Courts in Colonial Northern Rhodesia," in *African Women and the Law*, eds. Hay and Wright, 62; Karen Tranberg Hansen, *Distant Companions: Servants and Employers in Zambia, 1900–1985* (Ithaca, NY: Cornell University Press, 1989), 108–109.

81. If any administrators had known the legal history of adultery in Britain, a shift from compensation to criminalization would have seemed fit. In Great Britain into the eighteenth century compensation had been common for adultery, although this fell into great disfavor and eventually was eliminated. Indeed, when debating the question in the mid-nineteenth century many in Parliament thought criminalization or vigilantism preferable to

compensation. When compensation was awarded it was with the idea of appeasing a man for his loss of honor and of his wife's physical presence, "it being assumed that the husband could not condone the adultery by continuing to live with a guilty wife." Susan Staves, "Money for Honor: Damages for Criminal Conversation," *Studies in Eighteenth-Century Culture* 11 (1982), 279–297, quote from 279. The difference in Africa was that a marriage would not necessarily end in the event of unfaithfulness. Chanock, *Law, Custom, and Social Order*, 198; Arthur Phillips, "Marriage Laws in Africa," in *Survey of African Marriage and Family Life*, ed. Arthur Phillips (Oxford: Oxford University Press, for the International African Institute, 1953), 228. Adultery remained criminal in Great Britain and much of Europe into the 1960s. David I. Kertzer and Marzio Barbagli, *Family Life in the Twentieth Century* (New Haven, CT: Yale University Press, 2003), 119.

82. Chanock, "Making Customary Law," 62; idem, *Law, Custom, and Social Order*, chap. 11; Schmidt, *Peasants, Traders, and Wives*, 104–106; Diana Jeater, *Marriage, Perversion and Power: The Construction of Moral Discourse in Southern Rhodesia, 1894–1930* (Oxford: Oxford University Press, 1993), chaps. 5–6; Allman and Tashjian, *"I Will Not Eat Stone,"* 179; Margot Lovett, "Elders, Migrants and Wives: Labor Migration and the Renegotiation of Intergenerational, Patronage and Gender Relations in Highland Buha, Western Tanzania, 1921–1962," (Ph.D. dissertation, Columbia University, 1996), 324–329; Thaddeus Sunseri, *Vilimani: Labor Migration and Rural Change in Early Colonial Tanzania* (Portsmouth, NH: Heinemann, 2002), 179–180; H. F. Morris, "Indirect Rule and the Law of Marriage," in Morris and Read, *Indirect Rule and the Search for Justice*, 216; and Arthur Phillips, "Marriage Laws in Africa," 228. In colonial Nigeria (or least the Tiv area) men and women could be fined for acts of adultery. Paul Bohannan, *Justice and Judgment Among the Tiv* (London: Oxford University Press, for the International African Institute, 1957), 83–84.

83. For the origins of the IPC, see Eric Stokes, *The English Utilitarians and India* (Oxford: Oxford University Press, 1959), 219–233; Radhika Singha, *A Despotism of Law: Crime and Justice in Early Colonial India* (Delhi: Oxford University Press, 1998), esp. chap. 4.

84. H. F. Morris, "The Reception and Rejection of Indian Law," in Morris and Read, *Indirect Rule and the Search for Justice*, 113–114.

85. SK DARs 1907/08 to 1928.

86. H. F. Morris, "The Reception and Rejection of Indian Law," 119–126, and idem, "Indirect Rule and the Law of Marriage," 237, both in Morris and Read, *Indirect Rule and the Search for Justice*.

87. PCs' Meeting, Nov. 1, 1932, KNA: Adm 3/1/2; CNC to DCs, Aug. 12, 1932, KNA: PC/NZA 3/15/88.

88. DC NK to PC Nyanza, Feb. 20, 1928, KNA: PC/NZA 3/17/17.

89. Minute from DCs' meeting, Aug. 26, 1932, in PC Nyanza to CS, Aug. 29, 1932, KNA: PC/NZA 3/15/88.

90. DC SK to PC Nyanza, Nov. 2, 1932, KNA: PC/NZA 3/15/88.

91. DC NK quoted in PC Nyanza to CNC [ca. Nov. 1932]; DC NK to PC Nyanza, Jan. 19, 1933, both in KNA: PC/NZA 3/15/88.

92. DC NK quoted in PC Nyanza to CNC [ca. Nov. 1932]; DC NK to PC Nyanza, Jan. 16, 1933, both in KNA: PC/NZA 3/15/88.

93. DC SK to PC Nyanza, Nov. 2, 1932, KNA: PC/NZA 3/15/88.

94. Minute from DCs' meeting, Aug. 26, 1932, in PC Nyanza to CS, Aug. 29, 1932, KNA: PC/NZA 3/15/88.

95. DC NK to PC Nyanza, Jan. 16, 1933, KNA: PC/NZA 3/15/88. This DC had earlier noted such men could now "seduce married women, without any fear of reprisals, and are taking advantage of the situation." Quoted in PC Nyanza to CNC [ca. Nov. 1932], KNA: PC/NZA 3/15/88.

96. PCs' Meeting, Nov. 1, 1932, KNA: Adm 3/1/2. Other Europeans would share this opinion, including missionaries in Nyeri (Central Province) in the 1940s. Derek Peterson, *Creative Writing: Translation, Bookkeeping, and the Work of Imagination in Colonial Kenya*. Portsmouth, NH: Heinemann, 2004), 168–169.

97. The PC Nzoia thought imprisonment for adultery should only be used in very special circumstances, as identified by a PC. PCs' Meeting, Nov. 1, 1932, KNA: Adm 3/1/2.

98. CNC to PCs, June 28, 1933 KNA: PC/NZA 3/15/88.

99. A meeting of Nyanza DCs was "not in agreement that, under Native Law and Custom, the offence of adultery is punishable by imprisonment." Minute of DCs' Meeting, Aug. 26, 1932, quoted in PC Nyanza to CS, Aug. 29, 1932, KNA: PC/NZA 3/15/88.

100. Cf. Brett L. Shadle, "'Changing Traditions to Meet Current Altering Conditions': Customary Law, African Courts, and the Rejection of Codification in Kenya, 1930–60," *Journal of African History* 40 (1999), 411–431, esp. 429–430.

101. PCs' Meeting, Nov. 1, 1932, KNA: Adm 3/1/2. Records of these previous discussions have not been found.

102. Quoted in Robertson, *Trouble Showed the Way*, 98. This DC, Vidal, was by 1934 Acting PC Central, and found himself again in the midst of debates over criminalization of adultery, this time over the extension of the old IPC adultery sections into settled areas of Thika. Luo men working on white farms had been complaining that unemployed men from Nairobi were taking advantage of (as the DC put it) the "notoriously catholic" morality of Luo women. An offended husband had difficulty taking his wife back to Nyanza to recover bridewealth, and should he do so, her father would have difficulty receiving recompense ("for damages to his daughter's subsequent dowry-price") from the offender, since "as is most probable, the offender is a neer-do-wel[l]." Still, aside from DCs Thika and Nairobi, the general opinion in the province was "strongly opposed" to any changes. Two main reasons were given. First, "it was considered that adultery, at most, can only be regarded as a civil wrong," an opinion much more widely shared from the late 1930s on. Second, "the criminal liability of the male offender would constitute a gross injustice where, in many cases, the woman tempted him and he did eat." Ag. PC Central to PC Nyanza, June 15, 1934, KNA: MDS 2/3/4.

103. Robertson, *Trouble Showed the Way*, 98–99. Women in Nairobi also provided sexual services, companionship and cooking which helped stabilize the male workforce, and so the state did little to crack down on prostitution in the interwar years. White, *Comforts of Home*. On conflicting state needs regarding rural and urban women in Southern Rhodesia, see Barnes, "Fight for Control."

104. Antoinette Burton, "The Feminist Quest for Identity: British Imperial Suffragism and 'Global Sisterhood,' 1900–1915," *Journal of Women's History* 3 (1991), 46–81; idem, *Burdens of History: British Feminists, Indian Women, and Imperial Culture, 1865–1915* (Chapel Hill: University of North Carolina Press, 1994); Barbara Caine, *English Feminism, 1780–1980* (Oxford: Oxford University Press, 1997), 168–172.

105. The following paragraph is based on Leila J. Rupp, *Worlds of Women: The Making of an International Women's Movement* (Princeton, NJ: Princeton University Press, 1997).

106. Rupp, *Worlds of Women*, 42.

107. Suzanne Miers, "Slavery and the Slave Trade as International Issues, 1890–1939," in *Slavery and Colonial Rule in Africa*, eds. Suzanne Miers and Martin Klein (London: Frank Cass, 1999). Another area of interest to feminists was *mui tsai*, a kind of fosterage of girls in parts of China and Hong Kong that, critics charged, could easily slide over into domestic slavery and prostitution. The issue of *mui tsai* had first been raised in the House in 1920, but administrators in the colony retorted that it was certainly not as bad a practice as it had been described (laying claim, as did their colleagues in Africa, to the sole authority to "interpret this alien culture to London," as Pedersen puts it). In the words of the undersecretary of state, it was neither "possible nor advisable to enforce Western

ideals upon the family life of the Chinese." In 1929–1931, and again in 1936 feminists and liberal pushed the government to investigate the plight of *mui tsai*, which it eventually did in taking on the mantle of "reformers." Susan Pedersen, "The Maternalist Moment in British Colonial Policy: The Controversy over 'Child Slavery' in Hong Kong 1917–1941," *Past and Present* 171 (2001), 161–202; Maria Jaschok and Suzanne Miers, eds., *Women and Chinese Patriarchy: Submission, Servitude and Escape* (London: Zed Books, 1994).

108. Pedersen, "Maternalist Moment in British Colonial Policy," 201.

109. Susan Pedersen, "Eleanor Rathbone (1872–1946): The Victorian Family under the Daughter's Eye," in *After the Victorians: Private Conscience and Public Duty in Modern Britain*, eds. Susan Pedersen and Peter Mandler (London: Routledge, 1994); Brian Harrison, *Prudent Revolutionaries: Portraits of British Feminists between the Wars* (Oxford: Clarendon, 1987), chap. 4; Hilary Land, "Eleanor Rathbone and the Economy of the Family," in *British Feminism in the Twentieth Century*, ed. Harold L. Smith (Amherst: University of Massachusetts Press, 1990); Kumari Jayawadena, *The White Woman's Other Burden: Western Women and South Asia During British Colonial Rule* (New York: Routledge, 1995), 100–103.

110. R. M. Douglas, *Feminist Freikorps: The British Voluntary Women Police, 1914–1940* (Westport, CT: Praeger, 1999), 14, and passim; Susan Kingsley Kent, *Making Peace: The Reconstruction of Gender in Interwar Britain* (Princeton, NJ: Princeton University Press, 1993), 75, 155, n. 18; Rupp, *Worlds of Women*, 152.

111. "A History of St. Joan's Social and Political Alliance . . . 1911–1961," London: St. Joan's Alliance, 1961.

112. Angela Woolacott, "Australian Women's Metropolitan Activism: From Suffrage, to Imperial Vanguard, to Commonwealth Feminism," in *Women's Suffrage in the British Empire: Citizenship, Nation, and Race*, eds. Ian Christopher Fletcher, Laura E. Nym Mayhall, and Philippa Levine (London: Routledge, 2000).

113. Some of the groups who had members present at the BCL's inaugural meeting include: Women's Freedom League, The League of Church Militants, The National Union of Women's Teachers, The Federation of Women Civil Servants, The Association of Social and Moral Hygiene, Women's Liberal Association, The Conservative Women's Reform Association, and, from overseas, The Australian Federation of Women's Societies for Equal Citizenship, The Women's League of New South Wales, the Women's Enfranchisement League of South Africa, The Bermuda Women's Suffrage Society, as well as several from Canada and New Zealand.

114. See the frontispiece to the collection of BCL Conference Reports, Annual Conferences, 1925–1939.

115. "The Abolition of Slavery: A Catholic Centenary Commemoration," *The Tablet*, May 6, 1933, FL: 2/SJA/L14; Minutes of the 22nd Annual SJA Meeting, 1933, FL: 2/SJA/A1/7; *Catholic Citizen*, June 15, 1933; Nancy Stewart Parnell, "A Century of Emancipation," *Catholic Citizen*, July/Aug. 1933.

116. J. Wilbois, *Le Cameroun*, quoted in Christine Spender's review, *Catholic Citizen*, Oct. 15, 1934. Spender similarly argued that polygamy was incompatible with Christianity. Spender to Owen, Sept. 17, 1935, Church Missionary Society (CMS): ACC 83 O 16.

117. Father Hughes spoke at a June 1933 SJA conference on slavery as it affected women, and was paraphrased in "Domestic Slavery," *Catholic Citizen* July/Aug. 1933.

118. Christine Spender, "Polygamous Marriages in Equatorial Africa," *Catholic Citizen*, June 15, 1933; Spender, "Marriage and the Family in Mission Countries," *Catholic Citizen*, June 15, 1936; Grace Saunders, BCL 12th Annual Conference, 1936.

119. Robert W. Strayer, *The Making of Mission Communities in East Africa* (London: Heinemann, 1978), 80.

120. Nina Bolye, BCL 8th annual meeting, 1930; Alexandre LeRoy, "On the Position of Women in the British Cameroons and in Nigeria," *Catholic Citizen*, May 15, 1934;

Christine Spender, BCL 13th annual meeting, 1937; Statement of Mrs. Hooper, in Duchess of Atholl to CO, April 12, 1929, PRO: CO 323/1067/1.

121. See, for example, Strayer, *Making of Mission Communities*, 79; Statement of Mrs. Hooper, in Duchess of Atholl to CO, April 12, 1929, PRO: CO 323/1067/1.

122. Spender, BCL 13th Annual Conference, 1937.

123. BCL 11th Annual Conference, 1935. See also Nina Boyle, BCL 6th Annual Conference, 1930; N.a., "Domestic Slavery," *Catholic Citizen*, July/Aug. 1933; Archbishop LeRoy, "The Position of Women in the Cameroons and in Equatorial Africa," *Catholic Citizen* Oct. 15, 1933; Barbara Barclay Carter, "The White Sisters and African Women," *Catholic Citizen*, March 15, 1934; questions by SJA to CO, ca. Dec. 1935, in PRO: CO 847/5/6.

124. Boyle, BCL 6th Annual Meeting, 1930; *International Women's News*, Nov. 1932; SJA, minutes of meeting, July 17, 1933, FL: 2/SJA/A1/7; n.a., "Domestic Slavery," *Catholic Citizen*, July/Aug. 1933; Barbara Barclay Carter, "The White Sisters and African Women," *Catholic Citizen*, March 15, 1934. The leading anthropologists of the day weighed in against this position. "Modern writers on African sociology," commented Emmanuel Torday in the pages of *Man* in 1929, "are practically agreed that marriage among the natives does not consist of the buying and selling of the bride." He suggested that the term "bride price," then common currency, be replaced: "It is of more than academic importance that a better word should be substituted . . . Pagett, M. P., has been lately vigourously on the war-path and has acquainted us with the fantastic conclusions of slavery and traffic in daughters." Over the next two years in *Man* scholars conducted a debate over a working substitute; E. E. Evans-Pritchard was the ultimate victor, with his suggestion of "bridewealth" now nearly universally accepted. See E. Torday, "Bride Price, Dower, or Settlement," *Man* 29 (Jan. 1929), 5–7, and responses in the "Correspondence" sections of the July, Aug., Oct., and Dec. issues of 1929, and in the April 1930 issue.

125. Berman, *Control and Crisis in Colonial Kenya*, 184.

126. Berman, *Control and Crisis in Colonial Kenya*, 197, n. 176.

127. On the circumcision crisis, see Carl Rosberg and John Nottingham, *The Myth of "Mau Mau": Nationalism in Kenya* (New York: Meridian, 1966), chap. 4; John Lonsdale, "The Moral Economy of Mau Mau," in Bruce Berman and John Lonsdale, *Unhappy Valley: Conflict in Kenya and Africa* (London: James Currey, 1992); Strayer, *Making of Mission Communities*, chap. 8; David Sandgren, *Christianity and the Kikuyu: Religious Divisions and Social Conflict* (New York: Peter Lang, 1989), chaps. 4–5.

128. Lynn M. Thomas, *Politics of the Womb: Women, Reproduction, and the State in Kenya* (Berkeley: University of California Press, 2003), chap. 1.

129. Susan Pederson, "National Bodies, Unspeakable Acts: The Sexual Politics of Colonial Policy-making," *Journal of Modern History* 63 (1991), 656–659.

130. Pederson, "National Bodies, Unspeakable Acts," 657; Thomas, *Politics of the Womb*, 52–58.

131. Pederson, "National Bodies, Unspeakable Acts," 659.

132. [Indecipherable author], report on the meeting, Feb. 14, 1930, PRO: CO 1018/25. See also clipping from *Christian Science Monitor*, March 10, 1930, in the same file.

133. Florence Underwood, WFL, to SS, Feb. 6, 1930, PRO: CO 323/1067/1; Gertrude Horton, Gen. Secretary, National Union of Societies for Equal Citizenship, to SS, March 26, 1930, PRO: CO 533/394/10. My thanks to Lynn Thomas for copies of these papers.

134. "Notes of a meeting held in the Secretary of State's room . . . the 8th of April, 1930," April 9, 1930, PRO: CO 1018/25.

135. Draft, letter to Governors, March 1930, PRO: CO 822/27/10. My thanks to Lynn Thomas for a copy of this letter. The next several paragraphs follow Thomas, *Politics of the*

Womb, chap. 2, in which she places the circular in the context of metropolitan and colonial debates over African health and maternal policies.

136. The quotes come from, respectively: Memorandum by the Director of Medical and Sanitary Services, Zanzibar, May 5, 1930, in Resident, Zanzibar, to SS, June 10, 1930; A. J. Brackenbury, Ag. Snr. PC, and Murray, both quoted in T. S. W. Thomas, Gov. of Nyasaland, to SS, July 19, 1930; Ag. Gov. Uganda to SS, Sept. 30, 1930, all in PRO: CO: 323/1067/2; and for West Africa, [J. E. W. Hood?] "Notes on the Position of Women in West Africa," April 4, 1930, PRO: CO: 1018/25.

137. Mitchell, "Female Circumcision and the Status of Women," 63. On Mitchell and his career, see David W. Throup, *Economic and Social Origins of Mau Mau* (London: James Currey, 1988), chap. 3.

138. Quoted in Gov. Nyasaland to SS, July 19, 1930, PRO: CO 323/1067/2.

139. Gov. Uganda to SS, Sept. 30, 1930, PRO: CO 323/1067/2.

140. Mitchell, "Female Circumcision and the Status of Women," 67.

141. Pederson, "National Bodies, Unspeakable Acts," 665.

142. See file notes in PRO: CO 323/1067/1. My thanks to Lynn Thomas for copies of these notes.

143. Cf. Adam Ashforth, *The Politics of Official Discourse in Twentieth-Century South Africa* (Oxford: Clarendon, 1990).

144. Atholl to Shields, Aug. 6, 1931, PRO: CO 822/38/9.

145. Gov. Kenya to CO, Oct. 20, 1931, PRO: CO 822/38/9.

146. Owen, letter to *Manchester Guardian*, also published in *Manchester Guardian Weekly*, Aug. 30, 1935.

147. Owen to Christine Spender, Nov. 3, 1936, CMS: ACC 83 O 16. See also Cynthia Hoehler-Fatton, *Women of Fire and Spirit: History, Faith and Gender in Roho Religion in Western Kenya* (Oxford: Oxford University Press, 1996), 5–6. In 1931 Owen wrote that, "We have done much *for* Africans in the past. It remains to be seen how much we can do working *with* Africans in the future." He was also willing to take a swipe at colonial critics back home:

> Missions and other have been exercised for long about [bridewealth], and some urged that it be abolished. Even in England there are to be heard those who, knowing little of the constitution of the social life of an African tribe, call aloud for its abolition. It was been described as a system of slavery for African women, as degradation of womankind. But those who have dug below the surface of tribal organization know that it is most intimately bound up with the very admirable poor law system of native life, and that to abolish the "bride price" would call for reconstruction in realms which are not apparently, to the superficial observer, associated with it. In this connection the old saw that "a little learning is a dangerous thing" quite well applies.

W. E. Owen, "Some Thoughts on Native Development in East Africa," *Journal of the African Society* 30 (1931), 225–237.

148. Strayer, *Making of Mission Communities*, 107.

149. R. M. A. Van Zwanenberg, *Colonial Capitalism and Labour in Kenya, 1919–1939* (Nairobi: East Africa Literature Bureau, 1975), chap. 5; Owen, letter to *Manchester Guardian*, June 29, 1936, clipping in PRO: CO 847/6/11; Notes for Secretary of State before meeting with Owen, Oct. 9, 1938, and note, Oct. 13, 1938, both in PRO: CO 847/12/14.

150. Strayer, *Making of Mission Communities*, 107.

151. Hoehler-Fatton, *Women of Fire and Spirit*, 6, 45; Bethwell A. Ogot, "Alfayo Odongo Mango," in *Kenya Historical Biographies*, eds. Kenneth King and Ahmed Salim (Nairobi: East African Publishing House, 1971), 100–104.

152. Record of a Meeting at Government House, Oct. 22, 1930, PRO: CO 533/404/13; Hoehler-Fatton, *Women of Fire and Spirit*, 5; Rosberg and Nottingham, *Myth of 'Mau Mau'*, 96; Dobbs, Extract from letter, June 16, 1927, Dobbs Papers, Kenya 1906–31, RH: MSS Afr. s. 665; Berman, *Control and Crisis in Colonial Kenya*, 253, n. 116.

153. Quoted in Hoehler-Fatton, *Women of Fire and Spirit*, 10.

154. It was forced marriage that led Owen to question the entirety of African society: "I cannot think of the social life of an African tribe as civilized while its responsible leaders sanction such outrages on the personality of girlhood." Owen to *East African Standard*, June 18, 1936, in CMS: ACC 83 O 16.

155. In relating the case of a woman being dragged off by her "husband" that he had stumbled across and prevented, Owen recorded that he was "strongly tempted to give such brutes, with such a degrading attitude to the girlhood of their tribes, a taste of their own treatment to defenseless girls." Owen, "Notes on the case of [A], Jan. 3, 1940, CMS: ACC 83 O 16. At the request of Church Missionary Society archivists, I have left out the names of Africans mentioned in Owen's papers.

156. See, for example, Owen's untitled document of April 17, 1939; Owen, "Notes on the case of [A], Jan. 3, 1940; Owen to DC Central Kavirondo (CK), July 11, 1940, all in CMS: ACC 83 O 16.

157. Owen, "Notes on the case of [O]," in Owen to DC CK, Dec. 11, 1940, CMS: ACC 83 O 16.

158. Owen, "[Z], Seizures and Escapes," n.d. [Sept. 1942], CMS: ACC 83 O 16.

159. Letters to the editor, in FL: 2/SJA/L16.

160. Quoted in Rupert B. Howarth, Offices of the Cabinet, to E. B. Boyd, Colonial Office, Nov. 1, 1935, PRO: CO 847/5/6.

161. Luke to Vernon, Nov. 6, 1935, note in back of file, PRO: CO 323/1344/5.

162. Clipping in Christine Spender to Owen, Nov. 20, 1935, CMS: ACC 83 O 16.

163. The proceedings of the conference are described in an extract from *East Africa*, Nov. 14, 1935, in *Correspondence Relating to the Welfare of Women in Tropical Africa, 1935–37*, Cmd. 5784.

164. Several letters to the editor in the *East African Standard* supported this point. For example, "Common Sense" compared the "smiling happy faces of Kavirondo women" with "the drawn, care-worn unhappy faces of some of their fair-skinned civilised sisters." *East African Standard* Aug. 10, 1936. Jomo Kenyatta mused that "It seems to me that men, irrespective of race or colour, and may I even say cultural development, are always inclined to abuse women as members of a weaker sex . . ." Kenyatta to *Manchester Guardian*, Nov. 29, 1936. Both clippings can be found in CMS: ACC 83 O 16.

165. Pederson, "National Bodies, Unspeakable Acts."

166. Owen to *Manchester Guardian Weekly*, Nov. 22, 1935.

167. The judgment is reprinted in the *Welfare of Women in Tropical Africa*, enclosed in the response by the Gov. Tanganyika to SS. According to this transcript, the judge gave Kekwe fifteen, not eighteen, months imprisonment, with hard labor.

168. Owen to *Manchester Guardian*, June 16, 1936, reprinted in *Welfare of Women in Tropical Africa*.

169. Sec., SJA, to SS, July 10, 1936, PRO: CO 847/6/11.

170. BCL to SS, July 13, 1936; WFL to SS, Aug. 21, 1936, both in PRO: CO 847/6/11.

171. Alfred Milner to Colonial Minister, June 29, 1936, PRO: CO 847/6/11. (It is not clear if this Milner was related to Sir Alfred Milner, a leading figure in British imperial matters, who had died in 1925.) A clipping from the June 30 *East African Standard* titled "African Girlhood" was also pasted into this file. The author wrote that steps should be taken "to see that the romance which was so tragically interrupted is permitted to blossom into its natural happiness." In the margin a member of the CO scratched, "O You!"

172. SJA minutes, Sept. 14, 1936, FL: 2/SJA/A1/7.

173. This time excepting Somalia and Zanzibar.

174. Note at end of file, author illegible, Jan. 4, 1938, PRO: CO 847/11/12. This was in reference to the SJA. Men of the Colonial Office similarly dismissed female critics of *mui tsai* as "a lot of pretentious busybodies." Pedersen, "Maternalist Moment," 164.

175. Note at end of file, author illegible, ca. early July 1939, PRO: CO 859/15/7; notes at end of file, April 1932, PRO: CO 323/1176/16.

176. George Maxwell, "Lobolo," July 28, 1934, PRO: CO 323/1257/13. On Maxwell, see Suzanne Miers, *Slavery in the Twentieth Century: The Evolution of a Global Problem* (Walnut Creek, CA: AltaMira, 2003), chap. 7.

177. Note at end of file, author illegible, July 11, 1939, PRO: CO 859/15/7.

178. *Welfare of Women in Tropical Africa*, 8–10.

179. DC Fort Hall to PC Central, Oct. 9, 1936, KNA: PC/CP 19/1.

180. DC Meru to PC Central, Oct. 9, 1936, KNA: PC/CP 19/1.

181. It appears that only one officer willingly admitted the prevalence and negative effects of forced marriage. Beetham, a district officer in South Kavirondo, wrote that in Luo marriage if a girl resisted an arranged marriage her father would first employ verbal persuasion. If after the exchange of bridewealth she continued to refuse, "she is compelled if necessary by physical force to go to her husband, where she remains more or less a prisoner until she accepts the inevitable." Such cases, Beetham wrote, occurred frequently, especially when suitors were wealthy elders. He admitted that no women lodged complaints with African authorities, but this was because coercive marriages had existed for many decades, and women knew they would find no sympathy with senior men. Beetham was tardy in preparing his report, however, and his observations never reached London. DO SK to DC SK, Oct. 19, 1936, in DC SK to PC Nyanza, Oct. 21, 1936, KNA: MDS 2/3/5.

182. A definition to which Archdeacon Owen ascribed. He estimated that about three percent of marriages contracted every year were forced, "but it is certain that there are many more where extreme moral pressure is applied." Owen to Greaves, Secretary, Kenya Missionary Council, June 2, 1939, CMS: ACC 83 O 16.

183. DC Kiambu to PC Central, Oct. 8, 1936, and DC North Nyeri to PC Central, Oct. 21, 1936, both in KNA: PC/CP 19/1.

184. The DC SK also noted that cases of "real coercion involving physical effort" were infrequent, while the DC at Kitui stated that "*forced* marriage does not exist . . . though marriages de convenance are arranged." DC SK to PC Nyanza, Oct. 21, 1936, KNA: MDS 2/3/5; DC Kitui to PC Central, Nov. 2, 1936, KNA: PC/CP 19/1.

185. DC Meru to PC Central, Oct. 9, 1936, KNA: PC/CP 19/1. For similar arguments by Tanganyika administrators, see Mbilinyi, "Runaway Wives in Colonial Tanganyika," 23.

186. DC Fort Hall to PC Central, Oct. 9, 1936, KNA: PC/CP 19/1.

187. A. R. Barlow to DC Fort Hall, Jan. 1, 1940, and reply, Jan. 4, 1940, KNA: PC/CP 19/1.

188. In Embu, for example, at the meeting of the two families prior to bridewealth discussions, the bride was to pour beer for the guests. If she disliked the groom she would refuse to pour and thereafter, the DC was told, no coercion could be put on her "as the father would be the laughing stock of the clan." DC Embu to PC Central, Oct. 1, 1936, KNA: PC/CP 19/1. How many fathers might have been willing to risk ridicule to assert their will was a question the DC did not ask. The Central Kavirondo DC quoted Archdeacon Owen himself, who had pointed out the existence of an "ancient custom" whereby a bride had the right to refuse a prospective groom. The DC suggested that girls be alerted to this. DC CK to PC Nyanza, Oct. 3, 1936, KNA: MDS 2/3/5. Should a Meru girl publicly threaten suicide, the DC there wrote, "no Meru man would take the risk of resorting to coercion after the uttering of that formula." DC Meru to PC Central, Oct. 9, 1936, KNA: PC/CP 19/1.

189. DC Meru to PC Central, Oct. 9, 1936, KNA: PC/CP 19/1.

190. DC Kericho to PC Nyanza, Oct. 1, 1936, KNA: MDS 2/3/5.

191. Administrators were not the only ones to make this claim. Eleanor Hawarden, a strong supporter of African women's right but one who was less likely to see the subject in as stark terms as her colleagues, thought the debates were caught between two fields of knowledge: African experts who knew little of women's movements, and feminists who (like others) knew little about the Empire. Eleanor Hawarden, "The Status of African Women," *International Women's News*, Jan. 1936. The rather more conservative International Bureau for the Suppression of Traffic in Women also thought critics had little knowledge of actual conditions in Africa and that the administrators were good men who "certainly . . . would do anything possible to help improve the condition of either men or women, but it must be within the limits of the possible." Enforcing change against public opinion might produce "a little local war or disturbances." F. Sempkins, IBSTW, to J. D. Reelfs, Fédération Abolitionniste Internationale, Geneva, Feb. 25, 1935, FL: IBSTW Box 115, 26B. Similar comments were made after the publication of the 1938 White Paper.

192. DC SK to PC Nyanza, Oct. 21, 1936, KNA: MDS 2/3/5.

193. Ag. Gov. of Kenya to SS, in *Welfare of Women in Tropical Africa*, 21, quoting evidence of R. Southy, Reconditioning Officer. Southy's quote can also be found in DC CK to PC Nyanza, Oct. 10, 1936, KNA: MDS 2/3/5.

194. DC Fort Hall to PC Central, Oct. 9, 1936, KNA: PC/CP 19/1.

195. Ibid. This, of course, suggested that nonviolent coercion was rather morally objectionable, something most DC hesitated to say. In the margin of a letter from Atholl to the CO, where she wrote of girls being forced into marriage with wealthy elder men, an official scribbled, "This is not peculiar to Africa!" Atholl to SS, Aug. 6, 1931, PRO: CO 822/38/9.

196. DC Thika to PC Central, Sept. 25, 1936, KNA: PC/CP 19/1; DC Kisumu-Londiani to PC Nyanza, Sept. 25, 1936, KNA: MDS 2/3/5. The PC Nyanza also made certain to point out the questionable morality of Akumu, the girl who was forced into marriage and made a cause celebre by Owen in 1935. She had now, a chief reported, become pregnant but the father was neither her legal husband nor the man to whom she had run, but a third party. PC Nyanza to CS, Oct. 18, 1936, KNA: MDS 2/3/5.

197. DC Fort Hall to PC Central, Oct. 9, 1936, KNA: PC/CP 19/1.

198. Similar projects were proposed (and some implemented) in French West Africa, South Africa, and Southern Rhodesia. Arthur Phillips, "Marriage Laws in Africa," 204.

199. DC Meru to PC Central, Oct. 9, 1936, KNA: PC/CP 19/1. See also Schmidt, *Peasants, Traders, and Wives*, 112.

200. DC Machakos to PC Central, Oct. 6, 1936, KNA: PC/CP 19/1.

201. This was also the topic of debate in a series of letters to the *East African Standard* between July and Sept. 1936. Clippings of these letters can be found in CMS: ACC 83 O 16.

202. The following is based on responses from the governors to the Secretary of State, all printed in the *Welfare of Women in Tropical Africa*.

203. Gov. Nigeria to SS. See also the responses from the governors of the Gambia, Sierra Leone, Uganda, the Gold Coast, Nyasaland, and Tanganyika Territory.

204. Gov. Northern Rhodesia to SS.

205. Gov. Uganda to SS. See also Gov. Nigeria to SS.

206. Lee, notes in file, May 7, 1937, PRO: CO 847/9/5.

207. *Manchester Guardian Weekly*, July 29, 1938.

208. *Manchester Guardian Weekly*, Sept. 9, 1938.

209. "Extract from letter to St. Joan's Social and Political Alliance from: A Missioner (1) in Uganda," Sept. 23, 1938, PRO: CO 847/11/12.

210. N.a., "Forced Marriages in Africa," *Catholic Citizen*, Sept. 15, 1938.

211. "Report of Public Meeting . . . concerning Forced Marriages of African Girls," in Florence Barry, Secretary, St. Joan's, to MacDonald, Dec. 17, 1938, PRO: CO 847/11/12. See also *Catholic Citizen*, Jan. 15, 1939.

212. "Status of Women in Africa: Minutes of a Meeting held . . . Jan. 10, 1938," PRO: CO 847/11/12.

213. The delegation did present a memorandum by W. E. and L. Olive Owen, "Forced Marriages of African Girls," PRO: CO 847/11/12.

214. Kenya's Acting Chief Secretary wrote to the Secretary of the Kenya Missionary Council: "I am directed [by whom he did not say] to ask, with reference to the question of forced Marriages of African Girls, whether any such cases have come to your notice. If the answer is in the affirmative, I should be grateful for information as to the number and particulars of such cases in recent years." Owen excitedly passed along case after case, but few other missionaries followed his lead. Greaves, Secretary, Kenya Missionary Council, to all missions, May 25, 1939, CMS: ACC 83 O 16, and responses by Owen in the same file.

215. Pedersen, *Politics of Conscience*, 267, chaps. 14–17.

216. Correspondence from Owen to DC CK dated March 31 and April 19, 1939, and April 10, 1940, all in KNA: MDS 2/3/5; correspondence between Owen, DC CK, and PC Nyanza, KNA: L&O 1/1/2/2; SJA minutes of meeting, Oct. 16, 1939, FL: 2/SJA/A1/7.

217. Even among Owen's fellow missionaries. A meeting of the Kenya Missionary Council in 1939 on the topic of Forced Marriage of African Girls noted that "Several well-documented cases are reported, but all from one district and practically all by one missionary [i.e., Owen]. Other missions, including one in a neighboring district, have reported that they believe such marriages to be infrequent and decreasing." Minutes of Meeting of Standing Committee, Kenya Missionary Council, Sept. 11, 1939, CMS: ACC 83 O 16.

3

The Political Economy of Bridewealth, 1930s–1960s

As imperial debates over the status of African women dissipated, deep changes in the Gusii economy surfaced. Far from the relative isolation of earlier years, more and more homesteads were becoming irrevocably linked to the world market. The sale of cash crops was now basic to the Gusii economy, as was (at least for poorer men, particularly bachelors) the sale of labor. Demand and prices for cash crops meant that homesteads with plentiful labor—especially women's labor—could collect more wealth, more quickly, than had ever been true before. Veterans returned with pockets bulging with shillings. At the top were a small but powerful collection of men who combined privileged access to the state, highly paid employment, business ventures, and cash crops (particularly coffee) to lift themselves far above the common peasants. Remuneration for wage labor, however, rose only slowly, if at all; poorer men tended to stay poor. Of course, the highlands had always been host to the wealthy and the poor; this was what had caused men to seek out patrons. But now wealth begat wealth much more quickly than had been true before, and poverty was harder to escape.

The influx of wealth unequally distributed produced fantastic increases in bridewealth. The average bridewealth given in any marriage tended to rise to the highest bridewealth paid in the area. As P. Mayer puts it, "*individual* cases of [high bridewealth] quickly produce a *general* rise in the rate all round." Thus as those few men who grew even moderately wealthy gave more bridewealth, bridewealth rates rose to levels unattainable by many men. Attempts to limit bridewealth failed miserably in part due to wealthy men who refused to respect limits. But the state contributed to their failures as well. Administrators had no desire to prove its weakness by proclaiming bridwealth limits that no one would respect. Only if *all* Gusii agreed to abide by it would administrators institute a limit. For twenty-five years, as the local economy became more tightly linked to the world economy, and as administrators refused to back any limit that did not have virtually universal Gusii support, increases in bridewealth levels were uncontrollable.

THE GUSII ECONOMY TO THE 1930s

Trade

The establishment of colonial rule brought about new opportunities for trade. Land formerly left to bush because of raids could now be used to expand the area under crop. Mzee Jackson moved into southern South Mugirango in the 1920s when it was entirely without settlements. He and his agemates first established *egesirate*, and after some years brought their families to their new land. Jackson claimed large stretches of land and put them under crop, prospered, and eventually married six wives.[1] The building of markets offered new opportunities to dispose of surplus. Neither Luo nor Gusii had established permanent markets before colonial rule, but by 1912 eight trading centers served the district; by 1917 this number had risen to eleven, with seventy-seven shops.[2] As elsewhere in Kenya, Indians spearheaded the new commerce. They likely owned all the shops in Kisii town before the arrival of Richard Gethin in 1914, and alone or tagging along with administrative *safari*s headed into the hills to drum up trade.[3] Gusii and Luo farmers brought forward a wide variety of indigenous and newly introduced agricultural products.[4]

Despite numerous obstacles, trade boomed. Transport within the district was poor, including that to Kendu Bay and Homa Bay (where goods were shipped on to Kisumu and the railway), which was by ox-cart on torturously long, winding roads.[5] A forty-mile trip between Seventh-day Adventist (SDA) stations at Gendia (north of Kisii) and Kamagambo (to the southwest) took three days in 1913.[6] The marketplaces themselves left much to be desired. In 1912, the "Native Market" at Kisii consisted of a platform with a broken corner and a not entirely secure roof,[7] and the town itself was ill-kept, with scrub brush crowding unpaved streets.[8] Despite all this, imported goods found their way to African consumers. Africans bartered produce for axes, iron wire, knives, and beads, and in 1913–1914, "perhaps 12,000–15,000 English hoes," "thousands" of *panga*s (machetes), and "many thousands of rupees worth of clothing and enamelware."[9] Cash was also desirable for taxes and, as always, for purchasing cattle.[10]

Until the rise of maize exports during the 1940s, *wimbi* (finger millet) remained the most important crop, for subsistence and for sale. In a time when locusts and poor rains could devastate whole fields—1932–1933 is still remembered for the plagues of locusts that ravaged parts of Luoland and Gusiiland—the fact that *wimbi* could be stored for several years was an important consideration.[11] Although riverine-powered posho mills (for grinding grain) were becoming more common, *wimbi* had the advantage over maize of being relatively easy to grind at home.[12] Moreover, and perhaps most important, the asking price for *wimbi* remained higher than that for maize almost every season through the 1930s. Nonetheless, when the market promised significant returns Gusii farmers set aside land for maize. Increased prices prompted the planting of substantially more maize for the long rains in 1937, and sales shot to 2,378 tons, up from 689 tons in 1936.[13]

Wage labor offered another way to procure cash, but one which did not immediately introduce radical changes in the local political economy. As early as 1909 some Gusii (whether voluntarily or not) went to Machakos far to the east, and others in 1911 to areas even nearer the coast. The deaths of several of these men discouraged others from considering long-distance migrant labor,[14] and for some years Gusii were much more willing to come forward for work within the district than without.[15] Moreover, Gusii were motivated to earn wages primarily to pay taxes, and the sale of produce often brought in enough currency to cover these expenses.[16] To remedy the lack of labor, the administration turned to coercion. In 1913, four thousand men were "sent to work outside the district."[17] The brutality of the Carrier Corps failed to convince many of the benefits of going off to work, and another five thousand were forcibly turned out to wage labor in 1920.[18]

Over the 1920s and 1930s, wage labor became a somewhat more common experience for Gusii men. Many went to the European-owned tea estates in nearby Kericho. While the data on laborers were never exact, the district as a whole exported a few hundred laborers at the beginning of the decade, rising to ten thousand by 1930.[19] The depression sliced in half the selling price of produce in 1931, but the state would not allow an international economic crisis to deter them from collecting taxes.[20] More men were pushed toward the labor market. Unfortunately, the demand for labor was drying up, and wages had dropped by half as well.[21] The supply of labor for the first time exceeded demand. In 1933, a shockingly low number of men—sixty-two—left the district already on contract with employers.[22]

The Gusii economy survived the depression, however, and remained not yet fundamentally dependent upon the sale of produce and labor. After supplying their subsistence needs, Gusii exploited the demand for cash crops to the extent of keeping men detached from the wage labor market. In 1938, cash earned in South Kavirondo by the sale of agricultural goods, cattle, and animal products—£99,488—was nearly twice that brought in as wages, £51,300. The difference may have been greater. The district commissioner (DC) had estimated that £20,000 was earned in wage labor outside the district, but admitted that this may have been four times the actual amount. Moreover, the DC's computations drew not just on the earnings of Gusii workers but Luo as well, and it is almost certain that Gusiiland received an even smaller proportion of its income from wage labor than did Luoland.[23] For good or for bad, this relative detachment of Gusiiland from the broader colonial economy would not last long.

THE GUSII ECONOMY FROM 1940

The War and Wage Labor

More than in the first, in the Second World War the British relied on African muscle to achieve victory. Africans worked sisal, used for rope; tea, which boosted the morale of soldiers and civilians; and grains, which fed troops in the Middle East. Unlike the dirty, deadly portage East Africans performed in World War I, they now trained in a variety of skills, bore arms and learned to kill, and many thousands served outside the colony. Still, offering blood, toil, tears, and sweat for the Empire held little appeal to men from South Kavirondo. Rumors of war and memories of the Carrier Corps sent many men into hiding in 1939 and few volunteered to help defend the realm.[24]

Early in 1941, the South Kavirondo administration turned to conscription for the military, although by October gathering civilian labor had become the primary focus. Sidney Fazan, then the Nyanza provincial commissioner (PC), instructed district officers to lecture chiefs on their responsibilities to alleviate labor shortages.[25] They could not use force, he insisted, nor use it as an opportunity to settle personal grudges. This was not conscription, Fazan stressed, but "'assisted' recruitment."[26] The verbal niceties did nothing to soothe the conscience of the South Kavirondo DC, D. Storrs-Fox: this clearly was conscription. He pointed out to the PC that Africans currently received little remuneration for their labor, and that some Europeans were exploiting their captive labor force. This was, Storrs-Fox bitterly charged, the strong exploiting the weak, against which the Empire was fighting in their war with the "Huns." His request to be relieved of his post was granted.[27]

Storrs-Fox's protests did nothing to discourage the administration and chiefs from "recruiting" labor. While the PC issued another memorandum reaffirming that chiefs could "persuade" but not force or intimidate men into labor, his terminology was not always clear to Africans, perhaps intentionally so.[28] Africans were under the notion that a request for labor was in fact a requirement, and Luo chiefs advised the administration that compulsion might indeed be necessary.[29] Anticipating government demands on them for conscripts some chiefs were (according to tea estate companies) "advising or instructing people" against heading to Kericho to such an extent that the supply of labor at the tea estates fell off sharply. Other Luo and Gusii men fled to Tanganyika or hid with friends or relatives at Kericho.[30] During 1942, Tribal Police were seconded to chiefs to assist in conscription and arresting deserters.[31]

Whatever their methods, chiefs and the administration mobilized large numbers of Gusii men for the war effort. By the end of June 1942, 10,800 were in civil and military employment, equivalent (by administrative estimates) to 48 percent of able-bodied Gusii men.[32] Six months later 14,000 men were in civilian employ and 2,000 in the army, or 64 percent of eligible men. Over the last year of the war this percentage shrank, but remained within the 35–40 percent range.[33]

During the war, if given the choice between civilian wage labor on the one hand, and the military or farming on the other, wage labor always lost. "It appeared," the DC wrote in 1941, "that military work was in higher repute than civil, and dissatisfaction with current rates of pay on [European-owned farms] was frequently expressed."[34] Military pay did indeed surpass that on the tea estates. In 1942, army recruits earned shs. 15 per month, and privates shs. 17, while three years later tea pluckers took home only shs. 12 to shs. 14 per month.[35] Already by 1941 thousands of *askaris* were remitting hundreds of pounds back home to South Kavirondo.[36] At the end of the first full year of war, the DC noted that the number of wage laborers coming forward fluctuated inversely to peak labor periods in African farmers' agricultural cycle, and he noted that Africans "can become more prosperous under pleasanter conditions by cultivating at their own homes."[37] As the war wound down the government requested that, in the face of food shortages, tea growers release some workers to return to their own farms.[38] This was in February and March 1944, and by June the next year many had yet to return to Kericho. In 1944 labor was in such short supply that weeds amongst the tea bushes could no longer be kept at bay, and the companies began to import workers from Rwanda.[39] As peace replaced war and conscription ended, Gusii workers deserted the tea estates in their hundreds due to poor pay, a saturation of cash in the highlands, and the lack of consumer goods.[40] But this was temporary. In subsequent years many Gusii found themselves back at work, forced not by the administration but by poverty.

Cash Crops

The outbreak of World War II created huge new demands for cash crops, especially grains. The state hardly deviated from the privileges it granted white settlers—the Maize Control Board paid Africans one-half to one-third of what it paid white farmers for their grain—but the price farm goods attracted barreled up to new heights across the board. Both agricultural and administrative officers spent countless hours urging Gusii to plant maize and *mtama* (sorghum).[41] One DC browbeat chiefs whose subjects were considered not to be producing enough.[42] The Produce Control Board guaranteed maize prices, and considered requisitioning *mtama* if Gusii supplied an insufficient number of bags.[43]

Perhaps more in response to higher prices than to administrative pressure, farmers sowed ever more cash crops. Though never a popular crop in Gusiiland, *mtama* exports shot up from 18,000 bags in 1941, to 32,000 in 1943.[44] Maize exports doubled between 1941 and 1942, from 30,000 bags to 60,000, and doubled again by 1946, to 123,000 bags.[45] *Wimbi* exports too reached record levels in 1946.[46] Moreover, administrative reports on export numbers only tell part of the story. As always, some agricultural goods were sold within the district. The ever-active black market always paid more than did government purchasers, and it never discriminated on account of race.

Figure 3.1. Herding cattle, North Mugirango, 2004
Although land is in very short supply Gusii will keep cattle if at all possible, as does this homestead in North Mugirango. *Source:* Courtesy Calvin White, Jr.

By 1944, the administration proved increasingly unwilling to continue purchasing so much grain at artificially inflated prices. Yet when the Price Control Board mulled over suspending *mtama* purchases, the South Kavirondo DC, Perreau, warned that this was neither gentlemanly nor prudent. The administration had pledged high prices to induce greater production, and to revoke this now amounted to a "breach of faith." Perreau shuddered at how Africans (especially the Gusii) would react.[47] Price supports continued, and in 1945 cereal production in the district overwhelmed the road and water transport network.[48] Prices for and production of agricultural goods, especially maize, remained high for the next decade: the price per bag of maize doubled between 1949 and 1954.[49] In 1950, the availability of bags for maize could not keep pace with the harvest[50] and maize exports again overwhelmed road networks. Transporters were called in from outside the district, and storage facilities at Kisumu quickly filled.[51] Only adverse weather conditions could diminish harvests.[52] Wealth poured into the pockets of homesteads best able to take advantage of the export markets.[53]

An Emerging Elite

A few men managed to take advantage of the colonial economy most impressively. Early Christians composed much of the vanguard of these new elite. Only a handful of men had converted before the 1940s, and those who did often found themselves alienated from their erstwhile neighbors and clansmen. With a serious gender imbalance among converts, the special adversity Christian bachelors faced when pursuing wives meant that a man did not turn to Jesus on a whim.[54] But if the costs of following older paths to success proved prohibitive (at least in the early years) Christians blazed their own trails. Christianity lured many men with the promise of literacy and education. The colonial administration, strapped for personnel, sought out literate Africans to fill lower state posts. Already by 1913 the DC of South Kavirondo requested from the priest at Nyabururu a list of literate men who could assist chiefs and the tribunals.[55] Administrators hired educated young men for work as "houseboys" and cooks in the 1920s, their exposure to Western ways and knowledge of English or Swahili undoubtedly making them the most attractive candidates.[56] New missionaries without Swahili relied on "houseboys" with at least a working knowledge of English, which could be parleyed into decades of regular employment.[57] Work within the church had its own advantages. Paulo Nyamweya had first become acquainted with the value of the written word during his service in the Carrier Corps, helping to convince him to join the SDAs in 1922.[58] By 1949 he had become the first African mission director, with all the attendant privileges including a car allowance.[59] Others Christians found well-paying skilled work outside the district. Christians gained not just a new religion, but access to a new economy.

Privileged access to the state could bring fat paychecks to those with desirable skills. At the top were chiefs and court officials. In 1947, tribunal presidents, vice presidents and members earned, respectively, shs. 100, shs. 80 and shs. 75 per month.[60] Five years later their pay had shot up to shs. 240, shs. 180, and up to shs. 150 per month, respectively.[61] Members of the appeals court could earn even more. In the later 1940s a Local Native Council (LNC) secretary could earn between shs. 245 and shs. 320 per month.[62] Drivers' special skills could bring them shs. 50 to shs. 140 per month, and teachers at SDA schools earned shs. 120 per month. The next rung down included clerks (shs. 40 to shs. 90) and dressers (shs. 30 to shs. 60). In contrast, the government and missions paid their unskilled labor a pittance, between shs. 12 and shs. 30 per month.[63]

In the 1930s and 1940s, first generation Christians, along with non-Christian chiefs and other local government employees, invested their new wealth in businesses and cash crops. Maize-grinding mills sprouted along the Gucha River, later challenged by diesel-powered mills.[64] The most important new crop was coffee, introduced into the highlands in 1934. Although Africans had grown coffee in Tanganyika and Uganda, coffee growing in Kenya had officially been the domain of white settlers. In the early 1930s, however, the Colonial Office exerted enough pressure to force Nairobi to override settler protests and allow coffee growing in a few select African locations. The South Kavirondo LNC, with the vigorous support of District Commissioner C. E. V. Buxton, immediately began a campaign for the district to be included in the trials. Buxton's appeal, together with the fact that Gusiiland had already been proven (by a white trader and a priest) to be a fertile ground for coffee, persuaded Nairobi. After consultations with the Director of Agriculture and the construction of government nurseries, the first seedlings were sunk in Gusii soil in 1934.[65]

The first group of planters was a mixed lot. Despite government reassurances to the contrary, many Gusii had heard enough about land alienation elsewhere in the colony to suspect that the project was a means to probe the potential value of the land for white settlement. Frustrated officials' unceasing pronouncements on the virtue of coffee planting persuaded few Gusii to risk the possible loss of land. Those who did plant came from three groups. State officials encouraged their employees to take up coffee planting, and many did. It is not clear what form this "encouragement" took, but government workers tended to place more trust in their superiors' motives. "We were government people so we were not afraid," explained Mariera Angwenyi, who had served as an *askari*, clerk, and then in the administration, and was a half-brother of Chief Ooga. "We were sure that the government would not take the land."[66] The commoners should have feared white settlers less than "government people," some of whom expropriated land to put under coffee.[67] Others were "encouraged" by their chiefs to grow coffee. As was their wont, chiefs likely used something besides friendly advice to convince followers to plant.[68] The third group of coffee pioneers were entrepreneurs for whom the promise of easy profits outweighed the risk of losing land.

Within the next few years the less-committed planters dropped out and a more clearly defined elite began to take shape. The agricultural office had first confined plantings to three block farms (in Nyaribari and Bassi) in areas near larger roads. Although this scheme allowed officers easy access to the sites, it was of less utility for Gusii planters. Only three of eleven planters, for example, lived within two miles of the Bassi plot. By 1936, the administration admitted failure and the next year allowed more localized, even personal plots, but many planters deserted or sold their coffee bushes nonetheless.[69] The more dedicated growers, those who had voluntarily taken up the crop and who had the resources to keep the plants tended properly, persisted in their endeavors.

What is most striking about the early planters is that many had already begun climbing into the elite ranks. Fifty percent had worked full or part time for the local administration or the missions, an equal number had spent at least some time working outside the district (40 percent of them in skilled or semiskilled work), and two-thirds had had some exposure to western education, remarkable numbers all around. Several had scaled the ladder of state power as chiefs (such as Alexis of Machoge, Ooga of Getutu, and Musa of Nyaribari), headmen, or court elders. Nearly 60 percent had off-farm income.[70]

As the administration included new locations into gazetted coffee planting areas, new men signed on. Only those with capital on hand, however, could plant and maintain their plots for the five years before the bushes began to produce full yields.[71] Coffee requires significant inputs of labor. Mature bushes should ideally be weeded six to seven times per year, and pruned back as well.[72] While other Gusii farmers relied solely on household or *risaga* (joint work party) labor for subsistence and cash crop production, elite coffee planters ensured regular upkeep of their bushes by hiring laborers.[73] Indeed, coffee growers in the 1940s complained about the lack of labor available and in the war years petitioned the administration to exempt their workers from conscription.[74]

With their ties to the administration the coffee pioneers found ways to tap into state resources. From the very inception of the LNC members came under administrative criticism for their readiness to back projects that would benefit themselves and their friends. This practice would continue to be the case for many decades. For example, in the 1930s African entrepreneurs broke the Indian monopoly on dairies only with the assistance of the LNC, which extended them loans and refused to lease any further land for Indian dairies.[75] It is unsurprising that Musa Nyandusi influenced the LNC into allocating funds toward the support of coffee growing. Already by May 1934—only one month after the first precious seedlings were laid into Musa's plot—the LNC provided its plow for the block plantation in Nyaribari.[76] Hired hands at the nursery, inspectors and field staff all reported to the district agricultural officer, but drew their pay from the LNC. By January 1936, the LNC was employing twenty-three men for the benefit of the coffee growers, of whom there were only fifteen.[77]

The LNC also subsidized planters by marketing their coffee from 1939 to 1942. By 1941, the council had accumulated a deficit of £130, although with wartime increases in production and prices for coffee, it ended 1942 with an £850 surplus.[78] The growers hoped to continue to use the LNC as a safety net against hard times, but the DC successfully pushed them into a cooperative (though he was forced to concede a bonus on the previous season's production).[79] With LNC funds supporting them through the precarious first years of the industry coffee growers had now established themselves in this most profitable of crops.

While the pioneers remained atop production, and held on to the largest plots, coffee's popularity and profitability proceeded uninterrupted. The number of growers nearly doubled between 1950 and 1951, doubled again by 1953, again by 1955, and again by 1958, when 11,138 men[80] worked coffee bushes.[81] Indeed, through the 1950s and into the 1960s the demand for coffee seedlings well exceeded the supply, forcing some men to resort to theft—not for lack of cash, but simply to lay their hands on the precious plants.[82] In 1956, coffee sales brought in £110,000 for 5,764 growers, or about shs. 400 on average, although the larger planters earned rather more.[83] Few men could derive their primary income from the sale of coffee, but it did provide a very important secondary infusion of cash, equal to wages from two to three months' skilled labor or three to five months' unskilled labor.[84]

While coffee would remain the dominant high-return crop through to independence, the introduction of pyrethrum and tea offered other investment opportunities. Not surprisingly, it was the elite coffee growers who initiated pyrethrum planting. Trials had been made in Gusiiland in 1945, but only in 1949 did the state seriously discuss pyrethrum (its flowers used as an insecticide) as a cash crop. Coffee growers, through their cooperative society (dominated by the large planters), requested permission to begin planting and pledged £500 for equipment to dry the flowers. Chief Zachariah Angwenyi rounded up potential growers, some by force, to demonstrate Getutu's interest in the crop.[85] Planting began in 1950, with coffee elites, including Zacharia, amongst the pioneers.[86] Tea planting began later, in 1957, it too the preserve of those with access to labor and capital.[87]

Also benefitting from their access to the state were those interested in trading ventures. In 1953, the South Nyanza (as South Kavirondo was now known) African District Council copied North Nyanza's program of extending loans to traders.[88] By 1956, 26 loans had been made, disbursing £6,950.[89] Undoubtedly, elites, including councillors, chiefs, and their cronies, benefitted the most. Only in 1956 did the district Marketing Officer convince members of the council's Trades and Markets Committee that too many licences reduced average profits, and pointed to Gusiiland as an area particularly overflowing with traders. The councillors agreed to restrict new licenses, although they refused to revoke licenses already issued—some of which had undoubtedly been issued to themselves.[90]

David Ogega's career illustrates well the experience of the Gusii elites. Ogega, of Bassi location, began his climb as an early convert to Christianity. He was hired in the early 1930s as the cashier to the Kisii-Bakuria LNC, and was kept on when it merged with the Luo-Abasuba LNC.[91] With his steady cash income, he partnered in establishing a posho mill in 1932, branching out on his own the next year.[92] He then entered into coffee production. When coffee was still restricted to block plantings, Ogega collected ten acres (the largest holder was Musa with fourteen) primarily by "taking over" others' plots.[93] He continued to expand his holdings in the 1940s and was among those who relied heavily on hired labor. He became a member of the LNC in the 1940s, and was politically active in the Kisii Union, the South Nyanza Political Organization, and later the Kisii Highlands Abagusii Assocation (serving as treasurer in the first two groups).[94] In 1944 he asked to be considered to replace the retiring Chief Oirere of Bassi, but the DC refused: Ogega had "too many trading ventures" to allow him to fully dedicate himself to the many duties of a chief.[95] By 1945 he owned six or more posho mills, grew large amounts of maize as a cash crop, and was exploring investments in a transport business.[96]

Men's Crops and Women's Labor

Gusii agricultural harvests experienced phenomenal growth despite the fact that few farmers invested in more efficient means of production. A handful of plows had been used in Gusiiland from the 1930s, and in the war years a few more Gusii farmers purchased or rented them to expand their acreage under cultivation. The Kisii Coffee Growers association provided plows and cultivators for its members' use,[97] while one enterprising young man, living with his widowed mother and owning only two head of cattle, rented a plow to improve his life chances.[98] But these were exceptional cases. Overall, there is little evidence of qualitative improvements in productivity, especially among the bulk of Gusii farmers. Only plows, *panga*s (machetes), and *jembe*s (hoes) were in demand during the war, and only in 1948 did the Agricultural Officer in South Kavirondo suggest the provision of other devices such as wheelbarrows.[99]

If not from the introduction of new means of production, from whence did all these bushels of maize and bags coffee come? Some farmers introduced a second growing season for maize, an idea adopted from white settlers.[100] In addition, more land was put under cultivation for cash crops.[101] Changes in *emonga* (men's fields) were an important part of this. Previously men had worked *emonga* with crops for trade or for supplementing their homesteads' stores, but often now dedicated them solely to cash crops. P. Mayer noted that in the 1940s men with plows "generally increase[d] the proportion of [their] own *emonga* land as against the land cultivated for subsistence by [their] womenfolk," planting them with cash crops.[102]

In the absence of qualitative improvements in labor, cultivating extra land required quantitative increases in labor. Even the use of the plow required increased labor inputs, for while it could quickly turn soil it still left behind clods which had to be broken apart by hoe.[103] The answer was not wage labor. Hiring labor was the preserve of the elite,[104] and even up to the 1970s none but the most wealthy Gusii hired agricultural labor.[105]

Instead, increased production came primarily from unpaid female labor. Men investing in cash crops, especially coffee, drew on *egesangio*, women's voluntary rotating work parties. *Egesangio* worked only in women's plots, primarily to provide companionship to shorten long days in the sun. That *egesangio* came to be used on coffee plots is striking evidence at how successful men were at appropriating women's labor and land. Men extended their *emonga* by plowing up more and more of their wives' subsistence plots until the line between the two blurred and disappeared.[106] There remained only one field, treated like the older subsistence fields in that women labored on the whole field, but now including men's cash crops. By this sleight of hand *egesangio* could logically work coffee plants since these were now also part of women's daily work.[107]

Cash-cropping men, in particular men who had plowed up larger plots, also turned to *risaga* (joint work parties) for their labor needs. Even for those who might have considered employing farm workers *risaga* was thought more economical. Women's comradery, costing the host only the provision of beer and food for their husbands, provided labor harder-working and cheaper than hired labor.[108] The duty of brewing beer for the *risaga* fell to women, and over time the amount of beer needed could be quite substantial. One representative plow owner in 1948 called thirteen *risaga* (six from the nearby neighborhood, seven from a larger neighborhood) while only one large *risaga* came to work his wife's subsistence fields. This man received help at several points during the agricultural cycle—weeding and harvesting maize, digging, clearing, and weeding millet—while his wife had outside assistance only when harvesting her plot of millet. Since a typical small *risaga* required four to six pots of beer, and a large *risaga* a similar number of more sizeable pots, his wife prepared at least twenty-four small pots and twenty-eight larger pots of beer for the working of her husband's *emonga*.[109] The time and energy she dedicated to brewing certainly stretched further her already strained labor commitments.[110] Even if a husband provided the grain for the beer, the duty of brewing was still his wife's.[111] Thus even for those wives who did not *directly* labor on their husbands' cash crop plots, their labor was essential *indirectly*.[112]

Whatever labor women put to cash crops, men retained the proceeds. According to I. Mayer, men "monopolized" plowing and cash cropping.[113] Women were, however, often able to keep control over subsistence crop surplus, which they sold at local markets for soap and other household goods. Some women went on longer expeditions reminiscent of precolonial years, trading grain at Luo markets for pots which they brought back and sold at local Gusii markets.[114] Women who collected goats or cows put these toward their sons' bridewealth (or bridewealth for their own "wives"). Yet in Nyaribari some men extended claims over their wives' surplus as well.[115] While we as yet unfortunately know little about the processes of struggle that played out for control of these crops, men were the clear winners.[116]

The Cash Economy

If not all homesteads prospered, they all became irreversibly connected to the market as the need for cash increased steadily. More and more, daily necessities were not locally made. Imported hoes drove blacksmiths out of business. Soap, tobacco, and paraffin oil all became popular imports.[117] Girls living at the SDA mission received soap, while the boys worked plots and traded their agricultural surplus for school supplies.[118] In the late 1920s SDA missionaries launched "Operation Rat Dies" in their followers' mission villages and outschools. Depending on the number of vermin eliminated (proved by producing severed tails) the rat-killers received razors, soap, or scissors.[119] For most Gusii, however, such goods could be had only with currency.

Perhaps the most important new consumer good was western-style clothing. The first converts to Christianity invested in blankets, and later khaki shorts to replace goat skins, and were even complemented in 1932 by a touring American SDA as "neatly dressed."[120] But the desire for western clothing was spreading beyond Christians. One of the few changes DC Buxton noted among the non-Christian population in 1932 was an attraction to "flashy" clothes.[121] Getutu elders in 1936 complained of young women stealing their fathers' money to purchase clothes.[122] Cotton clothing for younger women had become a need, not a want.[123] Indians set up sewing machines in front of their shops to work imported cloth, taking advantage of "a general craving for more clothes."[124] In fact, clothing accounted for the largest share of all goods imported for sale in South Kavirondo, £37,000 out of a total of £48,000 in 1938.[125]

Gusii needed cash not only for imported goods but for taxes as well. In earlier decades the sale of produce or perhaps a short stint at wage labor could provide for the payment of hut taxes. But taxes steadily increased. Administrators continued to collect the King's due during the depression, even if it took them three times longer to do so in 1931 and 1932 than it had previously.[126] One of the first acts of the LNC was the imposition of a shs. 1 tax. (It was until 1937 "strictly voluntary," although we can be certain that most taxpayers did not willingly offer their money.)[127] By 1937, the poll tax (on men) had reached shs. 12, and the LNC tax shs. 2 per person; by 1946 it had risen to a combined shs. 17, along with an LNC special rate of another shs. 3—perhaps the highest tax burden in the colony.[128] A decade later the tax imposed by the African District Council was shs. 13, increased to shs. 18 the next year. This was in addition to a shs. 20 poll tax and taxes assessed by the Locational Advisory Councils (LACs), which could range from shs. 2 to shs. 7.[129]

Still other demands were made on Gusii pocketbooks. As maize supplanted *wimbi* as the main food crop, Gusii paid to have it ground at mills; unlike *wimbi*, maize could not easily be ground at home with mortar and pestle.[130] Gusii also invested large amounts of money in legal disputes. Administrators seemingly lay awake at night wondering how they might discourage Gusii from spending time and money filing their hundreds and thousands of court cases. Losers at the *ritongo* who continued on to the South Kavirondo Appeals Tribunal had to travel to Kisii town, a trip that today can take an hour by motor from the farthest reaches of North Mugirango and Machoge; too far to walk, and there was no free transportation. So too a life-saving trip to the main hospital in Kisii town. Health care itself could be expensive. All Health Centres and Dispensaries charged fees. When the ADC recommended in 1958 that minors receive free care, the (white) Medical Officer suggested that this be done only for children five years of age and younger so as not to lose a significant source of revenue.[131] In addition to the fees required to get treatment, more severe illnesses might also require cash for the purchase of medicines. Moreover, illness could reduce a farmer's productivity, or keep him or her out of the fields for days or weeks.

The Marginal Homesteads

All Gusii needed cash, but not all shared equally in the cash crop boom of the 1940s and 1950s. As was true across the colony, those with plentiful land and labor did very well,[132] while others struggled to survive. Which men adopted coffee had much to do with number of potential laborers in the homestead.[133] Some planted coffee but could not command enough labor to care for it properly. Complaints rolled in about farms where branches went unpruned and weeds choked the bushes, contributing to plant disease.[134] Unable to convince their wives to provide much labor and unable to marry more wives, such men had to invest a significant amount of their own time in the coffee plots and often had to drop from the ranks of the planters.[135]

Meanwhile, it was becoming harder and harder to rely on *wimbi* as a cash crop. Outside the immediate environs of Gusiiland *wimbi* had few consumers; only Luo and Kipsigis readily purchased it for food or beer.[136] The price for *wimbi* had dropped precipitously since the interwar years, and the poorer homesteads now looked to maize as their cash crop. Despite the monetary advantages of maize unforeseen problems could push farmers to the brink of disaster. On Christmas Eve, 1953, a storm destroyed Kendu Bay's primary storage building, leaving only half the normal space for grain collection. The Control Board slowed its maize purchases and many farmers held onto their crop until June, by which time much had been ruined by weevils.[137] Now in a pinch, farmers threw large amounts of *wimbi* on the market "no doubt" an administrator wrote, due to "shortage of ready cash."[138]

The situation for poorer farmers did not improve. In 1954–1955, apprehensive of low prices and recurrent problems with maize marketing, farmers increased *wimbi* planting at the expense of maize. This would provide for their subsistence needs, but it also reduced their potential cash income for basic necessities or unexpected expenses—and bridewealth cattle.[139] The next year Chief Musa Nyandusi, speaking more for his constituents than for himself, inquired if the price of *wimbi* could be increased (in 1955 it was half that of maize), hoping to give people the flexibility to grow *wimbi* for subsistence or as a cash crop as need be. The administration gave him no hearing. Poorer farmers continued precariously to balance their mix of cash and subsistence crops, until *wimbi* finally gave way, in the later 1950s, to maize as the grain fundamental to both the Gusii diet and economy.[140]

As compared to earlier years, after the war more Gusii men found themselves forced to spend time laboring for others. In the second half of the 1940s, the administration estimated that at any given time one third of able-bodied Gusii men were at work, the vast majority of them at Kericho.[141] "They are not

Figure 3.2. Tea fields in North Mugirango, near Kericho, 2004
Tea is one of the most important cash crops in Gusiiland. It is grown both in small family plots and large plantations, such as this one in North Mugirango near Kericho.
Source: Courtesy Calvin White, Jr.

popular as labour," the DC wrote in 1947, "except with the Kericho Tea Estates."[142] So few went farther afield, former administrator Chris Minter recalls, that the Gusii were "the *least known* of all the African communities" for many of his colleagues.[143] Even those Gusii who went to Kericho did not long keep themselves away from home. Only a minority spent more than a few months at a time in Kericho, and making multiple trips over a lifetime was more the exception than the rule.[144] Annual turnover of labor at the tea estates regularly exceeded 100 percent.[145]

Gusii men's reluctance to extend their stays at Kericho derived from high cash crop prices, low wages, and a fierce attachment to home. The 1948 census, though relatively unreliable, reported that of the Gusii population in Kenya, 93 percent lived in Gusiiland. The 1969 census placed it at 94 percent, as did estimates in 1975.[146] The year 1948 found Kericho without a significant labor shortage, but the next year's bountiful maize crop and high prices resulted in (in the eyes of the Labour Department) a "disappointing" supply of labor, Gusii and otherwise.[147] High cash crops prices might prevent a labor-rich Gusii patriarch from having to rely on wage labor, but this was not true for most young men who did not yet have wives and children of their own. Breaking down social standing of the wage laborers, especially those in Kericho, reveals that most were in fact young men between the years of circumcision and marriage. Wages, meager though they were, would be put toward bridewealth livestock. Indeed, few recently married men left their new households to seek wage labor.

Men looking for unskilled or semiskilled work found only low-paying employment. Unskilled labor for government departments and missions ranged between shs. 12 and shs. 30 per month.[148] Laborers for African coffee planters (paid by the LNC) generally earned shs. 25.[149] In Kericho, pay rates increased only slightly, and slowly, over the 1940s. A man in 1944 could earn from shs.12 to shs. 14 per month, barely surpassing rates common twenty years before,[150] while two years later monthly wages had actually slipped to between shs. 10 and shs. 14. A scandalized John Kebaso, touring the estates in 1946, found that workers' wages were "insufficient to meet their living!"[151] Wages in 1949 rose, but only slightly, to shs. 18 per month.[152]

The fact that juveniles (boys under sixteen years) constituted a significant percentage of Kericho's labor force did little to improve adult workers' position. From their earliest years the estates preferred boys under eighteen as tea pickers, believing that their small fingers were better suited than adults' to plucking leaves. Of course, children could also be paid less and kept under tighter discipline. Gusii juveniles accepted these terms, eager as they were for cash as well as for the education that was (falsely) promised them at the estates.[153] Juveniles constituted just under one-third of the total Gusii labor force in Kericho: 50 out of 180 workers John Kebaso met at one estate in 1946, and 6,800 out of 22,556 employed across the estates in 1952.[154] Parents and chiefs kept up a steady stream of complaints that estates were recruiting children without their parents' permission.[155] The PC in 1950 explained that the administration opposed child labor in principle, but that tea owners had reported insufficient supplies of adult labor. With 50 percent of production costs tied up in labor, growers' preference for children, who were paid one-third the adult rate, doubtless had less to do with lack of adult labor than with its relative cost.[156] Given the importance of the tea industry the government allowed the recruitment of juvenile labor, albeit with the restrictions on labor recruiters that children leaving the district be at least thirteen years old and taller than four feet eleven inches, and that parental permission be obtained. This, and all other administrative attempts to regulate child labor in Kericho, failed miserably.[157] Parents' and chiefs' complaints were never adequately addressed, and the virtually unrestricted supply of lower-paid and more easily controlled juvenile workers helped to depress adult workers' wages.

Conclusion

The cash that entered the highlands during and after the war was unprecedented. With the advent of cash crops a homestead with plentiful labor—women and children—could bring in more wealth than had been possible previously. This was especially true of those with off-farm income and access to the state. Households of limited labor fared not so well, and young men forced to raise even part of their bridewealth through wage labor despaired upon finding only low-paying jobs. Collecting bridewealth could be difficult enough, but low wages combined with steadily increasing bridewealth levels youths were pushed into ever more desperate positions. Wealth inequalities and low wages exacerbated the frustrations of men (and women) seeking marriage and adulthood.

GUSII BRIDEWEALTH AND THE FAILURE OF LIMITS

The nature of Gusii bridewealth was central to the crisis in Gusii marriage. Bridewealth tended to remain around a certain level, but the results of a few men paying high bridewealth were devastating, as P. Mayer explained. If a father sensed the level was about to rise or heard of wealthy men paying more, to protect his own interests he would demand this higher rate:

> Every father fears being left in the lurch by finding that the bridewealth which he has accepted for his daughter will not suffice to get him a daughter-in-law; therefore he is always on the look-out for any signs of a rise in the rate, and tends to raise his demands whenever he hears of other fathers doing so. This means in general terms, that *individual* cases of over-payment quickly produce a *general* rise in the rate all round.[158]

Essential to Gusii society and family life, to relations between seniors and juniors, men and women, was marriage and the exchange of bridewealth. Threats to these institutions—such as high bridewealth—were not to be taken lightly. The Gusii and the British well understood the troubles that could arise from excessive bridewealth. Judging by the volume of correspondence on the topic, administrators felt stock theft one of the most deplorable results of high bridewealth, and many Gusii agreed.[159] The rash of abductions in the 1890s and later in the middle decades of the twentieth century, along with increases in elopement and illicit sex, vividly illustrated the impact of excessive bridewealth levels. As one administrator put it in 1927, "young men cannot get wives and instead go in for fornication and seducing the young wives of hoary polygamists."[160] Elsewhere in the colony administrators and elders argued that high bridewealth reduced the young peoples' chances of marriage and pushed young women into prostitution.[161]

Interwar administrative dedication to preserving Gusii society thus required intervention in Gusii bridewealth, primarily through limiting the number of cattle to be exchanged. Some administrators felt bridewealth limits had to be voluntary, and perhaps that implementing limits would be beyond their authority.[162] These reservations were overcome, however, and over the first three decades of colonial rule Gusii elites and the local administration made repeated attempts to limit bridewealth. Few were effective for more than a year or two, and many had no impact whatsoever. For example, in 1926 the bridewealth rate was somewhere in the range of six to nine cows (along with one bull and three to thirteen goats). The DC along with Chief Onsongo of Getutu proclaimed a limit of three cows, but by the next year the rate was four to six cows, and by 1928 five to nine cows (plus a bull and three to ten goats). Again in August 1929 the DC and elders announced a limit of three cows; within a few months bridewealth was at eight head. In 1934 Chief Musa Nyandusi proposed a three-head limit, while the LNC passed a resolution that put it at six cows, one bull, and ten goats. The level the next year was six to ten cows, one bull, and six to fourteen goats.[163]

Why did so many of these attempts to limit bridewealth end in failure? As P. Mayer argued, the two which succeeded—Ogeto's (in 1903) and Ochwara's (in 1920)—combined elite participation, public agreement at a *baraza*, and some type of sanction.[164] Colonial-era limits usually lacked unanimous support. Most Gusii supported the limits. Nonetheless, some dissented. In 1926, DC S. O. V. Hodge found that while most men favored a lower bridewealth, "one or two of the elder men were not enthusiastic, probably because they had daughters for sale."[165] Hodge later noted that the proposed bridewealth limit "of course is unpopular with the Wazee [elders] as a whole who have marrigable [*sic*] daughters to get rid of who keep on putting up the price."[166] Chief Oirere of Bassi favored a limit (to help prevent stock theft) and while this gained young men's support their elders were less enamored with the idea.[167]

Moreover, most limits lacked effective sanctions; the failure of enforcement was the fundamental weakness of colonial-era bridewealth limits. Some men even found ways to break the spirit if not the letter of Ogeto's limit, despite the deadly oath attached to it. Fathers demanded extra "milk"—calves—that were not counted against the three-head limit.[168] Evading colonial limits could be easier still. In 1926, and again in 1928, administrators told Gusii that those paying or receiving bridewealth above the limit would be fined or imprisoned, but there is no evidence that such threats were ever carried out.[169] In 1929, the DC authorized the tribunals to impose three months imprisonment for offenders against the three head limit. Two years later he discovered that "there was only one Elder in the Native Tribunal who had not received marriage price of more than 3 head of cattle for his daughter." Punishment appeared to have been imposed only on those men whom the court elders disliked.[170] The Kisii-Bakoria LNC discussed what could be done, for even if extra cattle could be returned to the groom by the court the father-in-law simply again "extorted" them. The meeting suggested the cattle be collected, sold and the cash be given to the groom.[171] Only Chief Oirere of Bassi put this plan to work. Even there grooms hesitated to take part, for few men would dare alienate their fathers-in-law by filing charges. When on tour in Bassi in 1931, an administrator was asked by some young men how they could pay their taxes when no work was available. He replied, "had they last year accepted back the excess mahari [bridewealth] which they paid for their wives and Oirere had seized from their fathers-in-law, they would have plenty of stock to sell."[172]

Administrators made other attempts to regulate bridewealth via the Native Tribunals. They instructed court elders that when a marriage failed the husband should be refunded only the number of cattle allowed by the reigning limit, regardless of the number he had actually paid.[173] But this, again, placed on suitors the full onus to limit bridewealth. Fathers could continue to demand high bridewealth and it was up to grooms to refuse to pay above the standard rate. Aside from breaking off negotiations there was little a groom could do but pay the higher amount and risk losing the extra cattle should the marriage collapse.[174] SDA missionary Beavon fretted over the prospect of a young man having continually to pay over another cow or two (for "friendship's sake") only to see his wife run off, and then being able to reclaim only the standard rate. The resulting profit to a father would make this a not uncommon occurrence, Beavon felt. DC Hodge was "of the opinion that [Beavon] is taking an exaggerated view of the situation," while Fazan, the Nyanza PC, refuted each of the missionary's points in some detail.[175] His successor, however, admitted that a father was in "an unassailable position."[176]

K. L. Hunter, Bridewealth, and "Girl Cases"

The only state-sponsored bridewealth limit that had any lasting effect was that of District Commissioner K. L. Hunter in 1937. Hunter was of South African extraction, a former military man, and a strong disciplinarian,[177] and his ideas on marriage would shape administrative policy in Nyanza for many years. Hunter had in December 1935 called a *baraza* in Kitutu which some three thousand Gusii attended. They proposed that limiting bridewealth would be of "considerable assistance to the Kisii generally."[178] It appears, however, that no such limit was enacted and by 1937 the situation had not improved. In March, Hunter reported that high bridewealth had pushed many young men down one of two paths: "They either steal cattle to pay the bride price, or else steal the girl and run away with her."[179] After a girl was "stolen," Hunter explained, her father would file a civil case in a native tribunal to claim bridewealth. Should the young man have no property (as was typical) the debt was executed against his close relatives. This outraged stock owners, never sure when their cattle would be attached to pay for the marriage of some irresponsible youth. Hunter proposed that "to 'steal' an unmarried girl without payment of bridewealth or any prospect of doing so be criminally triable by a Native Tribunal."[180] The Attorney General demurred. "Stealing" a girl under sixteen years constituted a statutory offence and so could not be heard by Native Tribunals. Further, he insisted that elopement by girls over sixteen must remain purely civil.[181] (This policy was altered by the early 1940s, when elopement could be heard as an offense against customary law.)

With no clear strategy to combat "girl cases" the number of incidents continued to grow. By June, anxiety was mounting among members of the LNC. In Minute 78/37, "Abduction of unmarried girls," members recorded their distress over the "unsatisfactory state of affairs as regard such offences" which were on the increase. In September, members again brought up the issue of "youths running off with unmarried girls," and wished Government to compel "the girls and the youths to return home." The council, with Hunter presiding, requested of Nairobi permission to institute pass laws for both men and women.[182] Harsher measures appear to have been considered, but Hunter thought only pass laws might gain approval.[183]

Over the next weeks (before Nairobi had made a decision on the passes) Hunter became even more alarmed. In November, he called his huge *baraza* in Kisii town. He lectured those present on "the disgusting practice of indecent assaults on girls and defilement of girls under 16 years" and pointed out "the bestial nature of the offences [which he] likened to dogs and bitches." After several elders spoke in support Hunter administered an oath binding Gusii men:

1. To do all in their power to prevent the type of assaults on girls that were at present so common.
2. To demand not more than 11 head of cattle as marriage price.
3. To do all in their power to prevent stock theft.[184]

Hunter was so committed to preserving social order that far from using an oath in (as he put it) "native fashion" he devised a very new one. All present were ordered to strip naked, a departure from custom but one to which the elders acquiesced as a means dramatically to strengthen the oath.[185] According to Hunter, the Gusii overwhelmingly supported the *baraza* and no "girl cases" arose the next month.[186]

For the control of women, however, the state offered less support. Hunter had sent the LNC pass resolution to Nairobi (likely to the Attorney General) to gain approval, which was denied. He was forced to inform the councilors that "there was no chance of Government agreeing" to passes. Nonetheless, Hunter found a method to regulate the movement of young men and women and yet technically avoid pass laws. With the Acting PC present, Hunter informed the councilors that officers in South Kavirondo would "inquire" of African men leaving the district to work if "they are taking any woman." If a man answered yes, the officer would demand that he produce a letter from his chief confirming that the woman was his wife.[187] Young men "stealing" women would be prevented from leaving the district, offering the women's guardians a better chance of recovering them. Nonetheless, since this plan would require administrators to police all men exiting South Kavirondo—an impossibility — it ultimately proved to be a failure.

Hunter was not blind to senior men's own antisocial acts. If senior men contributed to disorder or dislocation then they too faced administrative criticism. In assigning responsibility for the "girl cases" Hunter charged that "elders were just as much to blame as the young people as the former demanded such prohibitive marriage prices for their daughters."[188] When fathers asked for high bridewealth many relatively poor men found themselves unable to marry. It was in this situation that young men "stole" women.

Gusii Bridewealth and the New Economy

Bad enough in 1937, during the war years bridewealth began climbing to levels never before seen in Gusiiland. In large part this was due to the wealth that was flowing into the highlands. Much of the wartime money was turned into cattle, and these large herds became large bridewealth herds. Speaking with Gusii in the 1940s, P. Mayer summarized their understanding of the recent rises in bridewealth:

> The rise in the rate that took place in the years following 1942 is attributed by the people largely to the increased cash that entered the Reserve in the hands of ex-askaris and others who profited by war conditions.[189]

Similarly, one elder recalled that "army used to buy grain from local people. When they got the money from selling, bridewealth began to rise."[190]

Yet the new wealth was not spread evenly, and at least part of the increase in bridewealth was due to the "unfair bargains" made by the nouveaux riches. Mayer continues:

> [The increase in bridewealth] is not regarded merely as a legitimate cause [such as when all or most Gusii could collect many cattle]: part of the rise is explained in terms of the unfair bargains made by these new rich.[191]

So long as cash crop prices remained high the elite grew wealthier and continued to upset bridewealth.

Even as Gusii watched in horror increases in bridewealth rates, young men also had to calculate wages and cattle prices. Those who relied on their sisters' bridewealth could not be certain of early marriage unless husbands could be found for their sisters—not a sure prospect given that so many other young men were in a similarly compromised position. Many young men pegged their hopes on natural reproduction of their herds and on wage labor. The former had always been a tried and true means of collecting bridewealth, but took time. Bridewealth typically was composed of equal numbers of cows and goats and one bull. The birth of a bull calf was not greeted with rejoicing. More than one or two bulls in a herd was a waste of pasturage and attention (and thus the cattle sold for meat to private butchers and to the army consisted primarily of bulls). Herd expansion by natural reproduction worked well only with the birth of heifers, and mother nature prefers to create male and female in relatively equal number.

For most men, the best avenue to collecting bridewealth quickly was through wage labor and the purchase of cows. In one sample from Wanjare, between World War II and Independence slightly over one half of young men had purchased their own bridewealth cattle.[192] The opportunities for work were by and large sufficient, especially at the labor-hungry Kericho tea estates so close by. In the colonial realm, however, ideal marketplace rules did not apply. High demand for labor did not always result in higher wages.

Along with low wages, equally distressing for young laborers were fluctuating cattle prices. In other parts of the colony, limited pasturage had pushed many people into replacing cattle with cash as bridewealth.[193] But into the 1950s, only the most densely settled areas of Gusiiland lacked ample pasturage. Indeed, the total number of cattle in South Nyanza only grew over the colonial period. A healthy trade in cattle over the essentially unregulated border with Tanganyika assured this. Administrators in the late 1940s calculated that 300,000–400,000 cattle were held in the district, but a 1950 census put it at 950,000. About one-third of these beasts resided in the Gusii highlands. Seven years later the district count had reached 1,100,000 head, fully one-sixth of the total cattle population of Kenya.[194]

Unlike wage labor rates, for cattle prices the laws of supply and demand operated in economically logical terms. Despite plentiful cattle, the always-high demand drove up their cost. Likely to arrest rising cattle prices, in 1950 the administration decreed that, for legal purposes, a cow was worth shs. 50. Nonetheless, one year later patrons of controlled markets willingly paid as much as shs. 135, and even more at uncontrolled ones.[195] The next year, 1952, the price of bulls had declined slightly, but cows remained quite expensive.[196] Even these extraordinary numbers may be underestimates. Håkansson's sources suggest cattle were dearer still: in 1943, cows may have cost shs. 140, shs. 400 in 1955, and shs. 300 in 1964.[197] Other sources suggest a 1956–1957 level of shs. 300.[198]

By tracing the trajectories of wages and cattle prices we can gain a sense of how long the average man had to labor in order to pay even minimal bridewealth. In 1943, an unskilled laborer would require between two years and nine months and eight years to acquire bridewealth; in 1946, four years, nine months; in 1952, two years and six months. If 1956 bridewealth rates stood at ten head, and if wage rates had remained at 1952 levels, a man would have had to have worked ten years to raise minimal bridewealth. Even with the most generous estimates—presuming that wage rates doubled over those four years—a man would labor away for five years to accumulate bridewealth.[199] These conclusions are, of course, limited in several ways. They assume that the worker began with no cattle whatsoever and had to earn all his cattle via wage labor, and so may overestimate the total time required to collect bridewealth.

Similarly, natural reproduction of the first cows purchased could move up the date of marriage. On the other hand, the estimates are calculated in terms of the bare minimum bridewealth without factoring in the number of goats and bulls fathers demanded of suitors. Even though goats reproduce more quickly than do cattle, a dozen or more goats were needed for bridewealth, and in the 1950s a single goat cost about shs. 35, or one month's salary.[200] As a confirmation of these estimates, R. LeVine and B. LeVine, based on their first-hand observations in Nyaribari in the 1950s, noted that it took a man a full forty months of labor at the Kericho tea estates to earn a minimal bridewealth.[201] Factoring in all these points, in 1940s and 1950s it took perhaps at least three to four years' steady work for a poor man to earn bridewealth, and probably longer. In contrast, in the 1920s it took perhaps six to eighteen months for a laborer to collect bridewealth sufficient for marriage.[202]

Gusiiland was not the only area in Kenya to experience increases in bridewealth, but, along with the Kuria, it was the hardest hit. The Native Catholic Union, situated mainly in Central and North Kavirondo, met with the PC in 1926 to discuss underage marriage and high bridewealth, and received the typical answer: turn not to limits but to the tribunals.[203] But, aside from an increase of complaints during the war years, thereafter these districts were relatively quiet. Polling PCs in 1950, the Chief Secretary learned that high bridewealth was a concern only in South Nyanza and Fort Hall districts. In all the others, bridewealth was either at a reasonable level or was declining. Only Kuria suffered increases in bridewealth comparable to that of the Gusii. Calls for bridewealth limits there also constantly arose only either to be rejected by the administration or to fail miserably. That Kuria lived on both sides of the porous Kenya–Tanganyika border made any administrative pronouncements compromised at best. But there is little evidence that marriage disputes that grew from high bridewealth struck Kuria in anything like the numbers that they did in Gusiiland.

Bridewealth Limits in the 1940s

As bridewealth began its unprecedented climb and more men found themselves unable to marry, Gusii again sought, in vain, some way to reduce or control it. Hunter's 1937 limit held for a few years, but certainly not past 1942. In the middle of 1944, Chief Musa and the elders in Nyaribari agreed to limit bridewealth to six cows, one bull, and ten goats. Those in North Mugirango likewise agreed that a limit was necessary, though they had not yet decided on the numbers.[204] In November, the whole of the South Kavirondo LNC took up the matter. Chief Agwata of North Mugirango reported that the elders had now decided on seven head of cattle and ten goats, and commented that all the Gusii locations favored some type of limit. Despite his location's prior decision to limit bridewealth Musa now pointed out that all previous attempts to cap bridewealth had failed; apparently he favored limits on a locational rather than a district-wide level. After much discussion the council decided to take no action. Within four months, however, the councilors admitted they were not satisfied with this decision, and proposed to put the question before local *baraza*s. By this time, however, the government had rejected the idea of an LNC-imposed limit. The frustrated councilors tossed out the hollow hope that bridewealth had peaked.[205]

Bridewealth had far from peaked. From ten to twelve head in 1944, it rose to fourteen in 1946, and sixteen, perhaps even twenty head by 1947.[206] That year LACs recommended bridewealth be held at six cows, one bull, and ten goats. This rate was adopted at chiefs' *baraza*s in Getutu and North Mugirango, as well at a combined meeting of elders from Majoge, Bassi, and South Mugirango. To discuss this limit, in September 1948 Musa called a huge *baraza*. LNC and LAC members, *etureti* elders, and a large number of people from across Gusiiland converged on Kisii town. All agreed to the six-cow rate. While a few questioned the ability to enforce a limitation, "[w]hen the proposal was put to the assembly as a whole, there was a loud cry of 'Eee' ['Yes'], and no voice was raised in answer to the call for dissentients."[207] The LNC endorsed the limit the next year. According to Musa, the public applauded the limit "which enabled some poor people [*sic*] to get wives, with small number of cattle."[208] Despite this enthusiasm, the decision seems to have had little effect. John Kebaso was "informed by reliable persons that the introduction of Dowry Control was never obeyed by the Kisii people, but [they] are shamelessly asking for more and more cattle for their daughters."[209] Rather than six, the rate was up to ten head in 1949, and District Commissioner Low in April again approached LACs to discuss bridewealth.[210] Low suggested at the end of 1950 that "It is believed that the Kisii have adhered" to the ADC limit.[211] In fact, 16 head were now commonly being exchanged.[212]

Kirera's Limit

By 1950, the state of Gusii bridewealth had reached a crisis, perhaps the worst since the 1890s. The cost of marriage now exceeded the means of not only poorer young men, but even the moderately well off. Fathers desperately sought suitors able to pay the going rate. So dire was the situation that young women were remaining at home past the normal years of marriage, in some cases to the point of breeching the "gray hair" rule: a homestead courted misfortune if a daughter lived there until growing gray. Brothers who relied on their sisters' bridewealth found themselves impatiently waiting for brothers-in-law, for so long as no bridewealth entered a homestead it was unlikely that bridewealth would go out. The steady movement of bridewealth between families on which Gusii marriage depended slowed nearly to a halt.[213]

By 1951, with anxiety mounting, among men and women, young and old, Chief Kirera of Getutu took action. To Kirera (as he was known locally; in British records he appears as Zacharia Angwenyi) the obvious solution to the crisis was to implement a bridewealth limit, reducing to a reasonable level the cost of marriage. Kirera called a *baraza* at Manga, site of his offices and *Ritongo* Manga, and pronounced that henceforth bridewealth should not exceed six cows, one bull, and perhaps one goat. His decree was greeted with great rejoicing across Gusiiland by youth and elders alike as the best and perhaps only way to resuscitate marriage. Songs were composed in Kirera's honor:

> Leader: Kirera son of Ooga
> Chorus: *Welcome the hero*
> He has issued a decree of six
> *Welcome the hero*
> And one for the plow
> *Welcome the hero*
> And another for its goatskin
> *Welcome the hero*
> Kirera son of Ooga
> *Welcome the hero*
> *He is a hero*
> *A living legend*
> *A hero*
> *A living legend, a hero*
> *A hero*[214]

A hero indeed. Six cows was within the means of many men, and the glut of aging maidens was rapidly reduced. The bridewealth and marriage circuit operated once again. In the year or two following Kirera's decree more marriages were consecrated than perhaps any other time in living memory.[215] For many older Gusii it is the bridewealth limit that first comes to mind when Kirera's name is mentioned.

For one or two years Kirera's limit held, only in part because of sanctions. When marriages collapsed the courts allowed only seven head of cattle to be refunded, regardless of what had actually been paid. Sub-chiefs were instructed each to bring an offender before the courts to serve as a deterrent, and *askari*s arrested those caught exchanging bridewealth above the limit.[216] But enforcing the limit, at least early on, was not imperative. Gusii, anxious over the imperilled state of marriage and bridewealth, almost universally applauded Kirera's limit. Nevertheless, as with every other bridewealth limit Kirera's disgruntled some senior men, particularly those with many daughters who resented this constraint on their acquiring large herds.[217] Moreover, as the ranks of the unmarried thinned, the urgency of the marriage crisis (momentarily) abated. For the moderately wealthy, Kirera's limit seemed increasingly irrelevant. In fact, from the day of Kirera's decree some marriages were sealed by more than six cows. By 1952, this had become common. The level soon reached as high as fifteen head, leading the ADC to propose enacting its own limit of seven.[218] And so the cycle began, and by 1953 or 1954 Kirera's limit had been eclipsed.[219] For the poorest Gusii and those who had yet to reach marriageable age the future again appeared bleak.

Subsequent years brought little hope. A Catholic priest in 1953 complained of the persistent rise in bridewealth. "There is a sort of 'maximum dowry' put down by the government," he noted, perhaps referring to Kirera's, "But nobody adheres to this arrangement any more." He spoke with a district officer about rectifying this, but admitted that he could not "see whether the government can do much. They could put a new 'okumu' [limit] but people would adhere to it a short time and they would break it again."[220] A few years later an ADC-sponsored rate of six to eight cows was ignored by a significant number of people in Nyaribari, where bridewealth exchanges soon reached ten to twelve head.[221] By 1961, Gusii Law Panel members recommended abolishing altogether the offense of taking or paying bridewealth above the limit, "since the limit was largely ignored by the people."[222]

The State and the Failure of Bridewealth Limits

Why did all of the wartime and postwar attempts to regulate bridewealth fail so miserably? Of the many attempts to limit bridewealth in the early colonial period all but two failed. Only Ochwara's (1920–1921) and Hunter's proved successful for any length of time. Each of these combined elite sponsorship, widespread consensus, and mystical sanctions. To enforce his limit Kirera relied partly on the use of his *askari*s and the courts (whether with or without the administration's knowledge) but more important was nearly unanimous public support. No other chief could replicate Kirera's feat, however, especially because the average Gusii saw chiefs simply as low-level state functionaries, far removed from the real seat of authority. Thus, Kirera notwithstanding, chiefs' pronouncements on bridewealth held little weight. One chief admitted this to P. Mayer:

> At my barazas I threaten people who pay more than six cows; for instance, I tell them I will come to their villages with the old men and women of the location and make *emuma* [a curse]. But in fact I can do nothing; I can call the offender to my baraza, but if he refuses to listen, I shall be forced to give up. This is the position at present.[223]

Chiefs, who regularly used compulsion to enforce unpopular policies, did of course have ways of inducing compliance to a variety of edicts. But for a chief to force all his followers to abide by a single rate was, undoubtedly, virtually impossible. Indeed, insofar as chiefs were likely allied with the wealthy men who paid high bridewealth, their positions were not without complications.

People who favored a limit on bridewealth—and they were many—were compelled to look to the state. Old men understood that *Serikali* (Government) really made law, and younger men knew that the LNC made specific laws, backed up by *Serikali.* As P. Mayer puts it, the average Gusii felt "that the Administration, and only the Administration, is the source of binding laws." Thus while Gusii might ignore bridewealth regulations emanating from chiefs, they believed the state stood a better chance at successfully imposing a limit. The 1949 LNC rate failed, according to Kebaso, because "some people think that probably the Res[olution] has not received the approval of His Excellency the Governor in Council."[224] Elders told Mayer that "[a]nyone who could make the rate binding through 'Serikali' would have done a good thing, and would have our gratitude."[225] Unfortunately, *Serikali* was of split mind on the subject, and this indecision meant very little state support was extended to where it was so desperately needed.

Administrators hesitated to regulate something so unwilling to be regulated. As early as May 1939 Chief Oirere informed the LNC that some men had already begun to ignore Hunter's 1937 limit. What could be done to prevent this, he asked desperately? The PC, in attendance, threw up his hands and replied that bridewealth was utterly "impossible to control." Even if the LNC did pass a resolution regulating bridewealth, he informed the councilors, "it would be disobeyed."[226] Administrative objections to bridewealth limits as unenforceable was a refrain heard over and over again during the next decade. At the November 1944 LNC meeting the DC encouraged the members to consider a limit. But within a couple of months the DC was forced to call a halt to the project, having been told that the government would not support such measures. Again, the government's reasoning was that the resolution would be impossible to enforce. Instead, the LNC might pass a "recommendation" that bridewealth should not rise above a certain number and then urge citizenry to abide by this. "I believe that we will achieve nothing by legislation," the PC insisted, "until public opinion is firmly against the practice" of exchanging high bridewealth.[227]

In 1945 the Nyanza PC explained to a Luo soldier, one of many who complained of the costs of bridewealth, that people could evade any limit by secretly paying higher amounts:

> When the majority of people in any area can see the difficulty as you have done, then surely they will all gather together and say "why do we go on with this custom which is like a stone around our necks, we must stop it."
>
> Then will be the time to say to Government we want a law to help us carry out what is our majority opinion, and Government will be able to help, to see that the one or two bad men do not offend against the opinion of the majority.[228]

Significantly, the author of this letter was K. L. Hunter. Despite having constructed the most successful administrative bridewealth limit in all the years of colonial rule, its collapse discouraged him. Hunter had now become convinced that bridewealth regulations were doomed to fail. Of course, in other areas of African life the state was ever willing to undertake projects that had virtually no popular support. But while noncompliance with, for example, terracing schemes could be easily observed and punished, bridewealth transactions were virtually invisible to the state. Administrators shuddered at the thought of Africans blithely evading bridewealth regulations, making a mockery of the state and bringing the law "into disrepute."[229]

Not all district officers had lost heart in the struggle to control bridewealth but they could generate only ineffectual methods of enforcing limits. In a 1945 chiefs' *baraza* South Kavirondo DC Perreau encouraged Gusii to revert to what (he imagined) bridewealth "used to be," two or three head. Nonetheless, he admitted that there was no sense in passing an LNC resolution until all the people were behind the plan.[230] In 1949, the DC supported the LNC's limit of six or seven head, and ordered that those paying or receiving more could be punished by the Native Tribunals.[231] For a short time this may have worked.[232] But ultimately this plan could hardly survive, for the onus of filing cases fell on grooms, and few youth were willing to alienate their fathers-in-law.[233]

While both Gusii and the administration recognized the perils of high bridewealth, they spent the postwar years talking past each other. Gusii were convinced that only *Serikali*'s bridewealth limits had any realistic chance of success. Until then, the vicious cycle of bridewealth increases would continue. For their part, administrators refused to enact any regulation until they could be convinced that virtually all Gusii would support it and so not make the law out to be a paper tiger. And here arose the problem. Only a small minority of Gusii men scoffed at limits, but the actions of these few forced the many continually to break limits. The state balked at establishing limits, since the failure of previous ones (supposedly) demonstrated that most Gusii were not yet fully behind bridewealth limits. Without state backing, limits proposed by chiefs and the LNC could not succeed, their failure only reinforcing the state's decision not to back a limit.

The result: bridewealth continued to rise.

CONCLUSION

The economic changes that began in the war years unleashed an explosive series of transformations in Gusiiland. Wealth flowed into the highlands during the war through sale of cash crops and through remits of *askari*s. The appropriation of women's labor and land meant that, given favorable weather and healthy prices, a man could catapult into relative wealth in a handful of years. Cash and cattle remained plentiful over the next two decades, but were not distributed equally. Some homesteads produced large amounts of maize, coffee, and other cash crops, supplementing their income through well-paying employment. Many more Gusii did less well. Those who relied on selling their labor faced wages that increased slightly if at all. The resulting dramatic rises in bridewealth levels, resistant to any attempts to limit it and increasingly lacking administrative attention, created social problems unseen for fifty or more years. Bridewealth outpaced the pay of wage laborers, leaving many unable to marry. Some fathers sought out any man able to marry their daughters. Many young couples eloped. Some men abducted women to be their "wives." Gusiiland slipped into a marriage crisis.

NOTES

1. Mzee Jackson, May 30, 2004.
2. SK DARs 1911/12, 1912/13; Nyanza PAR 1916/17.
3. SK DARs 1907/08, 1913/14; SK DQRs Sept. and Dec. 1911.
4. Already in 1909 locals had "eagerly accepted" sim-sim and groundnut seeds, within a couple of years some Gusii had energetically taken to the ghee trade, and in 1915 the DC reported that Gusii "seemed keen on having the [maize] seed . . ." By the war years items as diverse as English potatoes, animal hides, wheat, and chillies were among the many goods for sale in the district. SK DQRs Sept. 1909, June 1911; SK DARs 1912/13, 1914/15.
5. Robert Maxon, *Conflict and Accommodation in Western Kenya: The Gusii and the British, 1907–1963* (Cranbury, NJ: Associated University Presses, 1989), 69; Felix Oswald, "From the Victoria Nyanza to the Kisii Highlands," *The Geographical Journal* 41 (Jan.–June 1913), 124.
6. Nehemiah M. Nyaundi, *Seventh-day Adventism in Gusii, Kenya* (Kendu Bay, Kenya: Africa Herald Publishing House, 1997), 23.
7. Station Inspection, 1912, KNA: PC/NZA 2/2.
8. Nyaundi, *Seventh-day Adventism in Gusii*, 32–33.
9. SK DARs 1907/08, and between 1912 and 1917; Maxon, *Conflict and Accommodation in Western Kenya*, 54, 57; Richard Gethin, "An Old Settler Remembers," RH: MSS Afr. s. 1277, 6; W. F. G. Campbell, "Kitutu," Nov. 1918, SK PRB.
10. SK DQR Sept. 1911; SK DARs 1912/13, 1913/14.
11. Lacy Alvin Spake Jr., "A Micro-regional Geography Case Study of Tropical Highland Development: Gusii District, Kenya, East Africa" (M.A. thesis, San Francisco State College, 1965), 62.
12. Kirsten Alsaker Kjerland, "Cattle Breed; Shillings Don't: The Belated Incorporation of the abaKuria into Modern Kenya" (Ph.D. thesis, University of Bergen, 1995), 38–39.
13. Robert Maxon, *Going Their Separate Ways: Agrarian Transformation in Kenya, 1930–1950* (Cranbury, NJ: Associated University Presses, 2003), 74–75.
14. Maxon, *Conflict and Accommodation in Western Kenya*, 56.
15. SK DARs 1908/09, 1912/13; SK DQRs June 1909, June and Sept. 1911, March and June 1912. But for a contrary report, see SK DQR Sept. 1908.
16. SK DARs 1909/10, 1912/13; SK DQRs Sept. and Dec. 1910. In 1922 the DC reported that those Gusii youth who did not leave for labor instead busied themselves with "spirited work in the fields." SK DAR 1922.
17. SK DAR 1914/15.
18. SK DAR 1919/20.
19. Maxon, *Conflict and Accommodation in Western Kenya*, 79; SK DARs 1922, 1923, 1924, 1926, 1929, 1931. In 1920 several thousand went out on contract, with another three

thousand searching for labor on their own. How much of this was included in the forced labor of that year is not clear. H. E. Welby, "History of the District," SK PRB. In the 1929 SK DAR the DC considered that the Gusii received a "not inconsiderable" portion of their wealth from remittances by young men laboring outside the district.

20. On the administration's struggles to collect taxes see, for example, SK DAR 1932.

21. SK DAR 1931; W. W. Armstrong, "Kenya Colony," *Advent Review and Sabbath Herald* 110 (Jan. 26, 1933), 11–12.

22. Maxon, *Conflict and Accommodation in Western Kenya*, 106–107.

23. SK DAR 1938.

24. With the declaration of war there was "panic amongst the Kisii" and some young men "left their homes to hide in the bush lest they should be seized and taken as carriers." Men at the tea estates "flocked back to their homes, fearing they knew not what." SK DAR 1939.

25. SK DAR 1940.

26. PC Nyanza to DCs, Oct. 15, 1941, KNA: Lab 15/1.

27. DC SK to PC Nyanza, Oct. 20, 1941, KNA: Lab 15/1. He also worried that the administration was "laying up for [itself] all sorts of trouble by talking freedom and acting all Hitlerish." DC SK to PC Nyanza, Nov. 29, 1941, KNA: Agr 1/5/9.

28. PC Nyanza to DCs, Nov. 12, 1941, KNA: Lab 15/1.

29. DC SK to PC Nyanza, Nov. 29, 1941, KNA: Agr 1/5/9; Extract of Safari Diary [ca. Nov. 1941], in PC Nyanza to Chief Secretary, Dec. 4, 1941, KNA: Lab 15/1.

30. Labour Supervisor, The Tea Estates Labour Department (The African Highlands Produce Co., Ltd., and Kenya Tea Company Ltd.), to PC Nyanza, Nov. 22, 1941; DC SK to Labour Supervisor, Nov. 28, 1941, both in KNA: Lab 15/1; SK DAR 1942.

31. SK DAR 1942.

32. See Man Power Bulletins in KNA: Mil 6. Administrative records put 10,084 as volunteers and only 706 as conscripted but, given the discussion above, the line between the two was likely rather loose.

33. KNA: Mil 6.

34. SK DAR 1941.

35. Chief Secretary to East African Governors, Dec. 16, 1942, KNA: Mil 28; Labour Department, Nyanza, Annual Report, 1945, KNA: Pub 4/2/5.

36. See Family Remittance Monthly Return Form A and Form B, in KNA: Mil 4/6/9/1 and KNA: Mil 4/9/1/15B.

37. DC SK to PC Nyanza, Oct. 20, 1941, KNA: Lab 15/1.

38. M. P. Byers to Labour Officer, Feb. 6, 1945, KNA: Lab 2/1/19.

39. Intelligence Report for Dec. 1944, M. P. Byers to Labour Officer, Feb. 6, 1945, KNA: Lab 2/1/19; Labour Department, Nyanza, Annual Reports, 1944 and 1945, KNA: Pub 4/2/5.

40. LNC meeting July 30–31, Aug. 1, 1945; meeting of SK LNC and Representatives of Sotik Farmers, Dec. 3, 1945, KNA: Lab 2/1/9; SK DAR 1946; Minutes of chiefs' meeting, Kisii, Nov. 20, 1946, KNA: Adm 12/7/2.

41. DC SK to PC Nyanza, Sept. 11, 1944, KNA: TC 1/3/1.

42. Maxon, *Going their Separate Ways*, 222–223.

43. Maxon, *Conflict and Accommodation in Western Kenya*, 116; DC SK to PC Nyanza, Nov. 19, 1941; [PC Nyanza?] telegram to DC SK, Dec. 15, 1941, both in KNA: Agr 1/5/9; Dept. of Agriculture, Nyanza: Agricultural Program for 1942, Jan. 20, 1942, KNA: Adm 3/2/2; Dept. of Agriculture, Nyanza, Third Quarterly Report, 1944, KNA: Agr 3/2/1; PC Nyanza to DC SK, Jan. 13, 1945, KNA: Agr 1/2/3.

44. SK DAR 1943.

45. Maxon, *Conflict and Accommodation in Western Kenya*, 115.

46. Ibid, 115.

47. DC SK to PC Nyanza, Sept. 11, 1944, KNA: T&C, 1/3/1.
48. DC SK to PC Nyanza, Feb. 8, 1945, KNA: T&C 1/3/1.
49. Maxon, *Conflict and Accommodation in Western Kenya*, 132.
50. SK DAR 1950. Musa Nyandusi had warned of this already in late 1949. Nyaribari Annual Report, 1949, KNA: DP 1/16.
51. In 1943 an agricultural officer noted that transportation was the limiting factor on the production of more maize. Maxon, *Going their Separate Ways*, 223–224.
52. SK DARs 1953, 1954.
53. David Anderson and David Throup, "Africans and Agricultural Production in Colonial Kenya: The Myth of War as a Watershed," *Journal of African History* 26 (1985), 327–345.
54. Brett L. Shadle, "'Girl Cases': Runaway Wives, Eloped Daughters and Abducted Women in Gusiiland, Kenya, c. 1900–c. 1965" (Ph.D. dissertation, Northwestern University, 2000), 90.
55. Nyabururu Diary, entries for Oct. 1, Dec. 10 and 14, 1913 MH: Kisii Diaries; SK DAR 1913/14.
56. Stephen Orvis, *The Agrarian Question in Kenya* (Gainesville: University Press of Florida, 1997), 41–42.
57. Letter, Jessie Olson to mother, June 10, 1947.
58. Nyaundi, *Seventh-day Adventism in Gusii*, 50.
59. Gershom N. Amayo, "A History of the Adventist Christian Education in Kenya: Illustrated in the Light of its Impact on the Africans' Social, Economic, Religious and Political Development, 1906–1963" (Ph.D. dissertation, Howard University, 1973), 227–228.
60. Joint LNC, Oct. 28–31, 1947, KNA: Adm 15/7/13/1/2.
61. "South Nyanza African Court Elders," ca. Sept. 1952, KNA: L&O 2/1.
62. DC SK to PC Nyanza, Feb. 13, 1948, KNA: Lab 4/1/1.
63. DC SK to PC Nyanza, Feb. 13, 1948, KNA: Lab 4/1/1; "Kazi yao ni nini?" MFM: 12; Department of Agriculture (DA) SN, QR, Second Quarter, 1952, KNA: Agr 14/2/4.
64. Kennedy M. Moindi, "Peasants, Entrepreneurship, Capital Accumulation and Differentiation: The Gusii Maize Flour Millers of Western Kenya, 1920–1950," (paper presented at the African Studies Association Annual Conference, New Orleans, Nov. 2004).
65. Carolyn Barnes, "An Experiment with African Coffee Growing in Kenya: The Gusii, 1933–1950" (Ph.D. dissertation, Michigan State University, 1976); Maxon, *Conflict and Accommodation in Western Kenya*, 100–103; idem, "Stifling Capitalism in Rural Africa: The Gusii Coffee Industry in Kenya, 1932–1949," *Journal of Third World Studies* 11 (1994), 317–350.
66. Quoted in Barnes, "Experiment in African Coffee Growing in Kenya," 122, and 254 for his biographical details.
67. Philip Mayer and Iona Mayer, "Land Law in the Making," in *African Law: Adaptation and Development*, eds. Hilda Kuper and Leo Kuper (Berkely: University of California Press, 1965), 77–78. They refer to an unnamed chief, likely Musa.
68. Barnes, "Experiment in African Coffee Growing in Kenya," 121. Chiefs had done this before in regard to education, apparently intending to demonstrate their effective and progressive rule. Obadiah B. Nyarango, "Biography of Chief Musa Nyandusi" (Student Seminar Paper, Department of History, University of Nairobi, Dec. 1977); idem, "The Biography of Chief Musa Nyandusi" (B.A. thesis, Department of History, University of Nairobi, 1978). See below on the role of Chief Zacharia Angwenyi (Kirera) and his forcible promotion of pyrethrum.
69. Barnes, "Experiment in African Coffee Growing in Kenya," 106; Maxon, *Conflict and Accommodation in Western Kenya*, 102–103.

70. Barnes, "Experiment in African Coffee Growing in Kenya," 199, Table 22; Maxon, *Going their Separate Ways*, 80, 106.

71. PC Nyanza to Chief Secretary, March 11, 1944, KNA: Agr 1/2/2. See also Maxon, *Going their Separate Ways*, 237; Klemens Hubert, ed., "Agricultural Production in Kisii District/Kenya and Proposals for its Development," (Post-Graduate Training Center for Agricultural Development, Institute for Overseas Agriculture, Technical University of Berlin, 1972), 46.

72. Hubert, ed., "Agricultural Production in Kisii District," 47. The authors of this study estimate an annual expenditure of 15.8 "mandays [*sic*]" for weeding and another 15.3 for pruning. Ibid., 55. Weeding also helped check the spread of crop disease. Nyaribari Annual Report, 1949, KNA: DP 1/16.

73. Maxon, *Going Their Separate Ways*, 106–107.

74. Minutes of the Kisii Coffee Board, meetings of June 26, 1944, and Aug. 17, 1946; Special General Meeting of the Kisii Coffee Growers Cooperative, Oct. 13, 1946, all in KNA: Agr 1/2/9/3. See also John Lonsdale, "The Depression and the Second World War in the Transformation of Kenya," in *Africa and the Second World War*, eds. David Killingray and Richard Rathbone (New York: St. Martins, 1986), 127.

75. SK DARs 1935, 1937; Deputy Governor of Kenya to Secretary of State, Aug. 11, 1939, PRO: CO 533/515/7.

76. Agriculture Department, Monthly Report, May 1934, KNA: Agr 3/2/4.

77. Barnes, "Experiment in African Coffee Growing in Kenya," 104.

78. Maxon, *Conflict and Accommodation in Western Kenya*, 118.

79. Maxon, *Going Their Separate Ways*, 360.

80. Virtually all planters were men, although up to the 1950s some widowed women were able to grow coffee on their own plots. See the list of members in Chair, Kisii Coffee Board, to Members, April 24, 1944, KNA: Agr 1/2/9/3; Barnes, "Experiment in African Coffee Growing in Kenya," 120, n. 87.

81. Maxon, *Conflict and Accommodation in Western Kenya*, 119, Table 7.2, 134. The declining average acreage of coffee plots also illustrates that the moderately wealthy had joined the economic elite in coffee production. Those who had planted prior to 1939 had an average of 0.53 acres, while those who planted between 1940 and 1949 averaged only one-third an acre. Based on Ibid, Table 7.2.

82. DA, SN QR, Third Quarter, 1952; DA, SN QR, Second Quarter, 1954, both in KNA: Agr 14/2/4; Barnes, "Experiment in African Coffee Growing in Kenya," 165.

83. SN DAR 1956.

84. Orvis, *Agrarian Question in Kenya*, 52.

85. Maxon, *Conflict and Accommodation in Western Kenya*, 135–136.

86. Maxon, *Going their Separate Ways*, 244.

87. West Mugirango Monthly Report, Oct. 1963, KNA: DP 1/10; Maxon, *Conflict and Accommodation in Western Kenya*, 137.

88. Press Office Handout 409, Sept. 5, 1953, "Loans to traders in South Nyanza"; Press Office Handout 828, Dec. 14, 1953, "Scheme to encourage African traders," both in PRO: CO 822/305.

89. SN DAR 1956. Some agricultural loans had also been improperly diverted toward trading ventures. SN ADC, Agriculture and Natural Resources Committee, Jan. 17, 1955, KNA: Adm 7/15/5/3 III.

90. SN ADC Trades and Markets Committee, Jan. 20, 1956, Adm 7/15/5/3 IV.

91. Paul Mboya, *Utawala na Maendeleo ya Local Government South Nyanza, 1926–1957* (Nairobi: East African Literature Bureau, 1959) 5.

92. Maxon, *Going their Separate Ways*, 96.

93. Maxon, *Going their Separate Ways*, 106.

94. Maxon, *Conflict and Accommodation in Western Kenya*, 125, 129, 142–143. These groups were quite conservative, never really challenged the government, and were short-lived.

95. David Ogega to DC SK, Nov. 18, 1944, and reply, Nov. 20, 1944, both in KNA: DP 34/2.

96. Maxon, *Conflict and Accommodation in Western Kenya*, 125.

97. Minutes of the Kisii Coffee Growers Board, Dec. 18, 1946, KNA: Agr 1/2/9/3.

98. Provincial Exemption Tribunal, Aug. 25, 1942, KNA: Mil 4/9/1/2.

99. Senior Assistant Agricultural Officer, South Kavirondo, to Senior Agricultural Officer, Nyanza, Feb. 22, 1943; DC SN to PC Nyanza, May 21, 1949, both in KNA: Agr 10/1.

100. Orvis, *Agrarian Question in Kenya*. This proved easier to do in the lower-lying areas than in the higher parts, where the harvesting of the first crop could interfere with the planting of the second. Hubert, ed., "Agricultural Production in Kisii District," 31.

101. Maxon, *Conflict and Accommodation in Western Kenya*, 115; N. Thomas Håkansson, *Bridewealth, Women and Land: Social Change among the Gusii of Kenya* (Uppsala Studies in Cultural Anthropology, 10, Uppsala, 1988), 93.

102. Philip Mayer, *Two Studies in Applied Anthropology in Kenya* (London: Colonial Office, 1951), 14.

103. Edmund Alojzy Wilemski, *African Traditional Subsistence Economy in Change* (Cologne: R. J. Hundt, 1975), 74.

104. Nyaundi, *Seventh-day Adventism in Gusii*, 67.

105. Torben Bager, "Marketing Cooperatives and Peasants in Kenya" (CDR Publications 5, Uppsala, Scandinavian Institute of African Studies, 1980), 43. Hubert et al. calculated in 1972 that for basic production methods employing labor was not profitable, as it consumed all the earnings. With greater investments in fertilizer and other inputs, however, employing wage labor could bring a profit in a few years after planting. Hubert, ed., "Agricultural Production in Kisii District," 89–90.

106. Wilemski and Uchendu and Anthony argue that *emonga* disappeared when cash crops were introduced. That is, the distinction between men's and women's fields was erased and women's labor was incorporated into the working of the new larger field. Wilemski, *African Traditional Subsistence Economy*, 58–59; Victor C. Uchendu and Kenneth R. M. Anthony, *Agricultural Change in Kisii District, Kenya* (Nairobi: East African Literature Bureau, 1975), 28.

107. Barnes, "Experiment in African Coffee Growing in Kenya," 168; P. Mayer, *Two Studies in Applied Anthropology*, 6–7. I unfortunately have little information on the topic of women's involvement in and resistance to this process. For similar processes elsewhere, see Jean Allman and Victoria Tashjian, *"I Will Not Eat Stone": A Women's History of Colonial Asante* (Portsmouth, NH: Heinemann, 2000).

108. In the past any homestead head could join the beer drink, even if he had been unable or failed to provide female labor for the *risaga*. By the 1940s such men were made to feel increasingly unwelcome as hosts tried to reserve the food and drink for only those men who had delivered their wives' labor. While not yet wage labor, what had formerly been a communal activity took on the tone of an economic exchange. P. Mayer, *Two Studies in Applied Anthropology*, 14.

109. P. Mayer, *Two Studies in Applied Anthropology*, 12–14.

110. Although Orvis suggests that by the 1950s some men purchased beer. *Agrarian Question in Kenya*, 52.

111. See the example in "Justino: Risaga," MFM: 4.

112. Women's labor was also intensified on their own subsistence plots. In all but the poorest homesteads men were pulling out whatever labor they had previously contributed to subsistence crops, even as a second season of maize growing was introduced. Orvis,

Agrarian Question in Kenya, 53; Robert A. LeVine and Barbara B. LeVine, *Nyansongo: A Gusii Community* (New York: Wiley, 1966), 14.

113. Iona Mayer, "The Patriarchal Image: Routine Dissociation in Gusii Families," *African Studies* 34 (1975), 259–281, esp. 268.

114. Robert A. LeVine, "Wealth and Power in Gusiiland," in *Markets in Africa*, eds. Paul Bohannan and George Dalton (Evanston, IL: Northwestern University Press, 1962), 532, 534.

115. Robert A. LeVine "The Gusii Family," in *The Family Estate in Africa*, eds. Robert F. Gray and P. H. Gulliver (London: Routledge and Kegan Paul, 1964), 69.

116. According to Kitching, the same was true for Central Province: "It seems that by the early 1950s most Kikuyu male household heads had managed to achieve a position in which their wives (and daughters) undertook the major part of the labour in cultivation but in which the male heads had virtually untrammeled power of disposal over the product of that labour power." Gavin Kitching, *Class and Economic Change in Kenya: The Making of an African Petite-Bourgeoisie* (New Haven, CT: Yale University Press, 1980), 124.

117. SK DAR 1938.

118. E. A. Beavon, "Among the Kisiis in the Heart of Africa," *Advent Review and Sabbath Herald* 107 (April 19, 1923), 12–13.

119. Nyaundi, *Seventh-day Adventism in Gusii*, 76, 126–127. Similar campaigns were waged across colonial Africa. Megan Vaughan, *Curing their Ills: Colonial Power and African Illness* (Stanford: Stanford University Press, 1991), 41–42.

120. Beavon, "Among the Kisiis," 13; Amayo, "History of Adventist Christian Education," 121; J. J. Strahle, "What I Saw and Heard in East Africa," *Advent Review and Sabbath Herald* 109 (Aug. 4, 1932), 10.

121. SK DAR 1932.

122. SK MIR Feb. 1936.

123. Philip Mayer, *The Lineage Principle in Gusii Society* (International African Institute, Memorandum 24, Oxford, 1949), 4. Luo men and women had undergone similar struggles beginning as early as 1915. Margaret Jean Hay, "Changes in Clothing and Struggles over Identity in Colonial Western Kenya," in *Fashioning Africa: Power and the Politics of Dress*, ed. Jean Allman (Bloomington: Indiana University Press, 2004).

124. SK DAR 1946. Indian tailors were also frequented by whites in the district. Jessie Olson, personal communication, Dec. 31, 2002. Indian tailors were also active in Central Kavirondo, as were African ones as early as 1926. Margaret Jean Hay, "Fashioning a Modern Identity in Colonial Western Kenya: Struggles over Clothing in the Interwar Period" (Discussion Papers in the African Humanities number 35 [2002], African Studies Center, Boston University), 17; idem, "Changes in Clothing and Struggles over Identity," 78.

125. SK DAR 1938.

126. SK DAR 1932.

127. Mboya, *Utawala na Maendeleo ya Local Government*, 4; SK DAR 1937.

128. SK DARs 1937, 1946; Lord Hailey, meeting in South Kavirondo with DC Lawrence and DO Winser, Oct. 23, 1947, PRO: CO 1018/25.

129. SN DARs 1956, 1957.

130. Moindi, "Peasants, Entrepreneurship, Capital Accumulation," 18.

131. Special Committee, SN ADC, July 21, 1958; SN Public Health Committee, SN ADC, June 15, 1958.

132. Anderson and Throup, "Africans and Agricultural Production."

133. Ronald D. Garst, "Innovation Diffusion among the Gusii of Kenya," *Economic Geography* 50 (1974), 300–312.

134. See meetings of the Kisii Coffee Board, June 23, 1945; Aug. 17, 1946; Jan. 17, 1948; and June 26, 1948, all in KNA: Agr 1/2/9/3; Nyaribari Annual Report, 1949, KNA:

DP 1/16; DA, SN QR Second Quarter, 1952, KNA: Agr 14/2/4; Chiefs' meeting, May 17, 1956, KNA: DP 1/21; DC SN to Chiefs, South Nyanza, May 8, 1957, KNA: Agr 1/1 II; Barnes, "Experiment in African Coffee Growing in Kenya," 170–171.

135. Barnes, "Experiment in African Coffee Growing in Kenya," 168–170.

136. It found a market as far away as Moshi, again for the brewing of beer, but this was exceptional. SK DAR 1937.

137. SK DAR 1954.

138. DA, SN QR, Fourth Quarter, 1954, KNA: Agr 14/2/4.

139. DA, SN QR, Fourth Quarter, 1954, KNA: Agr 14/2/4; SN ADC, May 10–11, 1955, KNA: Adm 7/15/5/3 III; Chiefs' meeting, May 12, 1955, KNA: DP 1/21

140. The area under *wimbi* also decreased precipitously in the early 1960s, from 40,000 hectares in 1961, to 10,000 hectares the next year, although production increased from the mid-1970s. Omosa, *Re-conceptualizing Food Security*, 90, Figures 4.1 and 4.2.

141. SK DAR 1946; P. Mayer, *Lineage Principle in Gusii Society*, 4.

142. DC SK, "Short Description of South Kavirondo District," in Hailey Papers, PRO: CO 1018/25.

143. Chris Minter, personal communication, May 28, 2004.

144. P. Mayer, *Lineage Principle in Gusii Society*, 4.

145. Sally Jemngetich Kosgei, "Commodity Production, Tea and Social Change in Kericho, Kenya, 1895–1963" (Ph.D. dissertation, Stanford University, 1981).

146. Maxon, *Going their Separate Ways*, 246; Ronald D. Garst, "Population, Migration, and Communication in Kisii District, Kenya" (National Geographic Society Research Reports, Vol. 16, 1975), 293–303.

147. Labour Department, Nyanza, Annual Reports 1948, 1949, KNA: Pub 4/2/5.

148. DC SK to PC Nyanza, Feb. 13, 1948, KNA: Lab 4/1/1; "Kazi yao ni nini?" MFM: 12.

149. DA SN, QR, Second Quarter, 1952, KNA: Agr 14/2/4.

150. "Bride Price," *Baraza*, June 3, 1944, clipping in KNA: MDS 2/3/5; "Report by the President of the Kisii Union (Mr. John Kebaso) on His Visit to the Kericho Tea Estates and to Murera (Coffee) Estate, Ruiru," [hereafter, Kebaso, "Report"], Nov. 1946, KNA: Adm 8/33; Minutes of Chiefs' meeting, Kisii, Nov. 20, 1946, KNA: Adm 12/7/2. Samuel Oyieke, the South Kavirondo African Civil Liaison Officer to Tea Estates, reported that juveniles could earn shs. 50 by working overtime, certainly a great exaggeration. SK LNC, Aug. 13–16, 1946. On Kericho pay rates in the 1920s, see Kosgei, "Commodity Production, Tea and Social Change," 66.

151. Kebaso, "Report," KNA: Adm 8/33.

152. Labour Department, Nyanza, Annual Report 1949, KNA: Pub 4/2/5.

153. Kosgei, "Commodity Production, Tea and Social Change," 66–67. These schools offered little. One teacher informed John Kebaso that the grower had no intention of setting up proper schools, for fear that the boys would learn too much and run off elsewhere to take up clerical work. Another school had no slates or exercise books. The growers paid for nothing but the teacher, even though child workers and their parents surely did not have extra cash to buy school supplies. Kebaso, "Report," KNA: Adm 8/33. The South Nyanza Labor Inspector for Kisii, one Mr. Agutu, assured the ADC that estate owners' welfare facilities for children, including schools, were satisfactory. Despite Agutu's words, the ADC was not convinced, and stated that juvenile labor "did interfere with their educational chances." SN ADC, Finances and General Purpose Committee, May 2–3, 1955, KNA: Adm 7/15/5/3 III.

154. Kebaso, "Report," KNA: Adm 8/33; Deputy Chief Secretary to Secretary, Tea Board of Kenya, May 1, 1952, KNA: Lab 3/2. See also Kipkoech Mosonik arap Korir, "The Tea Plantation Economy in Kericho District and Related Phenomena to circa 1960" (B.A. thesis, University of Nairobi, 1976).

155. See, for example, chiefs' meetings of Aug 11, and Nov. 7, 1949, and Aug. 3, 1950, all in KNA: DP 34/7.

156. Kosgei, "Commodity Production, Tea and Social Change," 63; M. D. McWilliam, "The Kenya Tea Industry," *The East African Economic Review* 6 (July 1959), 32–48.

157. Joint ADC, Nyanza, Sept. 6, 1950, KNA: Adm 15/7/13/1/2 II; Agenda 11 from PC, notes on items on agenda, Joint LNC, Sept. 6, 1950, KNA: Lab 2/1/4. For the debates over juvenile labor, see letters from Labour Officer to Labour Commissioner, Oct. 4, 1946, April 2, 1947, and July 8, 1948, all in KNA: Lab 2/1/9; Minutes of Chiefs' Meetings, Kisii, Nov. 20, 1946, Nov. 17, 1949, and Aug. 3, 1950, all in KNA: Adm 12/7/2; Secretary, Labour Department, to PC Nyanza, April 3, 1951, KNA: Lab 2/1/4; SN ADC, Feb. 15–16, 1955, KNA: Adm 7/15/5/3 III; "Kuandika watoto wadogo kazi," *Sauti ya Bomani*, Nov.–Dec. 1949, 3–4; "Kuandika watoto kazi," *Sauti ya Bomani*, Feb. 1950, 3–4, both in RH: MSS Afr. s. 1488 Winser, box 1, file 1.

158. P. Mayer, quoted in Lucy Mair, *African Marriage and Social Change* (London: Cass, 1969), 52. See also Arthur Phillips, *Report on Native Tribunals* (Nairobi: Colony and Protectorate of Kenya, 1944), 294.

159. SK DAR 1921; Nyabururu Diary, entry for May 29, 1926, MH: Kisii Diaries; Ag. DC SK to PC Nyanza, May 31, 1926, KNA: PC/NZA 3/28/4/1; SK DAR 1929; SK LNC meeting Dec. 4, 1934; SK Safari Diary, Aug. 1935, KNA: Adm 12/4/1. See also NK LNC Resolution 5/1931, KNA: MDS 2/3/5; on Kuria bridewealth, DC SK to PC Nyanza, July 2, 1936, KNA: MDS 2/3/3.

160. SC Nyanza to CNC, Sept. 6, 1927, and Ag. DC, note on LNC Resolution 2/27, ca. 1927, both in KNA: PC/NZA 3/28/4/1; NK LNC Resolution 5/1931, KNA: MDS 2/3/5.

161. Address to LNC at Marenga, Provincial Diary, Feb. 1927, KNA: PC/NZA 3/26/4/3; Claire C. Robertson, *Trouble Showed the Way: Women, Men, and Trade in the Nairobi Area, 1890–1990* (Bloomington: Indiana University Press, 1997), 197–198.

162. Provincial Diary, at North Mugirango, June 1927, KNA: PC/NZA 3/26/4/3; PC's note in margin of DC SK to PC Nyanza, May 31, 1926, KNA: PC/NZA 3/28/4/1. The Nyanza Provincial Council (made up of representatives of LNCs across the province) requested the limitation of bridewealth in 1936. The PC said he would inquire of PC Central if there was a similar desire there, and if so legislation would be introduced. There is no evidence that this ever came to fruition. Provincial Native Council, Sept. 9–10, 1936, KNA: Adm 7/13/1/2.

163. For a more detailed examination of bridewealth levels and limits, see Shadle, "'Girl Cases,'" chap. 5.

164. P. Mayer, *Two Studies in Applied Anthropology*, 23.

165. DC SK to SC Nyanza, May 31, 1926, KNA: PC/NZA 3/28/4/1.

166. Note by DC on SK LNC resolution 6/27, c. 1927, KNA: PC/NZA 3/28/4/1.

167. SK Safari Diary, Aug. 1935, KNA: Adm 12/4/1. On similar attitudes in Kuria, see Kjerland, "Cattle Breed, Shillings Don't," 91. A headman in North Mugirango was in 1930 coming into conflict with his subjects over attempts to keep bridewealth low, although we know nothing more than this. NPIR June 1930.

168. Philip Mayer, *Gusii Bridewealth Law and Custom* (Rhodes-Livingstone Papers, 8 (Oxford, 1950) 16.

169. Nyabururu Diary, entry for May 29, 1926, MH: Kisii Diaries; "Codification of some Kisii Customs," March 27, 1928, KNA: PC/NZA 3/17/12/2. Later, the DC admitted that the use of fines in such cases "would never for a moment be considered" by the administration. DC SK to PC Nyanza, Sept. 30, 1926, KNA: PC/NZA 3/28/4/1. The next year at a North Mugirango *baraza* the PC reaffirmed that bridewealth could not be fixed by law, but suggested that lowering the age of marriage for girls to sixteen might alleviate the problem. Provincial Diary, June 1927, KNA: PC/NZA 3/26/4/3. One administrator tried a more informal method. At a *baraza* in Buregi (Kuria), he was told that many girls remained

unmarried, and he surmised the cause being "that the old men are hoping for a better price." He later related that he had told the crowd that he "expected to see them all married next safari. Pure bluff of course but I expect it will work." If it did, we do not know. Safari Diary, Aug. 1928, Buregi, KNA: PC/NZA 3/26/4/4.

170. SK Safari Diary, Oct.–Nov. 1931, KNA: Adm 12/4/1.

171. SK LNC Aug. 13, 1931, Adm 7/1/6/3. Chief Onsongo recommended this again at a *baraza* with the DC. Safari Diary, Oct.–Nov. 1931, *baraza* in Kitutu, KNA: Adm 10/4/1.

172. Safari Diary, July–Aug. 1931, KNA: Adm 12/4/1.

173. Nyabururu Diary, entry for Aug. 29, 1926; PC Nyanza to DCs Nyanza, Oct. 2, 1926, KNA: PC/NZA 3/28/4/1; SK LNC, Dec. 4, 1934; Provincial Native Council, Oct. 1, 1935, KNA: Adm 7/13/1/2.

174. In 1952 the ADC, concerned by the reluctance of grooms to charge avaricious fathers-in-law in the courts, urged that chiefs or sub-headmen should file the charges; there is no evidence that this plan was ever taken up seriously by the government. SN ADC, Nov. 11–13, 1952, KNA: Adm 7/15/5/3.

175. They admitted, however, nothing prevented fathers from encouraging daughters to desert their husbands and profiting from the marriage. The PC said that under the Christian Marriage Ordinance this would not be possible, but since there were no Christian SDA women this did not come into play. See extracts of letters from Beavon dated Aug. 27, Sept. 7, and Sept. 17, 1926, all in DC SK to SC Nyanza, Sept. 30, 1926; SC Nyanza to DC SK, Sept. 2, 1926 [mistakenly dated 1925], all in KNA: PC/NZA 3/28/4/1.

176. Ag. PC Nyanza to CS, Dec. 29, 1931, KNA: Adm 7/1/6/3; SK Safari Diary, Feb. 1928, KNA: PC/NZA 3/26/4/4; SK LNC, Aug. 13, 1931; P. Mayer, *Two Studies in Applied Anthropology*, 30.

177. Gavaghan, *Of Lions and Dungbeetles*, 60.

178. Safari Diary, Dec. 1935, Adm 12/4/1.

179. In the documents used for the following discussion, it is never clear what crimes were being committed. At times elders and the DC seem to be speaking of elopement, at other times something closer to abduction or rape. Much of this confusion can be attributed to the tendency to place women in passive roles (common in adultery cases as well) even when they willingly left with new men.

180. DC SK to PC Nyanza, March 16, 1937, KNA: MAA 10/43.

181. AG to DC SK, June 7, 1937, KNA: MAA 10/43.

182. The South Kavirondo LNC was not alone in Kenya in their desire to guard women more closely. In 1932 Father Brandsma, rather uncharacteristically for a missionary, urged the state to require passes for women, given the number of couples who eloped "with disastrous results for the [Luo] tribe" Brandsma to PC Nyanza, July 26, 1932, KNA: MDS 2/3/4. The DC in North Kavirondo in 1941 also spoke out in favor of pass laws. DC NK to PC Nyanza, Jan. 7, 1941, KNA: MDS 2/3/4. The South Kavirondo LNC again in 1947 called for passes for women to prevent them running off with men. This time, the request was met by the DC's curt reply that passes "were retrograde. The matter was dropped." SK LNC Feb. 25–27, 1947. But compare this to the Meru LNC's successful 1947 resolution to implement pass laws to control women leaving the district. Lynn M. Thomas, "Regulating Reproduction: State Interventions into Fertility and Sexuality in Rural Kenya, c. 1920–70," (Ph.D. dissertation, University of Michigan, 1997), 136. On pass laws for women elsewhere in Africa, see Elizabeth Schmidt, *Peasants, Traders and Wives: Shona Women in the History of Zimbabwe, 1870–1939* (Portsmouth, NH: Heinemann, 1992), 119–121, 163–165; Julia Wells, "Passes and Bypasses: Freedom of Movement for African Women under the Urban Areas Act of South Africa," in *African Women and the Law: Historical Perspectives*, eds. Margaret Jean Hay and Marcia Wright (Boston University Papers on Africa, VII, 1982).

183. LNC meetings June 24–25 and Sept. 21, 1937. From the early 1920s all African men had been required to carry a *kipande*, a small metal cylinder containing personal information and, most importantly, the place of employment or the signature of the employer releasing him from his contract. This policy was created to ensure that those deserting labor contracts could be traced and punished. See R. M. A. Van Zwanenberg, *Colonial Capitalism and Labour in Kenya, 1919–1939* (Nairobi: East African Literature Bureau, 1975).

184. "War—Aspects and Reactions 1939," SK PRB, 1930–1940.

185. P. Mayer, *Two Studies in Applied Anthropology*, 24. In his own report Hunter writes that the oath merely involved elders tossing grass in a hole, with the meaning that he who broke the oath would go into his grave just as the grass fell into the ground. SK MIR, Nov. 1937. Juma Nyokang recalls that elders poured milk into termite holes, swearing that those who demanded or offered more than three head would die. Juma Nyokangi, June 11, 2002. Robert Maxon has suggested to me that Hunter also warned that should the disturbances continue the Gusii might face a punitive expedition along the lines of those of three decades before.

186. SK DAR 1937; "War—Aspects and Reactions 1939," SK PRB, 1930–1940; SK MIR, Dec. 1938. A few years later, as district commissioner in Central Kavirondo, Hunter held another *baraza* to order that no woman should be "dragged." Owen, "Notes on the case of ["O"], in Owen to Hunter, DC CK, July 11, 1940, CMS: ACC 83 O 16.

187. SK LNC, 22 Feb. 1938.

188. "War—Aspects and Reactions, 1930–40," SK PRB.

189. P. Mayer, *Two Studies in Applied Anthropology*, 22.

190. Quoted in Håkansson, *Bridewealth, Women and Land*, 87.

191. P. Mayer, *Two Studies in Applied Anthropology*, 22. Similarly, ex-*askari*s with new-found wealth in parts of North Kavirondo helped push up the bridewealth to very high levels in the 1940s. Kenda Beatrice Mutongi, "Generations of Grief and Grievances: A History of Widows and Widowhood in Maragoli, Western Kenya, 1900 to the Present" (Ph.D. dissertation, University of Virginia, 1996), 107–108, 119–123. The story was the same for Central Kavirondo, as T. A. Watts later reported. Writing in 1955, he explained that there had been no call for bridewealth limits "since the immediate post-war rush of discharged soldiers for brides which raised their costs rather excessively." DC CN to DC SN, June 27, 1955, KNA: MDS 2/3/4. It was at this time in Iteso that cash bridewealth was introduced by ex-*askari*s who wished to marry quickly, without even waiting to convert currency into cattle. Nobuhiro Nagashima, "Aspects of Change in Bridewealth among the Iteso of Kenya," in *Transformations of African Marriage*, eds. David Parkin and David Nyamwaya (Manchester: Manchester University Press for International African Institute, 1987).

192. Orvis, *Agrarian Question in Kenya*, 71.

193. Kitching, *Class and Economic Change*, 233–240.

194. On the trade from Tanganyika and Butende, see Ag. Provincial Veterinary Officer (PVO), Nyanza Province, Kericho, to Veterinary Officer, Maseno, and Livestock Officer, South Kavirondo, March 28, 1950, KNA: Vet 9/1/2; DC SN to PC Nyanza, Sept. 8, 1950, KNA: Vet 9/1/1; PVO, Nyanza, to Director of Veterinary Services (DVS), June 1, 1951, KNA: Vet 2/2; Map, c. 1952, showing flow of cattle through the province, in KNA: Vet 10/4/1. On cattle censuses, see DC SK to PC Nyanza, Jan. 4, 1946, KNA: Vet 2/4; *Sauti ya Bomani*, Aug. 1950, MFM: 4; DVS, Kenya, to DVS, Tanganyika, Oct. 10, 1950, KNA: Vet 9/1/1; PVO, Nyanza, to DVS, June 1, 1951, KNA: Vet 2/2; Asst. DVS, Nyanza, to DVS, April 23, 1957, KNA: Agr 1/1 II.

195. Provincial Native Courts Officer, Nyanza to DC SN, Aug. 1950, KNA: L&O 2/8; PVO, Nyanza, to DVS, June 1, 1951, KNA: Vet 2/2.

196. DA, SN QR, Second Quarter, 1952, KNA: Agr 14/2/4.

197. Håkansson, *Bridewealth, Women and Land*, 92.

198. R. LeVine notes the price of a cow at $42, and elsewhere he and B. LeVine estimate the exchange rate at $1 to shs. 7. Robert A. LeVine, "Omoriori: Smeller of Witches," *Natural History* 67 (March 1953), 145; LeVine and LeVine, *Nyansongo*, 72.

199. These estimates are based on pay rates and cattle prices listed above, and levels of bridewealth provided by P. Mayer and Håkansson. The 1952 figure is slightly skewed due to Kirera's briefly successful bridewealth limit. Some men who had already collected some cattle were able to marry, but those who had just begun this process were unable to take advantage of the temporary reduction.

200. In 1956–1957, goats ran at $5, or shs. 35 each. R. LeVine, "Omoriori," 145.

201. LeVine and LeVine, *Nyansongo*, 50.

202. Based on earning and cow price estimates in Eric A. Beavon, "A Sketch of Gospel Triumphs in Kisii," *Advent Review and Sabbath Herald* 103 (18 March 1926), 11–13, and SK Safari Diary, Feb. 1928, KNA: PC/NZA 3/26/4/4.

203. PC Nyanza to DCs Nyanza, Oct. 2, 1926, PC/NZA 3/28/4/1.

204. "South Kavirondo: Mahari," *Askari*, Sept. 27, 1944, KNA: MDS 2/3/3. Rumors of such a limit had reached *askari*s off at war already by January 1944. Conference of East African Governors to Secretariat, Nairobi, Jan. 27, 1944, KNA: MDS 2/3/3.

205. SK LNC, meetings of Nov. 1–2, 1944; March 7–8, July 30–31–Aug. 1, and Dec. 5–7, 1945. Around 1941, some young men of the district (it is not clear if they were of Luo, Gusii, or Kuria areas) were using physical violence to restrict the bridewealth level to ten head. SK LNC, Oct. 21–22, 1941.

206. P. Mayer, *Two Studies in Applied Anthropology*, 25; Jason Ouko to PC Nyanza, July 10, 1946, KNA: MDS 2/3/6. See also Håkannson, *Bridewealth, Women, and Land*, 90–94. When his estimates overlap with Mayer's, Håkansson's tend to be somewhat lower. He explains that his were averages, while Mayer's appear to have been medians. Personal communication, Sept. 19, 1999.

207. SN DARs 1948, 1949; Mayer, *Two Studies in Applied Anthropology*, 19–20; SN ADC, Nov. 11–13, 1952, KNA: Adm 7/15/5/3 I; "Mahari," *Sauti ya Bomani*, July 1949, RH: MSS Afr. s. 1488 Winser, box 1, file 1.

208. Nyaribari Annual Report, 1949, KNA: DP 1/16.

209. John Kebaso to DC SN, Nov. 14, 1949, KNA: DP 34/7.

210. Baraza at Manga, April 11, 1949, MFM: 13.

211. SN DAR 1950.

212. Håkansson, *Bridewealth, Women, and Land*, 94.

213. Nyakeyo Abuga, April 24, 1998; John Kombo, May 25, 1998; Ondieki Bosire, July 1–2, 1998; Minda Omwenga, July 3 and 5, 1998; Aguncha Maina, July 6 and 7, 1998; Kwamboka Oyugi, Aug. 12 and 13, 1998; Omongina Onduru, Aug. 14 1998.

214. Nyakeyo Abuga, April 24, 1998; Peter M. Nyarang'o, *Sunset in Africa* (Nairobi: East African Educational Publishers, 1994), 29.

215. Aguncha Maina, July 6–7, 1998.

216. Juma Nyokangi, June 11, 2002. Not all were made to return the excess bridewealth, however, but were only fined. Mzee Jackson, May 30, 2004.

217. Nyakina Kemunto Mainye, July 7, 1997; Ondieki Bosire, July 1 and 2, 1998; Minda Omwenga, July 3 and 5, 1998; Aguncha Maina, July 6 and 7, 1998; Kontinanto Onyango, July 1998; Kwamboka Oyugi, Aug. 12 and 13, 1998.

218. Mission Diary, Catholic Mission at Rangenyo, entry for Feb. 16, 1953, MH: Kisii Diaries; ADC meeting May 27–29, 1952, Adm 7/15/5/3 I. The DC supported a limit, at least in theory, but told the councilors he would have to discuss the legality of the limit with the PC.

219. Nyakina Kemunto Mainye, July 7, 1997; Ondieki Bosire, July 1–2, 1998; Kontinanto Onyango, July 1998; Kwamboka Oyugi, Aug. 12–13, 1998; Omongina Onduru,

Aug. 14, 1998; Jeremiah Kingoina Obegi, Oct. 1–2, 1998; Cathaline Kerubo Ochoki, Oct. 4–5, 1998.

220. Diary of the Catholic Mission at Rangenyo, entry for Feb. 16, 1953, MH: Kisii Diaries.

221. LeVine and LeVine, *Nyansongo*, 46–47.

222. Eugene Cotran, *Report on Customary Criminal Offenses in Kenya* (Nairobi: Government of Kenya, 1963), 15.

223. Quoted in P. Mayer, *Two Studies in Applied Anthropology*, 26.

224. John Kebaso to DC SN, Nov. 14, 1949, KNA: DP 34/7.

225. P. Mayer, *Two Studies in Applied Anthropology*, 26.

226. SK LNC, May, 5, 1939, KNA: ARC (MAA) 2/2/35.

227. SK LNC, Nov. 1–2, 1944; March 7–8, 1945; July 30–31, 1945; PC Nyanza to DC SK, July 7, 1945, KNA: MDS 2/3/3; Recommendations of DC Kericho and PC Nyanza on Kipsigis LNC Resolution 12/45, KNA: MDS 2/3/3. A meeting of chiefs in 1949 concurred. Chiefs' meeting, March 10, 1949, KNA: DP 34/7.

228. PC Nyanza to Samson Agare Othieno, Sept. 28, 1945, in PC Nyanza to CS, Sept. 28, 1945 KNA: MDS 2/3/3. See also PC Nyanza to DC SK, April 23, 1946, in the same file.

229. PC Nyanza to DC SK, April 23, 1946, KNA: MDS 2/3/3.

230. Notes for Baraza with Chiefs, Dec. 4, 1945, in DC SK to PC Nyanza, Jan. 8, 1946, KNA: Adm 12/4/3. This opinion was shared by LNCs in Central and North Kavirondo. NK LNC Minute 34/44, June 30 –July 1, 1944, and Minute 90/44, Nov. 22–24, 1944, in DC NK to PC Nyanza, March 12, 1945; CK LNC Minute 71/44, Aug. 1944, untitled document, all in KNA: MDS 2/3/3.

231. Minutes of Chiefs' meetings at Kisii, Nov. 17, 1949, and March 2, 1950, KNA: Adm 12/7/2; "Mahari," *Sauti ya Bomani*, July 1949, RH: MSS Afr. s. 1488 Winser, box 1, file 1.

232. Minutes, chiefs' meetings, Nov. 17, 1949, and March 2, 1950, KNA: Adm 12/7/2.

233. DC SN to PC Nyanza, July 9, 1952, KNA: Adm 7/3/3/4/15; SN ADC, Nov. 11–13, 1952; SN ADC, May 27–29, 1952, both in KNA: Adm 7/15/5/3; Native Courts Officer (NCO) to DC SN, Aug. 29, 1952; DC SN to NCO, Sept. 27, 1952; NCO to DC SN, Oct. 9, 1952; Provincial African Courts Officer to African Courts Officer, Oct. 6, 1952, all in KNA: MAA 10/43; SN ADC, Finance and General Purposes Committee, Nov. 1, 1954, KNA: Adm 7/15/5/3; DO Knowles, for DC SN, to PC Nyanza, Feb. 17, 1955, KNA: MDS 2/3/4. Requests that chiefs or headmen, rather than grooms, be empowered to file cases seem to have been ignored, and few men were deterred by the threat of legal action as by 1955 courts (for reasons unclear) imposed relatively small fines. SN ADC Nov. 11–12, 1953; DO Knowles, for DC SN, to PC Nyanza, Feb. 17, 1955, KNA: MDS 2/3/4.

4

The Course of Marriage Disputes

Gusii women had long claimed the right to reject unwanted suitors and husbands, although there was always a tension between men's and women's rights to make marriage. In the later 1800s, negotiations over these questions shaped individual marriages, but they did not threaten the institution of Gusii marriage. Only in the 1890s did the decimation of cattle herds bring Gusii marriage to the brink of collapse. As herds were restored, so too was the stability in marriage.

The tension over male and female rights in making marriage intensified, along with rising bridewealth, from the Second World War. Fathers and daughters, husbands and wives, brothers and sisters—all engaged in struggles over making marriage. Fathers hoped that their daughters would consent to arranged marriages as a matter of course. At the same time, fathers recognized that daughters might not be amenable to their appointed husbands and could desert them. A senior man in the 1940s described it this way to I. Mayer:

> A good daughter will accept the husband I have found for her. 'But father, is this a good man?' 'Yes my child, he is like other men.' 'Then I will go with him, or if I have to leave him I will come straight back to you, so that you can quickly marry me to another.' A bad daughter runs off just as she likes, she does not think of her father and brother.[1]

Depending on a whole host of factors, conflicts between fathers and "bad daughters" (or, seen from the other direction, daughters and "bad fathers") could vary from the trivial to the all-consuming. Men and women fought in silence, in words, in violence. Their battles took place within homesteads, in neighborhoods, across clan boundaries.

The more bridewealth, rose the more "bad daughters" and "bad fathers" there were. Fathers found it ever more difficult to come upon young men with enough cattle to offer as bridewealth. Simply in order to assure themselves of getting the cattle necessary to marry into the homestead of another woman—*nyaika*, replacement—some fathers forced their daughters into marriages with wealthy men. For women wealth did not necessarily equal desirability, and many deserted their would-be husbands. Not all returned directly to their fathers, however, fearful that they would be turned away or pushed into marrying another well-off but unwanted man. Other women eloped with lovers who lacked the cattle that could even begin to approximate proper bridewealth. Many a poor young man with no woman likely to elope with him resorted to abducting one, hoping forcibly to create a "marriage."

SEX, MARRIAGE, AND FEMALE CONSENT

Youth, Sexuality, and Marriage

Young people in Gusiiland enjoyed relative freedom in sexual matters. Though fathers were consumed by matters of marriage and bridewealth, they cared less about the sexual lives of their daughters. It was "considered heinous . . . for an uncircumcized girl to have sexual intercourse or to become pregnant," P. Mayer explains.[2] But unlike other parts of east Africa there was no Gusii "cult of virginity" for unmarried women.[3] Parents certainly knew that their children engaged in postinitiation, premarital sex, but by the rules of *nsoni* they would never inquire about nor acknowledge it.[4] So long as young people carried on their affairs quietly they would not be disturbed.[5] In the 1940s, some Gusii even praised girls' premarital sex, "because she will not be frightened when she marries" or "because it shows she has no *ekiona* (sexual abnormality preventing intercourse)."[6] Lost virginity did nothing to lower the bridewealth given for a woman.[7]

Premarital pregnancy would not ruin a girl, though it might limit her appeal as a wife. Apparently no abortifacients were known aside from "deliberate jumping and falling," though some elder woman professed to know ways to prevent the growth of the fetus until a girl was properly married.[8] Otherwise, if the lovers came from intermarrying clans a marriage would be set up with little fuss. Should the young man rebuff his pregnant lover another suitor could always be found—no woman, with or without child, went unmarried. One early colonial official claimed that a single mother could command only half the normal bridewealth and would likely be married to a polygamist, happy to see proof of her fertility.[9] Later informants suggested that some mild disdain might be had for an unwed mother. She would either end up in a polygamous homestead or the wife of a poorer youth willing to endure playful teasing by his seniors.[10] In the end, elders dismissed premarital pregnancy with the proverb, "The boy only opened the gate for the cattle."[11] A woman rebuffed by her child's father may have been less sanguine about her situation and her future.

Potential spouses had several ways of encountering each other. Friends' and relatives' marriages allowed young people to mingle with their opposites of other clans, as did women's *ribina* fertility dances.[12] Schools, churches, and markets provided new meeting places. More commonly, a bachelor assigned a friend to be his *esigani*, whose duty it was to locate a promising maiden. The *esigani* sweated up and down hills, along paths, looking in particular for young women out working in the fields. He would chat with members of the homestead, all the while surveying the beauty and industry of the girls. Having come across a girl suitable for his friend, the *esigani* would inquire of her character, and generally investigate the family: was there a history of mental illness? were there witches in the family?[13] The *esigani* then reported his findings to his friend.

Marriage and Consent

A suitor could not be sure his advances would be welcomed by the woman he desired. An interested man and his agemates would come to call on a woman's homestead, the meaning of their visit unspoken but understood. She would size him up, perhaps seeking advice from her friends who might be present. If she found him attractive and agreeable, she offered him *uji* (a thin porridge).[14] If she believed he would make a poor husband, she might spit in his direction and say, "Step aside, let me sweep where you have stepped,"[15] or tell him to "leave our front yard," her intentions unmistakable to all those present.[16]

Other ceremonies offered women opportunities to end a marriage. At the completion of the "honeymoon" period (*egechabero*), the first month or so of cohabitation, a woman returned to her natal home at which point she might refuse to continue the marriage.[17] The possibility of leaving a husband continued until *enyangi*. According to one woman, even if a wife had borne a child, but the *enyangi* ceremony had not yet been performed, "She can go away and back to her father, and no bad words! She is no ritinge [loose woman] if she does so."[18]

Enyangi made a woman a "full" wife and cemented her place in her homestead. After *enyangi* a wife (but not a husband) who committed adultery brought on *amasangia*, a mystical uncleanliness that could wreak havoc on the homestead. Should she leave her husband she would be considered *ritinge*.[19] *Ebetinge*, the anklets placed on women at the completion of the *enyangi* ceremony, displayed a woman's status as a wife and could not be removed without courting mystical retribution. Fathers lost whatever lingering rights they had over daughters, including the ability unilaterally to return the bridewealth and dissolve the union. At *enyangi* fathers instructed daughters to obey their husbands, and the *enyangi* priest told the bride to "go to [your husband] and not look back."[20]

Yet the *enyangi* ceremony also extended a woman the chance to call a halt to the proceedings and leave her husband. *Enyangi* priests in the

Figure 4.1. *Ebetinge*
Made of iron and sinew, *ebetinge* marked a woman as fully married. *Source:* Courtesy N. Thomas Håkansson.

1940s insisted that skipping any steps in the ceremony would "spoil the enyangi," and continuing would be "not only useless but dangerous."[21] P. Mayer sat in on several *enyangi* ceremonies in the 1940s, which appear not to have changed fundamentally over the previous generation or two.[22] Certain actors in the *enyangi*, most importantly the bride, practiced "privileged obstruction"—holding up of the ceremony. She delayed dressing in her ceremonial garb, took excessive time preparing herself, and again later refused her husband entrance into the home. "Then comes her most characteristic obstruction," Mayer writes, "repeated postponement of the first great moment of 'showing her love,'" handing the groom a calabash.[23] Based on her own interviews, I. Mayer explained that "Gusii say that the giving of the calabash signifies the bride's 'love' or consent. Without it there can be no enyangi."[24] Again the next day the bride would hold out for some time before taking a calabash shared by all at the ceremony—the "loving cup (*egesingero*)." While all these obstructions were expected, "the underlying tension is always a real one—so much so that the outcome of the struggle is not always beyond doubt."[25] Thus the excited exclamation of one bridegroom's friend, apparently to no one in particular, when the bride finally took the calabash: "And you said she did not love him!"[26] after which "a loud shout went up."[27]

Figure 4.2. Elder woman with *ebetinge*
Women no longer don *ebetinge* at marriage, and many older women removed them upon conversion to Christianity. This woman, in a photo from the 1980s, would have been one of the last women to carry on the custom. *Source:* Courtesy N. Thomas Håkansson.

THE NATURE OF MARRIAGE DISPUTES

In the later 1940s Philip and Iona Mayer collected marital histories in one Gusii community. Three examples illustrate how difficult it could be to live out the ideal of a peaceful, stable family life:[28]

By the mid-1940s, Kinyuri was an old man of some 80 years. He married in what must have been the 1890s, as he gave only one cow. This woman left him for a time, but eventually returned, and he succeeded in marrying two more women by 1931. When interviewed by the Mayers, he had fathered twelve children, of whom five were adult daughters. Two had been married properly, one for six and the other for twelve head of cattle. Two other daughters had each eloped, and each had later deserted for new men. The fifth daughter had also eloped. She had borne four children with her lover, but Kinyuri had yet to receive anything in the way of bridewealth.

At the time of the Mayers' research Gisemba was 42. His first wife had deserted her husband (who had performed *enyangi*) for calling her a witch. Once the bridewealth had been returned and the first marriage dissolved, Gisemba married her properly. She later deserted to her first husband, but Gisemba had her brought back (how he did so is not recorded). Gisemba married a second wife and performed *enyangi*, but she left him for another man. Twice he had her returned, twice she ran off. She eventually returned to Gisemba on her own. He married a third wife in 1945. She too deserted him, but her father took her back to Gisemba. Gisemba married off one daughter for twelve head of cattle, but she left her husband for another man and Gisemba returned the bridewealth. Three times he brought his daughter home from her lover, who had no cattle. She finally returned to Gisemba of her own volition, for although her lover had begun to collect cattle, he had opened up marriage negotiations for a different woman.

Another man, also named Gesimba, born around 1905, had taken in a widow in 1930 as there was no one to "inherit" her; he later gave bridewealth. Together they had three daughters, none of whom were in proper marriages. The first had been married but left her husband when he failed to provide sufficient bridewealth. The second daughter had also left her husband. The third had eloped, and Gesimba had yet to receive any cattle from her lover.

Forced Marriage and Runaway Wives

As Gesimba and the others could attest, a marriage dispute could play out in any number of ways depending on the character of the men and women involved. Some women quickly succeeded in breaking undesirable marriages. A minority of husbands had no patience for dealing with runaway women, preferring to wipe their hands of the whole affair. Especially in the early stages of the marriage it might have appeared that the woman would cause more trouble than she was worth. One man preferred simply to sue for his bridewealth after his wife ran off and "married somebody somewhere."[29] Another put it bluntly: his wife "left me to another man, therefore I want my cattle."[30] Some parents and "husbands" quickly resolved their disputes: "we both found," a father said of his former son-in-law, "that my daughter was of no use to him."[31] Moenga married his daughter to Oyugi, but she "refused him" and so Moenge "returned to [Oyugi] all of his cattle and all of his goats before the Etureti elders."[32]

Acquiescing to a woman's demands was not always without its complications. One man received eight head of cattle for his sister. She ran off, but rather than challenging her, her brother replaced her with another sister. When she too deserted the "husband," the brother refused to fight, instead admitting the necessity of returning the bridewealth. The conflict then became how many cattle had been exchanged over the course of the two marriages and how many had been returned, a debate the "husband" took to the *ritongo*.[33] Such cases would be especially common if the cattle had already been used. When his sister left her husband one man willingly refunded all the bridewealth except a bull calf (which he had sold in order to pay his poll tax) resulting in a court case.[34]

If tension had for decades existed between men and women over making marriage, high bridewealth forced them into increasingly heated battles. Fathers or brothers, desperate for bridewealth, often put women's wishes second to considerations of cattle.[35] When Moguche eloped, her father Onyiego laid a court case to claim her. Onyiego succeeded and married her off to Obare for eight head of cattle and, therefore, he "want[ed] her to stay [with Obare] even though she refuses."[36] Another father, Ogoro, explained how his daughter Moraa had eloped with Joel. When Ogoro traced his daughter, Joel offered him only one cow. Not surprisingly Ogoro instead accepted eight head of cattle from another man, Ondara. Ogoro later had cause to tell the *ritongo* that John had "offended Ondara by causing his wife to desert him."[37] One brother found it easy to ignore his sister's wishes: her chosen man could offer only seven head, while another man gave eighteen.[38]

Many parents inclined to reconcile themselves to a daughter's wishes did so only so long as matters of cattle could be resolved. Okongo initially seemed receptive to the wishes of his daughter, Nyamunsi. Okongo and his family had first gone to Nyang'au to negotiate a marriage, but when Nyamunsi heard of it she ran to Nyabinge. Not an inconsiderate father, Okongo proceeded to ask bridewealth of this young man. Unfortunately, the cattle were unacceptable. Her family again went to Nyang'au but, as a relative explained, took from him only three head "to see if this girl will accept his home." As it turned out, "she [did] not agree." She remained with her lover Nyabinge, and Nyang'au filed an adultery case against his rival. Still hoping to please his daughter, during a court recess Okongo and the *etureti* elders visited Nyabinge to assess his herd. He now had seven head, still too few, and moreover of these only three were satisfactory. Okongo would no longer consider his daughter's wishes, for matters of cattle had determined her fate. She would be returned to Nyang'au.[39]

Another father related a story similar to Okongo's. His daughter had been married in 1956, but after two or three years she had yet to bear a child. This was a complaint a father could appreciate. She left her husband, her father told the court, for a man she loved and with whom she bore children. If the new man would give bridewealth, her father said, he would accept the union and return bridewealth to the first husband. But her chosen man had no cattle. The woman's father saw no option but to send his daughter back to her husband.[40] Indeed, fathers of runaway women commonly decided against their daughters if the bridewealth had already been disposed of. One man sued his father-in-law for custody of his wife. The father-in-law admitted that he could offer no defense: "I've used all of his cattle."[41]

Once the bridewealth had been expended, not only parents and siblings, but friends also might also pressure a woman to accept an undesirable marriage. Bethsheba first met Oenga when he came to her home to begin marriage negotiations. Oenga was physically strong, which appealed to her; she served him *uji* to signal her approval. The families duly exchanged bridewealth and she was taken to her new home. When she arrived, however, she quickly began to have doubts. The terrain was covered in steep hills, which she disliked, but more importantly Oenga's first wife had little desire for a co-wife. She encouraged Bethsheba to hide in the storage area above her kitchen and run off early the next morning. Bethsheba readily agreed, and kept silent when Oenga searched for her. At last he found her, foiling their plan. Unwilling to admit defeat, Bethsheba later succeeded in running to her parents. They refused to break the marriage. Her parents and brothers sat down with her, patiently explaining that Oenga's bridewealth had already been used by a brother for his marriage. Bethsheba's agemates fell into two camps. One group urged her not to return to Oenga: if the homelife would be unsatisfactory, they said, why should she return? But in the other group was her new sister-in-law, the woman her brother had married with Oenga's cattle. The woman pointed out that she loved Bethsheba's brother, despite his physical disability (he was hunchbacked). If she could love him, she asked, why could Bethsheba not love Oenga? A point she certainly did not need to make was that should Bethsheba break the marriage Oenga would demand the return of his bridewealth, which would require Bethsheba's family to claim back the bridewealth already used by (and thus break the marriage of) her brother. The collapse of Bethsheba's marriage had consequences for many others. Bethsheba mulled over her limited options. She had no boyfriend to whom she could go, and so no other ready prospects for marriage. She ultimately returned to Oenga, and she and her co-wife settled down to what ended up being a long and peaceful life together.

Figure 4.3. Bethsheba Kemunto
Bethsheba Kemunto, like others of her generation, struggled to balance the rights of her family against her own in matters of selecting a husband.

Elopement

Couples who eloped gambled that they could draw an otherwise reluctant father into marriage negotiations. Eloped couples often stole off to the Kericho tea estates, but these were temporary moves: they always intended quickly to return and set up proper marriages. While women's families hardly endorsed elopement, neither did they always condemn such unions out of hand. Often, parents' first step was to trace the couple and assess the size of the young man's herd. If he could offer a reasonable bridewealth a father might acquiesce to a marriage.[42] As I. Mayer points out, elopement "ranked as 'normal' youthful behavior,"[43] and *ritongo* elders also thought elopement less serious than adultery and abduction. Two former elders stated that parents' first duty was to determine if the daughter had willingly gone with the man. If she had, bridewealth negotiations should be opened; if she had not, then a court case should be filed.[44]

Elopement did not always lead to marriage, of course. Some parents disliked their daughter's chosen man or his family, or had another potential groom in mind.[45] More often the decisive factor was the youth's lack of cattle. It was the relative poverty of young men and their inability to follow normal marriage procedures that gave impetus to so many elopements. Indeed, this was one of the commonest results of excessively high bridewealth rates.

Given the circumstances it is understandable why elopement would so vex fathers. There was "nothing more heartily detested by fathers as a class," P. Mayer observed:

> The man who is forced to let his daughter go for a few cattle and a promise of more will bitterly quote the proverbial phrase 'A debt (*esira*) takes the girl'; that is, 'In return for my daughter I have got a mere promise.'[46]

When parents ascertained that a daughter's chosen mate owned few cattle, their reactions can be imagined. Some proved unwilling or unable to overcome the apparently unbreakable will of the daughter.[47] Such fathers had few attractive options. They might waive part of the bridewealth, grudgingly accepting as little as two-thirds of the going rate. Others made public declarations that the few cattle exchanged had not fulfilled the bridewealth contract, and that a certain number more remained outstanding.[48]

For a father to accept his daughter's elopement was more the exception than the rule. Having hunted down an eloped daughter, a father (often with other male relatives) dragged her home, and very many employed violence.[49] Ochora Ogoro, while employed by white missionaries but entirely without cattle, eloped with several women over the course of his long bachelorhood. On each occasion, relatives came with young men to drag home the wayward woman, beating her as they went.[50]

Parents also forced eloped daughters into marriages with more well-off men. A woman might then surrender, settling down with the new man: perhaps a real marriage with an undesirable man was in the long run preferable to an informal union with a more desirable mate.[51] Despite the requirement that during *enyangi* the bride assent to her marriage, certainly some were intimidated into keeping their objections to themselves. Once *enyangi* had been completed leaving a husband was an even more daunting prospect. Such was the case with Bethsheba after her marriage to Oenga. Leaving him after *enyangi* was no longer an option, she believed, because of the mystical sanctions that came with removing *ebetinge*. Similarly, Yunesi Kemuma ran away from her polygamist husband only two days into their marriage. Her parents and siblings convinced her to return since the bridewealth had already been used for a brother's marriage. Taking no chances, her husband suggested that *enyangi* immediately be performed to prevent any further resistance. He paid another cow and two goats, *ebetinge* were attached, and she never ran away again.[52]

Their unions having been cleaved, some women wept bitterly and surrendered to apparently irresistible parental wishes. But not all did so, instead shaking off bruises and returning to their chosen mates. The case of Prisilla and Juma is among the most wrenching of such stories.[53]

Juma and Prisilla met at a market in Majoge in 1952. She came to love him, and after a month she agreed to elope. She based her fateful decision on the certainty that her parents would have rejected Juma, for he had no cattle. Her parents reacted as expected. They instead struck a bargain with Osano,[54] a well-off subchief. Prisilla's parents set off to Juma's home with *askari*s lent them by Osano. Outnumbered, Juma could do nothing but stand to the side and quietly watch his would-be wife caned and dragged off by representatives of the state, operating far outside the boundaries of the law though they were. Yet Prisilla and Juma were a deeply committed couple—we loved one another, he explains—and she later escaped and returned to him. Again she was violently dragged off; again she returned. Escape and recapture: the cycle continued over several years, eventually producing three children. Prisilla's family availed themselves of *Ritongo* Kuja, but the case was dismissed.[55] At one point Osano came to her home to collect Prisilla who (still surprisingly energetic fifty years later) swung a *panga* (machete) at him, cutting his hand raised in defense. But Juma was the one who gave in, admitting the futility of continuing their fight. Prisilla surrendered to her fate. She finally married Osano and stayed with him until his death in 1975.

Nyaabe too suffered bitterly so that she might stay with her lover. She related her travails in his 1959 elopement case:

> [O]ne week [after I eloped] my brother brought government[56] and took me away from the home of the accused. That was when my older brother came and told me that I should go to live with him until he is given cattle.
>
> When I was at our home they went to see cattle near Nyaramba in order to marry me off by force. I then ran away and I went to the accused. Those brothers of mine came [to the accused] and were given 11 cows.

Insufficient, Nyaabe's brothers said. Her would-be husband promised he would deliver more cattle after harvest. All seemed well, but when Nyaabe returned to help her mother harvest maize her brothers dragged her off to another "husband." Another bridewealth dispute ensued with this man, and Nyaabe's brothers soon retrieved her.

> When we arrived home [my brother] tied me up with rope and beat me so much. After two days he told me he wanted to take me to Utende [south of Gusiiland]. We went and when we arrived at Raneni I ran off and hid . . . and I went to the accused where I am living up to today.[57]

Unfortunately, we do not know who emerged victorious, Nyaabe or her avaricious brothers.

Abduction

In the later 1800s, some men resorted to abduction to gain wives. This could well provoke a pitched battle between the clans, but if an abductor could hold his victim long enough his gamble might pay off. As disease decimated herds in the 1890s accumulating bridewealth became virtually impossible, and the number of abductions proliferated. As cattle numbers grew after 1900 and the chances of marriage became more realistic, the number of abductions fell to unremarkable numbers.[58]

Abductors ultimately had the same goal—marriage—as did men taking in runaway women. That they were expected to become wives was clear enough to abducted women: the accused man "kept me . . . 20 days as his wife" one woman said; "he had sex with me . . . as if he were my husband" (*alizini nami . . . kama bwanangu*) explained another.[59] Abductors' tools were violence and rape. They almost universally threatened or used physical assault. They used punches, kicks, clubs, knives. One woman was beaten so cruelly that she vomited blood.[60]

While brutality might be enough to break a woman's spirit, abductors raped their victims as well. What abductors sought to do, quite simply, was to impregnate their victims.[61] A girl's chance of marriage was not ruined by premarital pregnancy, but it was impaired. Some women impregnated by an abductor might be branded, unjustly, *ritinge*.[62] One might also wonder how a husband would treat his new bride's child, conceived by rape by another man. Should an abductee become pregnant she saw few options. Most in fact resigned themselves to the unions. As one woman put it, after having been kept for three months by her captor, "Now I am pregnant and do not know what to do." Later, in a still more desperate position, she admitted that she would "agree to be married to [her abductor] but he has no cattle to pay."[63]

Nyabonyi also succumbed once impregnated by her abductor, Ndonyo. When word reached him of his daughter's abduction, Ochwati searched desperately for them. He asked his chief for an *askari* and expended over shs. 300 tracing her, but to no avail. His case at *Ritongo* Kuja was dismissed since Ndonyo could not be found. In the meantime, Ndonyo raped and impregnated Nyabonyi, and she gave up her resistance to the union. It was only some four years later, after he beat and killed their child, that she laid an abduction charge against him.[64]

If it appeared that a marriage might come to be, an abductor's father conveyed a message to the woman's family: I've stolen (*naibire*) from your home—come see what I've stolen.[65] If she had become pregnant, her father might reluctantly accept whatever bridewealth he could get. Some fathers even negotiated bridewealth with abductors despite their daughters having escaped pregnancy;[66] more than once this provoked victims to hang themselves.[67] That some women and their families eventually acquiesced to marriage, and that other Gusii then treated them as legitimate marriages, was what made abduction a realistic option for the most desperate of men.

Abductors generally struck along paths that crisscrossed the hills of Gusiiland. Interclan dance competitions (which arose in the later 1930s or early 1940s) attracted many young men and women. While young people chatted and flirted and identified potential lovers or spouses, abductors identified potential victims.[68] The most beautiful and the best dancers were at heightened risk as they left for their homes. Other abductors quietly lingered near a woman's home timing her daily schedule to determine when best to strike, such as when she fetched water. Trips to relatives and to grinding mills could prove dangerous, as it did for Nyangeri who, returning home from a mill, was abducted, beaten and threatened with murder.[69] Market days could be the most perilous for young women. At times, they did not dare attend market without an escort of strong male relatives.[70]

Rael Kemuma Kururia discovered the dangers of market days. She fell victim to an abductor around 1953 when in her early teens. While at the market she met some young men with whom she had previously chatted. One, Ondieki,[71] had fancied her, but she had rebuffed his advances as she did again this day. As she followed the path home with a girlfriend, Ondieki with two young men pounced on her from the bush. (Rael's friend was from a clan that did not intermarry with the boys' hence abducting her was out of the question; they slapped her and sent her running.) Rael resisted desperately. She grasped tree branches, but one of the men pried apart her fingers and beat her. Thankfully, they neared an area from where her brother had married. She called out to her relatives, "Ooi! Ooi! I'm being abducted!" Rescuers rushed onto the path brandishing *panga*s and *rungu*s (clubs) and Ondieki and his fellows ran for their lives.[72]

Once at the abductor's safe haven, escape proved a formidable task. Abductors rarely withdrew to their own homes where rescuers would be sure to

Figure 4.4. Rael Kemuma Kururia
When in her teens, Rael Kemuma Kururia successfully fended off would-be abductors and charged them before the *ritongo*.

look. Instead, most sought shelter with friends or relatives.[73] Like couples in consensual relationships, many abductors stole off to the Kericho tea estates.[74] An abductor's hosts might help police their unwilling guest if they approved of his actions. Not all did so, fearing legal consequences.[75] Often, abducted women found themselves dragged from place to place as their captors sought to stay ahead of the law and enraged relatives. Nyambeki was grabbed by four men as she went home from church; she was kept for thirteen days at three different homesteads before being rescued.[76] Moraa was returning home from a visit to her sister's home when she was accosted by two men. She was taken to one of their homes, and then transferred to another's. That night, she was held down by three men and raped by a fourth, and the next day moved again from Wanjare location to Majoge. On her third day there she escaped, only to be intercepted by two friends of her would-be husband. Only after a week of captivity did she gain freedom, apparently after being rescued by her father and brother.[77]

The immediate reaction of abducted women was escape, and of their families, rescue. That most private of times, the trip to the latrine, could furnish an opening for women to escape.[78] The bravest exploited the smallest windows of opportunity, like Mary, who snuck from her captor's home, naked and bound, and ran for safety.[79] Upon learning of the crime, relatives of abducted women attempted to liberate them. Hearing that Sabaniah had abducted Moraa, her family immediately descended on his homestead. Sabaniah was not present (he had run to a relative's home) but Moraa's infuriated family found his young cousin, John. They pressed him for information, of which he had none, and subjected him to a sound thrashing.[80] Similarly, in the early 1940s one man abducted a woman and stole off to Kericho. Her relatives set upon his homestead, assaulting his family and demolishing many of their belongings.[81] But tracing an abducted woman could be both difficult and dangerous: some abductors fought off relatives of their would-be wives, in one case allegedly swinging *panga*s at the rescuers.[82]

State Representatives and Marriage Disputes

The power of chiefs, headmen, and other "indirect rulers" could prove essential to men hunting down "their" women. This was one of the most important differences between colonial and precolonial marriage disputes. With no overarching authority in the precolonial highlands, fathers and husbands had little chance of tracking down a woman who had run to an enemy clan. Now, with the *pax Britannia*, men could travel between clans in relative safety and draw on representatives of the state for assistance.

Administrators encouraged litigants to avail themselves of *etureti* (councils of elders) before going to the *ritongo*. The status of the *etureti* was, at best, contradictory. The administration saw in the *etureti* a resuscitation of "indigenous authorities," although Gusii recall *etureti* councils as strictly a colonial-era invention. People continued to seek the guidance of their "home elders," *abanyamaiga*, which predated colonial rule and which included all the elders of the lineage. *Etureti* elders, in contrast, were few, elected and/or appointed by headmen, and served over large geographically-bounded areas rather than lineages. Administrators insisted that *etureti* could accept only as much food and drink as they could consume on the spot, but also admitted the elders regularly took larger gifts and bribes. *Etureti* were empowered to arbitrate only, but many imposed fines and, one administrator complained, tended toward "overstepping the bounds and degenerating in places into an unofficial courts system."[83] Particularly in civil cases *ritongo* elders encouraged, even required the parties first to bring their disputes to the *etureti*, yet in very few cases did they call *etureti* elders to give evidence of their deliberations. It appears that, for a time, many Gusii did make use of the *etureti* for a variety of disputes, if only as a preliminary step toward their real destination, the *ritongo*.[84] The efficacy of the *etureti*, however, depended on the willingness of the disputants to attend the councils and abide by their decisions, for the elders had no powers of compulsion. By the later 1950s the administration admitted that the experiment of "resuscitating" *etureti* had failed.[85]

Chiefs also held regular *baraza*s to issue orders and hear minor disputes, including marriage disputes and subsequent bridewealth and child custody cases.[86] One such case involved a former chief's clerk. He had come upon a woman who claimed to be disliked by her co-wives. She had been very ill at her husband's home, she told him; the likely implication was that she had been bewitched. The clerk agreed to take her in, then "reported it to chief, so she became my wife ever since."[87]

As helpful as *etureti* and *baraza*s might be as arenas for mediation, chiefs' and headmen's authority was always backed by the very real threat of physical force. These government servants had *askari*s at the ready, to be dispatched for any number of purposes, strictly legal or not. Sanduki explained how he had met up with Omare, who "wanted to deny [that he was living with my married daughter], but I grabbed him and he told me [the truth]. I got [my son-in-law] and informed him that we must go to [Sub-Headman] Andrea [who] gave us his *askari* and we went with him and found my daughter with [Omare]."[88] Another man went to Chief Ooga to complain about his runaway wife. Ooga sent the aggrieved husband with a letter to his subheadman, where he was given an *askari* to go and arrest his wife's lover.[89]

Ritongo elders typically demanded that before coming to court fathers and husbands had made good-faith efforts to recover their eloped daughters and runaway wives. Oyaro's 1963 case against his wife's alleged lover failed for precisely this reason. "We the court," the elders pronounced in disgust,

> see that the complainant, when he discovered that his wife had been stolen, did not do a single thing, nor did he himself charge [the accused] before the sub-chief nor the chief. He just came running here. Therefore this complainant has no case.[90]

If the man himself had not even gone to his opponent's home, making a criminal charge was futile. Masese inquired of his accuser: how did you know that I had your wife?

> A: I knew she was with you because I found her at your home.
> Q: You found her at my home?
> A: I did not see her with my own eyes, although I know that my wife was there at your home.
> Q: Did you bring an Etureti elder to take hold of her?
> A: I was unable to bring an Etureti elder because I had filed a case here in court.

Masese's line of inquiry quickly produced a not guilty verdict.[91]

Elders required such evidence even at risk of complainants' lives. Kosnel found his wife living with another man and reported it to the subchief, who told him and his party to go the next day to claim the woman. "But on our return from s/chief," a shaken Kosnel explained, the accused man "and his relatives way laid us on the way and wanted to fight us. This scared us from returning to the s/chief as appointed." Without evidence from the subchief or other witnesses, the *ritongo* elders determined the accused had no case to answer and acquitted him.[92]

As in cases of runaway women, men came to state representatives for assistance in rescuing abducted women. Subchiefs or headmen would be called on for help; they would either go themselves or lend their *askari*s to her deliverers. One mother called on a subheadman when tracing her daughter. With several *askari*s she went to the abductor's house (in order to rescue the girl and inform the man he would be wanted at the *ritongo*), but he managed to drive them off. The *askari*s reported this to the *ritongo*, and a letter was despatched to Chief Hezron. Now reinforced by the chief's *askari*s, the band returned and found only the woman—her abductor had fled. The *askari* liberated the woman as well as twelve head of cattle from the offender's homestead.[93]

Upon escape or rescue, women took their abductors before either the *etureti* or the *ritongo*. After her relatives saved her, Rael Kemuma went to her *etureti* elders to lay charges where the three men were each (illegally) assessed fines of shs. 300. They refused to pay, however, and Rael proceeded with her brother to *Ritongo* Manga. All three ran off to Sotik, where court *askari*s managed to serve summons on two. They both pleaded guilty and were fined shs. 400 each. The third man had gone into hiding at Kericho, and now willingly sent Rael the shs. 300 as assessed by the *etureti*. Similarly, a 1946 *Ritongo* Kuja abduction case began when the accused abductor had ignored a compensation order levied by the *etureti*. The woman's father proceeded directly to the district commissioner who instructed the chief to bring the man and his accomplices to court. Unlike adultery and elopement cases *ritongo* elders thought abduction

Figure 4.5. Rael Kemuma Kururia and Nyasani Omanua
Nyasani Omanua, former *ritongo* elder, convicted Rael's attackers.

a serious enough crime to allow victims to come straight to court rather than first going before the *etureti*.

EXPANSION IN MARRIAGE DISPUTES

If the number of marriage disputes began to attract administrative attention by the late 1930s, with Hunter's concern over the increasing number of "girl cases," they burst onto the scene across the colony during the war years. By early 1941, the Nyanza Provincial Native Council and the South Kavirondo Local Native Council took the time to point out that a man living with an *askari*'s wife should be punished.[94] Even so, a great many soldiers continued to express their apprehensions to their commanding officers, and a circular was sent instructing all provincial commissioners, district commissioners and chiefs take a greater interest in ensuring that *askari*s' wives did not roam about.[95] Nevertheless, the number of adultery cases (one administrator wrote) "multiplied" across Kenya due to the absence of so many men during the war.[96]

As marriage disputes became distressingly common, particularly in Gusiiland, African elites scrambled to restore husbands' and fathers' flagging control over women and junior men. Facing an increasing numbers of runaway wives, the South Kavirondo LNC in 1945 encouraged the tribunals to hand down harsher punishments in these cases. The court elders did so, but it did not get past the doubtful eye of the Attorney General who ended the practice.[97] Two years later the growing number of men leaving the district with married or unmarried women spurred the LNC again to request pass laws for women exiting the highlands, a plan rejected by the DC.[98]

Abduction too began to demand more attention. At a Provincial Native Council meeting in 1944, African elites from across Nyanza expressed some anxiety over the extent of abduction, although several maintained that many supposed abductions were only rituals played out between happy, properly wed couples. In any event, the councillors resolved that propaganda was the best means of teaching people the ways of *ustaarabu*, civilization. But within three years Gusii elders had become increasingly alarmed at what were truly forcible abductions, and, as with adultery, demanded harsher punishments for offenders.[99]

The number of Gusii marriage disputes continued apace through the 1940s and 1950s. In the 1940s, the Mayers reported on their rising numbers, including distressingly common instances of the "pulling" of girls. While acting chief of North Mugirango in 1949, Musa Nyandusi saw a deterioration in law and order, including the "dragging of girls during market days."[100] Elders complained unceasingly about these trends, and dreaded the possibility of their daughters eloping. Some men in Bassi location complained to P. Mayer that nowadays "Boys and girls marry themselves."[101] As many as half the women I. Mayer knew had at some point in their lives run off from a husband or father.[102]

In May 1953, members of the LNC spent a considerable amount of time discussing abduction "which was now prevalent in [the] Kisii Highlands." They again encouraged the African Courts to impose more severe punishments for abductors, if necessary transferring offenders to magistrates' courts for longer sentences of imprisonment or for corporal punishment.[103] The same year, the priest at Rangenyo mission recorded that bridewealth now outstripped the resources of many young men, "Hence this abduction craze."[104] Gusii members of the South Nyanza Law Panel in late 1955 inserted their voices to the growing chorus of alarm over the innumerable abductions striking the highlands.[105] The next year Musa told fellow chiefs that the large numbers of indecent assault on young girls "applied particularly to Kisii Highlands [and] that this was a longstanding complaint against Kisii."[106]

Records from Gusii courts substantiate contemporary accounts of the multiplying numbers of marriage disputes. Extant registers from South Kavirondo locational courts provide information for twenty-four of the thirty months between January 1, 1925 and June 30, 1927. During these months 1,001 criminal

Table 4.1. *Ritongo* Manga Marriage Cases, 1943–1962

Year	Months of register extant	Marriage cases	Total criminal cases	Marriage cases as percent of total cases
1943	2	35	161	22
1944	0.5	19	89	21
1955	2	43	213	20
1956	1.5	52	163	32
1957	3.25	80	372	22
1958	1	20	121	17
1960	1.75	32	183	17
1961	5	66	553	12
1962	8.5	147	935	6

Source: Ritongo Manga Criminal Court Registers.

cases were heard in South Kavirondo as a whole, 422 of these in Gusii courts. Of the 1,001 cases, 52 involved illicit sex, cohabiting with a married woman and rape; 25 of these came from Gusii courts. Thus during these twenty-four months, 6 percent of all Gusii criminal cases involved sexual or marital matters.[107] By 1938 these numbers had risen only slightly. Over a five-month period between July and December, Gusii courts heard 232 criminal cases, of which 17 (7.3 percent) concerned marriage. The next year between January and July, 28 of 373 Gusii criminal cases, or 7.5 percent, dealt with marriage disputes.[108]

Already by the early 1940s the number of marriage disputes in the courts had shot up dramatically. Extant registers of criminal cases from *Ritongo* Manga show that the percentage of adultery, elopement, and abduction cases was consistently three to four times greater than the 7 percent common in the late 1930s (Table 4.1). Another source covering *Ritongo* Manga and *Ritongo* Kuja over four months in 1952–1953 shows marriage disputes reaching 20, 30,

Table 4.2. *Ritongo* Manga and *Ritongo* Kuja Marriage Cases, Nov. 1952–Feb. 1953

Month, Year	Court	Marriage cases	Total criminal cases	Marriage cases as percent of total cases
Nov. 1952	Manga	15	68	22
	Kuja	24	67	34
Dec. 1952	Manga	7	32	21
	Kuja	16	37	42
Jan. 1953	Manga	6	28	21
	Kuja	11	23	47
Feb. 1953	Manga	2	22	9
	Kuja	9	15	33

Source: KNA: ARC (MAA) 2/9/3.

Table 4.3. *Ritongo* Gesima Marriage Cases, 1956–1959

Year	Total marriage cases found	Total criminal cases heard	Marriage cases as a percent of total cases
1956	161	751	25
1957	125	642	19
1958	146	714	29
1959	98	621	16

Source: Ritongo Gesima court files, SN DARs 1956–1959.

even 40 percent of all criminal cases (Table 4.2). Evidence for *Ritongo* Gesima reveals similar numbers (Table 4.3). Between 1943 and 1962, elopement, adultery, and abduction cases almost always accounted for at least 15 percent of all criminal cases, generally more than 20 percent, and at least once as high as 47 percent.

In absolute terms too the number criminal cases involving women filed in the interwar years paled next to those of postwar years. The total number of criminal cases coming before Gusii courts increased significantly over the decades from the 1930s; marital disputes constituted a larger percentage a larger number of cases. Based on the numbers available, in 1925 approximately one marital case came before the courts per month; in 1938 this number was three, and in 1939, four. By 1943 about seventeen cases per month were filed in *Ritongo* Manga alone, and in 1944, thirty-eight per month; if the numbers from *Ritongo* Kuja were available this number would undoubtedly be much higher.[109] By 1951–1952 the number of all these cases dropped slightly: in November 1951, there were thirty-nine cases in Manga and Kuja combined, and only eleven in February of the next year. But this must have been due to Kirera's bridewealth limit, which allowed many couples to marry and so reduced the numbers of elopements and abductions. As the limit collapsed the number of court cases climbed again. In 1956, *Ritongo* Gesima and *Ritongo* Manga combined for an average of about forty-seven cases per month, and *Ritongo* Kuja probably saw another ten or more. Moreover, many parties settled their disputes outside of the courts, hundreds of men filed civil claims over women, and many hundreds of women filed divorce cases. The number of criminal cases can only hint at the tremendous numbers of marriage disputes erupting in these years.

CONCLUSION

Bridewealth rose, as did cattle prices, while wages stagnated. Young men found it increasingly difficult to be married, and increasing numbers of women found themselves without desirable husbands, or without any husband whatsoever. Young people saw their best option to be creating illicit unions. Some young men believed that their only option was to force both a woman and her father to accept a union. Gusii tried every avenue to reestablish order, although the meaning of "order" was up to dispute. As other options were exhausted, men and women entered the courts to hash out their disputes, and to offer up their ideas about what made a proper marriage. It was in the *ritongo* that Gusii articulated their views of marriage; it is on the transcripts of the *ritongo* that their words have been preserved.

NOTES

1. Iona Mayer, "The Patriarchal Image: Routine Dissociation in Gusii Families," *African Studies* 34 (1975), 259–281, quote from 276.

2. Philip Mayer, "Gusii Initiation Ceremonies," *Journal of the Royal Anthropological Institute* 83 (1953), 9–36, quote from 26.

3. As was the case in central Kenya. Carolyn Martin Shaw, *Colonial Inscriptions: Race, Sex and Class in Kenya* (Minneapolis: University of Minneapolis Press, 1995). The loss of virginity was a major consideration in determining the return of bridewealth in collapsed Luo marriages, as demonstrated in the uncatalogued court cases from South Kavirondo/South Nyanza held in the Kenya National Archive, Nairobi.

4. Philip Mayer, *Two Studies in Applied Anthropology in Kenya* (London: Colonial Office, 1951), 67.

5. DC SK to PC Nyanza, July 15, 1920, KNA: KSI/32. See also Philip Mayer, *Gusii Bridewealth Law and Custom* (Rhodes-Livingston Papers, 18, Oxford, 1950), 12; Iona Mayer, "The Gusii of Western Kenya," in *Cultural Source Materials for Population Planning in East Africa, Vol. III: Beliefs and Practices,* ed. Angela Molnos (Nairobi: East African Publishing House, 1973), 131.

6. Iona Mayer, "Studies in Gusii Kinship" (Ph.D. dissertation, Rhodes University, 1965), 135, n. 1.

7. G. A. S. Northcote, "History of the District," SK DQR Dec. 31, 1909; Untitled document, ca. 1910, 387, KNA: Lib. 572.Ken 83–947; [Questionnaire on marriage, 1930], KNA: PC/NZA 19/27; DC SK to PC Nyanza, July 15, 1920, KNA: KSI/32. See also I. Mayer, "Gusii of Western Kenya," 129–130.

8. I. Mayer, "Gusii of Western Kenya," 123, 130; Robert A. LeVine and Barbara B. LeVine, *Nyansongo: A Gusii Community* (New York: Wiley, 1966), 114–115; Agostin Makworo, Aug. 5, 1997; N. Z. Moturi, "Pregnancy in Ntana," *Bulletin of the Cardinal Otunga Historical Society* 80 (May 1980), 14–18.

9. W. M. Logan, "History of the Wakisii or Abagusii," SK PRB.

10. "Pre-marital adventures," MFM: 17; I. Mayer, "Gusii of Western Kenya," 132.

11. I. Mayer, "Gusii of Western Kenya," 132.

12. Moanda, in Robert A. LeVine and Donald T. Campbell, *Gusii of Kenya* (New Haven, CT: Human Resource Area Files, 1972), 363.

13. Father Doyle, "Marriage," ca. 1930, COHS: MAA/KIS/GEN/1/6.

14. P. Mayer, *Gusii Bridewealth Law and Custom*, 50; Northcote, "The Kisii," SK DQR Dec. 31, 1909.

15. Josiah Mochama, Jeremiah Ogechi, Elemeleck Chaga, Thomas Choti, July 16, 1997.

16. P. Mayer, *Gusii Bridewealth Law and Custom*, 50.

17. P. Mayer, *Gusii Bridewealth Law and Custom*, 10, 50–51; "Enyangi," discussion with Justino and Oscar, MFM: 8.

18. This came during P. Mayer's interview with a man named Nyang'wara. They were discussing the rights and duties of a wife prior to *enyangi*, when "(Sudden interpolation by

Nyang'wara's junior wife, who has child but not Enyangi) . . ." "Enyangi of Nanyuki and Mwango, Part II," Dec. 1948, MFM: 8.

19. I. Mayer, "Studies in Gusii Kinship," 131.

20. I. Mayer, "Patriarchal Image," 277. As one father told his daughter at *enyangi*, "Obey him! If he beats you, go under the bed. Obey him! . . . You must obey him as your mother obeyed me." Ibid., 131.

21. Philip Mayer, "Privileged Obstruction of Marriage Rites Among the Gusii," *Africa* 20 (1950), 113–125, quote from 121.

22. P. Mayer, "Privileged Obstruction of Marriage Rites"; "Enyangi," MFM: 8.

23. P. Mayer, "Privileged Obstruction of Marriage Rites," 116; I. Mayer, "Studies in Gusii Kinship," 100.

24. I. Mayer, "Studies in Gusii Kinship," 100.

25. P. Mayer, "Privileged Obstruction of Marriage Rites," 119. While wealthy men might afford *enyangi* soon after the exchange of bridewealth, others waited many years before amassing the resources necessary for the ceremony. In the latter instance, the couple would have been together years, perhaps decades, becoming parents and grandparents. In these circumstances, it was very unlikely she would refuse *enyangi*; the rituals of consent might be more a formality than in the cases Mayer observed.

26. P. Mayer, "Privileged Obstruction of Marriage Rites," 116.

27. I. Mayer, "Studies in Gusii Kinship," 100. She here draws on the same example as does P. Mayer in "Privileged Obstruction of Marriage Rites."

28. These are summarized from MFM: 12.

29. RK bw 60/47.

30. RK bw 91/47.

31. RM cw 521/46.

32. RG ad 96/56. See also RG ad 305/61.

33. RM cattle 660/46. This case ended up in the courts when the brother returned only two of seven or eight he owed, and was sued for the remainder by his former brother-in-law.

34. RM cattle 504/46. For similar disputes over outstanding bridewealth, see RK cattle 183/47, 185/47; RM cattle 56/46, 504/46, 583/46, 641/46, 659/46, 738/46.

35. RG ad 277/56.

36. RG ad 313/56.

37. RG ad 29/60.

38. RK ad 998/59.

39. RG ad 326/56.

40. RK ad 927/59.

41. RM cw 737/46. The translation is the Mayers'. See also RK cw 22/47.

42. Bethsheba Kemunto, June 23, 1997; Nelson King'oina Nyang'era, July 19, 1997; Pliscah Kerubo, Sept. 22, 1997; Nyasani Omanua, Oct. 22, 1997; Paul Nyangoto Ogeturenga, Oct. 1997; Nyakango Obiero, Nov. 3, 1997; Juma Nyokangi, June 11, 2002.

43. I. Mayer, "Gusii of Western Kenya," 133.

44. Nyasani Omanua, Oct. 22, 1997; Paul Nyangoto Ogeturenga, Oct. 24, 1997.

45. Jepheth Ondieki, Sept. 23, 1997; Helen Kerubo, Nov. 17, 1997; Kiage Kiage, Feb. 1998.

46. P. Mayer, *Gusii Bridewealth Law and Custom*, 13.

47. Samwel Mose, June 27, 1997; Jepheth Ondieki, Sept. 23, 1997.

48. P. Mayer, *Gusii Bridewealth Law and Custom*, 12–13.

49. Helen Kerubo, Nov. 17, 1997; Pauline Marwa, Nov. 23, 1997; Juma Nyokangi, June 11, 2002.

50. Ochora Ogoro, July 4, 1997.

51. Ochora Ogoro, July 15, 1997.

52. Yunesi Kemuma, June 8, 2002.

53. Juma spoke openly about his history, and much of what follows is based on his information. "Prisilla" (pseudonym) confirmed much of the story, but was more reticent and did not wish to have her name used.

54. Pseudonym.

55. They may have mistakenly filed it as an abduction case. According to Juma, the elders judged him innocent because Prisilla went to him willingly. In an elopement case this would not have been grounds for acquittal.

56. She most likely refers to a chief's or subchief's *askari*.

57. RK rug 844/59. While many men used violence to push women into unwanted marriages, at least two women used violence to prevent forced marriage. As one woman told the court: " . . . I was sent to the home of the complainant by force, then I hit him in the head with a hoe because I do not want him, [not] even a little." RG ad 523/62. See also RG ad 387/58.

58. Tangurera Omwenga, Aug. 6, 1997; Jeremiah Kingoina Obegi, Oct. 1–2, 1998.

59. RG ia 662/62, 702/58. The verb the second woman used, *kuzini*, has a negative connotation—illicit or immoral sex.

60. RK ia 859/59.

61. Josiah Mochama, Jeremiah Ogechi, Elemeleck Chaga, and Thomas Choti, July 16, 1997; Samwel Mose, June 27, 1997; David Ongera and Erasto Nyambwere, Oct. 3, 1997; Alexina Nyatuka, April 21, 1998.

62. Josiah Mochama, Jeremiah Ogechi, Elemeleck Chaga, and Thomas Choti, July 16, 1997; Nathan Ongayo, May 25, 1998; Sabaniah Aroni Omayo and Maoga Onkundi, May 28, 2002. In only a few cases, fathers in abduction cases made a it point to charge that a daughter's virginity had been "ruined." SKAT rug 23/47, 190/48; RK rug 231/46. According to Robertson, in central Kenya after only one night with her abductor a girl would have gained a bad reputation and so would resign herself to stay with him. Claire C. Robertson, *Trouble Showed the Way: Women, Men, and Trade in the Nairobi Area, 1890–1990* (Bloomington: Indiana University Press, 1997), 208.

63. RK rug 520/47; SKAT 61/48.

64. RK ia 361/58.

65. Sabaniah Aroni Omayo and Maoga Onkundi, May 28, 2002.

66. Arigisendera Mosioma, Sept. 24, 1997.

67. Nyasani Omanua and Rael Kemuma Kururia, June 3, 2002.

68. Bethsheba Kemunto, June 23, 1997; Arigisendera Mosioma, Sept. 24, 1997; Lawrence Nyatigo, Sept. 25, 1997; Onkaga Maina, Sept. 28, 1997.

69. RK ia 88/63.

70. Nyasani Omanua and Rael Kemuma Kururia, June 3, 2002; Musa Nyandusi, Annual Report, Nyaribari Location, 1949, KNA: DP 1/61. This was true in Central Kavirondo as well. Archdeacon Owen to DC CK, Dec. 11, 1940, CMS: ACC 83 O 16.

71. Pseudonym.

72. Nyasani Omanua and Rael Kemuma Kururia, June 3, 2002.

73. Josiah Mochama, Jeremiah Ogechi, Elemeleck Chaga, and Thomas Choti, July 16, 1997; Nyakeo Abuga, Aug. 8, 1997; Jepheth Ondieki, Sept. 23, 1997; Tangurera Omwenga, Aug. 6, 1997; Onkaga Maina, Sept. 28, 1997; Mary Nyangau, Nov. 25, 1997.

74. Josiah Mochama, Jeremiah Ogechi, Elemeleck Chaga, and Thomas Choti, July 16, 1997; Pauline Moraa Mosoti, July 23, 1997; Samwel Mose, June 27, 1997; Ochora Ogoro, July 4, 1997; Lawrence Nyatigo, Sept. 25, 1997; Samwel Mokaya Sangaka, Sept. 26, 1997; David Ongera and Erasto Nyambwere, Oct. 3, 1997; Nathan Ongayo, May 25, 1998; Alexina Nyatuka, April 21, 1998. Others went to the lumbering areas near Molo. David Ongera, Oct. 3, 1997; Helen Kerubo, Nov. 17, 1997.

75. RG ia 514/61.

76. RK ia 845/59.

77. RK rug 204/46.
78. Sabaniah Aroni Omayo and Maoga Onkundi, May 28, 2002.
79. RG ia case 41/69.
80. Sabaniah Aroni Omayo and Maoga Onkundi, May 28, 2002.
81. Samwel Mokaya Sangaka, Sept. 26, 1997.
82. RK rug 111/48. See also RK assault 87/47.
83. SN DAR 1952. See also SN DARs 1950 and 1954; SN ADC Aug. 5–7, 1952.
84. Philip Mayer, *The Lineage Principle in Gusii Society* (International African Institute, Memorandum 24, Oxford, 1949), 18; SK DAR 1948; SN DARs 1950, 1954; Jepheth Ondieki, Sept. 23, 1997, Nyasani Omanua, Oct. 22, 1997.
85. SN DARs 1956, 1957.
86. RM cattle 127/46; RM child custody 27/46.
87. RM cwc 730/46. The translation is the Mayers'. See also RM cw 565/46.
88. RK ad 694/59. On the use of subheadmen, see also RK ad 694/59, 827/63, and of chiefs, RK ad 353/56, 387/56, 422/61; RK ad 353/56, 19/63. See also P. Mayer, *Lineage Principle in Gusii Society*, 18. In Central Kavirondo Archdeacon Owen reported numerous cases of sub-headmen, headmen, and chiefs' and tribunal *askaris* forcibly returning women to their husbands and fathers. See, for example, Owen, "Notes on the case of [T.], Nov. 6, 1940, CMS: ACC 83 O 16.
89. RM child custody 27/46. P. Mayer explained to Lucy Mair that Gusii men believed it futile to use force to control would-be runaways, but that it had become far easier to reclaim women with the assistance of court *askaris*. L. P. Mair, "African Marriage and Social Change," in *Survey of African Marriage and Family Life*, ed. Arthur Phillips (London: Oxford University Press for the International African Institute, 1953), 66.
90. RK ad 20/63. See also RK ad 1152/59; RG ad 591/61 93/62, 446/65.
91. RG ad 582/62.
92. RG ad 446/65. See also, for example, RK ad 919/56, 814/59, 998/59, 1156/59, 258/60, 837/62; RG ad 122/56, 552/57, 696/57, 360/58, 917/59, 270/61, 125/64, 188/64. In some cases, the woman had been seen bringing water or wood toward the accused's home, even working in his field, but the elders determined that this was insufficient evidence to prove she actually lived with him. See RK ad 503/63, 354/63, 474/63, 635/64; RG ad 653/59, 834/59, 54/65.
93. DOA rug 30/45.
94. Nyanza Provincial Native Council, Jan. 17–18, 1941, KNA: Adm 7/13/1/2; SK LNC, 12 Feb. 1941.
95. Some men tried to push illegitimate claims by taking advantage of their military commanders' ignorance of local conditions. One Gusii man complained to his officer that his wife had run off, and eventually demanded that his bridewealth be returned. As it turned out, the "wife" was a woman he had abducted and for whom he had paid no bridewealth. Secretariat to all PCs, DCs, June 3, 1943; DC SK to PC Nyanza, May 18, 1943; PC Nyanza to Officer Commanding, EAASC, Nairobi, May 25, 1943, all in KNA: Mil 17/1/2. In the same file, see also DC North Kavirondo to PC Nyanza, Feb. 11, 1944; PC Nyanza to Officer Commanding, Nairobi Depot, March 18, 1944; DC CK to Principal Information Officer, Oct. 4, 1944.
96. Arthur Phillips, *Report on Native Tribunals* (Nairobi: Colony and Protectorate of Kenya, 1944), 266.
97. SK LNC, July 30–31, 1945; DC SK to AG, Aug. 15, 1945, KNA: MAA 10/43. In heavily Christian Nyeri (Central Province) many marriage disputes were hashed out before church councils or (much to men's chagrin) aired publicly by women followers of the East African Revival. Derek R. Peterson, "Wordy Women: Gender Trouble and the Oral Politics of the East African Revival in Northern Gikuyuland," *Journal of African History* 42 (2001), 469–489.

98. SK LNC, Feb. 25–27, 1947.

99. Provincial Native Council, Aug. 30–Sept. 1, 1944, KNA: Adm 7/13/1/2; DC SK to Judicial Adviser, Jan. 13, 1947, KNA: MAA 10/43.

100. Musa Nyandusi, Annual Report, Nyaribari Location, 1949, KNA: DP 1/61.

101. "Enyangi," meeting with Bassi elders, MFM: 8.

102. I. Mayer, "Gusii of Western Kenya," 133; I. Mayer, "Patriarchal Image," 276–278. In "Nyansongo," the village in which Robert LeVine and Barbara LeVine lived in the 1950s, fourteen of the fifty-one married women had previously been married. These earlier marriages had all been completed by the payment of bridewealth, but on one account or another had collapsed. We can guess that many of these unions failed due to the refusal of women to stay in them. LeVine and LeVine, *Nyansongo*, 49–50.

103. SN ADC, May 12–14, 1953, KNA: Adm 7/15/5/3.

104. Mission Diary, Catholic Mission at Rangenyo, entry for Feb. 16, 1953, MH: Kisii Diaries. See also entry for Nov. 3, 1952.

105. Minutes of the SNLP (Kisii Section), Nov. 28–29, 1955, KNA: RR 8/10.

106. Chiefs' meeting, May 17, 1956, KNA: DP 1/21.

107. KNA: PC/NZA 3/33/6.

108. Register of Criminal Cases, *Ritongo* Manga.

109. *Ritongo* Gesima was not established until 1953.

5

"Girl Cases" in the Courts

As bridewealth continued to spiral upwards, and more and more women ran off or were abducted, disputes over women streamed into Gusiiland's colonial courts. As men and women angrily debated who should be married to whom, the cases coalesced into two all-encompassing questions: the significance of female consent in making marriage, and the nature of female consent. Fathers and husbands refused to admit the right of women to have any voice in making marriage; all that was necessary to create a marriage was agreement between men and the exchange of bridewealth. Young couples vehemently disputed this, arguing that bridewealth was certainly necessary but was not the only part of a proper marriage. Any marriage that did not consider the desires of the woman was no marriage at all. In abduction disputes, however, the significance of women's will was assumed, and instead the question became how women's consent could be measured. Put simply, women's consent lay at the heart of the struggle over marriage.

THE COURTROOM

Depending on their residence, litigants brought their disputes before *Ritongo* Manga or *Ritongo* Gesima (for Getutu, North Mugirango, and Nyaribari locations) or *Ritongo* Kuja (for Bassi, Majoge, South Mugirango, and Wanjare). Litigants first approached the registering clerk, probably already surrounded by a crowd of people. When a litigant finally gained the clerk's attention the latter would demand to know the nature of the complaint. In matters of runaway wives the charge was "adultery" or, in the 1960s, "removing a married woman from the custody of her husband"; elopement was "removing an unmarried girl from the custody of her parents without their consent"; abduction was, prior to 1949, also "removing an unmarried girl," and later, "indecent assault." Husbands filed adultery cases, fathers or brothers filed elopement cases. (The name of the charge might have been more properly termed "removing an unmarried girl from the custody of her male guardian.") Abducted women themselves brought charges against their attackers. Men filed civil claims for "their" women, and women filed divorce cases. The state considered adultery, elopement, and abduction to be quasi-criminal. A guilty man could be fined and, in default of payment, imprisoned; only in abduction cases (when filed as indecent assaults) could elders sentence a man to peremptory imprisonment. But unlike purely criminal charges, the individual wronged (the husband, father, or the abducted woman) personally prosecuted the case and paid a fee to register it. The burden of calling witnesses, cross-examining the defendant and his witnesses, and presenting a reasonable case fell to the complainant.

The clerk wrote down the charge in the casebook, assigned it a number and a hearing date and assessed fees. For a criminal case in 1946, for example, complainants paid shs. 6; in 1955 they paid shs. 7 (shs. 5 for filing and shs. 2 for summons), which increased the next year to shs. 10 (shs. 6 for filing, shs. 4 for summons). For a civil case, the plaintiff's costs could be much higher. In 1955 a claim for a woman or a divorce petition cost shs. 42 to file, while six years later this had risen to shs. 66. The clerk filled out a summons (a three-inch by three-inch paper) containing the charge, the date of hearing, and the parties involved. The court would despatch a process server to deliver the summons. Depending on how full the court calendar was and when (and if) the summons was delivered, the case might be heard the next week or several months down the road.

The accuser (in criminal cases) or plaintiff (in civil claims) testified first, laying out the case, followed by the accused or defendant, and finally any witnesses, usually one or two per litigant. After each person spoke, the recording clerk read back the testimony, then placed the speaker's fingerprint next to his or her words on the transcripts. The elders might interject questions, but this was uncommon. The crowd gathered in and around the court—other litigants, witnesses, curious onlookers—would be kept quite by order of the elders, enforced by their *askaris*.[1] Once all the testimony had been presented the elders conferred either on their dias or in an adjoining room. Their decision was written down and the elders either signed or placed a thumbprint on the transcript. The judgment would then be read out, all the members of the case directed out of the courtroom, and the dispensation of justice continued.[2]

ADULTERY AND ELOPEMENT: COMPLAINTS

Adultery charges dealt first and foremost with illicit cohabitation. In only one case did the complaint involve just sex: a man had caught his wife having sex with the accused in the reeds near a river, and he resorted to the courts only because the two had enjoyed each other's company several times before.[3]

Words like *kuzini* (to commit adultery, to fornicate) appear very rarely in case files,[4] in contrast to commonly used verbs such as *kuchukua* (to carry off) or *kutorosha* (to cause to desert). As described by members of the South Nyanza Law Panel, complainants did not have to prove sexual infidelity "so long as there is an intention to deprive the husband" of the custody of his wife.[5]

However, intercourse between the accused man and the woman may have been presumed.[6] In one case not all the initial marriage ceremonies had been completed before the woman left her husband. The elders set her lover free, having decided that without a marriage no illicit sex (*uzinifu*) could have occurred.[7] This was rare, however, and in most cases the fact of *uzinifu* was irrelevant. Moreover, elders and complainants never mentioned *amasangia*, the mystical uncleanliness associated with a wife's unfaithfulness that required a sacrifice to remove. Illicit cohabitation demanded attention; *uzinifu* and *amasangia* could wait. Given the relative freedom young people had in conducting their love affairs, it is likewise clear that cohabitation rather than illicit sex lay at the core of elopement cases.

Husbands typically offered few details in setting out their complaints. They began by enumerating the bridewealth they had given, and then sought to establish that their wives now lived with the accused men. Husbands often said little more. The testimony of Kerege Keroro in an August, 1959, adultery case is instructive:

> I charge this accused man Ongechi because around the date of April 26, 1959, he took my wife of the name Nyanchara whom I married with bridewealth of 17 head of cattle, one cow has died leaving 16 head of cattle, and 14 goats, because 3 goats have been slaughtered. My wife has two children, one is there at my home and the other is there together with my wife with the accused.[8]

In contrast to his detailed exposition on his bridewealth, Kerege had virtually nothing to say about circumstances of the dispute, including why his wife had left him.

Complainants in elopement cases similarly focused their testimony on two topics: bridewealth and parental authority in making marriages. Most provided the bare facts only ("he took my daughter, I found her with him"). When they deigned to explain themselves further, complainants harped on bridewealth and parental consent. As one man told the *ritongo* elders, the accused had taken his daughter "without giving me bridewealth as is custom."[9] The failure to give bridewealth, in turn, presumed that her father had not consented to the union. (Recall that the name of the charge itself was "removing an unmarried girl from the custody of her parents *without their consent*.") Many complainants echoed Meshak, who charged a defendant with living with his daughter "like his wife without my permission."[10] The curious *Ritongo* Kuja case 700 of 1963 can only make sense in this regard. John, the accused, had already given bridewealth to Nyanchoka. Only one set of ceremonies remained before John could take home his bride. In the meantime Nyanchoka diligently guarded his daughter from other would-be suitors. An anxious John could not contain himself and "carried off" his bride-to-be. Nyanchoka successfully prosecuted John for elopement since he had not yet granted John permission to remove the girl. Even bridewealth did not make a marriage without a father' consent.

What men left out of their testimony was as important as what they included. Complainants presumed that if they persuaded elders on questions of bridewealth (and demonstrated that their wives or daughters had been found with the accused) they had proved their cases. The point complainants felt unnecessary to make was that bridewealth and fatherly consent alone made marriage, and that women's consent did not really factor into the equation. Since this was the "proper" interpretation of marriage they saw little reason to expound on it; they assumed elders shared their point of view. Complainants made the dispute one of facts alone: the status of the bridewealth and the location of the woman. Their interpretation of marriage permeated the cases but remained unstated.

Only one father explicated the nature of marriage. His daughter recounted running to her lover to escape Jason, a headman, to whom her father had forced her to marry. The elders inquired of her father if this was true. "I agreed myself [to the marriage]," he replied without hesitation, "but the girl did not like [him] and Jason brought people and they dragged my daughter, they carried her off, because I wished it."[11] Under questioning, this father articulated the assumption that lay within all complainants' words: daughters married whom fathers wished.

ADULTERY AND ELOPEMENT: DEFENSES

Breaking Marriages

With complainants having established the terms of debate, accused men and their "wives" tried to divert the cases onto new tracks; this was true in civil claims over women as well.[12] Rather than becoming bogged down in questions of cattle (which was, in any event, a point they could not win), they challenged complainants' interpretation of marriage itself. They posed questions about when a wife could legitimately desert her husband and when a woman could rightfully elope with a young man. Couples pushed the elders to look beyond the cold facts of cattle exchanges to what was (to their minds) the other essential aspect of marriage, a woman's consent.

The 1964 adultery case between John (the complainant) and Obara (the accused) encapsulated these debates. John had given bridewealth for Nyanchera (her father said) but Obara later took her "and retained her as his wife." Obara admitted that they had eloped when she was living at home, and therefore before she had been married, meaning he could not be guilty of adultery. He did not know, he said, if she was presently married. Nyanchera herself redefined the lines of debate:

> I have never been married to John. I went to the accused when I was very young. Obara was also very young. I finished one year with Obara. My father came for want of bride price. [Obara had none, but promised to collect some cattle and so her father left.] The second time my father came with [Tribal Policeman] Nyabwari and removed me from Obara. When I reached home I was told that he want[ed] to take me to someone else who had cattle. I ran and returned to Obara. I came from Obara's home today. I swear before the court that I [have] never go[ne] to John and I [have] never see[n] him but today.[13]

Nyanchera could not refute the facts: John had given bridewealth, and Obara had been unable to offer any. Nonetheless, she had not consented to marry John, and had successfully avoided ever even meeting him. In comparison she spoke of her longstanding commitment to Obara. She told the court that she continued to reside with him, which, on strictly factual grounds, could do nothing but hurt Obara's case. Nyanchera demanded that the court ponder who would be her legitimate mate, the man with whom she had lived for over a year, or a man whom she had never met.[14]

Consent also meant, women argued, that in certain circumstances a wife could rightfully desert her husband. Such was the case of childless women. The South Nyanza Law Panel (composed of court elders, chiefs, and other elites) agreed that a childless marriage could be dissolved with parental consent. These women took a different tack. They argued that they could unilaterally end a childless marriage. Why did they not first consult their parents? Some women rightly suspected that their fathers, fiercely attached to the bridewealth cattle crowding their compounds (or, more likely, already used), would be averse to allowing the marriage to end. For others, referring their troubles to their parents was unnecessary: they had specific goals and knew how to achieve them. These were the women who deserted their husbands and sought out new men, and hopefully not sterile men.

Morangi in 1960 left her husband Bosire (who had married her with a herd of sixteen head of cattle, three calves and five goats in 1957, he took pains to point out to the *ritongo*) since they had had no children. The accused man had taken her in, but upon hearing she was already married ("to a sterile man") he turned her out. Morangi defended her actions:

> The complainant is the one who married me. He is sterile, he is not fertile. This reason, to get pregnant, made me desert to the accused and I lived at his home for three days, and then he chased me out of there, and I wandered to the place where my sister lives. But I got pregnant by the accused. I do not wish to return to the complainant because of [his] infertility.[15]

Both men agreed that a husband's infertility was no excuse for desertion, and that bridewealth outweighed all other considerations. Morangi vehemently disagreed. She argued that a true marriage required children, and having proven her husband infertile she supposed the marriage was over. A public airing of his most private failings likely did not pacify Bosire's rage, something Morangi was willing to risk in order to produce a family.[16]

One woman found herself trapped between parental pressure, bridewealth exchanges, and her own choice of husband.[17] Moraa's marriage threatened to collapse when her husband Omwenga's bridewealth was short. Omwenga begged Moraa's father to wait, for once his sister had married he would have more cattle to give. In the meantime, however, another man, Nyakundi, gave her father bridewealth. Moraa protested this new marriage, saying that so long as her first husband was alive she could not marry another man. Nonetheless, her parents forced her into the marriage in order to secure a full bridewealth. She was left, Moraa told the court, no option but to go to Nyakundi. But Nyakundi verbally abused her son (by Omwenga), telling him that he was not truly of the family. Moraa finally decided to ignore her family's pressure and return with her child to Omwenga. A court case resulted, with Nyakundi suing Omwenga for custody of Moraa.[18]

In women's estimation a whole host of factors could render a marriage dead. While most Gusii accepted domestic violence as a part of married life, many adultery cases arose when women felt the beatings had risen to an unacceptable level of brutality and ran off.[19] Certainly, brothers and fathers might intervene if a female relative had been subjected to excessive violence, especially if the husband had used something besides his hand or fist or had caused real physical injuries. The Law Panel allowed that, if beatings "are alleged to be frequent, the parents should go into the matter first." If they found the charges true, and had the support of the *etureti* elders, a divorce could be granted.[20] Many abused women declined to follow the channels senior men had laid out for them. They simply fled. Women who had been chased off by their husbands also refused to return.[21] Should a husband fail to build his wife a granary,[22] if he sexually abused her children,[23] if he called her a prostitute or a witch,[24] he might one day find her gone.

Making Marriage

Women wished also to declare their devotion to their chosen mates. Standing before an array of senior men, women disclosed that their lovers had replaced their husbands in fundamental ways. Their words make this patently clear: "I love [the accused] and want to live with him"; "I know that [the] accused is my husband"; [the accused] should be my husband." As one man charged with elopement said, "I love this girl and am willing to marry her."[25] The most poignant witness was Moraa. She was clearly breaking down in court when faced with permanent separation from the man with whom she had eloped.

"Truthfully," she told the court, "I loved Moase, and I went to him, I alone by my own wishes, and Mose, I loved him very much, and up to this day I love him."[26]

Only if women had repudiated bridewealth could they have more decisively challenged senior men's interpretations of marriage, but this was not a step that they were willing to take. Indeed, it likely did not even occur to them as a viable option. Only marriage through bridewealth transformed young people into adults and put them on the road to being respected elders. These couples were not revolutionaries. They shared with senior men an abiding faith in the promise of marriage, and the presumption that bridewealth made marriage. Even if a woman called her mate her *bwana* (husband), she and everyone around her—family, friends, neighbors, indeed, all Gusii—knew this could never be true until he had paid bridewealth. Only one desperate woman was willing to stay with her impoverished mate indefinitely—"I will never leave him any more even if he has nothing to pay"—yet without denying that he should pay if and when he had the means.[27]

Young people's belief in bridewealth helps explain why, compared with adultery and abduction cases, exceptional numbers of men accused of elopement pleaded guilty. Fully two-thirds of these young men did not contest the charge. On the surface this seems illogical. Charges often collapsed for lack of evidence or because of conflicting testimony. Moreover, men who admitted their guilt received no consideration from the *ritongo* elders. But if elopement is understood as a failed bid at marriage, pleading guilty makes more sense. Eloped couples sincerely wished to marry rather than simply cohabitate, and only bridewealth could transform an illicit union into marriage. Eloping was not a rejection of marriage or of bridewealth, but a pragmatic decision foisted upon young people because of poverty. By pleading guilty men hoped to placate complainants, disputing neither the facts presented nor the importance of gaining a father's consent. Ingratiating themselves with complainants, accused men hoped, would soften them to the idea of consenting to a real marriage.[28]

It was this hope—of transforming illicit into licit marriage—that prompted young women and men to float offers of bridewealth during court proceedings. On occasion this succeeded.[29] Yet such offers often rung hollow, since it was the inability to pay bridewealth that had led to elopement in the first place. Some men could offer a substantial but insufficient herd, others a few head only, as in one case in which the complainant (apparently in dire financial straits himself) was willing to compromise: "[I]f she loves [the accused], that is a good thing. [He] should give me cattle, and I will be able to pay [my own] debts." The court recessed for the parties to examine the accused's herd. He could produce only five cows and two calves, which the complainant refused as far too few. The young man was duly convicted.[30] Similarly, Johana claimed in court to have enough cattle to pay bridewealth. He either lied or deceived himself, since his four head, as the elders stated, "is not a bridewealth which a person will be paid."[31] Other men made only vague promises that complainants were probably wise to ignore. Women too felt out the possibilities of their lovers and fathers coming to some agreement over bridewealth.[32] Perhaps the most poignant instance came in a 1956 case, in which a young man expressed his desire to offer bridewealth. His father, anxious to see his son properly married, seconded the offer. But before the women's parents, the *ritongo* elders, the various assembled onlookers, the father quietly admitted that he did not own a single cow. His son would be found guilty and neither man had any means of making a husband of the youth.[33]

No matter how long lovers had spent together they did not regard themselves as *truly* married until bridewealth had been paid. Kemunto, for example, coupled her right to choose men with her belief in the importance of bridewealth. "I refuse the complainant Sambeye," she told the court, "so I wish to live with Meroka [accused of adultery] and he shall show bridewealth cattle because I have lived with Meroka three years."[34] Even a woman who had spent ten years and had borne two children with her lover did not consider herself married since bridewealth had not been paid.[35] Others squabbled over previous attempts to pay bridewealth. In a 1960 case, Joel claimed that he did not have his accuser's wife, but his own: "I do not have the wife of [the complainant], rather, I know that Moraa is my wife who came to my home in the year 1958 . . . I called her father to come to see cattle and he refused." Moraa concurred: "My husband is the accused."[36] Since bridewealth had been offered they felt some justification for calling each other husband and wife. But Joel remained ready to give his cattle at any time.

From without, this dedication to bridewealth appears irrational. Surely these young couples had the least to gain by the perpetuation of bridewealth marriage. But it was not bridewealth per se that caused them such headaches. Their forced marriages and extended bachelorhoods resulted directly from the cripplingly high bridewealth *rates*, and senior men's *interpretation* of bridewealth, not the *existence* of bridewealth. Young people desperately wanted all the social amenities that went with a bridewealth marriage, but were unwilling to let the importance of bridewealth overshadow the importance of consent.

A 1960 case is the exception that proves the rule. Obiri had been charged with taking Kemuma, wife of Ntebo. Obiri admitted the woman had briefly lived with him, but, having learnt she was married, he chased her off the second time she came to him. The court questioned Obiri:

> Q: You found out that when a person carries off the wife of a man it is wrong?
> A: Yes, it is a great mistake, but the time I took her I found that she had entered the work of prostitution . . .
> . . .
> Q: Ntebo, is that wife of yours a prostitute?
> A: No!
> . . .

> Kemuma . . . woman who is being fought over: I do not know either of these two, the complainant and the accused, although I heard that this accused is charged that he had carried me to be his wife. And this complainant, he found me in the road and abducted me and I slept at his home one day and returned with my child which I got at home [i.e., before she was married]. That is the time I filed a divorce case against this complainant here in *Ritongo* Kuja, and that time . . . I was living with Obiri, it was one and a half years without having a child there. When the divorce case was dismissed, [meaning] that I should return to this complainant, I entered the way of prostitution, I even lived in Nubian Village [on the outskirts of Kisii town] to continue my prostitution, and all the three children I have I got there in Nubia. Their fathers – I am unable to know [them], not at all. And now I have no husband between the complainant and the accused, rather I want this complainant to return to me my two children because I was auctioned by my father to go to this complainant.[37]

Kemuma not only rejected her supposed husband, but also any man who might claim her. (Significantly, she realized that until her father returned the cattle to Ntebo and the connection severed, she could never truly be free of the man.) But Kemuma was atypical. In fact, of all the women who gave evidence in adultery and elopement cases only Kemuma disdained marriage entirely. Every other woman aspired to marriage sanctified by bridewealth, albeit marriage made on their own terms.

Arguing Female Agency

Lovers fought for the significance of female consent on another front: they had to establish the simple fact that women were active agents in the creation of illicit unions. Husbands and fathers sought to isolate cases from questions of female consent. One strategy was to attribute full responsibility to the accused man. Complainants most commonly used the verb *kuchukua*, to carry off, while others employed the verb *kutorosha*, the causative form of the verb *kutoroka*, to desert or run away. Thus women did not run away, but accused men carried them off or caused them to desert. In part, this made sense in the context of the colonial legal system. Men, not women, could be charged with adultery and elopement. Logically, litigants tried to affix blame to those who could be held criminally accountable. Yet in civil cases plaintiffs used the same verbs, although the salient point insofar as the law was concerned was very different. Civil cases concerned claim over a woman, and responsibility for her desertion was legally of little import. Of course, complainants knew full well that women entered illicit unions of their own volition. But, as their choice of words demonstrates, husbands and fathers very clearly wanted to keep women's agency entirely out of the discussion.[38]

In contrast, women said that they had deserted (*kutoroka*) their supposed husbands, or had gone (*kwenda*) from one man or had come (*kuja*) to another. For example, Osugo placed blame for his wife's desertion squarely on the shoulders of the accused: "I am charging Bichanga because *he has carried off my wife*, who is called Yunuke. Bichanga *took my wife away* in January, 1958." Bichanga submitted a very different interpretation. "Truthfully," he told the court, "Yunuke *wished on her own* [to come] and *she came* to my home in 1956." Yunuke concurred. "*I went* to the home of the accused," she insisted.[39]

Aside from their choice of verbs, some women assumed full responsibility for their actions. "I went by my own choice" (*kwa hiari yangu*) many said, or "by my own desire" (*kwa upendo wangu*). Kerubo, for one, was baffled why her (now former) lover had been charged for deeds of her own doing. "I don't know a thing [about] this Ayiera who is being tried here in *Ritongo* Kuja. Rather, it is I alone who went to him (*ila ni mimi peke y[angu] niliyemwendea*)."[40] One woman put the logic of the law itself into question. She maintained that the accused "is not guilty, because I went to his home by my own choice."[41]

More than just denying female agency, in a few cases complainants' rhetoric slipped so far as to commodify women. Some litigants portrayed accused men as thieves. In support of Ngare's adultery case his father-in-law testified on his behalf. Ngare had married his daughter for fourteen head of cattle, one calf and three goats, he told the court, but the accused had taken her, "and in that way [the accused] is guilty, that is to say, he's a thief."[42] Similarly, Nyaanga had traced his runaway wife to Kipsigisland, and there at the subchief's baraza he "said that he was following his cow of two legs which he had lost . . ."[43]

Women resentfully accused their parents of treating them like cattle or a commodity, pressuring elders to recognize just how far women's status had been degraded. In the late 1940s, Gusii women commonly moaned that "We are bought like cattle,"[44] and repeated this in the courtroom. Kemunto, for example, indicted her father since he had "auctioned [her] like a goat" to the complainant.[45] This theme of being sold off like a commodity or beast was repeated by more women: "my brother auctioned me to the complainant;" "I was auctioned by my father to go to the complainant."[46]

ADULTERY AND ELOPEMENT: JUDGMENTS

Ritongo elders had their feet planted in two worlds. They were very much local men, committed to Gusii norms about the centrality of marriage to a proper life, and the importance of bridewealth to creating a proper marriage. They were all fathers and husbands, and often polygamists. Keeping wives and daughters under male control was thus of very personal interest. Yet their horizons were much broader than those of the litigants before them. As the years passed, more and more elders came from the ranks of businessmen, state employees, and the educated. They had regular interaction with British administrators and white missionaries, and as teachers, evangelists, and traders had likely traveled across Gusiiland. They perceived and discussed problems facing all of South Kavirondo. They well appreciated the details of the cases that came before them, yet they could also place these disputes within the context of Gusiiland as a whole. They would be tools of neither local senior men nor a western legal tradition, and their decisions reflected this.[47]

Law Panels

Unlike officials elsewhere in Africa, Kenya administrators did little in the way of collecting and codifying customary law. Colonial officials across Africa regularly pestered senior men for information on the customary law of each "tribe" on every conceivable topic. Many African men exploited this, feeding officials versions of customary law which granted seniors terrific powers over juniors and women, which officials then applied. Providing partial definitions of customary law to the state had its advantages. In Kenya, however, the profits of defining customary law were less clear. Officials rejected the notion that there should be a single unalterable definition of customary law and avoided codifying anyone's interpretation of the law.[48] At times, officials consulted elders on points of customary law, and when hearing appeals from African courts Britons turned to African assessors for enlightenment on the more intricate aspects of the law. Nonetheless, elders never had the final word. Administrators did not always accept elders' interpretations,[49] and even called on Luo and Kuria elders to help sort out Gusii customary law cases, and vice versa.[50]

The state's inauguration of Law Panels appeared to blaze a new trail. Arthur Phillips first broached the idea of district level (but "tribal") Law Panels in the early 1940s. The panels' minutes would systematize the study of customary law and officers could more easily track (and guide) concurrent evolution of the law. Administrators made clear that the minutes would have limited practical application. They explained that African Courts would not be required strictly (or even loosely) to adhere to the panels' minutes when adjudicating cases. Until the mid-1960s Law Panel minutes were largely irrelevant to disputes in the African Courts.[51]

Yet Law Panel members must have been suspicious of the state's motives: why collect customary law if not to influence the courts? Might not the administration impose Law Panel minutes on the African Courts, or even draft new laws modeled after panels' definitions of customary law? Perhaps if panel members granted that in some circumstances a woman could rightfully leave her husband, the state might curtail courts' powers to return runaway women. District officers hearing cases on appeal might treat the minutes as definitive rather than suggestive.

Thus, undoubtedly wary of the implications their words might have, members of the Gusii section of the South Nyanza Law Panel outlined a very conservative customary law. Customary law, they informed the district officer chairing the panel, granted fathers and husbands vast powers over daughters and wives. In the application of the law, the panelists continued, little heed was paid to the circumstances of the cases. The customary law of adultery (in the minutes, "removing a wife from the custody of her husband" to distinguish it from illicit sex per se) is particularly instructive. The panelists in 1961 identified two defenses against an adultery charge: if the husband had granted permission for the accused to live with his wife, or if the accused had paid bridewealth.[52] The first was admittedly rare—indeed, in no surviving case did an accused make this claim—and the level of proof prohibitive ("strong evidence is required e.g. a letter from the husband"). No other defense, the elders stated, could acquit a man. According to the Law Panel members, the rights of husbands over wives were unassailable. A woman's consent mattered nil ("It is not a defense to prove that the married woman consented to being removed") and an accused had virtually no way to avoid punishment.[53]

Adultery

In adultery cases, *ritongo* elders applied a law that resembled but did not replicate what was said in the Law Panels. In the panels, elders imparted a customary law that suited that situation: to prevent the state from loosening senior men's hold on women. In criminal court cases the stakes were different. The raison d'etre of adultery prosecutions was to punish men who did not act like proper men, men who transgressed the rights of a husband over his wife. Elders thus championed husbands attempting to recover their wives. But husbands too could fail to live up to the standards elders expected of them: they chased wives away or failed to impregnate them; they waited years before tracing runaway women. While these circumstances did not entitle a woman to create a new union, they were mitigating factors in assessing the guilt of and levying punishment on accused men.

To win his adultery case, a husband had to establish two things: that he had paid bridewealth and that his wife had been found with the accused. The former could be proved through evidence of the father or brother of the woman. Should the accused deny having cohabitated with the woman (not an uncommon defence) the complainant might call other witnesses, such as her relatives who had assisted in retrieving the woman, or the *etureti* or sub-headman of the accused's area. Some charges did founder on this point (in particular if the complainant had not gone personally to collect his wife). Other charges failed when it emerged that all or most of the complainant's bridewealth had been returned to him by the woman's father, or that the woman had successfully divorced the man in court. If it were proven that the informal union had preceded the complainant's payment of full bridewealth, or before the legal couple had lived together, elders decided that no marriage had existed to be broken.[54] (In such an instance an elopement case should instead have been filed.) It was on these types of questions that complainants most often saw their cases fail. Indeed, elders dismissed one-third of the cases reviewed for these reasons.[55]

Some men escaped conviction when the accuser had let lapse his rights over his wife. By making no effort to seek out his wife for months or years a husband had (in elders' and the couple's eyes) essentially condoned the offense. Court elders threw out cases if the husband and wife had been living separately for some years. Adultery charges were intended to punish men who failed to respect other men's rights over women. If a husband did not exercise his rights over his wife he had little room to complain when other men transgressed them.

Elders (and women and their lovers) insisted that a man could not be punished for flouting another man's rights that had long since fallen dormant. Nyangau's wife had left him and lived with another man for many years before he filed an adultery case. The elders acquitted the accused because "a person [who] lives with the wife of [another] person for a period of five years has [committed] no wrong."[56] Women tried to expand on this idea, arguing that an extended coresidence could establish a legitimate union. Sigara, the woman under dispute in a 1962 case, told the elders that

> My husband is [the accused] Nyangwona because I have lived with him for a period of four years, and the complainant, I lived at his place a period of one year.[57]

Elders rejected Sigara's claim of marriage with Nyangwona, but concurred that he could not be punished. Of twenty-nine similar cases only one man was fined.[58] Nevertheless, court elders declared that the original marriages survived. Once a man resurrected his claims over his wife she was expected to return to him, and the accused no longer to live with her. A long separation did not extinguish rights gained via bridewealth.

Elders also discharged men who had sheltered "wandering" women. Some men who stole off to Kericho with their lovers subsequently cut the women adrift, leaving them to fend for themselves. These women might roam or "wander" (*kutangatanga*) from man to man, searching for stable relationships. For elders dedicated to restraining the unfettered movement of women this was clearly a disturbing situation. When a man took in a wandering woman, protecting her and exerting a measure of male authority over her, elders were inclined to absolve him of the crime of adultery.[59] Again, however, elders believed these relationships had to be terminated once the woman's husband reasserted his claim over his wife.

Elders posited that in a few circumstances wives had rights that outweighed those of husbands. Given the centrality of children to a successful marriage and to women's status, elders trivialized the sheltering of runaway, childless wives. Morangi had left her husband because they had failed to have children. The elders found her lover guilty, but levied a relatively light fine. He paid only shs. 100 (less than half the average fine for that year, 1960) "because the wife of the complainant deserted [due to] the complainant's infertility, that is why the accused will pay a small fine."[60] Women, like men, had certain rights in a marriage.

In a handful of cases elders took it upon themselves to comment on forced marriages, although this did not always influence their decisions. In *Ritongo* Kuja adultery case 641 of 1946 female consent clearly outweighed other factors. Makori had previously and successfully sued Oseko for his wife (who is not named in the case file). She nonetheless returned to Oseko. He tried to chase her off, but she refused to leave him. The elders determined "that she came to Oseko on her own. Therefore the case is dismissed."[61] Similarly, elders ruled that since Yunuke had gone to Bichanga on her own, he was guilty of no crime. Nonetheless, the court ordered Yunuke to be returned to her father, who would then turn her over to the man who had given bridewealth for her.[62] More commonly, elders simply noted the fact that a forced marriage had been contracted, perhaps as a critique of men who would make such marriages, but without allowing this overly to affect their decisions. The elders in one case fined a man "for carrying . . . the wife of Nyang'au even though . . . she refused Nyang'au but [her] parents agreed that she must live with Nyang'au."[63]

Elopement

As in adultery cases, in elopement cases *ritongo* elders tended to share complainants' ideas of marriage. If the couple had lived together without bridewealth having been paid, elders usually entered a guilty verdict regardless of the woman's desires. Elders often scolded young men, making sure that they realized the scope of their mistake. In one case they assessed a fine "so that [the convicted man] should not do this again."[64] Other elders explained that Gusii customary law had been broached,[65] or induced the accused to admit the errors of his ways.[66]

Yet in certain circumstances elders adopted more liberal views. If some bridewealth had been given or negotiations had been opened, elders presumed that the father had consented to a marriage. Elders encouraged such complainants to drop their criminal charges and instead open civil suits for the cattle outstanding.[67] Elders clearly hesitated to break apart these unions, illicit though they were. Rather than separating couples who seemed well on their way to making successful marriages, elders tried to cement their unions. Elders inquired of complainants if they would accept bridewealth, turning a criminal act into a preliminary to marriage.[68] In fact, Gusii members of the South Nyanza Law Panel encouraged this practice. Couples often eloped, they explained, if the woman's parents objected to the union. At this point, "the girl's father tries to determine the intention of the boy and if the latter is willing to marry the girl the matter is settled without recourse to the courts." Only if the "boy" was unwilling (or, more to the point, unable) to marry did the dispute enter the courts.[69] If a young man willingly produced sufficient cattle, elders saw little sense in punishing him. That is, they felt that fathers should respect their daughters' wishes so long as bridewealth could be paid. Similarly, if the couple had lived together for some time or had had a child, elders usually dismissed the charges and encouraged the complainant to accept the union as a fait accompli. Nevertheless, if the father rejected elders' suggestions of marriage the court would convict the young man.

ABDUCTION

Abduction cases, in terms of presentation, resolution, and roles of the disputants, differed markedly from adultery and elopement cases. The existence of female consent, disputed in adultery and elopement cases, was freely admitted by all parties in abduction cases. Furthermore, senior men generally considered abduction the most deplorable of the three crimes. That is, an informal union made without a woman's consent was more heinous than one made with her consent, implicitly acknowledging *existence* and the *significance* of female consent. Debate then shifted to the *nature* of women's consent: how could that consent be ascertained? How could men and women determine whether a woman had agreed to a union?

Complaints

Women normally began their cases by detailing their travails. They explained where they had been when accosted and where they had been taken, if the abductors had used or threatened violence, and when and how they managed to escape. Often, women ended their testimony here. Some women, however, went into more detail. Lack of "love" could be offered as proof of lack of consent. Bonareri accused Sagero of abducting her while she was returning home from selling bananas at Kisii town. The accused said the father had agreed to the marriage but had later backed out. Bonareri insisted that at that time she herself had "refused him for I did not love him to marry me."[70] By giving this history, she emphasized that she had never had any consensual relationship with her abductor, but had in fact refused him once already. That she did not love him could prove this.

In 1947, Keroro charged four men with abducting his daughters (one of the very few cases in which a man filed an abduction case). Love was taken as central to determining if the girls had consented. "They dragged my daughters by force," Keroro told *Ritongo* Kuja. "[My] daughters did not love them at all." Buchere, one of his daughters, similarly pointed out that "If I loved [the third accused] I would not come here and accuse him."[71]

Fathers and brothers generally supported women in abduction cases. In part, relatives were disturbed by the violence suffered by abducted women. They also (if only implicitly) recognized the evil of the woman's consent having been ignored, as did Keroro. Yet fathers who supported their daughters' abduction charges did not always do so for the best of reasons. For many fathers, using force in establishing marriage was not in and of itself wrong. Force could be legitimate if performed by or with the permission of the father. Thus to some fathers, abductors' crime was less the use of force than the failure to gain parental permission. One man wondered why, if he had really wanted her as a wife, his daughter's abductor had not come to "make a bargain."[72]

Defenses

Men accused of abduction had three main lines of defense available. Very few pleaded guilty. The strategy men followed in elopement cases made little sense here. If they did wish to marry their victims admitting abduction would hardly have put abductors closer to that goal. One man who owned up to his offense did not impress the *ritongo* elders with his honesty: they thought him "a very guilty person, to pull the complainant and have sex with her by force." They backed up their opinion with an unusually heavy sentence of a shs. 200 fine and four months in prison.[73] Other men tried to deny that the attack had occurred, but this defense failed more often than it succeeded.

The commonest defense was to claim that the woman had in fact consented to the illicit sex. As one accused man put it, "This complainant herself came to my home, to my house, because we had been discussing that she should be my wife."[74] One man told the court that his accuser "came herself to my home because we had chatted that she should be my wife."[75] Another stated that the woman had come to him willingly after bridewealth negotiations had collapsed (two of his cattle were of poor quality and had been returned to him).[76]

Cases could often be reduced to two diametrically opposed recollection of events. Mwebi, for example, told the court that he "did not pull the complainant, rather, she came on her own, that is, I found her in the road, waiting for me." His accuser, however, said that he had ripped her clothes, displayed a *panga* (machete) and threatened to kill her if she screamed. If she was telling the truth (and the *ritongo* elders believed she was) then Mwebi simply lied to save his own skin. Some abductors anticipated this and tried to cover their tracks. Sabaniah, who with nineteen agemates accosted Kemunto along a path, made sure to carry her high off the ground: if she were dragged and fought back he knew that the resulting cuts and bruises could be crucial evidence against him if the case came before the *ritongo*.[77]

What is most interesting and perhaps most disturbing about abduction cases is that many accused men could not, or did not wish to, distinguish between force and consent. Some thought the two not incompatible at all. Granted, not all abductors could truly have believed their victims had consented. Those who beat, flashed weapons, and threatened murder knew very well that only force had sealed the union. But was force always illegitimate, men wondered? One would-be husband, Nyakundi, had paid some bridewealth, and so felt he had claim over Moraa. Yet he also felt the need to use force to ensure possession of her. Nyakundi gave his story in a suit he laid against Moraa's brother Oburi for injury compensation. He had paid bridewealth, Nyakundi claimed, but when he and his friends came to collect her, Oburi fell on them with a *panga*. Nyakundi left with a one-and-a-half-inch deep gash on his head. Oburi gave a different version of events, portraying Nyakundi clearly as an abductor and thus worthy of having his blood spilt. Nyakundi had paid only partial bridewealth, Oburi explained, and thus did not yet have legal claim over the woman. The proof: "Had they paid full bridewealth the[y] couldn't come in the night [4 a.m.], also they couldn't come [in a group of] 19 men for 1 girl." After shaking off a blow to the cheek by a *kiboko* (whip), Oburi jumped to his sister's defense and cracked the invader on the head with a stick (not, he said, a *panga*).[78] Perhaps Nyakundi did believe that he had legal claim over Moraa, or perhaps he did not have enough cattle to finish paying bridewealth. In either case, he believed that the use of force was permissible to claim his "wife."

It appears that some young men so broadly defined consent that they could believe, or convince themselves, that their abductees were willing partners to an elopement. One accused man seemed honestly taken aback, "surprised [that she] is charging me here falsely."[79] In another abduction case, Begi explained that he and Anna had talked of marriage but (according to Begi) she was "cheating" him, leading him on. "Then when I met her and told her we should go to my place, she started to refuse." She had previously consented, now she rejected him. Begi assumed he could rightfully use force: "I pulled her," he said. The *ritongo* elders, taken aback by this brazen admission of force, inquired, "Do you see that it is wrong to pull the complainant without her wishing to go with you?" Had she consented? Had he forced her? Begi no longer knew the difference. "I can't know if it is wrong, or what it is."[80]

Consider also the case of Andama. In his defense, he stated that the woman "came herself to my home, of her choice." His coaccused, Obutu, provided more telling testimony. The three had chatted before, he explained, and met one day as she collected water at the river. "That is when we grabbed her and took her to another place to hide her. Of course, she tried to cry a little, because [that is] custom even if a woman wishes, it's necessary that one try a little to cover her mouth."[81] For Andama and Obutu her struggles and cries did not denote unwillingness on her part, but merely that she was playing the role expected of all good women. It was performance, nothing more. Or, at least this is what they claimed. In fact, standard marriage ceremonies did demand that new brides resist their grooms. When the groom and his friends came to collect the woman her relatives engaged them in a mock battle. The bride herself struggled—she screamed, grabbed hold of house supports, fell to the ground. This was not an expression of real resistance to the marriage, but not to do so would reflect negatively on the character of the woman. But a bride's resistance took place in her homestead, not at a river bank, and when she was with family, not when she was alone. Perhaps Andama and Obutu truly believed that their victim's resistance was feigned, but they would have been hard pressed to convince anyone else of that. Indeed, they were convicted.

Judgments

Elders did not usually find it difficult to determine if a woman had consented to a union or if she had been abducted. If a man denied any contact with his accuser he might force an inquiry into the facts: were there witnesses to the abduction? who had seen them together? Torn clothing or other evidence of a struggle were persuasive evidence. If a woman had not exploited a chance to escape or call for help, elders concluded that she had in fact consented.[82]

Men who admitted a relationship pushed their cases in another direction. It must have been clear to all involved that impugning the character of the woman was of no value. Indeed, not a single accused man brought up the sexual histories of their accusers. Despite occasional talk to the contrary, virginity at marriage was generally neither valued nor expected, except, perhaps, for some Christian converts. So long as their parents were not forced to confront their children's sexual adventures—a deeply offensive act according to *nsoni* rules—young people were free to engage in premarital sex. Fully aware that women could and did choose lovers, elders posed a question: if a woman had willingly gone to a lover, why would she later charge him with a crime? Rather than demanding that the woman prove lack of consent, elders instead demanded that the accused prove that consent had been granted. Mosioma claimed that he had begun bridewealth negotiations with his accuser's family, after which she came to him. The elders found him guilty. "The accused implicates himself that the complainant came to his home by her own choice," they wrote. "[I]t is not true because if this girl went to his home herself she would not come here to charge him."[83] Similarly, the elders at *Ritongo* Gesima convicted a man because, "although he admits [she was there] there is no evidence to show that they had had a [consensual] relationship."[84]

The willingness of *ritongo* elders to convict abductors, and the support fathers and brothers gave abducted women, reveals an important point about the use of force in making marriage. Ignoring women's consent and using physical violence was not necessarily wrong, according to fathers, husbands, and court elders. In cases of adultery and elopement the rights of fathers and husbands outweighed those of women, and men could enforce those rights as they saw fit, by violence if necessary. This did not mean that women did not have the intellectual *ability* to consent to, or reject, a union, men's rhetoric to the contrary notwithstanding. The very fact that violence had to be used to break women's spirits made this painfully clear. If a woman was exercising choices in ways that did not challenge her legal guardian—when a girl took lovers but did not elope with them—she would be left to her own devices.

(This did not, of course, apply to wives, for husbands had sole rights over them sexually.) All Gusii recognized a that girl's wishes here held sway, at least until the question of marriage arose and a father's wishes took precedence. Women's choices went thus far and no farther.

Abductors ignored women's wishes, a right that only fathers had. Still, abduction was not an offense against a father but against the woman abducted. The victim, and thus the prosecutor before the *ritongo*, was always the person whose rights were violated—in this case, the abducted woman. Abductors acted in the period when women exercised choices over sexual but not marriage partners, when fathers reserved but did not enforce their rights to marry off their daughters. Certainly fathers had much invested in the outcome of abductions: marriage and bridewealth were involved. But Gusii men, or at least the vast majority of them, would not go so far as completely to commodify their womenfolk. Despite their attempts to ignore women's agency in elopement and adultery cases, despite some who called women "cows of two legs," to most Gusii men women were not slaves to be sold or beasts to be bartered. The bridewealth-induced crisis in marriage may have forced men to act this way, to talk this way, but actions and words did not necessarily equal conviction. Thus if a woman willingly eloped her father might acquiesce to a marriage, which *ritongo* elders encouraged. If bridewealth was not a consideration—if her lover had cattle—a woman's choice in marriage partner might be respected.

Abductors were not thieves. Abductors did not abscond with a father's property. Abductors transgressed the rights of women. Even if an abductor had cattle most fathers would reject the union—because their daughters had rejected the union. Abductees, not their fathers or brothers, prosecuted their attackers in the *ritongo*. This was true even prior to 1949, when *ritongo* did not have jurisdiction over abduction. Abductions were instead filed as "removing an unmarried girl from the custody of her parents," but it was the unmarried girl and not her parents who laid out the charge. *Ritongo* elders punished abductors much more harshly than they did men guilty of elopement.[85] Fines in abduction cases were higher than in elopement cases, sometimes twice as much. Elders sentenced some abductors to peremptory imprisonment along with fines, which they never did in elopement cases. Abductors, and only abductors, believed that their circumstances justified their actions.

CIVIL CASES

Claims over Women and Children

It would not have been at all uncommon for *ritongo* elders one day to hear several adultery and elopement cases, and the next to hear several divorce petitions and civil claims for the custody of women. A husband could sue his "runaway wife's" lover for legal custody over her. About one-fifth of the

Table 5.1. Average Fines, in Shillings, for Elopement, Adultery and Abduction Cases for the Year 1960 in *Ritongo* Manga, *Ritongo* Kuja, and *Ritongo* Gesima

Case	*Ritongo* Manga	*Ritongo* Kuja	*Ritongo* Gesima
Elopement	117	100	125
Adultery	150	167	227
Abduction	240	217	150

Source: Court records, registers.

civil claims had originally come to court as adultery charges, which had been dismissed or had failed to break apart the illicit union.[86] Other plaintiffs may have thought it better to proceed directly to a civil claim, certainly a good idea if evidence for a criminal case appeared weak.

The process of filing a civil case and issuing summons was the same as in criminal cases, although the fees were higher and, if the plaintiff won, the defendant had to reimburse him the fees. Litigants told the same stories in civil and criminal cases. Plaintiffs generally stuck to matters of bridewealth and living arrangements, while defendants and women told of forced marriages and beatings, of men who were loved and husbands who were not.

Men used civil claims as an indirect method to regain women. A successful claim reasserted a man's legal rights over a woman, no matter where or with whom she might live, or for how long. This scuttled any plans the unwed couple might have had of getting married. The woman and her lover would be forced to realize that, regardless of their desire to live and to raise their children together, social recognition as a married couple could not be theirs.[87]

Perhaps most importantly, husbands claimed children as well as wives. All children, no matter who had fathered them, socially and legally belonged to the man who had given bridewealth. Thus a plaintiff claimed all the children his wife had borne regardless of their biological father. Unlike women, children could be given to the successful claimant at the time of the court hearing or, if not yet weaned, later by warrants of attachment. The significance of physical and legal control over children was twofold. First, while a daughter's bridewealth would always technically belong to her legal father, he stood a better chance of negotiating and realizing it should she live with him. Second, according to one administrator women were averse to remaining away from their children and would often remain with an unwanted husband rather than risk separation from children.[88] Mothers invested heavily, emotionally and otherwise, in their children. The relations between a mother and her boys could often be the closest in a homestead: mothers defended their sons' interests in bridewealth, and sons later provided for their mothers in their old age. Mothers and daughters retained deep emotional ties well after the latter had married and moved away.[89] The residence of children could well determine the residence of their mothers.

Divorce

Divorce cases differed fundamentally from all other marriage disputes. First, only women filed divorce cases; if men wished to end a marriage they simply demanded the return of their bridewealth. More important, women's thoughts about their marriages took center stage. Rather than debating whether or not a marriage existed, litigants debated whether or not their marriages should continue. A husband could not focus on bridewealth, for if he wished to retain his wife he had to answer her accusations of abuse, desertion, infertility, and forced marriage. Nonetheless, women's words alone did not determine the outcome of divorce cases. Court elders granted divorces less out of sympathy to women's complaints than to the wishes of the women's relatives.

Divorce proceedings opened with the words of dissatisfied women. Women, as they did in other cases, presented litanies of abuse suffered at the hands of their would-be husbands. Any number of actions, women insisted, could render a marriage dead. She had never wished to marry the man, a plaintiff might argue, as did Kwamboka: "I want to divorce [*Mimi nataka ili tuachane na*] this defendant Kinanga because I didn't love him since long ago, he is a good young man, but I don't love him."[90] Others complained of physical violence, or of having been accused of witchcraft or barrenness. For these women, their marriages had already essentially ended. They wished only officially to end the marriages, allowing them—legally—to create new marriages. Divorce cases proved the only legal context in which a woman could effectively present the argument that was otherwise so often ignored: that bridewealth alone did not make marriage.

To retain rights over his wife a husband had to convince *ritongo* elders that the divorce petition was baseless. As always they detailed the status of bridewealth: she is, and should remain, my wife because I paid bridewealth. "I don't want to divorce Sigara," stated Nyamboga, "because she is my wife, who I married with 10 head of cattle, and five calves, and two goats."[91] Yet husbands could not end their testimony there. Adultery and custody of women cases hinged primarily on men demonstrating the existence of a marriage sealed by bridewealth while, in contrast, divorce cases by definition *presumed* the existence of a marriage sealed by bridewealth. Proving that bridewealth had been exchanged was redundant. Unlike men charging adultery, respondents in divorce cases could not ignore their wives' accusations of mistreatment or forced marriage. Thus Nyamboga continued: "I've lived with her five years, also, I didn't call her a witch and barren, no!"

Women and Familial Support

Refuting women's accusations of mistreatment was all the more important given the number of successful divorce applications. As with criminal customary law, elders on the Kisii Law Panel related restrictive rules on divorce yet interpreted them very loosely in practice. In 1956, Oliver Knowles, officer in charge of courts in South Nyanza, explained that elders in Gusii, Luo and Kuria courts "recognize the truth of the maxim that 'hard cases make bad law' and give judgement accordingly." Knowles reported that in 1955 *ritongo* approved slightly over half of all divorce petitions, despite Law Panel minutes that would have kept divorces to a fraction of that number.[92] This year was not exceptional. Of 164 extant divorce cases from 1952 to 1961, forty-three were dismissed ex parte or on technical grounds. In eighty-six (or 71 percent) of the remaining cases elders granted divorces.

Why were elders so willing to follow the wishes of unsatisfied women? In fact, it was not women's words that counted so much as those of their brothers or parents. The plaintiff who had the support of her family could expect a favorable hearing by the court elders. Recognizing the continuing rights (at least until *enyangi*) of a family over a married-off daughter, elders nearly always followed the wishes of the plaintiff's kin. Of the eighty-six divorces granted, parents lent their support in seventy-six of the cases, in three others only the litigants testified, and of the remaining seven there is little information. In not a single case did the elders grant a woman a divorce against the wishes of her relatives.[93]

Perhaps more than anything else, the difference between fathers' attitudes in criminal and in civil cases came down to a woman's respect for parental rights.[94] What incensed fathers most was daughters taking matters into their own hands, living with new men without first seeking familial approval. All Gusii agreed that childlessness, accusations of witchcraft, and excessive domestic violence could dangerously weaken a marriage. The crucial questions centered on when these issues entirely and irrevocably undermined a marriage and, most important, who could make that determination. Women's arguments remained relatively constant across criminal and civil cases; whether they would be received favorably by court elders depended on their kins' testimony.

By supporting divorce petitions fathers and brothers (and in some few cases, mothers)[95] admitted circumstances in which a marriage should be dissolved, agreeing with the claims made by so many women. Excessive physical violence, the failure to produce children, and accusations and counter-accusations of witchcraft might lead relatives to support a woman who had left her husband.[96] Kin might also agree that a marriage could not be preserved because of what might be called irreconcilable differences.[97] A man who chased off his wife or called her a prostitute could alienate his in-laws.[98]

Two newly-sympathetic fathers admitted that they had done wrong to force their daughters into marriage. Kwamboka sued Kinanga for divorce in 1957 on two grounds: that she did not love him and that he had failed to support her when she fell ill. Kinanga denied both accusations, claiming that "she is my wife, when I married her she loved me very much." Kwamboka's father backed her fully. Truly, he told the court, "when [Kinanga] married the plaintiff

Kwamboka she didn't love him. Then, I forced her to go to the defendant Kinanga."[99] Nyamesa made a similar admission in his daughter's 1960 divorce case. "I wish that my daughter [Sese] should leave Oteyo," he told the court, "because I forced [her] to Oteyo, then, [she] utterly refused [him]."[100]

In divorce and civil claims matters of bridewealth loomed large in determining the support a woman could expect from her family. Should a marriage end bridewealth would have to be returned; no one would dispute this point. Perhaps the cattle remained in the family homestead, which made returning bridewealth a simple matter. But a woman filing for divorce would be unlikely to hear kind words from her family if the bridewealth had already been used. The second marriage would have to be broken, the bridewealth reclaimed and the wife sent home, all in order to satisfy the unhappy daughter. Not all families would be willing to take such steps. In other cases, new suitors had already been found. It was a less daunting proposition to end a marriage and turn loose cattle when new beasts were patiently chewing their cuds, waiting to join the homestead herd.[101] Some women were blessed with families willing to refund bridewealth even if no new source of bridewealth had yet been found. But too often questions of bridewealth bested any desire to release a relative from an unwanted marriage. "Truly," one father told *Ritongo* Kuja, "my daughter has refused her husband, and because she bore five kids who died, now I want to be given a period of five months to collect cattle." Nonetheless, he admitted, "if I fail, my daughter will return to her husband."[102] In seven cases litigants had negotiated divorces contingent on the return of bridewealth. When the cattle could not be produced the agreements were off, the divorces rescinded.

Civil Cases: Judgments

Elders generally, but not always, acquiesced to the desires of women's families in custody and divorce cases. In a few civil cases elders felt compelled to overrule parental wishes, or at least to comment unfavorably on the marriages parents had contracted for their daughters. Elders generally simply stated their findings, but sometimes detailed the grounds on which divorces could be granted. They maintained that a husband could do wrong, so much so that he effectively relinquished his rights over his wife. Witchcraft, if proved, could warrant the dissolution of a marriage,[103] as could chasing off a wife, especially "without reason, without any wrongdoing" by the wife.[104] So too a man's sterility and domestic abuse, as elders of *Ritongo* Gesima explained in denying Bina's divorce petition. The elders stated that her petition "isn't good, even a little, because there isn't reason enough to divorce ... her husband didn't hit her, he didn't even chase her off [nor was he sterile, as she had claimed]. And so, we don't see a reason for a divorce."[105] As in adultery cases, elders looked askance at men who failed to inquire after wives who had long ago left them. Such inaction could invalidate a man's claim over his wife.[106]

In theory, upon a man's death his family continued to exercise rights over his widow, but in practice court elders believed that a widow's choice might be of greater importance. *Ritongo* Kuja elders approved Kerubo's divorce application, following her brother's wishes, but also because "her husband had died."[107] A widow's desires could even trump those of her sibling. In a 1959 custody case, Siriba claimed Aencha (his brother's widow). Aencha's brother supported the claim. The elders, however, favored Aencha and overruled her brother and brother-in-law. "We see no reason," they wrote, "to return this women to another person who is not her husband, rather is just the family of her late husband."[108]

Elders on occasion granted women the right simply to reject a man, as so many women and young men demanded. Magara claimed Miruka in 1965. Miruka explained that she had been forced to marry Magara in 1959 when still a young girl. After only one month she had run off, was forced back to him, only to escape again. The elders dismissed Magara's claim over her. They pointed to Magara's previous bridewealth suits which suggested that he had agreed to end the marriage. Moreover, they ruled that Miruka "did not stay long with [Magara]" and she "has refused to return to [him]. The court has seen no right to order her forcible return to him."[109] Even a man who won legal claim over his wife might not gain permanent custody. The elders awarded Obara custody of his wife and children but ruled that "if the woman refuses Obara he will sue for his bridewealth."[110] Similarly, in *Ritongo* Kuja case 709/49 elders granted a man custody of his wife and children, but ordered that if she again refused him she would be allowed to remain with the defendant, her lover.[111] *Ritongo* Manga elders dismissed custody case 448/46 outright. They pointed out that the defendant had given bridewealth but also noted that the woman in dispute "loves him."[112]

Some elders went so far as to criticize the senior men standing before them, at times even in the same language used by dissatisfied women. In a 1957 custody case, the elders of *Ritongo* Kuja chastised Bwari for making and breaking his daughter's marriages for no reason other than to gain more cattle. Bwari had married his daughter first to the defendant, but ended that marriage after the plaintiff offered more cattle. Now in court Bwari stated that his daughter would be the wife of neither litigant. Clearly, he had found or was seeking yet another, wealthier son-in-law. Disgusted, the elders denounced Bwari for treating his daughter's marriages "like commerce."[113] In one exceptional custody case the elders saw that neither litigant could be blamed for the dispute:

> we find that the father of the woman is indeed the guilty one, because first his daughter went to the defendant [and the father recovered her through a court case and he] seized his daughter to sell her like a goat, and his daughter did not want the second husband. She will live at home [i.e., in her father's homestead] so that she will be married to another husband. Therefore we dismiss the case.[114]

As did so many women and young men, these elders believed a marriage borne of coercion not to be a legitimate marriage.

LEAVING THE COURTROOM

As the elders read the verdict finding her lover guilty and perhaps confirming an unwanted man as her husband, a woman's desperation must have been profound and her future bleak. The *ritongo*, essentially the highest level of dispute resolution for criminal cases (since so few guilty men filed appeals, and those who did rarely succeeded) had passed legal sentence supporting all that she had fought against. Such a woman, undoubtedly having already been subjected to physical violence, faced only more beatings. Fathers and husbands, having had their authority publicly challenged, certainly would pull no punches.

Upon returning home from court a father likely undertook another round of harangues or beatings. Some women surrendered at this point. Her lover had been fined or quite likely imprisoned in default of payment; fines in adultery and elopement cases could equal several months' worth of wages. With her lover imprisoned for some months she would have to suffer through this period with her own family.[115] This may have pushed some women into despair and surrender.[116] Fines or incarceration may well have soured men to the idea of taking in another woman.

Yet the very hopelessness of such women necessitated that senior men measure their actions. At the end of an adultery trial elders instructed the woman's father, not her husband, to take her home. In part this followed general Gusii practice. After a quarrel a husband had the right to drive his wife back to her parents. Her father, after reprimanding her, would send his daughter back with a goat to appease her husband. It would seem natural for a woman to leave the court with her father and later be returned to her husband.

Court elders were also taking into account a very real possibility that a woman, seeing no future and no options, would commit suicide if immediately given over to her husband. Committing suicide seems long to have been the last desperate act of women trapped in unwanted marriages. As early as the 1920s, female suicide (especially by drowning) was remarked upon by European observers. In a novel based on his experiences in Gusiiland, Seventh-day Adventist missionary Eric Beavon told the tale of Nyamwita. Having been forced into marriage with an unwanted man she threw herself ("with a wild cry and arms upflung") into the River Gucha.[117] A Gusii novelist, writing of his childhood in the 1950s, told of a similar case. Upon hearing *Ritongo* Kuja convict her lover of adultery one woman ran down the hill on which the courthouse was perched and threatened to plunge into the Gucha.[118] Iona Mayer too knew of cases in which "desperate [women] drowned themselves rather than return to a hated husband . . ."[119] The hopelessness of these women was matched by many women elsewhere in Africa who preferred death to unhappy marriages.[120]

Court elders and fathers took seriously threats of suicide. Prior to 1949 a man could file multiple adultery charges against his wife's lover, and elders would return such a woman at least twice to her lawful husband before considering the marriage ended. "The exception to [this] rule," the district commissioner reported, "is when a girl threatens suicide should she be returned. In such an instance, if the Elders are satisfied that [she] is serious, she will not be returned to her husband, but the marriage price will be returned forthwith."[121] Two former *ritongo* elders confirmed that women, if dragged away from the court by their husbands, would be likely to kill themselves.[122] Women who threatened suicide sometimes swayed their kin. One father explained that,

> I agreed that my daughter should go to the plaintiff, [but] today I've seen that it's difficult to go to the plaintiff, because she wanted to strangle herself. So, I've seen that I will lose my child. Now I want this plaintiff to get his cattle which remain at my place, that is, my daughter should live at home, and she will be married to a different man.[123]

Thus even as senior men saw their legal control over runaway wives affirmed by a state body, even as they chastised the impudent men who had challenged their rights, even as they successfully denied the significance of women's consent, they were forced to reckon with the reality of women's will.

CONCLUSION

Thousands of Gusii men and women came before the *ritongo* from the 1940s to the 1960s. Minus the one exception the archives reveal, to a man (and to a woman) all Gusii agreed that there could be no life without marriage. They all also concurred that marriage and bridewealth were inseparable. From here, opinions diverged. It was a much more difficult proposition to balance out the rights of fathers and of daughters, and of husbands and of wives. Elders usually favored the rights of senior men over their womenfolk, but did not always dismiss women's wishes. In turn, women and their lovers would not allow senior men to walk away from court unchallenged. Yet in the midst of debates so often polarized, some women and their families could come to a meeting of the minds: women had the right to choose and refuse lovers, or the right to divorce an unwanted husband.

From the war years on, thousands of angry Gusii men availed themselves of the *ritongo* and could generally expect the elders' support. Nonetheless, they found some *ritongo* policies unsettling. Colonial officials no longer enthusiastically promoted the value of "traditional" African society. "Modernization" and "development" became the new fascinations. Among the areas to be "modernized" were African family life and the courts. Here, at the intersection of family life and the law—the very place that Gusii men and women put forward their ideas about marriage—colonial officials set to work. They proceeded to rein in the power of the courts, limiting the number of adultery prosecutions and placing new burdens on complainants in bringing offenders to court. Complainants did not stop exploiting the courts, but neither would they find the courts as strong an ally as they might have wished.

NOTES

1. Nyasani Omanua and Rael Kemuma Kururia, June 3, 2002.

2. Few defeated parties filed appeals to the South Kavirondo Appeal Tribunal (later, the South Nyanza African Appeals Court) and even fewer from there to a district officer. Fathers and husbands were more likely to turn to civil suits for custody of women or for bridewealth. Men found guilty would likely not have had the cash available to file an appeal. All appeal court elders had served on the *ritongo* and the few surviving transcripts reveal that they adjudicated marriage disputes similarly in both arenas.

3. RG ad 38/65. The court elders thought this quite serious, seeing as how the complainant might easily have killed either of them in his rage. The adulterer was sentenced to six months imprisonment, although this was overturned on revision.

4. For example, one man complained that the accused "carried off my wife Kemunto and fornicated with her." RK ad 892/59. See also RK ad 354/63; RG ad 319/62, 480/62, 373/63. None of the civil cases consulted included references to sexual matters.

5. Special Law Panel meetings to Record customary criminal Offences in Kisii District 16/8/61, COHS: MAA/KIS/LAW/1/11.

6. As in Soga courts. Lloyd A. Fallers, *Law without Precedent: Legal Ideas in Action in the Courts of Colonial Busoga* (Chicago: University of Chicago Press, 1969), 112.

7. RK ad 998/59.

8. RK ad 610/59.

9. RG rug 658/58. See also RG rug 293/56, 310/56, 543/56, 714/56, 344/57, 507/57, 121/58, 1332/58, 388/59, 383/62, 684/62; RK rug 321/58, 935/59.

10. RK rug 1157/59. See also RG rug 293/56, 310/56, 481/56, 174/57, 13/59, 32/61, 151/61, 322/61, 487/62, 684/62, 662/63, 24/64, 115/64, 106/65; RK rug 844/57.

11. RK ad 641/46.

12. I include civil claims in the examples used in this section. For more on civil claims, see below.

13. RK ad 732/64.

14. See also RK ad 340/58, 643/58, 1165/58, 619/59, 658/59, 997/59, 769/60, 680/60, 1150/60, 689/63, 731/64, 53/66; RG ad 226/56, 268/56, 613/56, 850/56, 696/57, 359/58, 117/61, 305/61, 335/61, 472/62, 858/63, 17/64; RK cw 396/45, 709/49, 1006/58, 421/65, 817/66; RG cw 423/57, 897/57, 8/68.

15. RG ad 742/60. See also RK ad 673/59, 927/59, 1164/59, 255/60; RG ad 387/58, 934/60, 46/62; RK cw 1493/45, 1175/52.

16. Given the highly charged atmosphere surrounding infertility, simple accusations of barrenness could sour a woman to her marriage:

> Osugo married me, but, I went to his home and I lived there a period of three years without having children with him, and so I went to the accused's home and I have had a boy with him. Now, I do not wish to return to Osugo's home because he thinks that I was bad by failing to have children, but no! it is he who was infertile.

RK ad 927/59. See also RK ad 832/58, 673/59; RG cw 215/60; RK cw 461/50. Other women pointed to the continual sickness or deaths of children as just cause for repudiating a husband. See RK ad 306/58, 610/59, 934/60; RG cw 203/54.

17. This case is taken from the Mayers' notes. In the court cases they recorded, they did not put down the litigants' names, and so, for convenience sake, I've inserted common Gusii names.

18. RM cw 113/46.

19. See RK ad 886/46; RG ads 397/56, 659/60, 225/61, 21/62, 356/62; RG civil 1040/54; RK cw 1400/45. For a discussion of domestic violence in Gusiiland in the 1980s, see Margrethe Silberschmidt, *"Women Forget That Men are the Masters" : Gender Antagonism and Socio-economic Change in Kisii District, Kenya* (Uppsala: Nordiska Afrikainstitutet, 1999), 122–123. Her arguments on the historical antecedents of contemporary male violence are, however, unconvincing.

20. Minutes of the Law Panel Committee (Kisii Section), Nov. 29–30, 1954, KNA: DP 18/13.

21. RK ad 673/59, 259/60, 260/60, 758/60; RG ad 580/57, 308/60, 269/61, 540/62; RK civil nn/40s (no number, late 1940s), 39/65; RG cw 511/53, 219/56, 186/60, 634/60; RK cw 99/46, 600/47, 394/50, 461/50; RM cw 2/46. It is not clear in many of these cases why the husband had turned out his wife. Sometimes it seems unceasing arguments or the death of several children had produced intense mutual hostility. In cases where a wife had clearly offended a husband he could send her back to her parents, who should provide her with a goat to appease him. Some cases may have begun like this, only to escalate when the wife refused to return.

22. RG ad 621/56. Elena, a woman whose husband had been off at work for almost three years and (we can presume) did not contribute much to help support the homestead, went off to another man. RG ad 276/66.

23. RG ad 281/56, 338/61.

24. On prostitution, see RK ad 823/58. One man called his wife both sexually loose and a prostitute: RK cw 300/50. On accusations that the woman practiced witchcraft, see RK ad 673/59; RG ad 329/61; RK cw 1207/47, 1741/47, 1475/57; RG cw 982/54, 111/57, 333/60; RM div 189/57; RM cw 358/46. Other women charged that their husbands or in-laws had tried to teach them witchcraft. See RK cw 1480/45.

25. RG ad 17/64, 858/63, 188/61; RK rug 758/64. See also RK ad 770/59; RG ad 196/66; RK cw 396/45, 927/54, 433/55, 910/62; RG cw 257/56; RM cw 11/57, 157/57, 1447/57.

26. RK rug 770/60.

27. RM cw 411/46.

28. It made less sense for a man to plead guilty to adultery even though marriage was the ultimate goal of accused men. In adultery cases, pleading guilty would only prove that the complainant had incontestable rights over his wife. In fact, many an accused man denied that he had the complainant's wife: instead, he would said, she is *my* wife.

29. RG rug 1157/59, 769/64; RK 1127/46.

30. RG rug 435/57.

31. RG rug 373/59.

32. RG rug 153/56, 728/56, 173/57, 507/57, 51/58, 132/58, 174/58, 13/59, 373/59, 388/59, 619/60, 322/61.

33. RG rug 905/56. See also RG rug 310/56, 543/56, 728/56, 174/57, 435/57, 13/59, 388/59, 322/61, 325/61, 659/62, 106/65, 274/65; RK rug 844/59, 729/64, 758/64.

34. RG ad 32/59. See also RK ad 658/59; RG ad 397/56; RK cw 554/47, 1795/47, 709/49, 254/54, 584/56, 474/59; RG rug 173/57, 174/57, 103/58, 373/59.

35. RG rug 121/58.

36. RG ad 29/60. See also RK ad 643/58, 997/59, 1120/60, 472/62; RG ad 226/56, 313/56, 560/57, 420/63, 53/66; RK cw 1662/57; RG cw 224/53, 894/56, 67/67, 263/67.

37. RK ad 1150/60.

38. Like husbands, elders ignored the agency of women. As did many other women, Kwamboka told the court that "I *went* to the accused." The court heard this very differently: "[T]oday the woman herself has come before the court and she has said that in fact she was *carried off by* the accused." RK ad 770/59, emphases added. Elders hoped to brush aside Kwamboka's attempt to force herself into debates over whom she would marry. To an extent they succeeded: since they were the ones to judge her lover, she could not prevent him from being punished.

39. RK ad 927/59. Emphases added. While men and women in elopement cases often used *kuja* (to come) and *kwenda* (to go), (i.e., "She came to me," "I went to him"), they also employed *kuchukua* (to carry). Yet even *kuchukua* could be balanced by insistence that the woman had been "carried" consensually. RG rug 151/61, 742/64.

40. RG ad 164/58. See also RK ad 641/46, 832/58, 10/59, 694/59, 769/60; RG ad 621/56, 580/57, 690/60, 335/61; RK cw 86/47, 1402/57, 1475/57; RM cw 60/57, 1447/57.

41. RG ad 329/61. See also RK ad 610/59; RG ad 225/61.

42. RG ad 335/61. See also RK ad 240/58; RG ad 114/61.

43. RG ad 319/62. A woman from the Buha highlands of Tanzania recalled that parents, when forcing a girl into marriage, would "pull her like a goat until she agreed to the marriage." Margot Lovett, "Elders, Migrants and Wives: Labor Migration and the Renegotiation of Intergenerational, Patronage and Gender Relations in Highland Buha, Western Tanzania, 1921–1962" (Ph.D. dissertation, Columbia University, 1996), 277. Similarly, a Gikuyu man in 1956 referred to his new sister-in-law as a "two-legged goat." Claire C. Robertson, *Trouble Showed the Way: Women, Men, and Trade in the Nairobi Area, 1890–1990* (Bloomington: Indiana University Press, 1997), 208. Kershaw, however, suggests that for Gikuyu "a common term of endearment from a brother to a sister was 'my *mburi*', my goats." Greet Kershaw, *Mau Mau from Below* (Oxford: James Currey, 1997), 24.

44. Iona Mayer, "The Gusii of Western Kenya," in *Cultural Source Materials for Population Planning in East Africa*, Vol. III, *Beliefs and Practices*, ed. Angela Molnos (Nairobi: East African Publishing House, 1973), 131.

45. RG ad 696/57.

46. RK ad 680/60,1150/60. See also RG ad 613/56; RK cw 503/66; RG cw 894/56.

47. For more on the background of court elders, see Brett L. Shadle, "African Court Elders in Nyanza Province, Kenya, c. 1930–1960: From 'Traditional' to 'Modern,'" in *Intermediaries, Interpreters and Clerks: African Employees and the Making of Colonial Africa*, eds. Benjamin Lawrance, Emily Lynn Osborn, and Richard Roberts (Madison: University of Wisconsin Press, [in press]).

48. Brett L. Shadle, "'Changing Traditions to Meet Current Altering Conditions': Customary Law, African Courts, and the Rejection of Codification in Kenya, 1930–60," *Journal of African History* 40 (1999), 411–431.

49. Tribunal elders in Kuria explained that in the past many DOs had been displeased with their judgments based on customary law and consequently varied a large number of the their decisions. Safari Diary of K. L. Hunter, Aug. 1937, KNA: Adm 12/4/1.

50. DC SK to PC Nyanza, Dec. 3, 1947, KNA: L&O 2/1.

51. Shadle, "'Changing Traditions to Meet Current Altering Conditions.'"

52. Some accused men received a father's permission to live with the woman, and some even paid bridewealth, without knowing her father had already married her off elsewhere. In such cases fathers were considered at fault for having accepted two bridewealths. A father who married his daughter to two men simultaneously so disturbed social stability—claims over women and cattle were thrown into disarray and could lead to violence—that most Gusii condemned the practice and it was in fact a criminal act. One father, the elders said, "has been very dishonest according [to] the demeanour noticed in court. This important witness seems to have got into some secret agreement with the accused about his daughter's

marriage." The accused had followed all that he should have to gain rights over a woman, and so the elders could not convict him. RG ad 585/65. See also RK ad 620/59, 996/59, 260/60; RG ad 54/65.

53. Special Law Panel meetings to record customary criminal offences in Kisii District, Aug. 16, 1961, COHS: MAA/KIS/LAW/1/11.

54. RK ad 26/59, 604/59, 814/59, 998/59, 20/63; RG ad 277/56, 560/57, 29/60, 277/61, 93/62, 858/63, 496/62, 17/64, 124/65.

55. That so many cases were dismissed on these grounds does not lessen the importance of the large number of cases filed. If a husband failed to prove that his wife was with the accused it still meant she was a runaway wife, though to parts unknown.

56. RG ad 107/62.

57. RG ad 350/57.

58. See RK ad 673/59, 942/59, 997/59, 1164/59, 255/60, 260/60, 69/63, 344/63, 385/63, 715/64, 90/66; RG ad 529/56, 350/57, 444/57, 482/57, 558/58, 251/59, 42/61, 241/61, 107/62, 442/62, 450/62, 523/62, 376/63, 555/63, 11/64, 158/65, 221/65, 270/66.

59. See RK ad 306/58; RG ad 529/56, 580/57, 164/58, 114/61, 225/61, 46/62; RK ad 16/47, 169/48. If the woman's situation was not clearly fraught with danger, and especially if the father did not defend the accused, the elders would find him guilty. RG ad 359/58, 387/58, 319/62.

60. RG ad 742/60. See also RK ad 832/58, 927/59, 1164/59, 255/60. But court elders in two cases ignored this line of defense: in RK ad 832/58 the accused was fined shs. 150 (when the average fine for that year in *Ritongo* Kuja was shs. 170), and in RG ad 387/58 the elders also handed down a shs. 150 fine, compared to the average fine for that court in 1958 of just under shs. 140.

61. RK ad 641/46. In *Ritongo* Kuja Nyambebe accused Orondo of "stealing" his wife. Orondo admitted having lived with the woman, but asserted that "the wife came to me by herself." Not surprisingly, this defense did not sway the *ritongo* elders, who convicted him. Orondo appealed. Now, however, Kerubo ("the wife," the transcriber wrote) appeared and explained that she was the wife of (and had had a child with) a third man. While both litigants were "eager" to marry her, Kerubo said, "neither is my husband." The SKAT elders overturned the *ritongo's* decision. While in most adultery cases the role of the woman was ignored, Kerubo's actions were too extreme to be overlooked. The elders stated that "this wife is like a harlot she is wandering everywhere." More surprising, the elders made it a point to note that "the wife herself admits that she was not forced, she went there with her own free will." Appeal 16/47.

62. RK ad 927/59.

63. RG ad 326/56. See also RK ad 10/59, 942/59, 1133/59.

64. RK rug 1134/60. See also RG rug 310/56, 2/58; RK rug 935/59, 770/60.

65. RG rug 379/57, 480/57, 103/58, 431/61, 739/61.

66. RG rug 502/61, 383/62; RK rug 10/63.

67. RG rug 489/57, 501/57, 582/57, 174/58, 656/58, 32/61; RK rug 321/58, 16/59, 716/59.

68. RG rug 435/57, 132/58, 373/59; RK rug 844/59, 1157/59.

69. Kisii (or Gusii) Law Panel, Dec. 10–11, 1962, COHS: MAA/KIS/LAW/1/13.

70. RK rug 1/47. The translation is the Mayers'.

71. RK rug 65/47. The translation is the Mayers'.

72. RK rug 190/48. See also RK rug 231/46.

73. RK abd 771/60. See also RG abd 108/61; RG rug 648/58 (an abduction misfiled as an elopement case).

74. RG abd 18/55.

75. RK abd 859/59.

76. RG abd 702/58.

77. Sabaniah Aroni Omayo and Maoga Onkundi, May 28, 2002.
78. RM injury suit 391/46.
79. RG abd 225/59.
80. RK rug 1012/59.
81. RK rug 216/46.
82. SKAT 1/47.
83. RG abd 702/58.
84. RG abd 472/63. RG abd 662/62. See also RG abd 172/56, 16/57, 636/57, 702/58, 25/61, 227/67; RK abd 859/59, 88/63, 372/66.
85. As shown in Table 5.1, in *Ritongo* Manga and *Ritongo* Kuja fines were highest in abduction cases—over twice as high as those in elopement. *Ritongo* Gesima is here unusual, in that the fines for adultery are exceptionally high, and those for abduction low, but abduction fines remain higher than those for elopement. In addition, elders at Gesima and Kuja (and probably Manga as well, although the sources are unavailable) took advantage of their powers to imprison men in Indecent Assault cases. They sent ten men to prison for terms ranging from two to six months, and usually fined them as well. *Ritongo* Gesima elders did sentence two men to prison in adultery cases, one for a strictly sexual crime, although both sentences were quashed on review.
86. This includes only those cases which had a full hearing. Another 16 were dismissed either after passing one year without either party arriving in court or ex parte. Many more cases must have been moved to the provincial archives in Kisumu, where the process of sorting court records had just begun during my research. Those that had previously been heard as adultery cases: RM cw 11/57, 60/57, 69/57, 153/57, 175/57, 328/57, 1422/57; RG cw 472/53, 943/54, 79/59; RK cw 1043/52, 799/54, 433/55, 1394/55, 1332/56, 654/57, 284/61, 910/62, 806/64, 421/65.
87. One former court elder suggested that some civil claims preceded criminal cases, although no records confirm this. Paul Nyangoto Ogeturenga, Oct. 24, 1997.
88. This was in reference to divorces. Many women, after having obtained divorces in African Courts, returned to their husbands upon discovering that they would lose custody of their children. DOs i/c courts, at DCs' meeting, Nyanza, May 16, 1955, KNA: MAA 9/842.
89. See chap. 1.
90. RG div 447/57.
91. RG div 320/59.
92. Oliver Knowles, "Some Modern Adaptations of Customary Law in the Settlement of Matrimonial Disputes in the Luo, Kisii and Kuria Tribes of South Nyanza," *Journal of African Administration* 8 (1956), 11–15.
93. While elders never granted divorces against the wishes of the petitioners' kin, they did dismiss some divorce claims despite a relative's support. Elders followed parental wishes in ten of the dismissed cases, but they overruled parents in five cases.
94. I here disagree with Agnes Odinga. She examined eighty divorce cases from South Nyanza Luo courts and also found that many fathers supported their daughters' petitions. She argues that this is evidence of senior men's decreasing willingness to collaborate among themselves and with the state to control women. This is unconvincing if divorce cases are put in the context of other marriage disputes in the courts. Agnes Adhiambo Odinga, "Women's Medicine and Fertility: A Social History of Reproduction in South Nyanza, Kenya, 1920–1980" (Ph.D. dissertation, University of Minnesota, 2001), chap. 5.
95. If a woman petitioning for divorce had no living father or brother, her mother might appear in court to speak on her behalf.
96. On violence, see RG div 236/55, 616/57, 19/58, 320/59, 455/59, 119/60, 149/60, 261/60, 670/60, 144/61, 193/61, 220/61; RK div 1469/52, 863/53, 71/55, 1040/56, 1349/58, 1052/59; RM div 844/57; KAC 1/63, 321/63, 77/64, 6/65; on lack of children, see RG div

296/53, 57/56, 237/59, 180/57, 310/59; RK div 192/55, 180/57, 1145/58, 523/60; RM div 1159/57, 1290/57; on witchcraft, see RG div 236/55, 168/57, 542/59, 267/60, 448/60; RK div 1446/51, 1276/52, 1462/52 1470/54, 1040/56, 1459/58, 219/59, 320/59, 220/61; RK div 1059/56; RM div 976/57.

97. RG div 353/56, 320/59, 356/59, 173/60, 247/60, 34/60, 193/61, 246/61; RK div 246/58, 1146/58; RM div 1342/57, 17/60; RG cw 215/60; RK cw 254/54.

98. On chasing a wife, see RG div 353/56, 417/57, 570/57, 557/61, 616/57, 159/58, 186/59, 187/59, 257/59, 356/59, 455/59, 149/60, 173/60, 224/60, 247/60, 261/60, 347/60, 448/60, 670/60, 193/61, 246/61, 557/61; RK div 1771/52, 284/53, 379/54, 1470/54, 22/55, 172/55, 1040/56, 1041/56, 933/58, 1459/58, 246/59, 1052/59; RM div 20/60; on prostitution, see RG div 251/59; RK div 300/50, 71/55, 246/58, 470/58, 1146/58. One man insulted his wife as a loose woman. RK div 1041/56.

99. RG div 447/57.

100. RG div 478/60.

101. RM div 1053/57; RK cw 1221/51, 1501/47.

102. RK div 1459/58.

103. RG div 267/60; KAC div 169/65.

104. RK div 215/59. See also RK div 1469/52; RM cw 175/57; RM div 17/60.

105. RG div 57/56.

106. RG cw 469/64, 1064/59; RK cw 433/55, 1081/56, 450/63, 39/65, 421/65; RK div 1276/52, 284/53, 246/59, 1034/59.

107. RK div 190/52. See also RG cw 22/60. In 1968 the District Magistrate at Kuja heard a similar case, and ruled that "The court cannot force her back since [her husband] is dead." DM Kuja cw 472/68.

108. RK cw 474/59.

109. RK div 421/65. See also RK div 863/53; KAC div 50/64.

110. RK cw 1207/47. See also RK cw 396/45; RM div 20/60.

111. The children, however, would remain the plaintiff's. RK cw 709/49.

112. RM cw 448/46. See also RK cw 1493/45, 806/64.

113. RK cw 926/57.

114. RG cw 257/56. See also RK cw 396/45, 1207/47, 709/49, 1102/52, 806/64, 421/65, 472/68; RG cw 554/53, 894/56.

115. Ambros Bwoma suggested that when her lover had been imprisoned a woman would despair and return to her husband. Bwoma, July 19, 1997.

116. Paul Nyagoto Ogeturenga, Oct. 24, 1997.

117. Eric A. Beavon, *Sindiga, the Savage: A Tale of the Wilds* (New York: Harper, 1930), 228.

118. Peter M. Nyarang'o, *Sunset in Africa* (Nairobi: East African Educational Publishers, 1994). Arani Nyaberi recalls a similar case involving *Ritongo* Gesima. Personal communication, Dec. 7, 1997. A new court sits where *Ritongo* Kuja once stood, and the location remains a problem. In April 2006 a prisoner broke free of his guards at the court, ran down the hill, and dove into the Gucha, making good his escape.

119. Iona Mayer, "The Patriarchal Image: Routine Dissociation in Gusii Families." *African Studies* 34 (1975), 277.

120. Escaping a forced or unhappy marriage was the leading cause of suicide among women in most of the societies examined in Paul Bohannan, ed., *African Homicide and Suicide* (New York: Atheneum, 1967 [1960]). See also, for example, DC Meru to PC Central, Oct. 9, 1936, KNA: PC/CP 19/1; "Notes of meeting by W. E. Owen, between Owen and CS," in Ag. PC Nyanza to CS, March 3, 1944, KNA: MAA 7/700; Archdeacon Owen, "Comments on Report of Committee of L.N.C., Central Kavirondo, on Forced Marriages and Runaway Wives," June 5, 1944, CMS: ACC 83 O 22/1; PC Nyanza [note of Feb. 2, 1950 on the marriage of Agnes Othieno and Dan Nyanjom], KNA: Leg 28/1;

Monica Wilson, *For Men and Elders: Change in the Relations of Generations and of Men and Women among the Nyakyusa-Ngonde People 1875–1971* (New York: Africana, for the International African Institute, 1977), 111; L. P. Mair, "African Marriage and Social Change," in *Survey of African Marriage and Family Life*, ed. Arthur Phillips (London: Oxford University Press, for the International African Institute, 1953), 13, 122; Barthazar Aloys Rwezaura, *Traditional Family Law and Change in Tanzania: A Study of the Kuria Social System* (Hamburg: Institut für Internationale Angelegenheiten der Universität Hamburg, 1985), 65; Sally Falk Moore, *Social Facts and Fabrications: "Customary" Law on Kilimanjaro, 1880–1980* (Cambridge, UK: Cambridge University Press, 1986), 205; Steven Feierman, *Peasant Intellectuals: Anthropology and History in Tanzania* (Madison: University of Wisconsin Press, 1990), 61. A study in the United States found that with the introduction of unilateral divorce law female suicide rates dropped by as much as twenty per cent. Betsey Stevenson and Justin Wolfers, "Bargaining in the Shadow of the Law: Divorce Laws and Family Distress" (NBER Working Paper 10175, Dec. 2003).

121. DC SK to PC Nyanza, Oct. 21, 1936, KNA: MDS 2/3/5. See also N. K. Nyang'era, *The Making of Man and Woman under Abagusii Customary Law* (Kisii: self published, 1999), 64.

122. Nyasani Omanua, Oct. 22, 1997; Paul Nyangoto Ogeturenga, Oct. 24, 1997.

123. RK cw 1081/56. See also RG div 816/56; RK cw 274/46.

6

The State, African Society, and Limits of the *Ritongo*

As Gusiiland fell into its marriage crisis and the *ritongo* were clogged with marriage disputes, colonial administrators were reassessing their own ideas about African society. The tenor of colonial rule—in Kisii, Nairobi, and London—shifted from a dedication to preserving "traditional" Africa to the creation of a "modern" one; the 1937 White Paper on "The Status of Women in Africa" was both the best and the last major articulation of the older sentiments. The Second World War forced the British to reconsider the place of its empire in a very new international context. Previous beliefs in the inherent goodness of African society—in particular, the place of senior men atop African societies—no longer went unquestioned, and the need to defend "tribal" institutions from the degrading influences of the outside world seemed less an imperative. Administrators were not yet confident enough, however, to enact policies that would directly alter the balance of power between men and women, young and old.

The modernization of Africa also required revamping the legal system. African tribunals could not be allowed to continue on its present course with few set policies, little regular oversight, and staffed by old, illiterate men. Already in the later 1930s and on through independence, colonial officials undertook a series of reforms meant to bring African courts closer to "proper" courts. Rulebooks were put together, more educated elders were taken on, and administrative posts were created dealing solely with the tribunals. It was here that administrators could implement their ideas about reforming African society. They eliminated husbands' ability to file multiple adultery charges; a successful complainant could not ask for a warrant of attachment be issued for his wife; responsibility for bringing an accused man to court fell to husbands and fathers. With greater oversight of the tribunals and better educated elders, administrators could, on the whole, be assured that these policies were followed. The state would not allow the courts to be tools in the hands of senior men.

ADMINISTRATIVE THOUGHTS ON GENDER AND GENERATION IN THE POSTWAR WORLD

As the 1930s drew to a close, and with the controversy over the "Status of African Women" only just settled, administrators in Kenya began to doubt their previous attitudes toward African women, marriage, and bridewealth. As wartime came and went, minds began to change. In Britain and across the African empire "development" became the new mantra: Africa should be put on a faster pace toward joining the modern world. Many administrators reflected whether those decidedly "traditional" practices that kept women subordinated (at least in comparison to contemporary Britain) might present a barrier to Africa's path toward modernity. Administrators posed questions not recently heard from within their own ranks: Did bridewealth in fact reduce women to the status of slaves? How common was forced marriage and how could it be prevented? Were husbands and fathers deserving of extensive state support? The positions that administrators had so recently and so vehemently defended no longer seemed unassailable.

Developing Africa

By the late 1930s, there was a growing sense in colonial circles that preserving the "traditional" no longer served the purpose of European rule. A wave of strikes across Africa and elsewhere in the British empire forced colonial officials to reappraise whether they should recognize an emerging working class. Malcolm MacDonald, Secretary of State for the Colonies from 1938 to 1940, was particularly interested in social and economic causes, and labor actions in the colonies only gave impetus to his agenda. Under pressure from the metropole, the colonies established labor departments, removing workers' concerns from the larger rubric of African affairs handled by provincial administrations. On the home front, the war also made commonplace daily government involvement in citizens' lives, with such things as food rationing and assisting the London poor; in Africa, social services were expanded to include discussions of health and impoverishment. In 1940, Parliament passed the Colonial Development and Welfare Act, setting the stage for even deeper colonial involvement in daily African life after the war.[1] The idea of intense administrative involvement toward "developing" and "modernizing" Africa became increasingly accepted.

During the 1940s, Britain and France faced a new world order, one in which colonialism seemed less easily justifiable. London well understood that developing Africa could give concrete evidence of how Africans benefitted from colonial rule. Similarly, bringing Africans more in touch with modern ways demonstrated Britain's commitment to setting her colonies on the road (long though it might be) toward independence.[2] Of special importance, a developed Africa could help heal Britain's economy, bled dry by the war. To accomplish this, Britain colonized its African colonies a second time. Armies of Britons entered the colonial service, especially in technical areas: the number of agricultural officers in Kenya increased nearly 850 percent (from 298 to 2,519) between 1945 and 1957, dwarfing the increase in administrative officers (from 117 to 213).[3]

A new generation of administrators entered Kenya with new ideas about African life. Furse at the CO had for decades filled administrative ranks with Oxbridge men of a decidedly conservative outlook, deeply paternalistic and patriarchal. Already by the 1930s, the winds of change could begin to be felt; one official lamented the entry of some "fake gentlemen" into the service.[4] During the war Furse recognized that indirect rule was on the way out. Many recruits now came from outside the public schools, and practical skills were more emphasized. While the promise of adventure remained a lure to some, there were also idealists intent on preparing Africans for independence within their tenures (rather than the generations, or centuries, previously envisioned).[5] Some new administrators thought differently about Africans, having fought alongside them to defeat Axis dictators.[6] Older officials also changed with the times. Sidney Fazan began his career in Kenya in 1911, but in the later 1930s took active part in pushing for alterations in bridewealth customs. K. L. Hunter, appointed in 1919, took up the same issue in 1943 and appointed the first African Assistant Administrative Officers. As one former colonial official put it, the ethos of the interwar years was by 1945 "dead and done with."[7]

Development and African Women

A much broader, world-wide discussion of population and demography helped stimulate administrative interest in African family life. Colonial officials had long been concerned with Africa's population levels, from the 1890s to the 1920s observing that the numbers of their subjects had stagnated or declined (owing to disease, conquest, and the evils of forced labor). After the war demography captured the attention of Britons in new ways, as both African population and British dedication to development increased. Some argued that development would prevent overpopulation, others that only a precise counting of the African population would permit the effective implementation of modernization programs. In either event, if development were to proceed more thought had to be given to the place of fertility, reproduction, and family in Africans' lives.[8]

The evolution of African family life, in turn, called for new policies for African women. In his 1944 report on Kenya's native tribunals, Arthur Phillips "forecast ... that, for better or worse, the emancipation of African women will proceed, and with increasing rapidity." Rather than forestalling this, Phillips admitted the necessity of adapting marriage laws "so as to improve the status of the African wife."[9] Chris Minter recalled that he and fellow administrators "deplored (among [them]selves) the status of African women in certain [respects]."[10] Many argued that it was the progress of women that would ultimately determine the evolution of African societies. As the Nyanza Provincial Courts Officer wrote in 1950, "progressive development of African Society is relative to the increase in the status of African women."[11]

To encourage development the state (with assistance from the Colonial Welfare and Development Act)[12] began investing more time and money in training and education for African women, albeit in areas which reflected European (men's) ideas about gendered divisions of labor. At the Jeanes School at Kabete, men enrolled in commercial classes, grooming themselves to be the new business elite, as well as curricula in areas such as cooperatives and community development which would allow them to slide into positions eventually left empty by Britons. Education for women was rather different. African women too could take courses at Kabete, but in needlework, cooking, and laundry.[13]

A handful of administrators felt African women needed education beyond household chores. Elite African men required the companionship of educated wives to prevent them from slinking off to beerhalls and potentially creating urban disorder. African women, Governor Brooke-Popham wrote in 1939,

> must receive education not only in cooking food and looking after babies ... but also sufficient to be able to read native books and papers so they shall be able to talk on an equal footing with their menfolk. I believe the African [man] who takes quite an intelligent interest in European affairs, gets fed up when he goes back to his hut and finds his wife can think and talk of nothing but maize, manure, and goats. Thereupon he goes off to his counterpart of the club ... which may become a sort of talking shop, and possibly a centre of disaffection.[14]

If some African men were to be molded into a petite bourgeoisie, Robertson points out, "then it was considered suitable that they marry Western-style housewives."[15] A few women began to be included in important bodies such as African District Councils and Law Panels, and some took part in a "fact finding" tour to Uganda with South Nyanza elites.[16]

Education remained the preserve of few women; administrators touched the lives of many more through the *Maendeleo ya Wanawake* (Development of Women) organization. The roots of *Maendeleo* lay in the 1940s, when wives of colonial officials, missionaries, and settlers began holding workshops for African women. These disparate courses came together under government sponsorship in late 1951, and *Maendeleo* clubs and membership expanded rapidly over the next several years: 300 clubs with 37,000 members by the end of 1954. In South Nyanza alone there were one hundred clubs and 2,400 members in 1955, expanding to 219 clubs with 5,225 women two years later.[17] The courses of instruction, like those at the Jeanes school, mostly involved homecrafts (health and hygiene, basket weaving, cooking), but also included agricultural information, something which African women had generally received only via their menfolk.[18]

Quickly enough administrators recognized how influential training and education could be in expanding women's horizons and enlightening them to the ways of the modern world. The district commissioner (DC) of North Nyanza, writing about the Women's Institutes from which *Maendeleo* emerged, saw them as concrete steps toward reaching women. "For years, we have somewhat mechanically repeated the phrase 'we must get at the women,'" he conceded, "but I suppose being men our efforts have mainly stopped there." Women's Institutes provided a real opportunity not only to improve women's lives, but also to lead African society that much farther toward modernity. "If we do 'get at' the women successfully," he continued, "there is no limit to the rapid improvement of African social life that will take place; health and hygiene, agriculture, education, morals all will be incalculably affected for the good."[19] Former administrator Chris Minter recalled an army officer in the early stages of Mau Mau advancing the idea that they "could best win if [they] enlisted the support of the women—what was later expressed in other parts of the world as the 'hearts and minds' approach."[20] Perhaps of most significance, administrators argued, *Maendeleo* clubs promoted "civilized" behavior, of inestimable importance in fighting the "atavism" of Mau Mau. "This is not," the Commissioner of Community Development pronounced, "just tea and buns."[21]

Developing Bridewealth

The need to "modernize" African social relations included, some administrators believed, a revamping of those most basic of African social institutions, marriage and bridewealth. In 1939, the Secretary of State for the Colonies again solicited from the governors information on the status of African women. While he sought opinions as to the desirability of education and wage labor for women, most of his questions involved marriage: should bridewealth and polygamy be discouraged? How much freedom did widows have? Should a uniform law be enacted to prevent underage and forced marriages?[22] Fazan, Provincial Commissioner of Nyanza in 1949, explained how in older times bridewealth had helped to cement wider alliances among families and to prevent in-breeding. But of late in a few areas (primarily North and Central Kavirondo districts and Central Province) cash had begun to replace cattle as bridewealth.[23] With the rise of cash bridewealth and its exchange between individual grooms and fathers-in-law (rather than between families), the advantages of bridewealth melted away. In fact, marriage became the sale of women. Yet Fazan did not suggest a return to idyllic communalism. Instead, he posited that in the several districts more advanced toward individualism and money economy bridewealth had irrevocably become more of a curse than a blessing. "Its progressive disappearance over one or two generations," he wrote, "is desirable."[24]

While DCs in Central and South Kavirondo agreed with Fazan's overall assessment of the situation, those in North Kavirondo and Kericho still felt bridewealth helped ensure the good behavior of wives. Facing the loss of bridewealth cattle should their married daughters run off, parents had a vested interest in daughters' actions. Fazan countered with the claim that multiple exchanges of cattle broke more marriages than it saved. Bridewealth brought into a homestead was quickly used to contract another marriage, linking a whole series of unions. The collapse of one marriage set off a chain reaction, as each man in turn had to demand the return of his bridewealth, leaving a trail of broken marriages.[25]

A few years later the new Nyanza provincial commissioner (PC), Hunter, asked the administrative officers in the province to consider the future of "native policy." Since the signing of the Atlantic Charter, Britons had been forced to re-examine the future of their African colonial possessions[26] and Hunter intended to prepare Nyanza for a very different postwar world. Along with perennial questions of native authority, land, and labor, he identified "Native Marriage" as an area in need of study and possibly reform. For his own part, Hunter advanced numerous reasons why bridewealth should be discouraged, if not abolished. Not surprisingly, issues of law and order and of administrative efficiency headed up his list. The work of white officers, chiefs, and tribunals would be "reduce[d] *very* considerably" if they did not have to contend with endless disputes over bridewealth cattle. Stock theft would also decline. Campaigns against overstocking were destined to fail, Hunter continued, so long as Africans kept large number of poor quality cattle to use as bridewealth. Yet Hunter also argued that bridewealth perpetuated the low, even slave-like status of African women. Few girls completed their education since their families benefitted more from a girl's marriage than from her education; fathers preferred to pull their daughters from school and marry them off. With bridewealth, Hunter despaired, "a girl remains a chattel."[27]

The district officers (DO) in Nyanza tended to be more conservative than Hunter. Many called attention to the positive aspects of bridewealth: it inspired the poor man to work hard; it lent stability to marriage. The state might fine tune the system—advocate the use of cash to prevent overstocking,[28] cap bridewealth to allow youth to marry[29]—but bridewealth would fade away only when African society as a whole had changed.[30] The one officer who shared Hunter's objections to bridewealth marriages (which he characterized as the "buying and selling of women") thought only Christianity could alter people's attitudes.[31] When summarizing for Nairobi the views of the Nyanza administrators, Hunter still felt compelled to detail the "evils" of bridewealth.

Nonetheless, he was forced to admit that unseen and potentially harmful results might arise from any direct government action, or even from simple propaganda.[32] Government should protect women from forced marriages, but the abolition of bridewealth itself would have to await broader changes in African society.[33]

The transformation of officials' opinions had begun, however. Hunter, apparently finding support in African-language newspapers,[34] continued to press home his point. In 1944, he queried if Nyanza's local native councils (LNCs) "share[d] the view that we should aim at gradual abolition [of bridewealth] in the course of evolution." He again stressed bridewealth's relation to soil erosion, stock theft, and overburdened Native Tribunals.[35] Hunter well understood that bridewealth was a delicate subject, and that even supplanting cattle with cash might evoke howls of protest. Nonetheless, he argued that very little progress could be made "in the application of an Agrarian Plan without cutting across many of the indigenous customs."[36] Some DCs now sided with Hunter. Atkins in Central Kavirondo favored propaganda "to try and wean Africans from the bride price system," while Low in South Kavirondo concurred that bridewealth should be abolished "in due course."[37] Remarkably, district commissioners in Central Province proposed that, even though the elimination of bridewealth would hardly influence cattle holdings, the state should discourage the practice nonetheless.[38]

Some administrators even came to describe bridewealth as had many missionaries and metropolitan critics: as a form of slavery. In South Kavirondo, District Commissioner Perreau in 1945 harangued chiefs and other male elites about changes in marriage customs, including bridewealth. At a *baraza* Perreau outlined the myriad troubles attendant with high bridewealth. In particular, he stated that bridewealth cattle from a daughter's marriage,

> is promptly used to buy a girl for the son . . . You will notice I use the word 'BUY' instead of 'bride price.' This is intentional. For the actions of these days are getting like a slave market. Yes, you are buying and selling women; slavery, which is supposed to have been driven out, a badge o[f] shame! All the old significance and meaning of the payment of bride price is being turned into a vulgar and ugly greed for wealth. Wealth from *selling*, yes, selling, the seed of your bodies: your own blood! We Europeans, it is true, used at one time to trade in slaves but we stopped that about 100 years ago, but even at our worst we never made a trade of selling our own daughters.[39]

Perreau scolded members of the LNC as well, denouncing fathers for "selling their daughters as if they were traffic[k]ing in slaves."[40] The DC at Kericho in 1944 despaired that due to rising bridewealth marrying "a wife is a pure auction and the highest bidder obtains the maiden."[41] Administrators certainly only spoke such inflammatory language when conferring with each other or in palavers with African elite.[42] Nonetheless, perhaps more than anything else this demonstrates how increasingly disturbed officials had become with bridewealth and forced marriage.

Forced Marriage

Concomitant with their declining appreciation of bridewealth administrators were becoming more vocal in their condemnation of forced marriage. In 1937, even as the "Status of Women in Africa" inquiry was being published in London, Nyanza PC Fazan admitted that he remained unclear on the incidence of forced marriage. He hesitantly explored stronger methods to prevent those that did occur. Fazan composed an extended memorandum considering the means and ends the government should pursue regarding African marriage. He began by addressing forced marriage:

> The principal complaint made by missionaries is that girls are sometimes forced by their parents or guardians to marry against their will and that the parent often chooses a husband for his daughter from the size of the consideration he offers rather than from his suitability as a husband. There have been few complaints from natives but that may be due to the fact that girls have been brought up in the tradition that they must marry as their father pleases and, having experience of no other system, find no cause of complaint. I believe that girls have all along had more choice in the matter than the missionaries allege but I do not doubt the broad statement that a girl seldom stands out against her father in his choice of a husband and that the universal opinion of the native elders is that he has the best right and probably the best ability to judge.[43]

Not surprisingly, Fazan discounted missionary reports on the prevalence of forced marriages, but some of his ideas were very new. Fazan seemed ill at ease with existing African marriage customs and the degree of senior male authority. Perhaps the senior male discourse of marriage was so dominant that brides simply *did not know* that they could critique or resist forced marriage. Of course, this was not the case. Women did resist forced marriages, though rarely through complaints to legal authorities. Nevertheless, Fazan had stumbled across a potentially revolutionary insight. If women silently endured forced marriage only because of ignorance of other options, to eliminate forced marriages women would have to be educated to a radically different language of marriage, to be given "experience" of another "system" which extended them the right to reject unwanted mates.

Certainly no administrator had ever gainsaid the harm of forced marriages, although their interpretations of permissible force could be very generous. Fazan, perhaps dissembling a bit, noted in 1939 that it was "common ground . . . among all Administrative officers that a father's power over his children should not extend to forcing them to marry against their will."[44] Yet few officers had ever proposed any far-reaching solutions to prevent forced marriages. Fazan's memorandum, however, hinted at the need for an extensive reconfiguration of African marriage systems. He recommended the compulsory notification of intent to marry and the registration of marriages.[45] Since the woman would have to proclaim her consent to the marriage she would be given a formal opportunity to derail a coerced union. "There is," Fazan wrote, "so far as I can see, no other way of ensuring that cases of coercion are reduced to a minimum."[46] This policy, Fazan predicted, "would have indirect consequences of considerable magnitude." This was an eventuality he was now willing to risk. All the DCs in Nyanza supported Fazan's recommendation for marriage registration, although as it moved up the bureaucracy it was reworked to the point of irrelevance.[47]

As the 1940s progressed administrators condemned forced marriage in ever stronger terms. Even in such a tender area as ensuring the fidelity of *askari*s' (soldiers') wives during the war, administrators set plans to avoid trapping women in unwanted marriages.[48] When hearing the case of Achola Jeje, whose 1940 marriage had been consecrated by violence and (what Archdeacon Owen called) witchcraft, tribunal elders in Central Kavirondo decided that "all [was] according to native custom" and refused to release Achola from her husband. No longer looking favorably upon such judgments, the Provincial Commissioner applauded the Superior Native Tribunal when "more in accordance with civilised ideas" it set Achola free.[49] Even administrators unenthusiastic about female independence feared a rise in forced marriages. Such was E. J. A. Leslie, DC at Voi in 1939, an unabashed defender of "traditional" gender relations. Yet like the more liberal Perreau and Fazan, Leslie believed bridewealth was becoming the medium for the sale of women, parents allowing the lure of enrichment "to persuade them to marry their daughters at ridiculously premature ages and without their consent."[50]

Adultery and Elopement as Civil Wrongs

Adultery was briefly decriminalized in the early 1930s, but an outcry from the provincial administration forced the hand of the Attorney General. He refused to reinstate it as part of the Penal Code, but instead defined it as a crime against "native law and custom." Administrators knew full well that criminalization of adultery had no roots in the murky past of "tribal customary law," but rather in pragmatic concerns of the late 1920s and early 1930s.

In postwar years administrators began to question the legitimacy of the very new, noncustomary idea of adultery as a criminal act. Treating adultery (including cohabitation) as criminal, argued M. N. Evans, in 1947 a DO in Central Kavirondo, sustained the deplorable bridewealth system and, after all, "by native custom adultery was essentially a civil matter."[51] The DC in North Nyanza concurred. Adultery disputes ought to be settled in civil cases, he wrote in 1949, "especially as I can find no indication that in the past they were considered as Criminal offenses against the tribe."[52] Officers also reasoned that elopement was closer to a civil wrong than to a crime, and preserving it as criminal strengthened the ability of fathers to force daughters into marriages with unwanted men. In 1959, T. A. Watts, DC at Machakos, reflected on changes in customary law over the past four decades, the most momentous being Africans' (i.e., African men's) demand that adultery and elopement be classified as crimes rather than civil wrongs, as they had been prior to colonial rule.[53] In fact, whether these ideas were old or not was becoming irrelevant. When Nyanza Provincial African Courts Officer in 1957, Watts argued that most Africans had "abandoned most of their customary laws and tribal obligations." The continued use of quasi-criminal customary law charges (like adultery and elopement) was thus already "usually unfair and will soon be an anachronism."[54]

Until the 1960s, however, both adultery and elopement remained acts punishable by fine or, in default, imprisonment. Despite all their soul-searching, administrators hesitated to offend the sensibilities of senior African men. Watts continued to press for decriminalization but he was stymied (as he explained in 1949) by the fact that "native public opinion demands that this type of case should be treated as a criminal case."[55] It would take an independence-era constitution, with a proviso against the use of unwritten criminal law, to make the change.

Overruling Parents

Administrators also reflected on the rights of women to leave undesirable marriages despite parental objections. In 1955, South Nyanza district officer Raynor investigated with "considerable care" divorce procedure in the African courts. Appeals courts had been granting divorces without any attempt to ascertain if bridewealth could be returned. The ensuing civil cases, Raynor concluded, complicated matters for all involved. He thus suggested that only conditional divorce decrees be issued until the Appeals Court "is satisfied beyond all doubt that the whole question of bride price has been settled [in the African courts] according to customary law."[56] Although he wished only to eliminate some of the massive problems involving bridewealth disputes, two of his fellow DCs anticipated disastrous consequences for women. The DC at Kericho pointed out that making legal divorce dependant on the return of bridewealth put all the power in fathers' hands. Without a full divorce decree a woman could not remarry. In many cases a father wished to retain his bridewealth, "and is therefore deliberately dilatory and opposed his daughter's divorce."[57]

The Central Nyanza DC was even less receptive to the idea. He opposed "most emphatically any suggesion that divorce procedure should be tied up with bride price":

> Many years experience of divorce litigation especially in South Nyanza has convinced me that by being dilatory in returning bride price parents of women who have very good reasons for divorce have been able either to stop their daughters from remarrying, or have caused their daughters to live for years with men who are unable to pay bride price because the father says that he is unable first to repay the original dowry.

Instead, the courts should grant a divorce according only to the merits of the case, without reference to bridewealth. Rather than be forced to abide by the wishes of a father wedded to his bridewealth cattle, "the woman should be free to marry again."[58] (In practice, of course, *ritongo* granted divorces only with the concurrence of fathers or brothers.)

Discussion and Action

Debates over bridewealth, forced marriage, adultery, and divorce did not always produce policy changes. At times, administrators attempted to enact changes, but failed. They also had discovered that when Europeans tried directly to alter these practices the results could be as profound as they were unexpected; the Gikuyu female circumcision crisis had not been forgotten. Administrators shied away from full frontal attacks on these issues unless the practices themselves might have very dangerous consequences.[59] In the end, concerns over "law and order" trumped radical intervention into African marriage customs. Chris Minter recalls that the main issue was to ensure such matters were resolved in the African courts to prevent "physical reprisal[s]" and the upsetting of law and order: "This was really why apparently 'outdated' concepts of right and wrong were tolerated."[60]

More commonly, officers fell back on platitudes about propaganda and education, or encouraged Local Native Councils to regulate these affairs, in hopes that Africans would be more likely to listen to their black leaders and that the broader state would not be implicated in any resulting fiasco. The Member for African Affairs suggested that the government ought to work toward the limitation of bridewealth, but that the best method would be propaganda.[61] Other administrators were content to allow the process of social evolution to unfold. Parry, DO in North Kavirondo, drawing together all the debates over "Native Marriages" simply advanced that these problems "will in all probability solve [themselves] with the passing of time and the spread of education." Africans would have to show the initiative here: the state would be treading dangerous ground daring to legislate on "a custom which is so intimately bound up with the Africans' economic life."[62] The significant changes in administrative thinking about African marriage often produced only stillborn policy changes.

African men seem to have recognized that administrators were hesitant to involve themselves in domestic disputes and rarely came to officers to seek assistance. Terence Gavanagh, in Kisii in 1947–1948, recalled that "No one ever asked me (a boy!) about such things [marriage and bridewealth disputes] or to intervene. How and why?"[63] Chris Minter similarly thought it "most unusual" for Africans to bring marriage disputes to a DO, and "most irregular for a DO to intervene" unless it involved rape. One father complained to Minter of his out-of-control daughter who spent her time with "watu wa gitaa," guitar-playing youth. Minter replied that this was not a crime, and was in fact true of young people in the United Kingdom as well. He thought that, at best, it might in some way contravene customary law and directed the distraught father to go to his tribunal.[64]

A few (very few) marriage disputes did come to administrators when hearing appeals from the African courts. Britons might then apply their understanding of "proper" African marriage. A dozen appeals heard by district officer P. W. Low in 1945–1946 demonstrate his willingness to alter tribunal judgments he felt unfair to women. In some but not all appeals Low argued that Gusii women held certain rights of movement. For example, Marungu appealed his conviction on an elopement charge. He stated that the girl, Nyambuba, had gone to him willingly. Low's assessors proved unable to agree whether or not Marungu was telling the truth, but Low thought he was. For Low, the question then was: if Nyambuba had chosen to elope with Marungu, had Marungu committed an offense? "I should think not," Low ruled, "and Daudi [an assessor] agrees. It is no offense in Kisii custom for a girl to go and live with whom she pleases."[65] Fathers and court elders would have been shocked to hear this; indeed, Low's logic went against the very existence of elopement as an offense triable by the tribunals.[66]

Unsurprisingly, K. L. Hunter was also involved in writing appeals that favored women. Gwako Ombutora of Nyaribari in 1947 asked Hunter, then PC of Nyanza, to consider his case.[67] It was an extremely complex dispute over custody of Monyenye. Reviewing the record of the first appeal, Hunter found that Monyenye's first husband had been Ogoro, now deceased; Ogoro had given bridewealth, but Gwako had not; and Monyenye had had three daughters with Ogoro, and another daughter with Gwako. Having spent time in South Kavirondo, Hunter knew full well how the case should have been decided: Monyenye and her children should have been "inherited" by Ogoro's family. Hunter could not countenance this. "It is not equitable to force her [to remain with Ogoro's family]," he declared, "and therefore some departure from old native custom must be made." He ruled that Monyenye would stay with Gwako, as would her children. Upon the marriage of the first three children, the bridewealth would be sent to Ogoro's family. The bridewealth of the fourth child would go to Monyenye herself. This certainly was a "departure from old native custom." By all rights, the fourth daughter's bridewealth should also have gone to the family of Ogoro, the man who had given bridewealth for, and thus had legal rights over, Monyenye. In effect, Hunter ignored common practice and granted a woman personal control over considerable assets.[68]

G. A. Skipper, DC of South Nyanza in 1958, also determined that women should have some say in their residence. Rehona had unsuccessfully sued for divorce before the Resident Magistrate (hers had been a Christian marriage and thus not triable by a *ritongo*). Later, her husband had gone to *Ritongo* Kuja to sue for custody of her. Skipper reminded the president of Kuja that as it was a Christian marriage the court lacked jurisdiction. Moreover, Skipper wrote, even though Rehona's divorce petition had failed "this is no reason why she should return to [her husband] with whom she has not lived for about a quarter of a century." Skipper ordered that no more cases involving these parties were to be heard at *Ritongo* Kuja.[69]

Administrators' refusal more directly to address bridewealth and other marital matters did not go without criticism. At a 1941 meeting of the provincial commissioners they discouraged legislating changes in bridewealth, especially the substitution of cash for cattle. Such laws would be difficult to enforce (and so presumably suggest holes in state power) and would also write bridewealth into the law, making it "difficult, if not impossible, for the custom to die out."[70] But this explanation did not go far in satisfying the Director of Veterinary Services (DVS), who shot off a letter noting the "evils" of keeping large herds of bridewealth cattle. "[T]he bride-price custom," he charged, "does interfere with the plans approved for general agricultural development." The DVS surmised that the PCs would rather leave changes up to the gradual process of evolution. If this was to be policy, the Director spat, then the state might as well end all programs for "soil conservation and improvement in agriculture and animal husbandry, in fact on all progressive activities, until the necessary degree of evolution has occurred."[71] His concerns went unaddressed.

REMAKING THE COURTS

The reversal of administrative thinking about African marriage did not produce immediate reversal in policies; more effective were legal changes. The realms of African life administrators wished to "develop" included the law. No longer would they be content with African tribunals stocked with elderly, illiterate men, untrained in Western legal concepts, ignorant of colonial bureaucracy. The state created a whole new system of oversight and set of policies that would place more "modern" men on the benches and push the courts toward a more "modern" legal world. From the meshing of these two trends—administrative critiques of African society and the "development" of the African courts—emerged a legal system that placed limits on the ability of senior men (and abducted women) to track down and punish their adversaries.

Assessing the Courts System

From the 1910s the administration progressively isolated the African courts from the judiciary, yet it failed to introduce any other overarching and effective regulatory system.[72] The state into the 1940s never devised a single, consistent, colony-wide tribunal policy, while peripatetic DOs and inadequate records clouded local institutional memory of tribunal policies. In some districts "the policy regarding native tribunals had been completely changed several times during the course of a few years by successive District Commissioners."[73]

The Attorney General realized that the native tribunal system (a generous term for this anarchic collection of courts) was in desperate want of a meticulous examination. In April 1943, the AG called for "an investigation into the workings and procedure of native tribunals . . ." and in a subsequent meeting, "the want of a co-ordinated policy was still further emphasized."[74] The Attorney General tapped Crown Counsel Arthur Phillips to head the inquiry. Phillips spent three months over late 1943 and early 1944 traversing Kenya, observing courts, interviewing district officers, and reviewing administrative files.[75] When completed in August, his *Report on Native Tribunals* stretched to some 326 pages, with an exhaustive discourse on the history of each district's courts and seventy-eight points of conclusions and recommendations.

Phillips lobbied hard for a bureaucracy, headed up by a Judicial Advisor (JA), to oversee the African courts. After less than two years as JA, Phillips encountered serious health problems and accomplished few reforms before returning to Britain in 1947.[76] His successors (subsequently known as Native Courts Officer, NCO, and later African Courts Officer, ACO), however, made some advances toward implementing his recommendations. Central and Nyanza provinces saw the appointment of Provincial Native Courts Officers (PNCOs, later Provincial African Courts Officers, PACOs)[77] answerable to their PCs and directly superintending local court work. The two PACOs and the ACO communicated regularly, helping to fulfill Phillips' idea of coordinated courts planning. Within a few years, it was reported that the work of the PACOs "has been outstandingly successful."[78]

The ability of administrators to extend their oversight of the African courts was boosted by their success in isolating the courts from the judiciary. Their greatest victory was the 1951 African Courts Ordinance and the creation of a Court of Review. When this court was first proposed officers had staunchly opposed it,[79] but could hardly have been more pleased with its final incarnation. On the court would sit the Chief Native Commissioner, the ACO, and a person to be named by the Chief Justice: that is, two administrators and one judicial man. A case could come before the Court of Review only at the pleasure of a PC, only if the original tribunal's or African appeal tribunal's decision had been reversed by a district officer, and only if a significant point of law was involved. Most significantly, the Court of Review would hear all appeals: the Supreme Court could no longer hear cases that had originated in the tribunals, which is to say, virtually all intra-African disputes.[80] There had come into being two parallel legal systems—one for Africans under the administration, one for whites and Indians (and the most serious of crimes committed by

Africans) under the judiciary. Postwar direction of the courts came wholly into administrators' hands.

Remaking the Courts

While administrators resisted judicial interference with the tribunals they did not take issue with particular proposals to modernize and professionalize the courts. Administrators by and large agreed with Phillips: the African courts desperately needed attention. Many proposals advanced by Phillips and his successors were in fact greeted warmly by the administration. As in other areas of African life, the legal realm was to undergo "development" and "modernization" at the hands of eager and earnest DOs. "My great joy was the African Courts," recalled Thompson, who served in Kenya from 1947 to independence. "Not held back by Emergency restrictions [in northern Nyanza] DCs and DOs had put in a lot of time to very good effect training Court Clerks and Elders."[81]

Very soon administrators dedicated to courts work initiated conversations with (or, more often, monologues toward) African courts' staff. The Nyanza PACO, for example, devised a schedule of quarterly lectures to tribunal staff in each district.[82] District officers too invested more time in court oversight. Formerly, officers called on African courts when on tour, and then primarily to field complaints and hear appeals. The PACOs and the ACO now enjoined district officers to circuit the courts and evaluate the legality of fines levied, audit accounts and, where courts produced written transcripts, scrutinize a select number of civil and criminal files.[83] In Gusiiland, officers conducted one or two visits per month to the *ritongo*, examining files, listening to cases, and conferring with clerks (although not always with the elders).[84] By 1948, each district in Nyanza had an officer dedicated to court work and who (unlike other DOs) met periodically to address problems faced by the courts.[85] These officers were also in regular communication with the PACO and the ACO. From at least 1957, elders and tribunal staff attended training sessions headed by ACOs and PACOs on topics such as taking and assessing evidence and the hearing of customary law cases.[86]

Administrators also wished to bring in more "modern" elders for the courts. The status and composition of the courts in South Kavirondo varied over the years, until a near total overhaul of the system in 1936–1937. District officers undertook the consolidation of the many locational courts into a handful of divisional courts, in Gusiiland from seven to two. Chiefs were removed from the tribunals, and the type of elders sought by administrators began to change. Previously, they preferred elders of the "traditional" type. In the interwar years Britons had strived to preserve the influence of "tribal" elites, including (supposed) experts in customary law. It was thought that only as men progressed through their lives did they come to fathom the intricacies of customary law. Younger men knew little and were more likely than their elders to have been corrupted by the modern ways. As South Kavirondo district officer C. Farquhar Atkins explained in 1943, "on the whole the tribunals fulfil their present functions very adequately, but it is increasingly evident that the standard of education of Presidents and Vice-Presidents [of the courts] requires to be raised more and more to enable the tribunals to carry out properly their functions as criminal courts."[87]

The elders who took the benches from the late 1930s were increasingly of the "modern" class. Lists of elders from the 1940s and 1950s show that a majority had Western/Christian names. Several had served as teachers or elders in their churches; the president of the Kisii Appeal Tribunal in 1944 had formerly been a Seventh-day Adventist evangelist.[88] Many elders had advanced in the governmental and business worlds. Several had knowledge of the local courts system, having served as assessors for a DO's appeal court. Another set of elders included an assessor and a former member of an *etureti* council, evidence of their knowledge of customary law. Yet both men also had other notable achievements on their resumes, making their customary skills only one aspect of their attractiveness, and secondary at that. Three elders in South Kavirondo had served in the legal realm in positions that required bureaucratic knowledge and literacy: one had been a process server, and the others had been court clerks. Seven men had been "indirect rulers," one a headman, three subchiefs, and three chiefs. Other elders had served on local legislative or advisory bodies. Seven elders in South Kavirondo had been members of Location Advisory Councils and four had served on the LNC. Many elders had their hands in businesses of various types as traders, merchants, and so on.[89]

From the war years the administration breathed new life into the native tribunal system. Administrators dedicated to court work drafted new polices for the courts and, with few other administrative distractions, they could ensure their implementation. As younger, Western-educated African men took up positions as elders and clerks, administrators devised more—and more complex—procedural rules for the courts. As early as 1941, two DOs at Nyeri composed a "Guide and Instruction to Native Tribunals."[90] Later that decade the South Kavirondo officer in charge of courts initiated the distribution of periodic memoranda (later incorporated as Standing Orders) augmenting otherwise spare procedural rules. Books of Standing Orders were printed for tribunals across the colony in 1948 and 1954, and Standing Orders and the African Court Ordinance were translated into Swahili in 1952 for use by the courts.[91] Clerks were expected to have a grasp of a wide range of procedural and legal regulations. For promotion they were to pass exams in Criminal Procedure, Civil Procedure, Office Procedure, Accounting, and the African Court Ordinance.[92] The African courts were slowly molded into something like magistrates' courts.[93]

There were, of course, limits to how well this modernized court system worked. Many clerks failed their exams, and the legal knowledge and training of the European cadre was not always above suspicion.[94] In 1952 the ACO noted that, while the courts had steadily improved, some DOs had become rather lax and in reviewing African courts' records had failed to catch many ultra vires criminal sentences.[95] Three years later the South Nyanza DC despaired that the DO in charge of courts was having to spend the bulk of his time hearing appeals, leaving little time "for his very important duties of supervision."[96] Indeed, most *ritongo* transcripts have at most a scribbled initial of a district officer, suggesting only cursory review; this is hardly surprising given the vast number of cases heard by the African courts. Similarly, clerks had to deal with tremendous numbers of cases. T. A. Watts, Nyanza's PNCO, feared that the single registering clerk at *Ritongo* Manga was desperately overworked. In 1950 the clerk was being crushed by some 500 cases per month, and the standards of the overburdened court had fallen quite low.[97] As late as 1958, African Courts could not always be supplied with up-to-date guides on their statutory powers. When one DO requested such a handbook, the African Courts Officer replied that the "situation can be summed up in two words—im possible."[98] Despite all this, administrators invested more time and effort in court work than ever before, and the changes in the courts were real.

THE NEW COURTS AND THE CONTROL OF WOMEN

As administrators changed their views on African gender relations and began paying more attention to African Courts, they enacted policies that proved highly burdensome to complainants in marriage disputes. Administrators limited the powers of African Courts to return women to their husbands or fathers, and demanded complainants help the court serve summons on the accused. Policies regarding court appearances favored accused men. Should a complainant miss one appearance at court, or if the case had not been heard within one year of filing, the court would dismiss the charge. As administrators became more disturbed by women forced into marriage, and as women and young men flooded African courts with adultery and elopement cases, the state placed more restrictions on courts' powers to control and punish irresponsible youth.

Bringing Accused Men to Court

Among the strategies commonly employed by Gusii men who created illicit unions was to temporarily leave South Kavirondo District. Most stole off to the tea estates in neighboring Kericho District, while others headed farther away to Nakuru or Thompson Falls or south to Tanganyika. Since they ultimately desired marriage, most had every intention of returning to Gusiiland, but hiding outside the district could save a man from prosecution.

If an accused man could simply evade a court appearance chances were good he could escape punishment.[99] With the filing of a quasi-criminal case, the court clerk set a court date and issued a summons to the accused. Quite commonly, the accused could not be located and the summons would go unserved. Some summons, for whatever reasons, were never even issued by the court. On the appointed date, then, a complainant might enter court only to face several weeks' delay while the court issued another summons to the accused. In this way a case might drag on for months, the complainant walking miles to court only to discover another postponement. After three court dates without the appearance of the accused, one man in frustration withdrew his adultery case "because I am annoyed by coming here."[100] Should a complainant miss a single court date, however, the court would immediately dismiss his case. In one case filed in 1956, the court sent out eight summons to the accused, who could not be found. The complainant faithfully attended each of the first seven court dates. When he missed the eighth, the case was summarily dismissed.[101]

Even if a complainant expended the time and energy to come to court six, seven, eight times, he or she might still see the case dismissed at the expiration of one year. Hoping to clear the books of old outstanding cases, the Native Courts Officer in 1949 instructed courts to dismiss cases which had been left pending for over one year.[102] The DO in charge of courts in South Nyanza was adamant that in serious cases "we cannot allow a person to escape justice . . . because he has managed to run away and hide himself in Nakuru or Nairobi or elsewhere for a year." But in "trivial cases," quasi-criminal ones like adultery, elopement, and abduction, "it does not matter so much."[103] Many cases were thus dismissed one year, or even six months, after the date of filing. In theory, these cases could be filed again later, once the accused could be found. In practice this made little sense because court elders regularly dismissed adultery and elopement cases in which the couple had lived together for some time.

Simply tracking down the accused and ensuring he came to court was perhaps the most serious challenge facing a complainant, one for which the courts and the state offered precious little assistance. Native Courts Officer Desmond O'Hagan explained that it was "the duty of the Private Prosecutor to be diligent and to give every possible assistance to the Court to find the accused."[104] In many instances when an accused could not be found to serve summons,[105] the court directed the complainant to bring news of his whereabouts. A similar situation held, it is true, in civil suits between Europeans, where the plaintiff bore the duty of finding the address of the defendant.[106] But this only reinforces the conclusion that administrators considered these acts more like civil wrongs than criminal acts. As such, it was left to complainants to do the leg work in tracking down accused men. Tea companies sometimes gave free transport to fathers "who wanted to visit their children or to bring them back."[107] Nonetheless, following a woman and her lover could be quite expensive: one man expended shs. 316 tracing his daughter who had run off with a man to the Kericho area. If the outlay of money did not stop them, many men hesitated to go after an accused for fear of their lives. White tea farmers in Kericho, it was believed, shot Africans who trespassed or disrupted production by hauling laborers or their lovers back to Kisii.[108]

If a complainant anticipated that the accused would evade summons he could request issuance of an arrest warrant, but here too the state erected financial roadblocks. The Nyanza PNCO in 1949 complained of the large number of arrest warrants sent to the tribunals from outside the province in regard to adultery and elopement cases. This, he informed the NCO, involved "considerable expense against Government funds . . . for what is really a civil matter." He proposed requiring the complainant to deposit money enough to cover transport of the accused and round trip transport of an escort.[109] The policy was implemented later that year and was incorporated into the Standing Orders for African Courts in 1954.[110] If a man wished his daughter or wife to be present at the trial but she refused summons a similar procedure was followed, except that the complainant himself had to accompany the warrant.[111] The costs involved goes a long way toward explaining why complainants requested arrest warrants in less than ten of the cases recovered.

Handicapped by court policies, many complainants endured an excruciatingly long and difficult process simply to gain a court hearing. Consider the course of events over the twelve court dates set for one 1956 adultery case:

1. Complainant present, accused not served with summons
2. No summons sent
3. No summons sent
4. Complainant present, accused not served
5. No summons sent
6. Accused has run off to work
7. Summons sent to DC Londiani
8. Summons not yet back from Kericho
9. Complainant present, accused at work
10. No summons sent
11. All are at work
12. Dismissed after one year from date of filing[112]

These policies proved such an impediment to complainants that huge numbers of cases were eventually dismissed. Of the 714 adultery and elopement cases recovered from *Ritongo* Gesima, 305 (43 percent) were dismissed before trial. In *Ritongo* Kuja the numbers were slightly less: 40 percent, or seventy-three out of the 184 cases found were dismissed.[113] In short, if an accused man could flee the district or hide himself the complainant would be hard pressed to carry the case through, even to gain a hearing.

Restrictions on the Use of Court Authority

Administrators felt ill at ease with the forced marriage of women, yet balked at any real legal protection for women. When they discovered less inflammatory methods to prevent forced marriage, ones which would be less likely overly to antagonize senior men, administrators took action. The elimination of warrants of attachments on women was one example. In civil suits a plaintiff could apply for a warrant of attachment to claim property he had been awarded; the court's or a chief's *askari* would then retrieve the property from the defendant.[114] In civil claims over women, a successful plaintiff could ask to have the woman herself attached. By the late 1940s, administrative opinion had swung decidedly against this practice. Winser, DO in charge of Courts in South Nyanza, thought attaching women "entirely repugnant and furthermore ineffective." It was "obviously useless," he chided court elders, "to attach a woman and return her to her husband if she does not want to return and runs away again after a few days." The NCO agreed (he thought it "improper and wrong" to return a wife to her husband "against her wish") and in 1949 supported Winser in removing from courts the authority to attach women. Later that year all tribunals in Nyanza were ordered not to attach women, and by 1954 this was enforced colony-wide.[115]

It was this changing attitude toward attaching women, along with the actions of African women themselves, which led many officers to conclude that the state and the courts simply could not force women to stay with unwanted men. In reference to an African woman's status under British law, J. H. Flynn, magistrate at Kitale, posited that "in theory she is not a chattel, whatever she may be in practice." As such, he argued, African courts had no authority to order a woman to cohabit with a man, regardless of any bridewealth exchange.[116] For Flynn, this was a question of jurisprudence and the authority legally granted to courts in a British dependency: it was ultra vires for an African Court to order a woman to return to her husband.

In fact, administrators pointed out, it was simply impossible to force a woman to stay with an unwanted man. The DC at Elegyo told his LNC in 1941 that he deplored the instability caused by runaway wives, but lectured the councilors that "women could not be coerced like cattle." Though he was open to other suggestions on how to create more long-lasting marriages, he told the African elites that court orders for women to return to their husbands were usually "unenforceable."[117] Before the South Kavirondo LNC the DC said there was no point in repeatedly returning a runaway wife, so a husband would be better off ending the marriage and requesting his bridewealth back from her parents.[118] For courts to force a woman back to her legal but unwanted husband was "improper and wrong," "repugnant." By the late

1940s, courts could declare to whom a woman was legally married, but that woman was "free to choose whether she is going to return to her husband or not."[119]

What could a man do if, after the court had granted him legal authority over his wife, she refused to go to him? From the 1930s through the mid-1940s, most tribunals in South Kavirondo followed a procedure regarding repeat adultery cases, of which the administration knew and approved. The first two times a runaway woman appeared before a tribunal, the elders would "order her to return [to her husband], but the third time she deserted" the elders would dissolve the marriage, hand her over to her father, and order the bridewealth be refunded.[120] That is, a woman had to leave her husband at least three times (probably more, as the courts were the last resort for resolving these disputes) before the court elders terminated the marriage.

Soon, however, the state eliminated multiple adultery prosecutions. While he believed a court could not forcibly hand over a woman to an unwanted man, Winser defended the right of a husband to repeatedly prosecute his wife's lover until she either relented or filed for divorce. The Provincial Commissioner, Provincial Native Courts Officer, and Native Courts Officer all disagreed. The PNCO in 1949 informed Winser that when a woman had "definitely refused" to go back to her husband and was "living as the wife of another man, [that man] though not yet legally married to the woman, cannot be repeatedly prosecuted for adultery." The NCO concurred, and decreed that instead "her husband . . . should take action for the recovery of Bride Price."[121] This seriously limited the aggrieved husband's options. Even if a man successfully prosecuted his wife's lover, should the couple flaunt the court's decision the state became an impotent ally.

Not all courts staff took these changes quietly. In 1952, a document was prepared on "Criticisms of South Nyanza Clerks" on the courts' standing orders. One of their recommendations concerned the disposition of female children in a divorce:

> Once a case has been decided and if the child is of a reasonable age to leave the mother, the Court should hand over the child to the decree holder there and then rather than telling the decree holder to wait for the dowry when the child has been married. Very troublesome judgment.

The clerks' suggestion was disregarded. In the margin an administrator commented simply, "No."[122]

CONCLUSION

Colonial officials were never satisfied with Africa. This was the very nature of their work. Justifying colonialism meant doing something for Africans—whether Africans wished it or not. Certainly, most colonial officials were true believers. Improving Africa was not mere rhetoric to most. Yet the meaning of "improvement" was neither self-evident nor static. Improving Africa in the interwar years meant protecting the old Africa; in the postwar years it meant developing a new Africa. Yet one had to be careful. Africans were rarely consulted as to what, if anything, needed "developing," but they often had much to say after the fact. "Developing" the family, officials believed, might well be a noble goal, but the likelihood of negative, unintended consequences gave them pause. Scolding Africans was one thing, but in the end it was better to allow bridewealth to die off on its own, and hazard only the most inoffensive policies. Developing the legal system was easier. It was much less controversial (or at least, there was no obvious backlash) to select more educated men as elders, to train them in new methods, to watch and to guide them. Here officials could, indirectly, work on African family life.

Senior men could not put all their faith in the *ritongo*. Through no fault of their own their cases might never get heard, and the *ritongo* could not (legally) force women back to their menfolk. This is not to say that the *ritongo* did not have their uses. The fact that hundreds and thousands of Gusii turned to the *ritongo* is ample proof of that. Fines and imprisonment were nothing to be laughed at, and being granted legal custody of a woman and her children could be a powerful tool in gaining effective control over them. Nonetheless, in the end the *ritongo* were not all that senior men (and abducted women) would have wished of them. For these Gusii, the state picked exactly the wrong time to reassess their ideas about African society.

NOTES

1. D. A. Low and J. M. Lonsdale, "Towards the New Order, 1945–1963," in *History of East Africa,* Vol. 3, eds. D. A. Low and Allison Smith (Oxford: Oxford University Press, 1976); Frederick Cooper, *Decolonization and African Society: The Labor Question in French and British Africa* (Cambridge, UK: Cambridge University Press, 1996), chaps. 1–2; John Iliffe, *The African Poor: A History* (Cambridge, UK: Cambridge University Press, 1987), 200–203. On the prewar origins of postwar agricultural policy, see David Anderson and David Throup, "Africans and Agricultural Production in Colonial Kenya: The Myth of the War as a Watershed," *Journal of African History* 26 (1985), 327–345.

2. John D. Hargreaves, *Decolonization in Africa* (New York: Longman, 1996), 90–106; Bruce Berman, *Control and Crisis in Colonial Kenya: The Dialectic of Domination* (London: James Currey, 1990), 259–262.

3. David Throup, *Economic and Social Origins of Mau Mau, 1945–53* (London: James Currey, 1988), 25. The manner in which development projects were carried out, however, often did little else than alienate Africans. Ibid., 151–64; A. Fiona D. Mackenzie, *Land, Ecology and Resistance in Kenya, 1880–1952* (Edinburgh: Edinburgh University Press for the International African Institute, 1998), 1–2, 163–165.

4. Robert Heussler, *Yesterday's Rulers: The Making of the British Colonial Service* (Syracuse, NY: Syracuse University Press, 1963), 93.

5. David W. R. Evans, personal communication, May 17, 2004; Robin Williamson, "The Lure of Dust," 31, and Michael Wasilewski, "Apprenticeship in Kwale," 38, both in

Colony to Nation: British Administrators in Kenya, 1940–1963, ed. John Johnson (Norfolk: Erskine, 2002).

6. W. H. Thompson, "A Different Way into the Service," in *Colony to Nation*, ed. Johnson, 8.

7. Quoted in Heussler, *Yesterday's Rulers*, 163. See also Joanna Lewis, *Empire State-Building: War and Welfare in Kenya, 1925–52* (Oxford: James Currey, 2000), 245. Not all officials were immediately enamored with development plans. For several years after the end of the war Kenya administrators were troubled by emerging capitalists and the "excessive individualism" noticed especially among Gikuyu. Administrators turned to agricultural betterment schemes to discourage cash cropping and reinvigorate communalism and the authority of indigenous elders. Officers soon admitted defeat, however, and reversed policy to co-opt the peasantry and promote soil conservation through individual land tenure, now exploiting Gikuyu "individualism." As early as 1953, administrators began consolidating and registering land in Gikuyu locations. In Gusiiland, the administration directed government sociologist Philip Mayer to study "traditional" cooperative farming techniques, but soon gave up as peasants continued their spontaneous program of demarcating farm boundaries. Often, however, it was finance rather than desire that proved the limiting factor for administrative dreams of development, in Nyanza more than elsewhere. Throup, *Economic and Social Origins of Mau Mau*, 39; Mackenzie, *Land, Ecology, and Resistance in Kenya*, 157–162, 165–169; David F. Gordon, *Decolonization and the State in Kenya* (Boulder, CO: Westview, 1986), 88, 102–104, 120–121; Berman, *Control and Crisis in Colonial Kenya*, 274–276; Philip Mayer, *Two Studies in Applied Anthropology in Kenya*, (London: Colonial Office, 1951); SN ADC, Finance and General Purposes Committee, 28–29 July 1958; Minter, personal communication, May 28, 2004.

8. Lynn M. Thomas, "Regulating Reproduction: State Interventions into Fertility and Sexuality in Rural Kenya, c. 1920–70" (Ph.D. dissertation, University of Michigan, 1997), 218–267.

9. Arthur Phillips, *Report on Native Tribunals* (Nairobi: Colony and Protectorate of Kenya, 1944), 297.

10. Minter, personal communication, May 28, 2004.

11. PNCO Nyanza to DC SN, Jan. 18, 1950 KNA: MDS 2/3/5.

12. Phillips, *Report on Native Tribunals*, 296.

13. To extend the influence of this education, the state employed a few female graduates as homecraft officers to teach in the Reserves. Claire C. Robertson, *Trouble Showed the Way: Women, Men, and Trade in the Nairobi Area, 1890–1990* (Bloomington: Indiana University Press, 1997), 126–127; Audrey Wipper, "The Maendeleo ya Wanawake Movement in the Colonial Period: The Canadian Connection, Mau Mau, Embroidery and Agriculture," *Rural Africana* 29 (1975–76), 195–214, esp. 196–197. On the origins of the Jeanes School, see Kenneth James King, *Pan-Africanism and Education: A Study of Race Philanthropy and Education in the Southern States of America and East Africa* (Oxford: Clarendon, 1971), chap. 6. The South Nyanza ADC constructed centers for women to be taught similar skills, along with "*ustaarabu wa kisasa*" (modern civilization), by four European women. Paul Mboya, *Utawala na Maendeleo ya Local Government South Nyanza, 1926–1957* (Nairobi: East African Literature Bureau, 1959), 8. More centers came along in the 1950s, and were praised by the DC as "of great value, not only in raising the standard of the home, but as a means for the distribution of propaganda, information, and as the hub of community development schemes." SN DAR 1951. See also SN DARs 1953 and 1955. Women were also to undergo training in agriculture, and perhaps then be appointed Assistant Agriculture Instructors. DA QR, SN, First Quarter, 1954, KNA: Agr 14/2/4.

14. Henry Robert Brooke-Popham to Sir Henry Moore, Oct. 24, 1939, quoted in Luise White, *The Comforts of Home: Prostitution in Colonial Nairobi* (Chicago: University of Chicago Press, 1990), 142.

15. Robertson, *Trouble Showed the Way*, 127. The state did integrate a very few women directly into the state bureaucracy, but this was one tiny aspect of the much larger changes administrators envisioned.

16. One woman served on the South Nyanza Law Panel, two on the South Nyanza African District Council, and another on the Meru ADC. Minutes of the SNLP, KNA: RR 8/10; SN ADC minutes, 1956, KNA: Adm 7/15/5/3; Lynn M. Thomas, *Politics of the Womb: Women, Reproduction, and the State in Kenya* (Berkeley: University of California Press, 2003), 88–89. On the trip to Uganda, see Chiefs' meeting, May 12, 1955, KNA: DP 1/21. A handful of women from South Nyanza were selected to go to a several week course of instruction in Central Nyanza, at least some of whom were then taken on as Assistant Instructors, apparently in agriculture. DA, SN QRs, First Quarter, 1952, and First Quarter, 1954, both in KNA: Agr 14/2/4.

17. SN DAR 1957.

18. Wipper, "Maendeleo ya Wanawake Movement," 195–197; Audrey Wipper, "The Maendeleo ya Wanawake Organization: The Co-optation of Leadership," *African Studies Review* 18 (1975), 99–120, esp. 100, 102; Mackenzie, *Land, Ecology, and Resistance in Kenya*, 98–107; Cora Ann Presley, *Kikuyu Women, the Mau Mau Rebellion, and Social Change in Kenya* (Boulder, CO: Westview, 1992), 165–167.

19. North Nyanza Annual Report, 1950, quoted in Wipper, "Maendeleo ya Wanawake Movement," 196. Terence Gavaghan, *Of Lions and Dung Beetles* (Elms Court, UK: Arthur H. Stockwell, 1999), 161.

20. Minter, personal communication, May 28, 2004.

21. "Women's Clubs Aiding Anti-Mau Mau Fight," *East African Standard*, March 4, 1955.

22. Secretariat Circular, May 23, 1939, KNA: MDS 2/3/8. Replies from other parts of Africa have not yet been tracked down.

23. Gavin Kitching, *Class and Economic Change in Kenya: The Making of an African Petite-Bourgeoisie* (New Haven, CT: Yale University Press, 1980), 221–226.

24. PC Nyanza to CS, June 12, 1949, KNA: MDS 2/3/8.

25. DC CK to PC Nyanza, June 13, 1939; DC SK to PC Nyanza, June 26, 1939; DC NK to PC Nyanza, June 16, 1939; DC Kericho to PC Nyanza, June 21, 1939; PC Nyanza to CS, July 6, 1939, all in KNA: MDS 2/3/8.

26. Hargreaves, *Decolonization in Africa*, 59–60.

27. K. L. Hunter, "Native Policy," ca. 1943, KNA: Adm 1/1.

28. C. H. Williams, DO SK, "Native Policy," Dec. 8, 1943; E. J. A. Leslie, DO Kericho, "Native Policy: The Atlantic Charter in Relation of African Colonial Society," Dec. 7, 1943, both in KNA: Adm 1/1.

29. N. F. Kennaway, DO CK, "Notes on Native Policy," Nov. 27, 1943, KNA: Adm 1/1.

30. H. Carr, DC SK, "Memorandum on Native Policy," Dec. 7, 1943; R. S. Winser, DO CK, "Memorandum on Native Policy," Dec. 9, 1943, both in KNA: Adm 1/1.

31. Parry, DO NK, "Native Policy," Dec. 6, 1943, KNA: Adm 1/1.

32. As Hunter put it in a letter to Archdeacon Owen regarding forced marriage, he still felt "that we have much to learn. Until we are moderately certain that we have all the facts I think it would be wrong to precipitate action." Hunter, PC Nyanza, to Owen, June 12, 1944, CMS: ACC 83 O 22/1.

33. K. L. Hunter, "Memorandum on Native Policy in Kenya Presenting the Views of the Nyanza Provincial Administration," Feb. 2, 1944, KNA: Adm 1/1.

34. Copies of these papers have not yet been found. In 1945 some Africans stationed overseas formed the Anti-Dowry Association, but this collapsed the next year as more and more members broke their pledge and married with bridewealth. Bildad Kaggia, *Roots of Freedom, 1921–1963: The Autobiography of Bildad Kaggia* (Nairobi: East African Publishing House, 1975), 57.

35. PC Nyanza to DCs Nyanza, Nov. 19, 1944, KNA: MDS 2/3/3.

36. PC Nyanza, "Bride Price Stock," March 4, 1947, KNA: MDS 2/3/3.

37. DC CK to PC Nyanza, Sept. 22, 1945, and DC SK to PC Nyanza, Sept. 29, 1945, both in KNA: Leg 28/1.

38. Central Province DCs' Meeting, April 9–12, 1947, KNA: Adm 3/2/3.

39. Notes for Baraza with Chiefs, Dec. 4, 1945, in DC SK to PC Nyanza, Jan. 8, 1946, KNA: Adm 12/7/2. Archdeacon Owen had thanked Perreau for his "promptitude" in helping to deal with cases of forced marriage in Central Kavirdondo. Owen to DC CK, April 19, 1939, CMS: ACC 83 O 16. Only six years before Perreau (then in Central Kavirondo) had explained to Archdeacon Owen that, after having discussed the matter with the PC, administrators remained convinced that forced marriage was rare, although they did not deny that fathers "sometimes bring an undesirable amount of pressure on their daughters to persuade or compel them to marry husbands they would not have chosen." DC CK to Owen, May 11, 1939, CMS: ACC 83 O 16. See also PC Nyanza to DC CK May 9, 1939, KNA: MDS 2/3/5.

40. SK LNC, Dec. 5–7, 1945. See also CK LNC, Feb. 1945, KNA: MDS 2/3/3. Apparently in reaction to tribunal judgments regarding the custody of women, a former DC of Teita District failed to understand the "nice distinction" one elder made between precolonial slavery and "the Taveta customary treatment of women and children." Looking at the inability of women to select their husband, or even to reject unwanted ones, the DC argued that denying a woman these options amounted to enslaving her to a man. Quoted in Phillips, *Report on Native Tribunals*, 140. The postwar French West African administration made a similar comparison of forced marriage with slavery. Barbara M. Cooper, *Marriage in Maradi: Gender and Culture in a Hausa Society in Niger, 1900–1989* (Portsmouth, NH: Heinemann, 1997), 15.

41. DC Kericho to PC Nyanza, Feb. 18, 1944, KNA: MDS 2/3/3. According to one leading missionary, it was this rise in bridewealth, rather than bridewealth itself, which tended "to alter the basis [of marriage] from social contract to 'purchase.'" W. Scott Dickson, *Christian Marriage and Divorce Law in Kenya in Relation to Africans* (Nairobi: Ndia Kuu Press, 1947), 17.

42. In his published 1944 report, however, Arthur Philips wrote that "Luo custom apparently tends—perhaps even more than that of most tribes—to regard women as chattel." Phillips, *Report on Native Tribunals*, 28.

43. Fazan, PC Nyanza, "Memorandum Regarding Native Marriage and Kindred Problems," ca. 1937, in PC Nyanza to CS, Aug. 5, 1937, KNA: Leg 28/1.

44. PC Nyanza to CS, June 12, 1939, KNA: MDS 2/3/8.

45. Registration was instituted on a voluntary basis in some parts of South Kavirondo as early as 1928, but apparently was rarely employed. Extract from Minutes of SK LNC, Sept. 24–25, 1928, KNA: PC/NZA 3/28/4/1. This was noted as "Standard Resolution No. 4 re Registration of Native Pagan Marriages," suggesting registration had been debated and generally accepted by higher levels of the administration. On the lack of use of registration here and in Central Kavirondo, see CS to PC Nyanza, Sept. 21, 1938, KNA: Leg 28/1.

46. PC Nyanza to DC CK, May 9, 1939, and PC Nyanza to CS, May 27, 1939, both in KNA: MDS 2/3/5. See also Beetham, DO SK, to DC SK, Oct. 19, 1936, KNA: MDS 2/3/5; S. H. Fazan, "Memorandum," KNA: Leg 28/1; Winser, DO SK, to PC Nyanza, May 21, 1947, KNA: MAA 7/725.

47. Fazan, "Memorandum," KNA: Leg 28/1. See also DC CK to Archdeacon Owen, May 11, 1939, CMS: ACC 83 O 16.

48. PC Nyanza to DC SK, Nov. 1, 1940, KNA: Leg 28/1.

49. PC Nyanza to CS, Sept. 5, 1940; Archdeacon W. E. Owen, "Notes on the Case of Achola d/o Jeje," April 10, 1940; PC Nyanza to DC CN, Jan. 10, 1949, all in KNA:

MDS 2/3/5. For similar cases, see Hunter, DC CK, to Owen, July 13, 1940, CMS: ACC 83 O 22/1; Lambert, DO CK, to PC Nyanza, c.c. Archdeacon Owen, Nov. 20, 1940, CMS: ACC 83 O 16. Anthropologist Gordon Wilson questioned the rights of parents to force their daughters into marriage. Employed by the government to work amongst the Luo in the 1950s, his advice on marriage customs was not so easily dismissed. Gordon Wilson to PC Nyanza, for attention of Provincial Courts Officer, Sept. 29, 1956, KNA: Adm 13/2/1.

50. E. J. A. Leslie, "Marriages Between Detribalized Natives," 1939, copy in Leslie to PC Coast, May 11, 1945, KNA: Leg 28/1.

Kitching (*Class and Economic Change in Kenya*, 223–226) argues that changes in administrative attitudes were due to the monetization of bridewealth. From the 1930s bridewealth increased in much in Kenya, even as land holdings shrunk, so that the collection of large bridewealth herds was necessary but burdensome. The solution: by 1950 Gikuyu, Luhyia, and many Luo of Central and North Nyanza substituted cash for cattle as bridewealth. In the same period, numerous colonial officials commented that monetized bridewealth reduced women to chattel: as the Nyanza PC noted in 1948, "Often the custom has so far deteriorated that bride price is paid in cash. This is surely a human sale" (African Affairs Department Report for 1948, quoted in Kitching, 225). This opinion was not universal. H. R. Lambert, a postwar champion of resurrecting and strengthening tribal and clan ties, frowned on cash bridewealth not for mimicking slavery, but because it could more easily be disposed of and so left no bond between the families. Lambert, "Limitation of Bride Price," Aug. 4, 1948, Appendix II, to Desmond O'Hagan, NCO, to members of African Affairs Committee, Aug. 26, 1948, KNA: Adm 2/4.

In fact, more than one official positively favored the use of cash bridewealth as a solution to overstocking. As early as 1930, S. O. V. Hodge, DC of South Kavirondo, lamented the time and money Gusii spent on litigation over bridewealth cattle. Only the eventual replacement of cattle with money, he suggested, would solve these problems (SK DAR 1930). As more officials identified soil erosion as one of the preeminent problems facing African agriculture, the idea of using cash bridewealth as a method to eliminate overstocking attracted attention. (Director of Veterinary Services, "Bride Price Payment in Stock," Nov. 5, 1941, KNA: MDS 2/3/3.) Fazan noted that "some administrative officers" had argued this position, though he disagreed. (Fazan, "Memorandum," KNA: Leg 28/1.) On Africanists' arguments that monetization of bridewealth causes a breakdown in social relations, see Henrietta L. Moore and Megan Vaughan, *Cutting Down Trees: Gender, Nutrition, and Agricultural Change in the Northern Province of Zambia, 1890–1990* (Portsmouth, NH: Heinemann, 1994), 157–158. On state concern over soil erosion, see David Anderson, "Depression, Dust Bowl, Demography and Drought: The Colonial State and Soil Conservation in East Africa During the 1930s," *African Affairs* 83 (1984), 321–342; and idem, *Eroding the Commons: The Politics of Ecology in Baringo, Kenya 1890–1963* (Oxford: James Currey, 2002).

51. Evans, "Criminal Proceedings for Adultery," May 6, 1946, KNA: L&O 2/13. When this was considered by the DCs in Nyanza however, they balked at any changes because of the "known views of natives on this subject." Nyanza DCs' Meeting, June 21, 1946, KNA: Adm 3/2/2.

52. DC NN, to PACO Nyanza, Jan. 26, 1949, KNA: Adm 11/1. See also PNCO Nyanza to NCO, June 27, 1949, and PNCO Nyanza to DC NN, March 10, 1950, both in KNA: MAA 6/21; PACO Nyanza to DC NN, Jan. 12, 1949, KNA: Adm 11/1. As in some other instances, administrators in Coast Province held more conservative views. DCs there in 1949 agreed that adultery should be criminal not only for men but for women as well. Coast DCs' Meeting, Feb. 25–26, 1949, KNA: Adm 3/2/4.

53. T. A. Watts, "Comments on the Agenda" of the Conference on the Future of Law in Africa, n.d., in Watts to ACO, Oct. 13, 1959, PRO: CO 955/78.

54. PACO Nyanza, "Quasi-Criminal Offenses in African Courts," July 1, 1957, KNA: Adm 13/2/1 (II).

55. PNCO Nyanza to NCO, Oct. 21, 1949, KNA: MAA 10/43. See also DC CK, "Criminal Proceedings for Adultery," May 6, 1946, KNA: L&O 2/13; PC Coast to NCO, Aug. 30, 1949, KNA: MAA 6/21.

56. DO Raynor for DC SN to PC Nyanza, Nov. 2, 1955, KNA: PC/NZA 3/15/29.

57. DC Kericho to PC Nyanza, Dec. 19, 1955, KNA: PC/NZA 3/15/29.

58. DC CN to PC Nyanza, Nov. 16, 1955, KNA: PC/NZA 3/15/29. His colleague in North Nyanza agreed that the current system should be left in place. DC NN to PC Nyanza, Dec. 3, 1955, KNA: PC/NZA 3/15/29.

59. See, for example, Thomas, *Politics of the Womb*, chap. 1; idem, "Imperial Concerns and 'Women's Affairs': State Efforts to Regulate Clitoridectomy and Eradicate Abortion in Meru, Kenya, c. 1910–1950," *Journal of African History* 39 (1998), 121–145.

60. Chris Minter, personal communication, May 28, 2004.

61. Member for African Affairs to PCs, Dec. 21, 1948, quoted in Arthur Phillips (ed.), *Survey of African Marriage and Family Life* (London: Oxford University Press for the International African Institute, 1953), 219.

62. Parry, DO NK, Dec. 6, 1943, KNA: Adm 1/1.

63. Terence Gavanagh, personal communication, May 8, 2004.

64. Minter, personal communication, May 28, 2004. For similar examples of aggrieved men being redirect to the African courts, see PC Nyanza to Jackton Ayara [ca. Dec. 1947]; PC Nyanza to DC NK, Dec. 16, 1947, both in KNA: PC/NZA 3/15/15; DC SN to Zachary Ombongi, April 7, 1961, KNA: DP 5/4.

65. DO appeal rug 30/45. This could go for men as well as for women. In another district, Philip Jones heard a bridewealth appeal involving a young man who had refused to sleep with the nearly toothless "ancient lady" who was to be his wife via the levirate. Jones decided in favor of the young man, for his "sympathy was naturally" with him. Jones, "District Officer," 51.

66. However, in two adultery cases Low followed common *ritongo* logic. In one case, the appellant (the original defendant) claimed that he had not known that his lover was married. This was immaterial, Low commented, and the assessors also insisted it had been he man's duty first to determine her marital status. DO Appeal ad 14/46. See also DO Appeal ad 18/46.

67. Gwako s/o Ombutora to PC Nyanza, June 23, 1947, KNA: PC/NZA 3/15/15.

68. PC Nyanza to Gwako, Sept. 6, 1947, KNA: PC/NZA 3/15/15.

69. DC SN to President, *Ritongo* Kuja, June 6, 1958, KNA: DP 5/4.

70. CNC to Deputy CS, Oct. 29, 1941, KNA: MDS 2/3/3. On administrative resistance to codifying and crystallizing African custom and customary law, see Brett L. Shadle, "'Changing Traditions to Meet Current Altering Conditions': Customary Law, African Courts, and the Rejection of Codification in Kenya, 1930–60," *Journal of African History* 40 (1999), 411–431.

71. DVS, "Bride Price Payment in Stock," Nov. 5, 1941, copy in CNC to Deputy CS, KNA: MDS 2/3/3. Elsewhere, hesitancy to interfere with marriage practices could also work against the interests of senior men. When the Elegyo LNC in 1941 sought new ways of punishing illicit lovers, Nairobi replied that this was a "social problem in wh[ich] we can give practically no assistance." [CNC?] to Deputy CS, Jan. 16, 1942, KNA: ARC (MAA) 2/10/21.

72. Shadle, "'Changing Traditions to Meet Current Altering Conditions,'" 416–420; idem, "Law and the Nature of Colonial Rule: The Struggle to Control African Courts in Kenya." Department of History Faculty Research Seminar, Virginia Tech, April 21, 2006.

73. Phillips, *Report on Native Tribunals*, 1, 3, 13; A. N. Doorly, "Native Tribunals," *Journal of Comparative Legislation and International Law* 28 (1946), 25–34, esp. 25.

The Chief Justice in 1925 similarly disparaged the tendency for each district to have its own tribunal rules, while those set down by ordinance were largely ignored. Chief Justice, "Notes on Native Tribunals," c. 1925, KNA: Jud 1/1104.

74. Phillips, *Report on Native Tribunals*, 1.

75. Phillips, *Report on Native Tribunals*, 1–2.

76. AG to CS, Jan. 31, 1945, KNA: MAA 7/421; CNC to Deputy CS, Jan. 14, 1947; and CNC to CO, July 19, 1947, all in KNA: MAA 7/421; Y. P. Ghai and J. P. W. B. MacAuslan, *Public Law and Political Change in Kenya* (Oxford: Oxford University Press, 1970), 156–157. On Phillips' health problems, see Phillips to Officer Commanding 2nd Echelon, East Africa Command, July 7, 1945, KNA: ARC (MAA) 6/43, and for further biographical information, H. F. Morris and James S. Read, *Indirect Rule and the Search for Justice: Essays in East African Legal History* (Oxford: Clarendon, 1972), 343.

77. Ghai and MacAuslan, *Public Law and Political Change in Kenya*, 156–157.

78. Judicial Advisors' Conference, 1953, Special Supplement to *Journal of African Administration* 5 (1953), 14.

79. N/a, "Notes Re. Native Tribunals and Mr. O'Hagan's Paper," c. 1948, KNA: Jud 1/978.

80. H. F. Morris, "Native Courts: A Corner-stone of Indirect Rule," in Morris and Read, *Indirect Rule and the Search for Justice*, 161; Arthur Phillips, "The African Court System in Kenya," *Journal of African Administration* 4 (1952), 135–138.

81. W. H. (Tommy) Thompson, "Orderly Administration," in *Colony to Nation*, ed. Johnson, 145. See also in the same volume Alan Liddle, "Getting to Know the Kamba," 162.

82. Nyanza DCs' Meeting, Dec. 1–2, 1949, KNA: Adm 3/2/2.

83. Standing Orders to African Courts, Appendix C, 1954, KNA: MAA 2/117.

84. Administrators also wished to ensure that the court was kept tidy. The strategy here was to visit the elders' homes—they were provided housing in the court compound—and reduce the salary of those with poor housekeeping skills. Nyasani Omanua, Oct. 22, 1997.

85. PNCO Nyanza to NCO, Dec. 30, 1948, KNA: RR 8/8. See also Nyanza DCs' Meeting, Jan. 30–31, 1950, KNA: Adm 3/2/2. For the minutes of their meetings see appendices to Nyanza DCs' meetings, in KNA: MAA 9/842.

86. SN DARs 1957, 1959.

87. Quoted in Phillips, *Report on Native Tribunals*, 33, and see also 27, 34.

88. Phillips, *Report on Native Tribunals*, 32.

89. For more on changes in the courts and elders in Nyanza, see Brett L. Shadle, "African Court Elders in Nyanza Province, Kenya, c. 1930–1960: From 'Traditional' to 'Modern,'" in *Intermediaries, Interpreters and Clerks: African Employees and the Making of Colonial Africa*, eds. Benjamin Lawrance, Emily Lynn Osborn, and Richard Roberts (Madison: University of Wisconsin Press, [in press]).

90. Phillips, *Report on Native Tribunals*, 43.

91. T. A. Watts to J. L. Fairclough, Nov. 7, 1952, and May 7, 1953, both in KNA: PC/NZA 3/15/29.

92. DC NN to PACO Nyanza, Nov. 27, 1954, KNA: L&O 2/1. Yet book knowledge alone, administrators believed, did not necessarily a good clerk make: those with experience but without education were often preferred over those educated but untested.

93. Although in 1948 the Native Courts Officer admitted that, given the widely-varying standard of tribunals, DCs could delete those Standing Orders unsuitable for local use. NCO to PCs, DCs, May 21, 1948, KNA: MAA 6/21.

94. DC NN to PACO Nyanza, Nov. 27, 1954; DO i/c Courts, SN to PACO Nyanza, Dec. 14, 1954, both in KNA: L&O 2/1. One man had served as PNCO for several years, even though his legal knowledge was not yet quite up to par: he failed three of ten subjects on his Bar Final in 1952. PNCO Nyanza to NCO, July 3, 1952, KNA: MAA 6/40. When Philip

Jones was sent to Oxford for the Second Devonshire Course his request for training in law was denied, and he instead turned to agriculture. Nonetheless, his first assignment upon returning to Kenya was to deal with the courts in North Nyanza. Philip Jones, "A District Officer and the Law," in *Colony to Nation*, ed. Johnson, 48.

95. ACO to CNC, Nov. 10, 1952, KNA: RR 1/6.

96. SN DAR 1955. At least in the early 1950s there was also a regular turnover of men assigned to courts work. Min. 62/52, DCs' meeting, Oct. 1–2, 1952, KNA: PC/NZA 3/15/29.

97. PNCO Nyanza to DC SN, Aug. 12, 1950, KNA: L&O 2/1/3; SN DAR 1950. Several more clerks were later appointed. PNCO Nyanza to DC SN, Aug. 18, 1950; PNCO Nyanza to DC SN Nov. 9, 1950, both in L&O 2/1/3.

98. DO i/c Courts, NN, to ACO, Sept. 22, 1958, and ACO's reply, Sept. 27, 1958, both in KNA: MAA 2/119. Similarly, chiefs who wished to have a copy of the Penal Code were made to purchase them. Chiefs' Meetings Feb. 15, 1951, and May 17, 1951, KNA: DP 34/7. Even the Laws of Kenya books used by district officers were not always kept up to date. Chris Minter, "From KAR to Administration," in *Colony to Nation*, ed. Johnson, 22.

99. NCO to DC Nyeri, Jan. 20, 1949, KNA: MAA 6/33.

100. RG ad 318/56.

101. RG ad 259/56.

102. Native Tribunal Circular 4 of 1949 (South Nyanza), KNA: MAA 6/9. T. A. Watts, PNCO Nyanza, encouraged dismissal of long-standing private prosecutions: once an accused had been found, it often happened that the complainant could not then be found to serve him or her the summons. This, he feared, caused much distress for an accused man, who then had "the threat of this prosecution hanging over him indefinitely." PNCO Nyanza to NCO, Dec. 17, 1948, KNA: MAA 6/21.

103. Native Tribunal Circular 16 of 1949 (South Nyanza), KNA: MAA 6/9.

104. NCO to DC Nyeri, Jan. 20, 1949, KNA: MAA 6/33.

105. Joyce Kannan notes that in Central Province defendants in land cases tried to dodge process servers, postponing court dates and allowing them continued use of disputed land. Joyce Anwera Kannan, "The Cultural Politics of Bridewealth: Marriage, Custom and Land in Colonial Murang'a, c. 1880–1952" (Ph.D. dissertation, School of Oriental and African Studies).

106. Registrar, Supreme Court, to Ag. Resident Magistrate, Nakuru, March 1, 1940, KNA: Jud 1/1460.

107. Chiefs' meeting, May 30, 1952, KNA: DP 34/7.

108. Nyambweke Onchaba, Oct. 2, 1997.

109. PNCO Nyanza to NCO, June 27, 1949, and July 18, 1949, both in KNA: MAA 6/21.

110. PNCO Nyanza to NCO, Jan. 18, 1950, KNA: MAA 6/21; Standing Orders for African Courts, 1954, KNA: MAA 2/117.

111. DCs Nyanza meeting, Oct. 1–4, 1951, KNA: MAA 9/842. In North Nyanza the administration also put restrictions on the use of court lockups. Chiefs sometimes brought in men wanted for private prosecutions, but complainants might not appear for several days. The DC instructed tribunal presidents no longer to take these men into their lockups unless the prosecutor "appears with the accused on the same day." DC NN to Chiefs, cc Native Tribunals, Aug. 7, 1952, KNA: PC/NZA 3/15/29.

112. RG ad 619/56.

113. We can be less sure of the numbers for *Ritongo* Manga, though they may have be smaller. With only registers of cases preserved, and these only partial, it is difficult to make any firm conclusions. For example, only a one month portion of the 1958 register was found, in which it is recorded that ten of the twenty adultery, elopement and abduction cases filed were dismissed. From only two different years were more than six months of

a register discovered. In 1962, from which 34 weeks of the register was recovered, only eleven out of 147 cases, or 7 percent, were dismissed. From the extant thirty-four weeks of the 1965 register, thirteen (28 percent) of forty-six cases were dismissed. If the smaller percentages of cases dismissed from Manga are a reflection of incomplete sources or a real difference between the courts cannot be known.

114. NT Circular 10/49, KNA: MAA 6/9.

115. DO i/c Courts, SN, to NCO, July 9, 1949, and NCO to PNCO Nyanza, Aug. 2, 1949, both in KNA: L&O 2/14; PACO Nyanza to DC NN, Oct. 14, 1949, KNA: L&O 2/8; Standing Orders for African Courts, 1954, KNA: MAA 2/117. This policy may have originated as early as 1944 in Nyanza. See PNCO Nyanza to NCO, July 20, 1949, KNA: L&O 2/14.

116. J. H. Flynn, First Class Magistrate, Kitale, to Revenue Officer, Kitale, Nov. 9, 1948, in PC Rift Valley to NCO, Jan. 26, 1949, KNA: MAA 6/21.

117. Extract, Minutes of Elgeyo LNC, Dec. 4, 1941, with note by PC Rift Valley, Dec. 23, 1941, KNA: ARC(MAA) 2/10/21. Williams, a district officer in Central Kavirondo, admitted to Archdeacon Owen that the tribunals sometimes ordered the return unwilling women to their husbands but, he said, "I have found it quite impossible to enforce them even [if] I wanted to and I now take the line that the woman must be free to choose for herself." Williams to Owen, April 9, 1942, CMS: ACC 83 O 16.

118. SK LNC, Sept. 24–25, 1942.

119. NCO to PNCO Nyanza, Aug. 2, 1949, KNA: MAA 6/21; Winser, DO i/c Courts, to NCO, July 9, 1949, KNA: L&O 2/14; PNCO Nyanza to DC NN, Oct. 14, 1949, KNA: L&O 2/8. See also PNCO Nyanza to NCO, July 20, 1949, KNA: L&O 2/14; J. H. Flynn, First Class Magistrate, Kitale, to Revenue Officer, Nov. 9, 1948, KNA: MAA 6/21; Standing Orders for African Courts, 1954, KNA: MAA 2/117.

120. Archdeacon Owen to Christine Spender, SJA, Nov. 3, 1936, CMS: ACC 83 O 16; Despatch from Ag. Governor, Kenya, to Secretary of State for the Colonies, Dec. 31, 1937, in *Correspondence Relating to the Welfare of Women in Tropical Africa*, Cmd 5784, 1938; PC Nyanza to D. G. Givan, Church Missionary Society, Dec. 5, 1944, KNA: MDS 2/3/5. Nonetheless, in 1942, Luo Chief Pius Olima complained about the practice of Native Tribunals allowing runaway wives to continue living with their lovers. SK LNC, Sept. 24–25, 1942.

121. Winser to NCO, July 9, 1949; PNCO Nyanza to NCO, July 20, 1949; NCO to PNCO Nyanza, Aug. 2, 1949; PNCO Nyanza to DC SN, Aug. 10, 1949, all in KNA: L&O 2/14. An exception to this rule was made in cases of seduction only, as opposed to cohabitation. See DC SN to PC Nyanza, Feb. 20, 1952, and PACO Nyanza to DC SN, Oct. 27, 1952, both in KNA: L&O 2/13.

122. Standing Orders (Criticisms of South Nyanza Clerks), Oct. 30, 1952, KNA: PC/NZA 3/15/29.

7

The Demise of Marriage Disputes

> If someone steals your wife let him keep her.
>
> —label for sale in Kebirigo market, June 2002

The peculiarities of the colonial political economy and legal system helped to create the context for and to shape the crisis in Gusii marriage. Very different were the political economy and judiciary of independent Kenya, and thus so too were Gusii marriage disputes. Shrinking pasturage bode ill for the management of large herds. Fertile Gusii soils did not translate into consistently high income for peasants, and the sore muscles of wage laborers still did not earn them fat pay packets. A settlement scheme opened up new land to the east, but primogeniture reduced family farms toward increasingly uneconomic sizes. And so: less wealth to invest in bridewealth cattle, less land on which to graze them, decreasing viability of polygamous homesteads, decreasing ability of fathers to support unmarried daughters. Bridewealth levels dropped, the number of forced marriages and abductions declined, and eloped couples were left alone (in what came to be called "come-we-stay" unions). Women had thus won the war over the importance of their consent to marriage. They then stumbled into another war. Women remained committed to bridewealth marriage, but entrenched poverty and the acceptance of "come-we-stay" made bridewealth marriages harder to come by.

The government of independent Kenya, while not always breaking radically from its colonial predecessor, set about refashioning the legal landscape. The results were, at best, contradictory. Adultery and elopement were decriminalized. Governmental debates over marriage entered the public arena. The 1968 Commission on the Law of Marriage and Divorce came down against forced marriage, polygamy, and bridewealth. Like the colonial executive, however,

Kenya's parliament refused to challenge certain aspects of "traditional" marriage and did not write into law all of the Commission's recommendations. Similarly, while the judiciary released women from unwanted marriages it did not (or could not) champion eloped women in "come-we-stay."

DECLINE IN BRIDEWEALTH AND THE EMERGENCE OF "COME-WE-STAY"

Beginning in the 1960s, and increasingly so in the 1970s and 1980s, the Gusii political economy underwent series of changes that had as serious consequences for marriage as had those of the 1940s and 1950s.[1] Education became one of the most promising avenues of investment. While the cost of secondary and even primary school could quickly deplete a family's disposable income, most parents had few qualms about paying for as many years of schooling as possible for their children, especially sons. Educated men filled well-paying salaried jobs in the new nation's expanding (and nonracial) bureaucracy-cum-patronage system. This income could be put toward bridewealth or invested in school fees for younger brothers.

Declining land availability in Gusiiland created new aggravations. In previous generations a growing family could always expand into unoccupied bush beyond their clan boundaries. Already by the 1950s and 1960s nearly all of Gusiiland had been claimed. Now, as fathers divided their land between sons, plots shrank to barely sustainable acreage. A tiny farm might allow enough land for one wife but could hardly provide plots for multiple wives. Many children by many wives did little but spread homestead resources thinner than they already were. Recurrent expenditures mounted as did the potential for unexpected financial demands (medical costs, for example). The hope of educating even one child dimmed. A polygamous homestead could no longer be equated with a prosperous homestead.

Put crudely, in the decades after *Uhuru* women were no longer such a good investment for men and bridewealth steadily declined. According to Håkannson's statistics, by 1970 bridewealth was half of what it had been in 1965; it halved again by 1980. At the same time, household income rose in relation to cattle prices. Bridewealth declined in absolute and relative terms. Even so, bridewealth remained out of the reach of many young men, although the percentage of aging bachelors was certainly less than it had been in the 1950s.[2]

Yet marriage itself remained the hallmark of adulthood. All Gusii expected that all Gusii should marry. All believed that marriages must be sealed with bridewealth. Even the most pious Christians consecrated their unions with both solemn vows and fat cattle. More pragmatic concerns also led women to seek marriage. Women still gained land rights only through marriage. If their parents were not wed, children could make no claims on their biological fathers.

As before, dedication to bridewealth marriage did not mean it would be easily achieved. Changes in the law and in the Gusii economy, and decades of battles over women's consent in marriage, led to a growing recognition that elopement had become a standard preliminary to marriage. To alleviate the burden of supporting their daughters, fathers often agreed to delay bridewealth demands. As one Gusii man told Håkannson in the 1980s, "If a daughter goes you lose a member who has been using limited family resources. Therefore people can wait several years for the bridewealth."[3] The number of elopements and the time that passed before men gave bridewealth both rose. In Håkannson's sample, in 64 percent of the marriages made in 1957–1962, bridewealth was given upfront, and in every case the marriage contract had been fulfilled within three years. (Of course, this covers only unions that eventually became marriages, and leaves out elopements and marriages that collapsed before becoming legitimized.) What had been the rule in 1962 had become the exception by 1975–1980. Håkannson found that in those years less than half of all marriages were immediately sealed by bridewealth and one out of five husbands still owed bridewealth four years into their marriages.[4] Moreover, fathers no longer had legal recourse to recover a daughter. Parents might not approve of "come-we-stay" but they would—indeed, had to—accept it.

With no legal penalties for elopement and little pressure to quickly produce bridewealth, young men sensed the balance of power tilting toward them. Women slid into greater insecurity as their lovers adopted more cavalier attitudes toward these unions. Young men saw elopement as a chance to "try out" women, so to speak. As one youth in the 1980s said of his lover:

> If she proves worthy I will consider paying bridewealth. But I first want to know her character, if she is lazy or hard working, if she is dirty or cleans the house, if she is a witch, if she is harsh or kind, if she receives visitors warmly or not. She may be dirty in the way of baths, not cleaning the house or beddings, and if she will wash my young brothers and sisters, while she has no kids of her own. When I have learned her character fully I may pay, but if I don't like her I will chase her off.[5]

This young man knew that once he had tired of his lover he could send her away without consequence.

What could a spurned woman do? If she remained childless she might find another man with whom to live. In a more difficult position was a single mother, who had to bear the full burden of raising her children—since no bridewealth had been given, the biological father had no rights over and no responsibilities to his offspring. A family would hesitate to take on the expense of supporting a daughter and her child, and few men would be anxious to marry her and bear the burden of raising children born of another man.

One might wonder why women eloped at all. Considerable financial pressures forced some to leave their families. A daughter whose parents did not pay her school fees might feel that she had little reason to remain at home. Neighbors did give a greater measure of respect to a "wife" than they did women still living at home. Rather than being greeted as a daughter of her father, an eloped woman might be known as the wife of her lover.[6] Most important, every eloped woman prayed that the union would eventually be legitimized with bridewealth. In the early years of a come-we-stay the woman strove to please her lover and his family, proving herself "worthy," and giving them no reason to turn her out. Perhaps if she were not "lazy" or "dirty" she could become a real woman, a married woman. Come-we-stay offered some benefits and at least a possibility of marriage, enough to outweigh many women's reservations.

DECLINE IN ABDUCTION

Lower bridewealth eliminated the impetus for abduction and, although the evidence is not overwhelming, it appears that by the later 1960s instances of abduction had declined significantly.[7] Moreover, abduction cases of the late 1960s and 1970s were not like those of previous decades. In a 1967 *Ritongo* Gesima case Kwamboka charged that while on her way to visit her stepmother she had met up with Mongare (whom she knew). He ordered his five companions to grab her, she said, and they "took me to his home to be his wife." The prosecutor (by this time criminal cases were filed by the state) argued for a harsh sentence:

> the accused is a big man in the area and well educated and a business man who is supposed to know what is wrong and what is not. In this respect I ask the court to impose severe sentence on him to make others see as this offence is too common over here.

If crimes like Mongare's were becoming "too common" these were not abductions committed by desperate, impoverished youth. Mongare had the wherewithal to marry Kwamboka properly, and in fact already had two wives. Kwamboka also had a husband and children, which Mongare would have known; abducting her would not easily have led to marriage.[8]

The decline in abductions is also suggested by chiefs' reports. Although not all were conscientious in sending in their reports, many chiefs and subchiefs dutifully recorded matters regarding health, education, taxes, and law and order. Under the last heading they noted the many disputes that their subjects continued to bring before them. Few crimes against women were brought to chiefs' and subchiefs' attention. In October 1966, for example, only two recorded assaults: one subchief listed two cases of girls being "pulled" (for which two young men were imprisoned for ten months and fined shs. 600), and the chief of West Kitutu recorded a case of a man "reported for doing adultery forces [*sic*]."[9] Reports from 1967 similarly record few abductions. That year, chiefs and subchiefs reported a total of two cases of child sexual abuse, one of indecent assault, one of "two people pulling girls from the road," and "Two cases of eloping [i.e., abduction?]" for which "[suspects] arrested."[10] If not eradicated, abduction was no longer the scourge it had been even a decade before.[11]

DECRIMINALIZATION OF ADULTERY AND ELOPEMENT

With independence drawing neigh, Nairobi belatedly undertook the process of shifting responsibility for the African Courts from the administration to the judiciary and clearing up the murky status of customary law. While administrators had long fought off codification of customary law, others (including African Courts Officers) understood that these laws would have to be compiled and put to paper in order to provide some kind continuity and certainty in the law. Conferences of judicial advisors from various British colonies had come to similar conclusions. Under pressure from London some starts were made toward putting customary law on a more firm footing. In the late 1950s, the University of London's School of Oriental and African Studies seconded Eugene Cotran to the Kenya government as part of the Restatement of African Law Project. Cotran quickly went to work collecting and standardizing criminal customary law of "tribes" from across the colony.[12]

Ultimately, Cotran's interest lay less in defining any one group's customary law than in creating a national body of criminal law. The collection of criminal law was done "with a view, in due course, to getting these written into the statutory law of Kenya." After meetings with district or subdistrict "tribal" Law Panels, Cotran called representatives to provincial meetings where differences and variations in local customary laws were broken down. Cotran finally extracted a set of ten basic criminal customary laws, including adultery and elopement, shared by most "tribes."[13]

The implications of Cotran's findings set off a series of debates within an administration struggling to envision the nature of an independent Kenya. Cotran argued vehemently that the soon-to-be independent Kenya should have nondiscriminatory law. Thus a law criminalizing adultery should apply to all ethnic groups, all races.[14] Nairobi was rather taken aback by this.[15] White Kenyans, it was argued, would be outraged at this attack on their personal rights. Some apparently libertine (or comedic) administrators protested. One proposed constitution would have given regional assemblies control over customary law and thus, a member of the central administration argued, there was no sense in altering the penal code. "I favour leaving such matters as adultery to the Regions," he wrote, "and hope I can find a liberally minded Region to serve on in!"[16]

In the end, bed-hopping settlers had their rights preserved. Cotran's position had been supported by his academic contact in Britain, Anthony Alott, who pointed out that under the old Indian Penal Code adultery had been criminal for all residents of the colony. Cotran and Alott both insisted that resistance by a minority white population should not be allowed to determine national law.[17] Introducing racially-specific laws into a national penal code "for the sake of the 1 percent European population," Cotran charged, "is, to say the least, unreasonable."[18] He finally relented, however, and offered compromise language: adultery would be criminal only for those "subject to native law and custom."[19]

Ultimately, Cotran's gesture was made irrelevant by the Kenya Constitution, itself a part of nation building, which demanded a more British-style judicial system. No "modern" judiciary could apply unwritten customary laws and Cotran's *Report on Customary Criminal Offences in Kenya* (1963) should only inform, not determine, magistrates' rulings. T. A. Watts, African Courts Officer in both colonial and independent Kenya, instructed the courts that as of June 1966 customary law offenses could no longer be filed as criminal acts, but as civil claims only. Criminal prosecutions for adultery and elopement, on which Gusii men had so heavily relied in their battles with women and youth, were gone.[20]

REDEFINING MARRIAGE AND DIVORCE IN KENYA

The Commission on Marriage and Divorce

Charles Njonjo, the first Attorney General of independent Kenya, felt strongly that Kenya needed a more detailed and national set of laws on marriage. In 1967, he appointed a Commission on the Law of Marriage and Divorce to consider the creation of "a new law providing a comprehensive and, so far as may be practicable, uniform law of marriage and divorce applicable to all persons in Kenya" and to supercede customary, Hindu, Islamic, and statutory laws. The paramount consideration, the Commission later concluded, should be the promotion of marriage and family life. At the same time, creating a new nation also meant advancing women's status. The commission was instructed to "pay particular attention to the status of women in relation to marriage and divorce in a free democratic society."[21] Thus commissioners concluded that, whatever their desire to promote the family, the "law must be based on a recognition of human dignity, regardless of sex . . ."[22]

Much more than any colonial-era inquiry into marriage, the commission called on a cross-section of the populace. The commission itself was composed of fourteen people, of whom three were women—Pheobe Asiyo, Shirin Esmail, and Margaret Kenyatta (the new president's daughter).[23] The inquiry sought input from all sectors of the Kenya nation.[24] Those giving evidence included, inter alia, Christian and Muslim leaders, representatives of ethnic organizations, social workers, teachers, "traditional elders and chiefs"[25] and many women's groups.[26]

The commission's report crafted a balance between "traditional" and "modern" ideas about marriage and gender. Forced marriage came under withering attack. The commission hesitated to make generalizations about the status of women, given the many different customs in effect across the nation, but certain practices—forced marriage, restrictions on widows' marital lives—they regarded "as derogating from the dignity and status to which women are entitled." The very definition of marriage was "the voluntary union of a man and a woman, intended to last for their joint lives."[27] The commission members were "emphatically of the opinion that the consent, freely given, of both parties should be essential to the validity of every marriage," although marriage would still require parental consent for those under twenty-one.[28] The age of consent to marriage should be standardized for all ethnic, religious, and racial groups (eighteen years old for men, sixteen for women, which followed a recent UN decision).[29] This would protect girls from forced marriage as well as rape, for a man charged with defiling a minor could not claim to be exercising his conjugal rights.

The commission also came down hard against domestic abuse, polygamy and bridewealth. Wife-beating was "all too common" and the commissioners recommended that "the law provide expressly that no-one has the right to inflict corporal punishment on his or her spouse." Some witnesses opposed to polygamy argued that only in monogamous marriages was it possible "to find the mutual love and trust that are essential to a stable and happy home." Like European administrators before them, the commissioners concluded that the outright prohibition of polygamy would "cause considerable social disruption, without being really effective." At the same time, neither should the law be used to support polygamy as an institution. Indeed, the "law should do everything reasonably possible," they wrote, "to discourage the practice of polygamy."[30] Bridewealth (or dowry, the term they used) ought not to be abolished, but the validity of marriage and divorce should not be determined by the exchange of bridewealth because this would "impede change" away from the custom.[31]

The commissioners' discussion of adultery underscored their commitment to both the institution of marriage and the advancement of women's rights. It was recommended that a husband could make a civil claim for damages, up to shs. 1000, against his wife's lover. "We base this," they wrote, "both on the principle that where there is a wrong there should be a remedy and on the assumption that the liability to such proceedings will have some deterrent effect, however slight."[32] Moreover, they recommended that adultery or enticing away a wife be (re)criminalized. Hardly a radical proposal. The next was. The commission asserted that, except in polygamous marriages, wives also had sole claim to their husbands sexually. There was "no logical reason" why a wife could not lodge a civil claim against her husband's lover, for there was no "ground for discrimination in the law." Such too should be the case in criminal prosecutions for adultery and enticement. "[W]e see no reason," the commissioners argued, "to distinguish between adultery by men and women and we think the [criminal] law should be the same for both."[33] Like British administrators before them, the commission members hoped to create a new, "modern" marriage, and preserving marital unions was of enormous import. Unlike colonial officials, however, the commissioners were less afraid clearly and directly to advance women's rights under the law.

Legislation and Marriage

Despite the commission's strong defense of "traditional" marriage its more liberal proposals were too much for members of (the almost entirely male) parliament to swallow, and its recommendations were never enacted. Parliament was in general not amenable to advancing women's rights. For example, the Affiliation Act (1959) granted unwed mothers the legal right to claim child support from their former lovers. As Lynn Thomas has shown, after independence MPs charged that the Act encouraged promiscuity on the part of women, led fathers to discourage their pregnant daughters from marrying, and was financially burdensome to men. By 1969 these criticisms, along with the fact that some leading politicians were being sued by former lovers, led to the Act's repeal.[34]

The Marriage Bill of 1976 similarly faced fierce parliamentary opposition. Most controversial was the proposed criminalization of adultery. Outraged MPs argued that men, especially monogamists, had a biological need for extramarital sex. It was unfair to punish a man for that which he could not control. A compromise bill was reintroduced three years later with the clause criminalizing adultery removed (although lodging civil claims would still be allowed). MPs raised new objections to the bill, especially the discouragement of polygamy and the criminalization of domestic violence. The Bill, MPs claimed, contained too many "western" ideas incompatible with African traditions. As Cotran described it, after a "very heated debate" Parliament voted it down.[35] Yet another version of the Marriage Bill was proposed in 1985. This one eliminated the domestic violence clause and declared adultery and elopement "moral" matters not subject to civil suits. Nonetheless, this time the bill failed even to be introduced into Parliament.[36]

Marriage in the Courts

Parliament's refusal to pass a marriage bill left ill-defined women's legal rights. Judicial rulings complied by Cotran in 1987, however, showed that on one count the courts were unanimous: marriages had to be fully consensual. As the High Court at Kisumu ruled in 1978, to "compel a woman to go and live with a man whom she does not want . . . [is] contrary to natural justice and in possible contravention of a woman's constitutional right to personal liberty and movement."[37]

Some women were able to successfully use the courts to escape unwanted marriages, such as Marcella, a Gusii women. The District Magistrate at Kisii in 1980 granted Marcella a divorce from her woman–woman marriage with Maria. Maria appealed to the High Court. The facts were as follows: Maria had "married" Marcella in July 1974. Two months later Marcella ran off. Before Judge Aganyanya, Marcella "said that she had been forced into marrying the appellant by her mother" and had been treated cruelly by Maria. Aganyanya considered the evidence of her twice having run away (once to "a boy with whom she had earlier got two children"):

> What does this imply? Can a person of mature age, as [Marcella] then was, consent to a marriage only to break it after two months? And after deserting the matrimonial home, what special interest would her mother have to go out with [Maria] to look for her and return her to [Maria]? [Marcella] must have been right in saying that she had not initially consented to this arrangement freely.

In Gusii woman-to-woman marriage it had generally been the case that the "bride" be allowed to choose her lover. Aganyanya apparently did not understand this point, or thought it was not being applied in this case:

> Much as a people's customs should be respected, I am constrained to believe that custom which allows this sort of arrangement, where a woman will have no right to choose which man should have sexual intercourse with her, is repugnant to justice and an abuse of an individual freedom of choice . . . This is obviously against rules of natural justice and I feel the custom does not fit in with modern developments.

Aganyanya confirmed Marcella's divorce.[38]

Women seeking to make claims on former lovers fared less well. Some judges argued that long coresidence "as man and wife" created the presumption of marriage, and thus the burden was not to prove the marriage existed but that it did not.[39] But this was an uncommonly positive outcome for women. More often courts followed the restrictive rules in Cotran's 1968 *Restatement of the Law of Marriage and Divorce*.[40] Like his *Report on Criminal Customary Law*, the *Restatement* drew on minutes from Law Panels (long since defunct), which generally outlined a very conservative interpretation of customary law. One Luhyia women filed suit for child support from a former lover. The Affiliation Act had by this point been repealed and thus only if the two had been married could District Magistrate Mbaka order support. He turned to the *Restatement*. According to members of a circa 1960 Law Panel, under Luhyia customary law without bridewealth there could be no valid marriage. The couple before Mbaka had lived together for several years but bridewealth had never been given. It pained Mbaka to rule against the woman but he was compelled to follow the law.[41] A less sympathetic Judge Bennett in 1972 heard a case in which a Kipsigis woman's parents had not consented to her marriage. Following the *Restatement*'s declaration that no valid Kipsigis marriage could exist without parental consent, Bennett, perched on his dias, informed the woman that she was "no more than a concubine."[42]

CONCLUSION

In one of the ironies of which history is made, success in one endeavor only posed new and more distressing troubles for Gusii women. Few women of the 1970s would face the dangers of abduction or the trauma of forced marriage. They would elope, and their fathers would not subject them to violence and the state would not fine or jail their lovers. Yet Gusii women could not arrest the changes they had helped to introduce. Women won the right to choose or reject a husband, but found themselves caught precariously in unions with men who might not yet wish to be husbands. The new legal system too had mixed results for Kenyan women. The judiciary removed itself from the nasty business of splitting apart happy couples and returning women to unwanted husbands. Yet the courts could do nothing to protect the interests of unwed mothers. Discussions of marriage and how to reform it now took place among Kenyan men and women on a very public stage, rather than in memoranda and reports written by white men to be read by other white men. Too often, however, the results were the same: rights ill-defined, but tending to favor men.

NOTES

1. Unless otherwise noted, the following draws on N. Thomas Håkannson, *Bridewealth, Women, and Land: Social Change among the Gusii of Kenya* (Uppsala Studies in Cultural Anthropology, 10, Uppsala, 1988), chaps. 8–10.

2. Håkannson, *Bridewealth, Women, and Land*, chap. 9.

3. Håkannson, *Bridewealth, Women, and Land*, 186.

4. Håkannson, *Bridewealth, Women, and Land*, 179. See also Sarah Nerlove, "Trait Disposition and Situational Determinants of Behavior among Gusii Children of Southwestern Kenya" (Ph.D. dissertation, Stanford University, 1969).

5. Håkannson, *Bridewealth, Women, and Land*, 189.

6. Håkannson, *Bridewealth, Women, and Land*, 192.

7. For example, in 1956 *Ritongo* Gesima heard ten abduction cases; from 1967 to 1970 the new District Magistrate at Gesima tried only one abduction case. *Ritongo* Kuja in 1959 heard nine abduction cases, while between 1966–1969 there were only two abduction cases.

8. RG ia 213/67. Mongare escaped with a shs. 250 fine. In a rape case the next year, the prosecutor again suggested that "Such kind of the offence is on great increase in this area." The Magistrate agreed: "Offence serious and on increase." Given the youth and clean record of the offender, the magistrate applied what he considered a lenient sentence, shs. 250, the same as Mongare's supposedly harsh fine. This young man could not come up with the cash, and served four months in prison instead. DM Kuja ia 644/68.

9. Achoki Nyaombani, s/c Bomanono, Oct. 1966; E. Mayaka, West Kitutu, Oct. 1966, both in KNA: DP 1/10.

10. Evarasto Mayaka, West Kitutu, Jan. 1967; Chief of Nyaribari Masaba, June 1967; Chief, West Mugirango, Sept. 1967; Johnson Basigwa s/c Masige (Bassi), Jan. 1967; N. Nyanchoka, Bassi, Jan. 1967; all in KNA: DP 1/10.

11. Silberschmidt reports a case of abduction in 1970. Margrethe Silberschmidt, *"Women Forget That Men are the Masters": Gender Antagonism and Socio-economic Change in Kisii District, Kenya* (Uppsala: Nordiska Afrikainstitutet, 1999), 124.

12. Brett L. Shadle, " 'Changing Traditions to Meet Current Altering Conditions': Customary Law, African Courts, and the Rejection of Codification in Kenya, 1930–60," *Journal of African History* 40 (1999), 411–431.

13. These were adultery, "taking away or enticing a married woman," eloping, "sexual intercourse with a person within the 'prohibited degrees,' " receiving second bridewealth, forced circumcision, "taking property without consent" (covering such things as bridewealth or inheritance, where some claim to the property could be made), removing boundary markers, abusing a person of a higher age grade, and underage drinking. Cotran, *Report on Customary Criminal Offenses in Kenya*, (Nairobi: Government of Kenya, 1963).

14. Cotran to ACO, Dec. 22, 1962, KNA: RR 8/1.

15. The Advisory Committee on African Courts recommended acceptance of the Cotran Report except for his "recommendation that adultery and seduction be made criminal offences for members of all races." ACO to Cotran, Sept. 14, 1962, KNA: RR 8/1.

16. The ACO warned that "the more vocal elements of the European population" would not peacefully abide this attack on "their liberal 'rights' . . . and their 'freedom' under British law." ACO to Crown Counsel, Aug. 15, 1962, KNA: RR 8/1. The perhaps only partly tongue in cheek comment on the importance of administrative adultery came from DSF, penned message at bottom of this letter.

17. Alott to Cotran, Oct. 5, 1962, KNA: RR 8/1.

18. Cotran, *Report on Customary Criminal Offenses in Kenya*, 17. Part of the question of discrimination in the law grew from concern that a European could without fear of criminal sanction induce African women into having pre- or extramarital sex. Cotran refers to a similar argument made by Hastings Banda in Nyasaland, and suggested Kenya African politicians would have a corresponding view.

19. The Affiliation Act, however, was extended to cover women of all races. Lynn M. Thomas, *Politics of the Womb: Women, Reproduction, and the State in Kenya* (Berkeley: University of California Press, 2003), 140.

20. T. A. Watts, ACO, to African Court Registrars and Presidents, June 18, 1966, KNA: Jud 1/1941. See also Tudor Jackson, *The Law of Kenya*, 3rd ed. (Nairobi: Kenya Literature Bureau, 1988), 21–22, and chap. 6. Court records show that these polices were quickly implemented.

21. Quoted in Eugene Cotran, *Restatement of African Law: Kenya*, Vol. I: *The Law of Marriage and Divorce* (London: Sweet and Maxwell, 1968), 7–8.

22. *Report of the Commission on the Law of Marriage and Divorce* (Nairobi: Government of Kenya, 1968), 3.

23. The other members were Justice Spry (Chair); Rev. J. De Reeper (Bishop of Kisumu); J. F. H. Hamilton; Dr. D. F. Heisel; M. Jahazi, MP; Rev. J. T. Mpaayei; D. J. Coward (Registrar-General); G. S. Sandhu, Esq.; A. R. Tsalwa, MP; S. Waruhiu, Esq.; and Cotran (member and secretary).

24. The following draws on *Report of the Commission*, Appendix II.

25. Used in reference to those on whose behalf Paul Ngutu spoke at Naivasha. *Report of the Commission*, 136.

26. Those giving evidence included (in writing) *Maendeleo ya Wanawake*, the Y.W.C.A., Ikinu Women's Group, and Kakamega District Women, and (in oral presentations) representatives of the East African Women's League, National Council of Women, Young

Women Christian Organization, local *Maendeleo* branches, and Kenya Association of University Women.

27. This last point was important for the commissioners. Divorce, they wrote, "should not be made easy." The only ground for divorce should be that the marriage "has irreparably broken down." (Marriages could be annulled in such instances as impotency or a refusal to consummate the union.) The commission suggested the creation of "marriage tribunals" to which couples would first take their disputes. Only when a tribunal had failed to reconcile the two could a divorce case be filed at court.

28. The quotes are from *Report of the Commission*, 15, 28. To take part in a wedding that had not been given parental blessing should be an offense, and parents could appeal to a court to annul an unapproved marriage. Yet there were limits even here. The requirement of parental consent would not apply to couples over twenty-one, and any couple could apply to the court to overrule "unreasonably withheld" parental consent.

29. *Report of the Commission*, 16–17. It was recommended that a court could reduce the age for girls to fourteen in case of pregnancy.

30. *Report of the Commission*, 22–23.

31. *Report of the Commission*, 29–35.

32. *Report of the Commission*, 62.

33. *Report of the Commission*, 123.

34. Thomas, *Politics of the Womb*, 155–164.

35. Eugene Cotran, *Casebook on Kenya Customary Law* (Nairobi: Nairobi University Press, 1995 [1987]), 1.

36. Kivutha Kibwana, *Law and the Status of Women in Kenya* (Nairobi: Claripress, for the Faculty of Law, University of Nairobi, 1996), 142–143.

37. *Shem Ochola Okech v. Lazaro Owino*, High Court of Kenya at Kisumu, Civil Case No. 22 of 1978, in Cotran, *Casebook on Kenya Customary Law*, 127–132.

38. *Maria Gisese w/o Angoi v. Marcella Nyomenda*, High Court of Kenya at Kisii, Civil Appeal No. 1 of 1981, in Cotran, *Casebook on Kenya Customary Law*, 196–198.

39. *Hortensiah Wanjiku Yawe v. Public Trustee*, Court of Appeal for East Africa, Civil Appeal No. 13 of 1976, in Cotran, *Casebook on Kenya Customary Law*, 63–69.

40. Cotran, *Restatement of African Law*, 1.

41. *Gertrude Nelima Nalwa v. Francis Nalwa*, District Magistrates' Court at Nairobi, Maintenance Suit No. 7 of 1972, in Cotran, *Casebook on Kenya Customary Law*, 46–48.

42. In the matter of the Marriage Act, Cap. 150, Laws of Kenya, and In the Matter of Proposed Marriage between E. L. and E. C., and In the Matter of Caveat entered by G. C. L., High Court of Kenya at Nakuru, Civil Cause No. 6 of 1972, in Cotran, *Casebook on Kenya Customary Law*, 40.

Conclusion

The history of Gusii marriage is of course unique to time and place, but it can also tell us much about the history of marriage elsewhere in colonial Africa. Marriage was universal, although what marriage meant varied enormously. Many patrilineal societies followed marriage customs similar to those of the Gusii. Women became adults only upon marriage, only when widowed could rural women expect to be without a husband, and even then they remained closely aligned to the families of the deceased. Certainly, such customs were not shared by all Africans. In matrilineal Asante and on the Swahili coast women engaged in "serial monogamy," entering and exiting several marriages over their lifetimes, perhaps living happily as single women in their postreproductive years. Marriage in these societies was rather different than Gusii marriage; nevertheless, the nature and meaning of marriage was always up for grabs.

Nowhere in colonial Africa was marital stability a forgone conclusion. Many women were unwilling to remain in unhappy marriages with husbands who, for any number of reasons, did not satisfy them. Some set up shop as independent "market women." Others left for greener pastures far afield—these were the "runaway women" who absconded to Nairobi or Johannesburg or to the Rhodesian Copperbelt. At the other extreme were rural districts like Gusiiland and Kuria where an insignificant number of women left for city life. Despite the scholarly attention "runaway women" have attracted, Gusii women should be regarded as less the exception than the rule. African urban populations grew rapidly only after independence, and it remains a heavily rural continent. Women remained the bedrock of the African countryside throughout the colonial epoch.

If the vast majority of women stayed close to home we can expect to find communities across colonial Africa caught up in debates over the nature of marriage. Indeed, African writers have found this a rich vein to mine for their fiction.[1] Certainly such debates had taken place before colonial rule.[2] But colonial economies—with their cash crops, migrant labor, conscription, taxes, development programs, forced communal labor, and land hunger—reshaped household dynamics. Similarly, the new political order—with white rulers supporting black rulers and courts, granting them powers of compulsion, and often ignoring or ignorant of abuses of that power—altered the public realm, and extended itself into the private realm as well. Twentieth-century marriages were made, debated and broken, marriage customs preserved and reinvented, in a context much different from that of the nineteenth. The study of Gusii marriage suggests new ways of understanding the contours of African marriage disputes in the colonial world.

What nearly all Africans shared was the yolk of foreign domination. Colonial rule took on a variety of shapes, of course, depending upon the presence or absence of white settlers, demands for wage labor, the timing of conquest, and the ability of the state to implement its policies. Yet colonial rulers came from the same world. Especially between the wars British administrators' families, their schooling, and their views on life did not vary widely. If the social backgrounds of postwar officers were more varied they held an understanding of their duty to "develop" Africa and prepare it for independence. All British administrators were influenced by the political and social changes taking place across the ocean. The Colonial Office and Parliament involved themselves in events in all corners of the empire. As unique as Kenya's history might have been, Britons in Nairobi were of the same world as those in London, Salisbury, Accra, and Dar es Salaam. Neither would their ideas about African women and society have been entirely alien to their colleagues in Dakar, Leopoldville, and Lourenço Marques.

GUSIILAND: 1906 AND 2006

Gusiiland in 2006 is in many ways a very different place from what it was in 1906 (admittedly not particularly impressive insight). From *abagambi* and their limited powers, there are now African district commissioners, police, members of Parliament, and leaders of the only political party of any standing, Ford-P. The economy had been primarily subsistence with surplus traded locally or regionally. Today Gusii tea and coffee are drunk in Europe and the United States, their pyrethrum is used as a natural insecticide by farmers worldwide, and soapstone carvings crowd store shelves hundreds and thousands of miles away. These connections to world markets also mean that the Gusii economy is highly reactive to minor fluctuations in the economies of nations most will never see. Cash is essential to the local economy, but work is hard to come by and pay rates low. Most youth are un- or underemployed, although hundreds are finding their way to the United States and Great Britain for education and work. Gusii with any cash at all invest in education, although this no longer guarantees a bright future. Small businesses emerge and fail, college graduates hawk ties and batteries on street corners. One-hundred years ago land had been plentiful, and in the area south of the Gucha River not a single Gusii could be found. Most Gusii can now only dream of having land enough for themselves and their children.

In other ways a person of 1906 would find comfort in aspects of contemporary Gusii culture. Parents and children still refrain from discussing sexual matters. However much a mother wishes to become a grandmother she cannot bring herself to broach the subject with her adult child. Many fathers will now enter the homes of their married sons, but others still find this objectionable.[3] Grandparents and grandchildren retain their free relationship. No subject is out of bounds. A grandmother will offer her grandchildren advice on avoiding AIDS, and seeing each other naked carries no shame. All young people understand proper relations between the generations, even if they look puzzled when asked what "*nsoni*" is: the word is being lost, but not what it represents. Circumcision, male and female, is still nearly universal. The rate of female circumcision (or female genital mutilation) are among if not the highest in all of Kenya. *Yaa*—uncircumcised boy—can still be a demeaning term when used for one's junior. Some men of means will wed more than one wife. While "the Gusii" now exist as a community, an identity celebrated by some, exploited by others, it can still be trumped by the much older clan identities. When parliamentary elections come round it is clan affiliation that can determine votes. A politician has to stump across his constituency, but he can be assured of the bedrock support of his clansmen.

When one considers marriage there have been both deep continuities and striking changes between 1906 and 2006. Bridewealth remains, without a doubt, an essential part of marriage. Whether married before a judge, a pastor or a priest, no marriage *really* exists until cattle have been exchanged. Unlike other agricultural communities in Kenya, bridewealth exchanges in cattle have not been cast aside. Even if bridewealth is negotiated in terms of shillings, the shillings must be converted into cattle before delivery to the bride's family. The grinding poverty endemic to Gusiiland (and to much of Africa) means that, as in the 1890s and the middle decades of the twentieth century, few men can easily gather bridewealth. Now, however, couples resort to "come-we-stay" and set up unions with little reference to their parents.

The history of Gusii marriage in the colonial era cannot be separated from world history. Gusiiland in 1906 had been connected only indirectly with the wider region through trade with Luo, cattle raiding with Maasai and Kipsigis, and the occasional pawning of people and exchange of ritual and medicinal knowledge. During the colonial years Gusii vistas stretched farther. Gusiiland was influenced by actions taken or only proposed, ideas developed and discarded, fierce debates and contradictory policies, emanating from Kisii town, Kisumu, Nairobi, London, mission-sponsoring churches in the United States and Europe, the offices of the Manchester Guardian, labor strikes in

Jamaica and Northern Rhodesia, seminar rooms at Oxbridge ... At the same time, Gusii history was not determined by the outside world. Young lovers, incensed fathers and husbands, contemptible abductors, tea pickers, coffee planters, grain farmers, court elders, chiefs and headmen all influenced Britons in Kisii, Kisumu, Nairobi, the Colonial Office, Parliament, American, Dutch and British missionaries, soldiers in the Middle East, international firms ... The history of Gusii marriage is at once the story of one man and one woman, and of the world.

* * *

While researching the history of Gusii marriage I was told the story of my grandmother's aunt Sophie Althoff. Sophie was born in 1861, the fourth of nine children. Her family prospered on a farm in northwest Illinois, a place of rolling hills where cows graze and corn grows tall out of some of the richest soils one can hope to find. As a young woman Sophie's parents sent her to keep house for two bachelor brothers, now plowing their own fields. As are so many raised in rural parts, Sophie was a hard worker and she took up domestic chores for another bachelor on a nearby farm. Sophie's brothers soon recognized the signs of a budding romance of which, for reasons long since forgotten by my family, they strongly disapproved. Over her objections they sent her back to their parents' home. She was crushed by the separation from her beloved. A few weeks later Sophie was found hanging in the barn, her lifeless body testament to her dedication to the man she loved.

NOTES

1. See, for example, Seydou Badian, *Caught in the Storm*, trans. Marie-Theres Noiset (Boulder, CO: Lynne Rienner, 1998 [Originally published in 1954]), Buchi Emecheta, *The Bride Price* (New York: George Braziller, 1976), and Ngugi wa Thiong'o and Ngugi wa Mirii, *I Will Marry When I Want* (Portsmouth, NH: Heinemann, 1982).
2. And they certainly take place today. One need only peruse Kenya's *Daily Nation*, particularly around Valentine's Day, or chat with secondary school students to hear debates over what marriage and romance should be like.
3. One afternoon in 1997 my neighbor Arani Nyaberi's father came to pay him a visit. Arani pulled chairs outside his house for the two of them, and when it began to rain they moved into the home where I was staying. It took this dense foreigner some time to recognize this as manifestation of *nsoni*.

Bibliography

Magistrate's Office, Keroka

Criminal and civil case records, *Ritongo* Gesima.

Magistrate's Office, Nyamira

Civil case records, criminal and civil registers, *Ritongo* Manga.

Former District Headquarters, Ogembo

Criminal and civil case records, *Ritongo* Kuja.

Kenya National Archive, Nakuru

Civil case records, *Ritongo* Gesima and *Ritongo* Kuja.

Kenya National Archives, Nairobi and Center for Research Library's Microfilm Collection, Chicago

Nyanza Deposit

Nyanza Province Annual Reports
Nyanza Province Intelligence Reports
South Kavirondo District Quarterly and Annual Reports
South Nyanza District Annual Reports
South Kavirondo District Political Record Book
South Kavirondo Monthly Intelligence Reports, 1930–38
Adm 1/1 General Native Policy
Adm 2/4 Internal and External Relations: African Affairs Committee

Adm 3/1/2 Provincial Commissioners' Meetings: Minutes
Adm 3/2/2 Conferences, Committees, Commissions: District Commissioners: Agenda and Correspondence
Adm 3/2/3 Conferences, Committees, Commissions: District Commissioners' Meetings: Central Province Minutes and Agenda
Adm 3/2/4 Conferences, Committees, Commissions: District Commissioners' Meetings: Coast Province Minutes and Agenda
Adm 5/4/3/7 Conferences: Provincial District Teams: District Teams: South Nyanza Agenda and Minutes
Adm 7/1/6/3 Local Native Council (Kisii-Bakoria): Minutes and Agenda
Adm 7/3/3/4/15 African District Council: South Nyanza: Registration of Bride Price By-Laws
Adm 7/13/1/2 Local Native Council: Provincial Native Council: General Correspondence: Agenda and Minutes
Adm 7/15/5/3 African District Council: Nyanza Province: South Nyanza: Agenda and Minutes
Adm 8/33 Institutions and Associations: Kisii Union
Adm 12/4/1 Tours and Diaries: South Kavirondo: 1938–39
Adm 12/7/2 Nyanza Administration: Barazas: Chiefs' Barazas
Adm 13/2/1 II Provincial Commissioner Nyanza: Native Tribes and Their Customs: Native Law and Customs: General Correspondence
Adm 15/7/13/1/2 Provincial Native Council: Agenda and Minutes
Agr 1/1 Crop Production: General Correspondence
Agr 1/1 II Crop Production
Agr 1/1/1/1 Crop Production: Food Shortages and Famine: Nyanza: General
Agr 1/2/2 Crop Production: Specific Crops: Coffee
Agr 1/2/3 Crop Production: Specific Crops: Mtama
Agr 1/2/9/3 Crop Production: Specific Crops: Coffee: Kisii Coffee Growers Cooperative Society
Agr 1/5/9 Export of Agricultural Produce for Military Purposes from Nyanza
Agr 3/2/1 Statistics and Data: Reports: Monthly Reports—Nyanza
Agr 3/2/4 Monthly and Crop Reports: South Kavirondo, 1934–51
Agr 10/1 Agricultural Machinery and Implements: Introduction—Native Reserves
Agr 14/2/4 Statistics and Data: Agricultural Reports: South Nyanza, 1951–54
DP 1/16 Monthly Intelligence Reports: Chiefs
DP 1/21 Chiefs' meetings, 1954–61
DP 5/4 Provincial administration: Divorces, general
DP 18/13 Minutes of Law Panel Meeting
DP 30/24 Safari Diary 1936–1938
DP 34/7 Staff: Chiefs and headmen: Chiefs' meetings
KSI/3/2 District of South Kavirondo: Histories and Customs of Kisii and Luo between 1911–1924
KSI/4/1 G. A. S. Northcote's Diary
Lab 2/1/4 Labour: Standing Orders: Juvenile Labour
Lab 2/1/9 Labour: Standing Orders: Visits to Labour Conscripts
Lab 3/2 Labour: Labour Supply
Lab 4/1/1 Labour: Wages: Complaints
Lab 15/1 Assisted Labour: Standing Orders and General Correspondence
L&O 2/1 Native Tribunals: Appointments: General Correspondence
L&O 2/1/3 Native Tribunals: Appointments South Nyanza
L&O 2/13 African Courts: Adultery Cases
L&O 2/14 African Courts

MDS 2/3/3 Marriages: Natives: Bride Price
MDS 2/3/4 Marriage, Divorce and Succession: Runaway Wives and Girls and Prostitution
MDS 2/3/5 Native Marriages and Divorces: Registration of Native Marriages: Contracts in Accordance with Tribal Customs
MDS 2/3/8 Marriages and Divorces: Natives: Status of Women in Africa
Mil 4/6/9/1 Family Remittances: Monthly Returns: Form A
Mil 4/9/1/2 Exemption Tribunal
Mil 4/9/1/15B Family Remittances: Monthly Returns: Form B
Mil 6 Manpower: Returns
Mil 17/12 Domestic and Miscellaneous Affairs of African Troops
Mil 28 Recruitment for Military Africans
PC/NZA 3/15/29 African Courts: Hearing of Cases
PC/NZA 3/15/88 African Courts: Adultery Cases
PC/NZA 3/17/12/2 Orders and Regulations: Communicating List of to Natives: Translations into Swahili
PC/NZA 3/17/17 Comments on Bills before Legislative Council
PC/NZA 3/26/4/3 Traveling Diaries, 1927
PC/NZA 3/26/4/4 Traveling Diaries, 1928–1929
PC/NZA 3/28/4/1 Native Marriages and Dowries 1925–1928
PC/NZA 3/33/6 Native Tribunal Cases: South Kavirondo
PC/NZA 19/4 Judicial Cases: South Kavirondo
PC/NZA 19/27 Native Law and Cases
Pub 4/2/5 Annual Reports: General: Labour Department (Nyanza) 1942–50
Vet 2/2 Organization and Policy: Destocking Native Reserves
Vet 2/4 Organization and Policy: Castration of Bulls
Vet 6/1 Quarantines: General Correspondence
Vet 9/1/1 Stock Trading: General Correspondence: Export and Import of Livestock
Vet 9/1/2 Cattle Trade: Livestock Purchases in Reserves: Stock Purchases, 1931–50
Vet 10/4/1 Stock Trading: Marketing of Stock: General Correspondence

Other

AG 1/609 Indecent Assaults on Women and Children
ARC (MAA) 2/9/16 I African Courts: Complaints: Nyanza
ARC (MAA) 2/10/21 Native Tribunals: General 1941–52
ARC (MAA) 6/43 Native Tribunals Ordinance: 1930: Matters Arising From Mr. Phillips' Report on Native Tribunals
Jud 1/1104 Native Tribunals
Jud 1/1460 Service of Process
Jud 1/1941 African Courts 1963–67
Leg 28/1 Native Marriage and Divorce
MAA 2/117 Publications and Reports: Standing Orders: Native Tribunals
MAA 2/119 African Courts: Miscellaneous Correspondence: Nyanza 1952–66
MAA 6/9 Native Tribunals: Standing Orders: South Nyanza
MAA 6/21 Procedure of Native Tribunals
MAA 6/22 Procedure of Native Tribunals: General
MAA 6/29 Miscellaneous Correspondence: Native Tribunal Cases
MAA 6/33 Reorganization of Native Tribunals
MAA 6/40 Provincial Native Courts Officer Nyanza: Letters and Circulars
MAA 7/421 Legislation: Native Tribunals Ordinance: Appointment of Judicial Advisor
MAA 7/700 Native Tribes and Customs: Marriage of Girls: Forced Marriages of Girls

MAA 7/725 Tribunals (Native): Recording of Native Law
MAA 9/842 Boards, Commissions, Meetings, etc.: District Commissioners Nyanza 1950–57
MAA 10/43 Native Tribunals Ordinance: Native Tribunals Cases Kisii
PC/CP 19/1 Forced Marriage of African Girls
RR 1/4 African Courts: Proposed Amendments to Native Tribunal Ordinance, 1930: New African Courts Bill: 1945–52
RR 1/6 African Courts: Policy and Organization
RR 8/1 Native Law: Recording Native Law
RR 8/8 Native Law: Law Panels: Establishment and Function
RR 8/10 Native Law: Law Panels: South Nyanza

Gusii County Council, Kisii

South Kavirondo Local Native Council, Agenda and Minutes

Public Records Office, Kew (UK)

CO 323/1067/1 Status of Indigenous women and children: practice of female circumcision
CO 323/1067/2 Status of Indigenous women and children: East Africa, 1930
CO 323/1176/16 British Commonwealth League
CO 323/1244/12 Minimum Age of marriage and Age of Consent in the Colonies (Replies to Circ. Desp., July 24, 1933)
CO 323/1257/13 Proposals for the Reclassification of the Forms of Slavery, 1934
CO 323/1344/5 Marriage, Minimum Age of, and Age of Consent: Bride Price, Inheritance of Widow, etc. 1935
CO 533/392/10 Kikuyu circumcision ceremony, 1930
CO 533/394/10 Kikuyu circumcision ceremony, 1930
CO 533/404/13 Archdeacon Owen—Contributions to Press
CO 533/515/7 Eviction of Indians engaged in the dairy industry in South Kavirondo District, 1939
CO 822/27/10 Women and children: native customs, 1930
CO 822/38/9 Limitation of the "Bride-price" in Kenya and Tanganyika, 1931–1932
CO 822/305 Loans to African traders in Nyanza Province, Kenya, 1953
CO 847/5/6 Status of Women in Africa, 1935
CO 847/6/11 Status of Women in Africa, 1936
CO 847/11/12 Status of Women in Africa, 1937
CO 847/12/14 Discussions with Archdeacon Owen, 1938
CO 859/15/7 British Commonwealth League: Enquiries concerning employment of native labour in Africa, 1939,
CO 955/78 Conference on the Future of Law in Africa, Comments on Agenda, 1957–1959
CO 1018/25 Central, North, and South Kavirondo and Kericho districts, 1947–1948 [Lord Hailey's notes]

Rhodes House, Oxford University

MSS Afr. s. 665, Dobbs, Kenya 1906–31
MSS Afr. s. 1153, Kenya Native Affairs, Sidney Herbert Fazan
MSS Afr. s. 1277, Richard Gethin, "An Old Settler Remembers"
MSS Afr. s. 1488 Winser, box 1, file 1

MSS Afr. s. 1792, box 37 (Matson Papers), File 5/1. S. H. Fazan
MSS Afr. s. 1942, Memories of an Administrative Officer by K. L. Hunter, April 1975

Mill Hill Missionaries Archive, St. Joseph College, London

Kisii Diaries

Nyabururu Diary
Diary of Catholic Mission at Rangenyo
Diary of Catholic Mission at Gekendo

Archives of the Cardinal Otunga Historical Society, Mosocho, Kenya

MAA/KIS/GEN/1/1 Northcote, "History of the District"
MAA/KIS/GEN/1/6 Doyle, "Marriage," "Circumcision"
MAA/KIS/LAW/1 Minutes of the South Nyanza Law Panel
MAA/KIS/LAW/1/11 Minutes of the South Nyanza Law Panel
MAA/KIS/LAW/1/13 Minutes of the South Nyanza Law Panel
MAH/KIS/PRE/6/1 Abel Nyakundi, "Okaba Omochakano Bw'Abagusii na Mogikoyo Omwambo," trans. by John M. Omwenga as "Being the Beginnings of the Kisiis and their Brothers the Kikuyus"

Fawcett Library, London Guildhall University

Association for Moral and Social Hygiene

3/AMS/62.8: Kenya
3/AMS box 46: Executive Council Meeting Minutes
The Shield

British Commonwealth League

Conference Reports, Annual Conferences, 1925–1939

International Bureau for the Suppression of Traffic in Women

Box 115:
26B: Pre-marriage Rite and Marriage Problem amongst natives in the British Colonies of Africa
26D: Forced Marriages of African Girls

St. Joan's Alliance

2/SJA/A1/7 Saint Joan's Alliance meetings, Minutes Book, Dec. 12, 1932–Sept. 15, 1942
2/SJA/A1/8 Minutes Book, Sept. 15, 1942–May 11, 1944
2/SJA/L14–19 Clippings, 1933–38

Women's Freedom League

FL 6/1 Minutes

The International Women's News (formerly *Jus Suffragii*), London

The Catholic Citizen (formerly *The Catholic Suffragist*), London

Gusii Field Material, Philip and Iona Mayer (in the possession of Iona Mayer, Oxford)*

*Used with the kind permission of Professor Mayer.
1: History
4: Cattle, Land, Risaga
8: Enyangi Ritual
12: Iteresi Survey
13: Modern
17: Marriage, Sex, Gender
18: Miscellany

Correspondence

Harold Beavon, Dec. 20, 2002
David W. R. Evans, May 17, 2004
Terence Gavanagh, May 8, 2004
Chris Minter, May 28, 2004
Jessie Olson, Dec. 31, 2002

Jessie Olson Letters*

*Used with kind permission of Ms. Olson.

Correspondence

Jessie Olson to her mother, 1947.

Oral Interviews Cited

Nyangau Kiage, June 16, 1997
Bethsheba Kemunto, June 23, 1997; June 6 and 9, 2002
Ochara Ogoro, July 4 and 15, 1997
Josiah Mochama, Jeremiah Ogechi, Elemeleck Chaga, Thomas Choti, July 16, 1997
Ambros Bwoma, July 19, 1997
Benson Nyamari Moengi, July 22, 1997
Tangurera Omwengo, Aug. 6, 1997
Jepheth Ondieki, Sept. 23, 1997
Samwel Mokaya Sangaka, Sept. 26, 1997
Nyambweke Onchaba, Oct. 2, 1997
Nyasani Omanua, Oct. 22, 1997
Paul Nyangoto Ogeturenga, Oct. 24, 1997
Nyakango Obiero, Nov. 3, 1997

Helen Kerubo, Nov. 17, 1997
Kerubo Kiage, Nov. 19, 1997
Jeremiah Kingoina Obegi, Oct. 1–2, 1998
Sabina Gesare, Oct. 6–7, 1998
Sabaniah Aroni Omayo and Maoga Onkundi, May 28, 2002
Nyasani Omanua and Rael Kemuma Kururia, June 3, 2002
Yunesi Kemuma, June 8, 2002
Juma Nyokangi, June 11, 2002
Prisilla (pseudonym), June 11, 2002
Peter Ogaro Nyangoto, Agnes Kerebi, Saberah Moraa, Callen Mokeira (family of Paul Nyangoto Ogeturenga), June 12, 2002
Luke Gasuku, June 15, 2002
Mzee Jackson, May 30, 2004

Indiana University Archives of Traditional Music

Dobrin song collection, 85–346-F

Periodicals

East African Standard
Manchester Guardian Weekly

Government Publications

"Correspondence relating to the Welfare of Women in Tropical Africa, 1935–37," Cmd. 5784, July 1938.
Carothers, J. C. *The Psychology of Mau Mau.* Nairobi: Colony and Protectorate of Kenya, 1955.
Cotran, Eugene. *Report on Customary Criminal Offences in Kenya.* Nairobi: Government of Kenya, 1963.
"Health and Progress of Native Populations in Certain Parts of the Empire," Colonial Number 65. London: HMSO, 1931.
Mayer, Philip. *Two Studies in Applied Anthropology in Kenya.* London: Colonial Office, 1951.
Phillips, Arthur. *Report on Native Tribunals.* Nairobi: Colony and Protectorate of Kenya, 1944.
Report of the Commission on the Law of Marriage and Divorce. Nairobi: Government of Kenya, 1968.
Wilson, Gordon. *Luo Customary Law and Marriage Law Customs.* Nairobi: Colony and Protectorate of Kenya, 1961.

Books, Articles, and Dissertations

Abuya, Jackson, Samuel Ratemo, Saul Omweri, Japhet Ratemo Getugi, Zachary Sunda, Peter Ndemo, Zachary Omwenga, and Joseph Onserio. "The Seventh Day Adventists in Kisii District." *Bulletin of the Cardinal Otunga Historical Society* 41 (Jan. 30, 1972): 12–19.

Allman, Jean. "Adultery and State in Asante: Reflections on Gender, Class and Power from 1800–1950." In *The Cloth of Many Colored Silks*, edited by John Hunwick and Nancy Lawler. Evanston, IL: Northwestern University Press, 1996.

Allman, Jean, Susan Geiger, and Nakanyike Musisi, eds. *Women in African Colonial Histories*. Bloomington: Indiana University Press, 2002.

Allman, Jean, and Victoria Tashjian. *"I Will Not Eat Stone": A Women's History of Colonial Asante*. Portsmouth, NH: Heinemann, 2000.

Amayo, Gershom N. "A History of the Adventist Christian Education in Kenya: Illustrated in the Light of its Impact on the Africans' Social, Economic, Religious and Political Development, 1906–1963." Ph.D. dissertation, Howard University, 1973.

Ambler, Charles H. *Kenyan Communities in the Age of Imperialism*. New Haven, CT: Yale University Press, 1988.

———. "The Renovation of Custom in Colonial Kenya: The 1932 Generation Succession Ceremonies in Embu." *Journal of African History* 30 (1989): 139–156.

Anderson, David. "Depression, Dust Bowl, Demography and Drought: The Colonial State and Soil Conservation in East Africa during the 1930s." *African Affairs* 83 (1984): 321–342.

———. "Stock Theft and Moral Economy in Colonial Kenya." *Africa* 56 (1986): 399–415.

———. *Eroding the Commons: The Politics of Ecology in Baringo, Kenya 1890–1963*. Oxford: James Currey, 2002.

Anderson, David, and David Throup. "Africans and Agricultural Production in Colonial Kenya: The Myth of the War as a Watershed." *Journal of African History* 26 (1985): 327–345.

arap Korir, Kipkoech Mosonik. "The Tea Plantation Economy in Kericho District and Related Phenomena to circa 1960." B.A. thesis, University of Nairobi, 1976.

Armstrong, W. W. "Kenya Colony." *Advent Review and Sabbath Herald* 110 (Jan. 26, 1933): 11–12.

Ault, James M. "Making 'Modern' Marriage 'Traditional': State Power and the Regulation of Marriage in Colonial Zambia." *Theory and Society* 12 (1983): 181–210.

Bager, Torben. "Marketing Cooperatives and Peasants in Kenya." CDR Publications 5, Uppsala, Scandinavian Institute of African Studies, 1980.

Barnes, Theresa A. "The Fight for Control of African Women's Mobility in Colonial Zimbabwe, 1900–1939." *Signs* 17 (1992): 586–608.

Barnes, Carolyn. "An Experiment with African Coffee Growing in Kenya: The Gusii, 1933–1950." Ph.D. dissertation, Michigan State University, 1976.

Beavon, Eric. "Among the Kisiis in the Heart of Africa." *Advent Review and Sabbath Herald* (April 19, 1923), 12–13.

———. "In the Wilds of East Africa." *Advent Review and Sabbath Herald* (Jan. 31, 1924), 18.

———. "A Sketch of Gospel Triumphs in Kisii." *Advent Review and Sabbath Herald* (March 18, 1926), 11–13.

———. *Sindiga, the Savage: A Tale of the Wilds*. New York: Harper, 1930.

Beidleman, T. O. *Colonial Evangelism: A Socio-historical Study of an East African Mission at the Grassroots*. Bloomington: Indiana University Press, 1982.

Beinart, William. "Speaking for Themselves." In *Tradition and Transition in Southern Africa: Festschrift for Philip and Iona Mayer*, edited by Andrew D. Spiegel and Patrick A. McAllister. Johannesburg: Witwatersrand University Press, 1991.

Berman, Bruce. *Control and Crisis in Colonial Kenya: The Dialectic of Domination*. London: James Currey, 1990.

———. "Ethnography as Politics, Politics as Ethnography: Kenyatta, Malinowski, and the Making of *Facing Mount Kenya*." *Canadian Journal of African Studies* 30 (1996): 313–344.

Berman, Bruce, and John Lonsdale. *Unhappy Valley: Conflict in Kenya and Africa*. London: James Currey, 1992.
Bernhardsdotter, Ann-Britt. "The Power of Being: A Study of Poverty, Fertility and Sexuality among the Kuria in Kenya and Tanzania." Ph.D. dissertation, Uppsala University, 2001.
Binagi, Lloyd A. "Marriage among Kuria." *Mila* (Institute of African Studies, University of Nairobi) 5 (1976): 13–23.
Birundu, Sarah C. A. "Gusii Trade in the Nineteenth Century." B.A. thesis, University of Nairobi, 1973.
Bohannan, Paul. *Justice and Judgment Among the Tiv*. London: Oxford University Press, for the International African Institute, 1957.
Bozzoli, Belinda. "Marxism, Feminism and South African Studies." *Journal of Southern African Studies* 9 (1983): 139–171.
Bozzoli, Belinda, with Mmantho Nkotsoe. *Women of Phokeng: Consciousness, Life Strategy, and Migrancy in South Africa, 1900–1983*. Portsmouth, NH: Heinemann, 1991.
Bravman, Bill. *Making Ethnic Ways: Communities and Their Transformations in Taita, Kenya, 1800–1950*. Portsmouth, NH: Heinemann, 1998.
Bujra, Janet. "Production, Property, Prostitution: 'Sexual Politics' in Atu." *Cahiers d'Etudes africaines* 17 (1977): 13–39.
Burton, Antoinette. "The Feminist Quest for Identity: British Imperial Suffragism and 'Global Sisterhood,' 1900–1915." *Journal of Women's History* 3 (1991) 46–81.
———. *Burdens of History: British Feminists, Indian Women, and Imperial Culture, 1865–1915*. Chapel Hill: University of North Carolina Press, 1994.
———. "'States of Injury': Josephine Butler on Slavery, Citizenship and the Boer War." In *Women's Suffrage in the British Empire: Citizenship, Nation, and Race*, edited by Ian Christopher Fletcher, Laura E. Nym Mayhall, and Philippa Levine. London: Routledge, 2000.
Butterman, Judith Marianne. "Luo Social Formations in Change: Karachuonyo and Kanyamkago, c. 1800–1945." Ph.D. dissertation, Syracuse University, 1979.
Buxton, Clarence. *The Kenya Question*. Nairobi: East African Standard, 1948.
Byfield, Judith. "Women, Marriage, Divorce and the Emerging Colonial State in Abeokuta (Nigeria) 1892–1904." *Canadian Journal of African Studies* 30 (1996): 32–51.
Caine, Barbara. *English Feminism, 1780–1980*. Oxford: Oxford University Press, 1997.
Cashmore, T. H. R. "Studies in District Administration in the East Africa Protectorate, 1895–1918." Ph.D. dissertation, University of Cambridge, 1965.
Cell, John W. "Colonial Rule." In *The Oxford History of the British Empire*, Vol. 4, edited by Judith M. Brown and Wm. Roger Louis. Oxford: Oxford University Press, 1999.
Chanock, Martin. *Law, Custom, and Social Order: The Colonial Experience in Malawi and Zambia*. Cambridge, UK: Cambridge University Press, 1985.
Clark, Carolyn. "Land and Food, Women and Power in Nineteenth Century Kikuyu." *Africa* 50 (1980): 357–370.
Clough, Marshall. *Fighting Two Sides: Kenyan Chiefs and Politicians, 1918–1940*. Boulder: University Press of Colorado, 1990.
Cooper, Barbara M. *Marriage in Maradi: Gender and Culture in a Hausa Society in Niger, 1900–1989*. Portsmouth, NH: Heinemann, 1997.
Cooper, Frederick. *From Slaves to Squatters: Plantation Labor and Agriculture in Zanzibar and Coastal Kenya, 1890–1925*. New Haven, CT: Yale University Press, 1980.
———. *Decolonization and African Society: The Labor Question in French and British Africa*. Cambridge, UK: Cambridge University Press, 1996.

Cory, Hans, and M. M. Hartnoll. *Customary Law of the Haya Tribe, Tanganyika Territory*. London: International African Institute, 1945.

Cotran, Eugene. *Restatement of African Law: Kenya,* Vol. I: *The Law of Marriage and Divorce*. London: Sweet and Maxwell, 1968.

______. *Casebook on Kenya Customary Law*. Nairobi: Nairobi University Press, 1995 (1987).

Dickerman, Carol. "African Courts Under the Colonial Regime: Usumbura, Ruanda-Urundi, 1938–62." *Canadian Journal of African Studies* 26 (1992): 55–69.

Dickson, W. Scott. *Christian Marriage and Divorce Law in Kenya in Relation to Africans*. Nairobi: Ndia Kuu Press, 1947.

Doorly, A. N. "Native Tribunals." *Journal of Comparative Legislation and International Law* 28 (1946): 25–34.

Douglas, R. M. *Feminist Freikorps: The British Voluntary Women Police, 1914–1940*. Westport, CT: Praeger, 1999.

Engels, Dagmar. "The Age of Consent Act of 1891: Colonial Ideology in Bengal." *South Asia Research* 3 (1983): 107–134.

Epprecht, Marc. *"This Matter of Women is Getting Very Bad": Gender, Development and Politics in Colonial Lesotho*. Pietermaritzburg: University of Natal Press, 2000.

Fallers, Lloyd A. *Law without Precedent: Legal Ideas in Action in the Courts of Colonial Busoga*. Chicago: University of Chicago Press, 1969.

Feierman, Steven. *Peasant Intellectuals: History and Anthropology in Tanzania*. Madison: University of Wisconsin Press, 1990.

Fields, Karen E. *Revival and Rebellion in Colonial Central Africa*. Portsmouth, NH: Heinemann, 1997 (1985).

Fischer, G. A. "Am Ostufer des Victoria-Njansa." *Petermanns Mitteilungen* (1895): 42–46.

Forbes, Geraldine H. "Women and Modernity: The Issue of Child Marriage in India." *Women's Studies International Quarterly* 2 (1979): 407–419.

Garst, Ronald D. "Innovation Diffusion among the Gusii of Kenya." *Economic Geography* 50 (1974): 300–312.

______. "Population, Migration, and Communication in Kisii District, Kenya." National Geographic Society Research Reports, Vol. 16, 1975, 293–303.

Gartrell, Beverley. "The Ruling Ideas of a Ruling Elite: British Colonial Officials in Uganda, 1944–1952." Ph.D. dissertation, City University of New York, 1979.

Gavaghan, Terence. *Of Lions and Dung Beetles*. Elms Court, UK: Arthur H. Stockwell, 1999.

Geisler, Gisela. "Moving with Tradition: The Politics of Marriage among the Toka of Zambia." *Canadian Journal of African History* 26 (1992): 437–461.

Ghai, Y. P., and J. P. W. B. MacAuslan. *Public Law and Political Change in Kenya*. Oxford: Oxford University Press, 1970.

Glassman, Jonathon. *Feasts and Riot: Revelry, Rebellion, and Popular Consciousness on the Swahili Coast, 1856–1888*. Portsmouth, NH: Heinemann, 1995.

Gordon, David F. *Decolonization and the State in Kenya*. Boulder, CO: Westview, 1986.

Gorges, G. H. "A Journey from Lake Naivasha to the Victoria Nyanza." *The Geographical Journal* 16 (July 1900): 78–89.

Guyer, Jane I. *Family and Farm in Southern Cameroon*. African Research Studies No. 14, Boston University, 1984.

______. "The Value of Beti Bridewealth." In *Money Matters: Instability, Values and Social Payments in the Modern History of West African Communities*, edited by Jane I. Guyer. Portsmouth, NH: Heinemann, 1995.

Håkansson, Thomas. *Bridewealth, Women and Land: Social Change among the Gusii of Kenya*. Uppsala Studies in Cultural Anthropology, 10, Uppsala, 1988.

———. "Grain, Cattle, and Power: Social Processes of Intensive Cultivation and Exchange in Precolonial Western Kenya." *Journal of Anthropological Research* 50 (1994): 249–276.

Hargreaves, John D. *Decolonization in Africa*. New York: Longman, 1996.

Harries, Patrick. "Kinship, Ideology and the Nature of Pre-Colonial Labour Migration: Labour Migration from Delagoa Bay Hinterland to South Africa, up to 1895." In *Industrialisation and Social Change in South Africa: African Class Formation, Culture and Consciousness, 1870–1930*, edited by Shula Marks and Richard Rathbone. New York: Longman, 1982.

Hay, Margaret Jean. "Economic Change in Luoland: Kowe, 1890–1945." Ph.D. dissertation, University of Wisconsin, 1972.

———. "Local Trade and Ethnicity in Western Kenya." *African Economic History Review* 11 (1975): 1–12.

———. "Fashioning a Modern Identity in Colonial Western Kenya: Struggles over Clothing in the Interwar Period." Discussion Papers in the African Humanities number 35, 2002, African Studies Center, Boston University.

———. "Changes in Clothing and Struggles over Identity in Colonial Western Kenya." In *Fashioning Africa: Power and the Politics of Dress*, edited by Jean Allman. Bloomington: Indiana University Press, 2004.

Hay, Margaret Jean, and Marcia Wright, eds. *African Women and the Law: Historical Perspectives*. Boston University Papers on Africa, VII, 1982.

Heimsath, Charles H. "The Origin and Enactment of the Indian Age of Consent Bill, 1891." *Journal of Asian Studies* 21 (1962): 491–504.

Harrison, Brian. *Prudent Revolutionaries: Portraits of British Feminists between the Wars*. Oxford: Clarendon, 1987.

Heussler, Robert. *Yesterday's Rulers: The Making of the British Colonial Service*. Syracuse, NY: Syracuse University Press, 1963.

Hirsch, Susan F. *Pronouncing and Preserving: Gender and the Discourses of Disputing in an African Islamic Court*. Chicago: University of Chicago Press, 1998.

Hodgson, Dorothy L. "Pastoralism, Patriarchy and History: Changing Gender Relations among the Maasai in Tanganyika, 1890–1940." *Journal of African History* 40 (1999): 41–65.

Hodgson, Dorothy L., and Sheryl A. McCurdy. *"Wicked" Women and the Reconfiguration of Gender in Africa*. Portsmouth, NH: Heinemann, 2001.

Hoehler-Fatton, Cynthia. *Women of Fire and Spirit: History, Faith and Gender in Roho Religion in Western Kenya*. Oxford: Oxford University Press, 1996.

Holmquist, Frank W. "Peasant Organization, Clientelism and Dependency: A Case Study of an Agricultural Producers Cooperative in Kenya." Ph.D. dissertation, Indiana University, 1975.

Hubert, Klemens, ed. "Agricultural Production in Kisii District/Kenya and Proposals for its Development." Post-Graduate Training Center for Agricultural Development, Institute for Overseas Agriculture, Technical University of Berlin, 1972.

Hunt, Nancy Rose. "Placing African Women's History and Locating Gender." *Social History* 14 (1989): 359–379.

Iliffe, John. *The African Poor: A History*. Cambridge, UK: Cambridge University Press, 1987.

Jackson, Kennell A. "The Family Entity and Famine among the Nineteenth-Century Akamba of Kenya: Social Responses to Environmental Stress." *Journal of Family History* 1 (1976): 192–216.

Jackson, Tudor. *The Law of Kenya*, 3rd. ed. Nairobi: Kenya Literature Bureau, 1988.

Jaschok, Maria, and Suzanne Miers, eds. *Women and Chinese Patriarchy: Submission, Servitude and Escape*. London: Zed Books, 1994.

Jayawadena, Kumari. *The White Woman's Other Burden: Western Women and South Asia During British Colonial Rule*. New York: Routledge, 1995.

Jeater, Diana. *Marriage, Perversion and Power: The Construction of Moral Discourse in Southern Rhodesia, 1894–1930*. Oxford: Oxford University Press, 1993.

Johnson, John, ed. *Colony to Nation: British Administrators in Kenya, 1940–1963*. Norfolk: Erskine, 2002.

Johnstone, H. B. "Notes on the Customs of the Tribes Occupying Mombasa Sub-District, British East Africa." *The Journal of the Anthropological Institute of Great Britain and Ireland* 32 (Jan.–June, 1902): 263–272.

Judd, Dennis. *Empire: The British Imperial Experience from 1765 to the Present*. London: Harper Collins, 1996.

Judicial Advisors' Conference, 1953. Special Supplement to *Journal of African Administration* 5 (1953).

Kershaw, Greet. *Mau Mau from Below*. Oxford: James Currey, 1997.

Kibwana, Kivutha. *Law and the Status of Women in Kenya*. Nairobi: Claripress, for the Faculty of Law, University of Nairobi, 1996.

King, Kenneth James. *Pan-Africanism and Education: A Study of Race Philanthropy and Education in the Southern States of America and East Africa*. Oxford: Clarendon, 1971.

Kirk-Greene, A. H. M. "The Thin White Line: The Size of the British Colonial Service in Africa." *African Affairs* 79 (1980): 25–44.

Kitching, Gavin. *Class and Economic Change in Kenya: The Making of an African Petite-Bourgeoisie*. New Haven, CT: Yale University Press, 1980.

Kjerland, Kirsten Alsaker. "Cattle Breed; Shillings Don't: The Belated Incorporation of the abaKuria into Modern Kenya." Ph.D. thesis, University of Bergen, 1995.

______. "When African Women Take Wives: A Historiographical Overview." The Nordic Africa Institute, Poverty and Prosperity Occasional Papers 6, 1997.

Klein, Martin. *Slavery and Colonial Rule in French West Africa*. Cambridge, UK: Cambridge University Press, 1998.

Knowles, Oliver. "Some Modern Adaptations of Customary Law in the Settlement of Matrimonial Disputes in the Luo, Kisii and Kuria Tribes of South Nyanza." *Journal of African Administration* 8 (1956): 111–115.

Koenig, Anthony. *The Beginning of the Church in South Kavirondo*. Mosocho, Kenya: Cardinal Otunga High School, 1985.

Kosgei, Sally Jemngetich. "Commodity Production, Tea and Social Change in Kericho, Kenya, 1895–1963." Ph.D. dissertation, Stanford University, 1981.

Kuper, Adam. *Anthropologists and Anthropology: The British School, 1922–1972*. New York: Pica, 1973.

______. *Wives for Cattle: Bridewealth and Marriage in Southern Africa*. London: Routledge and Kegan Paul, 1982.

Land, Hilary. "Eleanor Rathbone and the Economy of the Family." In *British Feminism in the Twentieth Century*, edited by Harold L. Smith. Amherst: University of Massachusetts Press, 1990.

Langat, S. C. "Some Aspects of Kipsigis History before 1914." In *Ngano: Studies in Traditional and Modern East African History*, edited by B. G. McIntosh. Nairobi: East African Publishing House, for the Department of History, University College, Nairobi, 1969.

Lawrance, Benjamin, Emily Lynn Osborn, and Richard Roberts, eds. *Intermediaries, Interpreters and Clerks: African Employees and the Making of Colonial Africa*. Madison: University of Wisconsin Press, (in press).

LeVine, Robert A. "Omoriori: Smeller of Witches." *Natural History* 67 (March, 1953): 142–147.

———. "Gusii Sex Offenses: A Study in Social Control." *American Anthropologist* 61 (1959): 963–990.

———. "Wealth and Power in Gusiiland." In *Markets in Africa*, edited by Paul Bohannan and George Dalton. Evanston, IL: Northwestern University, 1962.

———. "The Gusii Family." In *The Family Estate in Africa*, edited by Robert F. Gray and P. H. Gulliver. London: Routledge and Kegan Paul, 1964.

LeVine, Robert A., and Barbara B. LeVine. *Nyansongo: A Gusii Community*. New York: Wiley, 1966.

LeVine, Robert A., and Donald T. Campbell. *Gusii of Kenya*. New Haven, CT: Human Relations Area Files, 1972.

Lewis, Joanna. *Empire State-Building: War and Welfare in Kenya, 1925–52*. Oxford: James Currey, 2000.

Lonsdale, John. "When did the Gusii (Or Any Other Group) Become a 'Tribe'?" *Kenya Historical Review* 5 (1977): 123–133.

———. "The European Scramble and Conquest in African history." In *The Cambridge History of Africa*, Vol. 6, edited by Roland Oliver and G. N. Sanderson. Cambridge, UK: Cambridge University Press, 1985.

———. "The Depression and the Second World War in the Transformation of Kenya." In *Africa and the Second World War*, edited by David Killingray and Richard Rathbone. New York: St. Martins, 1986.

Lovejoy, Paul. "Concubinage and the Status of Women Slaves in Early Colonial Northern Nigeria." *Journal of African History* 29 (1988): 245–266.

Lovejoy, Paul E., and Jan S. Hogendorn. *Slow Death for Slavery: The Course of Abolition in Northern Nigeria, 1897–1936*. Cambridge, UK: Cambridge University Press, 1993.

Lovett, Margot. "Gender Relations, Class Formation, and the Colonial State in Africa." In *Women and the State in Africa*, edited by Jane Parpart and Kathleen Staudt. Boulder, CO: Lynn Rienner, 1989.

———. "On Power and Powerlessness: Marriage and Political Metaphor in Colonial Western Tanzania." *International Journal of African Historical Studies* 27 (1994): 273–301.

———. "'She Thinks She's Like a Man': Marriage and (De)Constructing Gender Identity in Colonial Buha, Western Tanzania, 1943–1960." *Canadian Journal of African Studies* 30 (1996): 52–68.

———. "Elders, Migrants and Wives: Labor Migration and the Renegotiation of Intergenerational, Patronage and Gender Relations in Highland Buha, Western Tanzania, 1921–1962." Ph.D. dissertation, Columbia University, 1996.

Low, D. A. "British East Africa: The Establishment of British Rule, 1895–1912." In *History of East Africa*, Vol. 2, edited by Vincent Harlow and E. M. Chilver. Oxford: Clarendon, 1965.

Low, D. A., and J. M. Lonsdale, "Towards the New Order, 1945–1963." In *History of East Africa*, Vol. 3, edited by D. A. Low and Allison Smith. Oxford: Oxford University Press, 1976.

Lugard, Frederick. *The Dual Mandate in British Tropical Africa*. London: Frank Cass, 1965 (1922).

Mackenzie, A. Fiona D. *Land, Ecology and Resistance in Kenya, 1880–1952*. Edinburgh: Edinburgh University Press for the International African Institute, 1998.

Mair, Lucy. *African Marriage and Social Change*. London: Cass, 1969.

Mamdani, Mahmood. *Citizen and Subject: Contemporary Africa and the Legacy of Late Colonialism*. Princeton, NJ: Princeton University Press, 1996.

Matsuzono, Makio. "Adjacent Generations and Respect Attitudes among the Gusii." In *Themes in Socio-cultural Ideas and Behaviour among Six Ethnic Groups of Kenya*, edited by Nobuhiro Nagashima. Kunitachi: Hitotsubashi University, 1981.

Manicom, Linzi. "Ruling Relations: Rethinking State and Gender in South African History." *Journal of African History* 33 (1992): 441–465.
Manners, Robert A. "The Kipsigis of Kenya: Culture Change in a 'Model' East African Tribe." In *Three African Tribes in Transition.* Vol. 1 of *Contemporary Change in Traditional Societies*, edited by Julian Steward. Urbana: University of Illinois Press, 1972.
Maxon, Robert. "A Kenya Petite Bourgeoisie Enters Local Politics: The Kisii Union, 1945–1949." *International Journal of African Historical Studies* 19 (1986): 451–462.
———. *Conflict and Accommodation in Western Kenya: The Gusii and the British, 1907–1963*. Cranbury, NJ: Associated University Presses, 1989.
———. "Stifling Capitalism in Rural Africa: The Gusii Coffee Industry in Kenya, 1932–1949." *Journal of Third World Studies* 11 (1994): 317–350.
———. *Going Their Separate Ways: Agrarian Transformation in Kenya, 1930–1950.* Cranbury, NJ: Associated University Presses, 2003.
Mayer, Iona. "Studies in Gusii Kinship." Ph.D. dissertation, Rhodes University, 1965.
———. *The Nature of Kinship Relations: The Significance of the Use of Kinship Terms among the Gusii.* Manchester: Manchester University Press, for the Rhodes-Livingstone Institute, 1965.
———. "The Gusii of Western Kenya." In *Cultural Source Materials for Population Planning in East Africa*, Vol. III: *Beliefs and Practices*, edited by Angela Molnos. Nairobi: East African Publishing House, 1973.
———. "The Patriarchal Image: Routine Dissociation in Gusii Families." *African Studies* 34 (1975): 259–281.
Mayer, Philip. *The Lineage Principle in Gusii Society*. International African Institute, Memorandum 24, Oxford, 1949.
———. *Gusii Bridewealth Law and Custom.* Rhodes-Livingstone Papers, 18, Oxford, 1950.
———. "Privileged Obstruction of Marriage Rites Among the Gusii." *Africa* 20 (1950): 113–125.
———. "The Joking of 'Pals' in Gusii Age-Sets." *African Studies* 10 (1951): 27–41.
———. "Gusii Initiation Ceremonies." *Journal of the Royal Anthropological Institute* 83 (1953): 9–36.
Mayer, Philip, and Iona Mayer. "Land Law in the Making." In *African Law: Adaptation and Development*, edited by Hilda Kuper and Leo Kuper. Berkeley: University of California Press, 1965.
Mbilinyi, Marjorie. "Runaway Wives in Colonial Tanganyika: Forced Labour and Forced Marriage in Rungwe District 1919–1961." *International Journal of the Sociology of Law*, 16 (1988): 1–29.
Mboya, Paul. *Utawala na Maendeleo ya Local Government South Nyanza, 1926–1957.* Nairobi: East African Literature Bureau, 1959.
McClendon, Thomas. "Tradition and Domestic Struggle in the Courtroom: Customary Law and the Control of Women in Segregation-Era Natal." *International Journal of African Historical Studies* 28 (1995): 527–561.
———. *Genders and Generations Apart: Labor Tenants and Customary Law in Segregation-Era South Africa, 1920s to 1940s*. Portsmouth, NH: Heinemann, 2002.
McKibben, Ross. *Classes and Cultures: England 1918–1951*. Oxford: Oxford University Press, 1998.
McKittrick, Meredith. "The 'Burden' of Young Men: Property and Generational Conflict in Namibia, 1880–1945." *African Economic History* 24 (1996): 115–129.
McWilliam, M. D. "The Kenya Tea Industry." *The East African Economic Review* 6 (July 1959): 32–48.

Meillassoux, Claude. "'The Economy' in Agricultural Self-Sustaining Societies: A Preliminary Analysis." In *Relations of Production: Marxist Approaches to Economic Anthropology*, edited by David Seddon. London: Frank Cass, 1978.

———. *Maidens, Meal and Money: Capitalism and the Domestic Community*. Cambridge, UK: Cambridge University Press, 1981.

Miers, Suzanne. "Slavery and the Slave Trade as International Issues, 1890–1939." In *Slavery and Colonial Rule in Africa*, edited by Suzanne Miers and Martin Klein. London: Frank Cass, 1999.

Miers, Suzanne, and Richard Roberts, eds. *The End of Slavery in Africa*. Madison: University of Wisconsin Press, 1988.

Moindi, Kennedy M. "Peasants, Entrepreneurship, Capital Accumulation and Differentiation: The Gusii Maize Flour Millers of Western Kenya, 1920–1950." Paper presented at the African Studies Association Annual Conference, New Orleans, Nov. 2004.

Mokamba, David, Nyayiemi Moturi, Gabriel Metet, and David Achira. "The Kisii-Kipsigis Wars of the Late Nineteenth Century." *Kenya Historical Review* 2 (1974): 221–234.

Moore, Henrietta L., and Megan Vaughan. *Cutting Down Trees: Gender, Nutrition, and Agricultural Change in the Northern Province of Zambia, 1890–1990*. Portsmouth, NH: Heinemann, 1994.

Moore, Sally Falk. *Social Facts and Fabrications: "Customary" Law on Kilimanjaro, 1880–1980*. Cambridge, UK: Cambridge University Press, 1986.

———. *Anthropology and Africa: Changing Perspectives on a Changing Scene*. Charlottesville: University of Virginia Press, 1994.

Morombasi, James, and Barnabas Gabuna. "Trade in Kisii before 1907." *Bulletin of the Cardinal Otunga Historical Society* 64 (May 20, 1978): 3–8.

Morris, H. F., and James S. Read. *Indirect Rule and the Search for Justice: Essays in East African Legal History*. Oxford: Oxford University Press, 1972.

Moturi, N. Z. "Pregnancy in Ntana." *Bulletin of the Cardinal Otunga Historical Society* 80 (May 1980): 14–18.

Murray, Colin. "High Bridewealth, Migrant Labour and the Position of Women in Lesotho." *Journal of African Law* 21 (1977): 79–96.

Mutongi, Kenda Beatrice. "Generations of Grief and Grievances: A History of Widows and Widowhood in Maragoli, Western Kenya, 1900 to the Present." Ph.D. dissertation, University of Virginia, 1996.

N.a. "Native Routes through the Masai Country, from Information Obtained by the Rev. T. Wakefield." *Proceedings of the Royal Geographical Society and Monthly Record of Geography*, 4 (1882): 742–747.

N.a. "Neumann's Journey in East Africa." *The Geographical Journal*, 6 (Sept. 1895): 274–277.

Nast, Heidi J. "The Impact of British Imperialism on the Landscape of Female Slavery in the Kano Palace, Northern Nigeria." *Africa* 64 (1994): 34–73.

Nerlove, Sarah. "Trait Disposition and Situational Determinants of Behavior among Gusii Children of Southwestern Kenya." Ph.D. dissertation, Stanford University, 1969.

Nyang'era, N. K. *The Making of Man and Woman under Abagusii Customary Law*. Kisii: self-published, 1999.

Nyarang'o, Peter M. *Sunset in Africa*. Nairobi: East African Educational Publishers, 1994.

Nyarango, Obadiah B. "Biography of Chief Musa Nyandusi." Student Seminar Paper, Department of History, University of Nairobi, Dec. 1977.

———. "The Biography of Chief Musa Nyandusi." B.A. thesis, University of Nairobi, 1978.

Nyasani, Joseph M. *The British Massacre of the Gusii Freedom Defenders*. Nairobi: Nairobi Bookmen, 1984.
Nyaundi, Nehemiah M. *Seventh-day Adventism in Gusii, Kenya*. Kendu Bay, Kenya: Africa Herald Publishing House, 1997.
Ochieng', William R. "A Traditional History of the Gusii of Western Kenya, Appendix I: Southern Nyanza Historical Texts." Ph.D. dissertation, University of Nairobi, 1971.
———. *A Pre-Colonial History of the Gusii of Western Kenya, from c. A.D. 1500 to 1915*. Nairobi: East African Literature Bureau, 1974.
———. "In Search of a State among the Kitutu in the Nineteenth Century." In *State Formation in Eastern Africa*, edited by Ahmed Idha Salim. Nairobi: Heinemann, 1984.
Odinga, Agnes Adhiambo. "Women's Medicine and Fertility: A Social History of Reproduction in South Nyanza, Kenya, 1920–1980." Ph.D. dissertation, University of Minnesota, 2001.
Ogot, Bethwell A. "Alfayo Odongo Mango." In *Kenya Historical Biographies*, edited by Kenneth King and Ahmed Salim. Nairobi: East African Publishing House, 1971.
Okioma, Zebedeo. "Nyamosi, First Chief of Majoge." *Bulletin of the Cardinal Otunga Historical Society* 78 (Nov. 15, 1979): 19–20.
Omasire, Shem. "Milestones in the History of the Gusii: An Oral Tradition Perspective." *Bulletin of the Cardinal Otunga Historical Society* 100 (July 15, 1983): 43–46.
Omosa, Mary. "Re-conceptualizing Food Security: Interlocking Strategies, Unfolding Choices and Rural Livelihoods in Kisii District, Kenya." Ph.D. thesis, Landbouw Universteit Wageningen, 1998.
Ondieki, Cleophas. "Chiefs as Agents of Social Change in Gusii During the Colonial Period, c. 1905–1963, Part IV." *Bulletin of the Cardinal Otunga Historical Society* 117 (Aug. 1, 1987): 9–25.
Onguti, Zebedeo. "Some Kisii Riddles, Sayings and Proverbs." *Bulletin of the Cardinal Otunga Historical Society* 32 (July 25, 1970): 8–17.
Orvis, Stephen. *The Agrarian Question in Kenya*. Gainesville: University of Florida Press, 1997.
Osborn, Emily Lynn. "'Circle of Iron': African Colonial Employees and the Interpretation of Colonial Rule in French West Africa." *Journal of African History* 44 (2003): 29– 50.
Oswald, Felix. *Alone in Sleeping Sickness Country*. London: Kegan Paul, 1915.
———. "From the Victoria Nyanza to the Kisii Highlands." *The Geographical Journal* 41 (Jan.–June 1913), 114–126.
Parking, David, and David Nyamwaya, eds. *Transformations of African Marriage*. Manchester: Manchester University Press for the International African Institute, 1987.
Parpart, Jane L. "Class and Gender on the Copperbelt: Women in Northern Rhodesian Copper Mining Communities, 1926–64." In *Women and Class in Africa*, edited by Claire Robertson and Iris Berger. New York: Africana Publishing, 1986.
———. "Sexuality and Power on the Zambian Copperbelt: 1926–1964." In *Patriarchy and Class: African Women in the Home and the Workforce*, edited by Sharon B. Strichter and Jane L. Parpart. Boulder, CO: Westview, 1988.
———. "'Where is Your Mother?': Gender, Urban Marriage, and Colonial Discourse on the Zambian Copperbelt, 1924–1945." *International Journal of African Historical Studies* 27 (1994): 241–271.
Parsons, Timothy. *The African Rank-and-File: Social Implications of Colonial Military Service in the King's African Rifles, 1902–1964*. Portsmouth, NH: Heinemann, 1999.
Partington, H. B. "Some Notes on the Kisi People." *East Africa Quarterly* 2 (1905): 328–329.
Pedersen, Susan. "National Bodies, Unspeakable Acts: The Sexual Politics of Colonial Policy-Making." *Journal of Modern History* 63 (1991): 647–680.

———. "The Maternalist Moment in British Colonial Policy: The Controversy over 'Child Slavery' in Hong Kong 1917–1941." *Past and Present* 171 (2001): 161–202.

———. "Eleanor Rathbone (1872–1946): The Victorian Family under the Daughter's Eye." In *After the Victorians: Private Conscience and Public Duty in Modern Britain*, edited by Susan Pedersen and Peter Mandler. London: Routledge, 1994.

Peires, J. B. "Paradigm Deleted: The Materialist Interpretation of the Mfecane." *Journal of Southern African Studies* 19 (1993): 295–313.

Peterson, Derek R. "Wordy Women: Gender Trouble and the Oral Politics of the East African Revival in Northern Gikuyuland." *Journal of African History* 42 (2001): 469–489.

———. *Creative Writing: Translation, Bookkeeping, and the Work of Imagination in Colonial Kenya*. Portsmouth, NH: Heinemann, 2004.

Phillips, Anne. *The Enigma of Colonialism: British Policy in West Africa*. London: James Currey, 1989.

Phillips, Arthur. "The African Court System in Kenya." *Journal of African Administration* 4 (1952): 135–138.

———. ed. *Survey of African Marriage and Family Life*. London: Oxford University Press for the International African Institute, 1953.

Posel, Deborah. "State, Power and Gender: Conflict over the Registration of African Customary Marriage in South Africa c. 1910–1970." *Journal of Historical Sociology* 8 (1995): 223–256.

Presley, Cora Ann. *Kikuyu Women, the Mau Mau Rebellion, and Social Change in Kenya*. Boulder, CO: Westview, 1992.

Radcliffe-Brown, A. R., and Daryll Forde, eds. *African Systems of Kinship and Marriage*. London: KPI, 1987 (1950).

Raikes, Philip. "Monogamists Sit by the Doorway: Notes on the Construction of Gender, Ethnicity and Rank in Kisii, Western Kenya." CDR Working Paper 92.7, Center for Development Research, Copenhagen, Oct. 1992.

Ranger, Terence. "The Invention of Tradition in Africa." In *The Invention of Tradition*, edited by Eric Hobsbawm and Terence Ranger. Cambridge, UK: Cambridge University Press, 1983.

Roberts, Penelope A. "The State and the Regulation of Marriage: Sefwi Wiawso (Ghana) 1900–40." In *Women, State, Ideology: Studies from Africa and Asia*, edited by Haleh Afshar. Albany, NY: SUNY Press, 1987.

Roberts, Richard. "Text and Testimony in the Tribunal de Premiere Instance, Dakar, during the Early Twentieth Century." *Journal of African History* 31 (1990): 447–463.

———. "Representation, Structure and Agency: Divorce in the French Soudan during the Early Twentieth Century." *Journal of African History* 40 (1999): 389–410.

Roberts, Richard, and Kristin Mann. "Law in Colonial Africa." In *Law in Colonial Africa*, edited by Kristin Mann and Richard Roberts. Portsmouth, NH: Heinemann, 1991.

Robertson, Claire C. *Trouble Showed the Way: Women, Men, and Trade in the Nairobi Area, 1890–1990*. Bloomington: Indiana University Press, 1997.

Rosberg, Carl G., and John Nottingham. *The Myth of Mau Mau: Nationalism in Kenya*. New York: Meridian, 1966.

Rupp, Leila J. *Worlds of Women: The Making of an International Women's Movement*. Princeton, NJ: Princeton University Press, 1997.

Savage, Donald C., and J. Forbes Munro. "Carrier Corps Recruitment in the British East Africa Protectorate." *Journal of African History* 21 (1980): 313–342.

Schmidt, Elizabeth. "Negotiated Spaces and Contested Terrain: Men, Women, and the Law in Colonial Zimbabwe, 1890–1939." *Journal of Southern African Studies* 16 (1990): 622–648.

———. "Patriarchy, Capitalism, and the Colonial State in Zimbabwe." *Signs* 16 (1991): 732–756.

———. *Peasants, Traders and Wives: Shona Women in the History of Zimbabwe, 1870–1939*. Portsmouth, NH: Heinemann, 1992.

Shadle, Brett L. "Rape and Justice in Kenya, c. 1940–1970." Paper presented at the Stanford Conference on Colonialism, Law and Human Rights in Africa, Stanford University, May 1999.

———. "'Changing Traditions to Meet Current Altering Conditions': Customary Law, African Courts, and the Rejection of Codification in Kenya, 1930–60." *Journal of African History* 40 (1999): 411–431.

———. "'Girl Cases': Runaway Wives, Eloped Daughters and Abducted Women in Gusiiland, Kenya, c. 1900–c. 1965." Ph.D. dissertation, Northwestern University, 2000.

———. "Patronage, Millennialism and the Serpent-God Mumbo in Southwest Kenya, 1912–1934." *Africa* 72 (2002): 29–53.

———. "Bridewealth and Female Consent: Marriage Disputes in African Courts, Gusiiland, Kenya." *Journal of African History* 44 (2003): 241–262.

———. "Rape and the Law in Colonial Kenya." Paper presented at the African Studies Association Annual Conference, New Orleans, Nov. 2004.

———. "Law and the Nature of Colonial Rule: The Struggle to Control African Courts in Kenya." Department of History Faculty Research Seminar, Virginia Tech, April 21, 2006.

———. "African Court Elders in Nyanza Province, Kenya, c. 1930–1960: From 'Traditional' to 'Modern.'" In *Intermediaries, Interpreters and Clerks: African Employees and the Making of Colonial Africa*, edited by Benjamin Lawrance, Emily Lynn Osborn, and Richard Roberts. Madison: University of Wisconsin Press, (in press).

Shaw, Carolyn Clark. *Colonial Inscriptions: Race, Sex and Class in Kenya*. Minneapolis: University of Minnesota Press, 1995.

Shepard, Gill. "Rank, Gender, and Homosexuality: Mombasa as a Key to Understanding Sexual Options." In *The Cultural Construction of Sexuality*, edited by Pat Caplan. London: Routledge, 1987.

Shereikis, Rebecca. "Customized Courts: French Colonial Legal Institutions in Kayes, French Soudan, c. 1880–c. 1913." Ph.D. dissertation, Northwestern University, 2003.

Silberschmidt, Margrethe. *"Women Forget That Men are the Masters": Gender Antagonism and Socio-economic Change in Kisii District, Kenya*. Uppsala: Nordiska Afrikainstitutet, 1999.

Singha, Radhika. *A Despotism of Law: Crime and Justice in Early Colonial India*. Delhi: Oxford University Press, 1998.

Sinha, Mrinalini. *Colonial Masculinity: The "Manly Englishman" and the "Effeminate Bengali" in the Late Nineteenth Century*. Manchester: Manchester University Press, 1995.

Sandgren, David. *Christianity and the Kikuyu: Religious Divisions and Social Conflict*. New York: Peter Lang, 1989.

Spake, Lacy Alvin, Jr. "A Micro-regional Geography Case Study of Tropical Highland Development: Gusii District, Kenya, East Africa." M.A. thesis, San Francisco State College, 1965.

Spencer, John. *The Kenya African Union*. London: KPI, 1985.

Spencer, Paul. *The Maasai of Matapato: A Study of Rituals of Rebellion*. Bloomington: University of Indiana Press, 1988.

Staves, Susan. "Money for Honor: Damages for Criminal Conversation." *Studies in Eighteenth-Century Culture* 11 (1982): 279–297.

Stern, Steve J. *The Secret History of Gender: Women, Men, and Power in Late Colonial Mexico*. Chapel Hill: University of North Carolina Press, 1995.
Stevens, Lesley. "Bananas, Babies, and Women Who Buy Their Graves: Matrifocal Values in a Patrilineal Tanzanian Society." *Canadian Journal of African Studies* 29 (1995): 454–480.
Stevenson, John. *British Society, 1914–45*. London: Penguin, 1984.
Stichter, Sharon. *Migrant Labour in Kenya: Capitalism and African Response, 1895–1975*. Essex: Longman, 1982.
Stichter, Sharon B., and Jane L. Parpart, eds. *Patriarchy and Class: African Women in the Home and the Workforce*. Boulder, CO: Westview, 1988.
Stigand, C. H. *The Land of Zinj: Being an Account of British East Africa, its Ancient History and Present Inhabitants*. New York: Barnes and Noble, 1913.
Strahle, J. J. "What I Saw and Heard in East Africa." *Advent Review and Sabbath Herald* 31 (Aug. 4, 1932): 10.
Strayer, Robert W. *The Making of Mission Communities in East Africa*. London: Heinemann, 1978.
Stokes, Eric. *The English Utilitarians and India*. Oxford: Oxford University Press, 1959.
Stocking, George W. Jr. *After Tylor: British Social Anthropology, 1888–1951*. Madison: University of Wisconsin Press, 1995.
Sunseri, Thaddeus. *Vilimani: Labor Migration and Rural Change in Early Colonial Tanzania*. Portsmouth, NH: Heinemann, 2002.
Sytek, William. *Luo of Kenya*. New Haven, CT: Human Relations Area Files, 1972.
Thomas, Lynn M. "Regulating Reproduction: State Interventions into Fertility and Sexuality in Rural Kenya, c. 1920–70." Ph.D. dissertation, University of Michigan, 1997.
———. "Imperial Concerns and 'Women's Affairs': State Efforts to Regulate Clitoridectomy and Eradicate Abortion in Meru, Kenya, c. 1910–1950." *Journal of African History*, 39 (1998): 121–145.
———. *Politics of the Womb: Women, Reproduction, and the State in Kenya*. Berkeley: University of California Press, 2003.
Throup, David. *Economic and Social Origins of Mau Mau, 1945–53*. London: James Currey, 1988.
Torday, E. "Bride Price, Dower, or Settlement." *Man* (Jan. 1929): 5–7.
Trench, Charles Chenevix. *Men Who Ruled Kenya: The Kenya Administration, 1892–1963*. London: Radcliffe, 1993.
Uchendu, Victor C., and Kenneth R. M. Anthony. *Agricultural Change in Kisii District, Kenya*. Nairobi: East African Literature Bureau, 1975.
Van Zwanenberg, R. M. A. *Colonial Capitalism and Labour in Kenya 1919–1939*. Kampala: East African Literature Bureau, 1975.
Wakefield, T. "Notes on the Geography of Eastern Africa." *Journal of the Royal Geographical Society* 40 (1870): 303–328.
Walker, Cherryl, ed. *Women and Gender in Southern Africa to 1945*. Cape Town: James Currey, 1990.
Waller, Richard. "Emutai: Crisis and Response in Maasailand 1883–1902." In *The Ecology of Survival: Case Studies from Northeast African History*, edited by Douglas H. Johnson and David M. Anderson. Boulder, CO: Westview, 1988.
Watkins, Elizabeth. *Oscar from Africa: The Biography of Oscar Ferris Watkins, 1877–1943*. New York: Radcliffe Press, 1995.
White, Landeg. *Magomero: Portrait of an African Village*. Cambridge, UK: Cambridge University Press, 1987.
White, Luise. *The Comforts of Home: Prostitution in Colonial Nairobi*. Chicago: University of Chicago Press, 1990.

———. "Separating the Men from the Boys: Constructions of Sexuality, Gender, and Terrorism in Central Kenya, 1939–1959." *International Journal of African Historical Studies* 23 (1990): 1–26.

Wilemski, Edmund Alojzy. *African Traditional Subsistence Economy in Change*. Cologne: R. J. Hundt, 1975.

Wilson, Monica. *For Men and Elders: Change in the Relations of Generations and of Men and Women among the Nyakyusa-Ngonde People 1875–1971*. New York: Africana, for the International African Institute, 1977.

Wipper, Audrey. "The Maendeleo ya Wanawake Organization: The Co-optation of Leadership." *African Studies Review* 18 (1975): 99–120.

———. "The Maendeleo ya Wanawake Movement in the Colonial Period: The Canadian Connection, Mau Mau, Embroidery and Agriculture." *Rural Africana* 29 (1975–1976): 195–214.

Wolpe, Harold. "Capitalism and Cheap Labour-power in South Africa: From Segregation to Apartheid." *Economy and Society* 1 (1972): 425–456.

Woollacott, Angela. "Inventing Commonwealth and Pan-Pacific Feminisms: Australian Women's Internationalist Activism." In *Feminisms and Internationalism*, edited by Mrinalini Sinha, Donna Guy, and Angela Woollacott. Oxford: Blackwell, 1999.

Wright, Marcia. "Bwanika: Consciousness and Protest among Slave Women in Central Africa, 1886–1911." In *Women and Slavery in Africa*, edited by Claire C. Robertson and Martin A. Klein. Portsmouth, NH: Heinemann, 1997 (1983).

Index

About the Author

BRETT L. SHADLE teaches African History at Virginia Polytechnic Institute and State University. He received his Ph.D. from Northwestern University in 2000, where he worked under Professor Jonathon Glassman. Prior to joining Virginia Tech in 2005, Shadle taught at Bowdoin College and the University of Mississippi. He is currently researching the history of sexual crimes in twentieth-century Kenya, and the history of colonial Kenya's African courts system.

www.ingramcontent.com/pod-product-compliance
Ingram Content Group UK Ltd.
Pitfield, Milton Keynes, MK11 3LW, UK
UKHW021543041026
15470UKWH00019B/733

9 780325 070926